A Unified Theory of Justice and Crime

A Unified Theory of Justice and Crime

Justice That Love Gives

Michael J. DeValve, Tammy S. Garland,
and Elizabeth Q. Wright

LEXINGTON BOOKS
Lanham • Boulder • New York • London

Published by Lexington Books
An imprint of The Rowman & Littlefield Publishing Group, Inc.
4501 Forbes Boulevard, Suite 200, Lanham, Maryland 20706
www.rowman.com

Unit A, Whitacre Mews, 26-34 Stannary Street, London SE11 4AB, United Kingdom

British Library Cataloguing in Publication Information Available

Library of Congress Cataloging-in-Publication Data

Names: DeValve, Michael J., author. | Garland, Tammy S., author. | Wright, Elizabeth Q. (Elizabeth Quincy), author.
Title: A unified theory of justice and crime : justice that love gives / Michael J. DeValve, Tammy S. Garland, and Elizabeth Q. Wright.
Description: Lanham : Lexington Books, [2018] | Includes bibliographical references and index.
Identifiers: LCCN 2018022640 (print) | LCCN 2018025542 (ebook) | ISBN 9781498559911 (Electronic) | ISBN 9781498559904 (cloth : alk. paper)
Subjects: LCSH: Criminal justice, Administration of. | Criminology—Religious aspects. | Love.
Classification: LCC HV7419 (ebook) | LCC HV7419 .D444 2018 (print) | DDC 364.01—dc23
LC record available at https://lccn.loc.gov/2018022640

∞™ The paper used in this publication meets the minimum requirements of American National Standard for Information Sciences—Permanence of Paper for Printed Library Materials, ANSI/NISO Z39.48-1992.

Printed in the United States of America

Michael: For and because of Dad and Mom. For Phillip, Hal, Richard, Lindsay, Kin, and the rest of my teachers. And for my students. John, I hope this work is worthy of your art. Kin, thank you for making me the proudest dad. Tammy and Beth, thank you for being incredible, and for investing in this project. Thank you, Mom, for the edits once again. And the cookies. And for a billion other things. Lindsay, thank you for believing in me, for Muppets, for listening, for . . . everything.

Tammy: To my Aunt Wilma, thank you for showing me the true meaning of love, to Gracelynn who fills my heart with it, daily, and to Bradley for reminding me that love is messy, and sometimes even in our own despair, we must take our own academic advice and embrace forgiveness.

Beth: To Tammy and Michael—thank you for allowing me to join you on this work. I hope its reading sparks the changes this work intends. And to my dear family, my kiddo Kinsey who has taught me what true kindness is, as she is kind without even trying; and to my husband Jimmy who consistently challenges me to find commonality in difference and connection amid division. I strive each day to make these two proud.

Contents

Introduction

Everyone loves a hero. And there is nothing more exciting than when the hero defeats the villain, or in the case of Theseus, a beast, and saves his country. A torturous and harrowing path has led Theseus to this auspicious moment; he must face the frightening Minotaur at the heart of the labyrinth, with nothing but his wits and a ball of thread given to him by an amorous Ariadne (well, in some versions he has a sword). Unwinding the thread as he ventures into the labyrinth, Theseus eventually meets the Minotaur, destroys him, and finds his way back out of the labyrinth by following his love's thread. One mythical account has Theseus and Ariadne united after his struggle, the loving couple separated only by Ariadne's death during childbirth years later; however, most accounts of the Minotaur legend have Theseus abandoning Ariadne on the island of Naxos. Unskillful love often is just fickle like that. Regardless, without the love (and loving equipment) of Ariadne, Theseus would have failed in his quest and the continued loss of the flower of Athenian youth to the Minotaur likely would have continued unabated. We will consider again Ariadne's love and its significance in the last chapters of this book, but for now, the good guys win.

Eminent natural scientist Edward O. Wilson (1998) recalls Ariadne's non-lethal combat support for Theseus's ordeal; the thread she gave him winds through the labyrinth from its starting point, connecting outer chambers with inner sanctum in dramatic and functional fashion. This connection facilitated the success of his mission. For Wilson, the thread represents that unifying force among areas of human endeavor, from physics at the portal, past other natural sciences, to the social sciences, humanities and religion at the murky hub. The string, representing consilience, or theoretical unity, would connect natural and social sciences, humanities, and religion under one conceptual umbra. For him, only when we understand our culture and ourselves in light of roots as unearthed by the natural sciences will we begin to grasp why we are, writ large, The Way We Are. Coming to grips with our predecessors, *Homo ergaster* and *Homo erectus*, and understanding how they came to be as they were can shift the tumblers and unlock a more profound understanding of ourselves and our universe than we have previously known. Wilson crafts a powerful and compelling argument for his elegant and honorable vision, and we agree with almost all of it.

But there is a problem. Wilson has us tie one end of the string to physics at the gate of the labyrinth and argues that it is through the natural sciences like evolutionary biology that we, mirrorlike, must perceive ourselves in order to understand ourselves. He seems to end his analysis, and his analogy, at this point; if so, it is to his argument's cost, sadly. Recall that the string was given to brave Theseus by lovely Ariadne, so that should he defeat the Minotaur, he could return to her. The string did more than merely unite exterior and interior portions of the labyrinth; it secured Theseus's return from horror to the place where at least one loved one waited for him.

It is useful to note also that a "labyrinth" and a "maze" are not the same thing. Whereas a maze has dead ends and false turns, a proper labyrinth is a single path folded back upon itself. Technically speaking, if Theseus was in a true labyrinth, the string would have been superfluous. What would the value have been of a string to follow, when one can simply follow the path to inevitable freedom? We think there is more than syntactical imprecision here; we think there is more in the symbology than Wilson may see. More to the point, we will take what we think we see in Wilson's work as invitation to push to the limit of responsibility our own interpretation of the symbology in the story. Wilson views the Minotaur as our darker, monstrous tendencies; he views Theseus as humanity's better nature. The labyrinth represents the human world of the known and the unknown, and the thread represents the idea that we are both Theseus and the Minotaur, mutually understandable in light of our scientific, humanistic, and artistic discourses that are unified by the natural sciences. Poor Ariadne has no role in Wilson's metaphor system. While accepting Wilson's colorful metaphor in part, allow us to observe one additional point. The thread, as we have seen now a pointless endeavor, we argue has an altogether different meaning. Although brave Theseus did not need the thread, his lifeline, to escape, he needed it just as surely as if he *had* been in a maze. Wilson's connecting thread is indeed vital to unifying thought in disparate areas of human endeavor, and it does indeed connect how we came to be to who we are, and indeed who we seek to be. But it is not evolutionary biology. The thread's nature, in fact, is indicated by its source: it was a gift of love from Theseus's beloved, uniting her with him as he dangles in danger, binding nobility and monstrosity together. It turns out that Ariadne's love was not incidental; whether dying in childbirth or nursing a broken heart among the enigmatic and artistic Cycladic people, Ariadne loved Theseus as we too must love: she loved with her whole self without concern about the results of her loving sacrifice. The thread, you see, is the most significant part of the myth: it was the concrete reminder of why the fight mattered in the first place. The thread, dear friends, is love.

The consilience Wilson seeks is very much a possibility, but is not to be found where or how Wilson says it is. Certainly the natural and social sciences in defining the human paradox, at their deepest and most fundamental levels, have a common two-part question: "Who am I, and what is my place in the universe?" Answers to natural scientific questions tend to reframe how we understand, how we tell and retell stories (Kuhn, 1996), how we expend resources, why we fear what we fear, how we process and confront harm done by humans to other sentient beings, why we construct social institutions the way we do, and so on. The humanities, religion, and the social sciences are, however, as responsible for the development of natural, scientific inquiry (itself a social institution). Thus, Wilson's argument, as elegant as it is, fails on the mistaking part of the labyrinth for the thread. Certainly evolutionary biology, with roots in physics and branches in faith, helps us understand ourselves. But this understanding is partial, as it fails to recognize its own nature as human inquiry. Evolutionary biology is no more privileged a science than any other, any more than history is to the historian; all grapple with the core question of who we are and what we mean, only in different ways. The human today is a product of inquiry from the earliest times of recorded sentience, with Her roots in faith and branches in physics. Certainly, we can forgive Wilson for seeing his own discipline as being the axle of human wisdom. What binds disciplines together, what makes the question relevant, is the idea that *we are*. We pursue this foundational question by addressing our most fundamental nature because of our common connection, not only to each other, but to the humans who have been, to those who have yet to come, and to the rest of the universe. Wilson's premise, the idea of connection between star formation and the selection of the next Food Network star, presumes the existence of mutuality, of interbeing. Sadly, he trips over the string he had followed all the way to the end of the labyrinth. Perhaps Wilson's mistake is to confuse his science for his love for his science; we suspect that what Wilson was experiencing, at some level, was not his science, which he loved, but his love.

Wilson is undeniably correct when he speaks of the power of consilient scholarly and creative work to bring awareness to new and profound understandings of who we are. Consilient work even offers the promise of allaying fears that may stem from asking such aboriginal and paradigmatic questions.

Part of the challenge with understanding consilience, though, is the issue of prepotency. By that we mean whether it makes sound sense to seek consilience itself, or to inquire normally and to celebrate the discovery of Truth by coincidence. This is no minor distinction, mind you. Scientific endeavors, which set out to discover consilient explanations, may well discover them, but the very fact that they would seek them means that they risk finding them where they are not present. It would seem to be more compelling to allow consilience to emerge from the regolith beneath us as we search for something else, provided scientific training prepares scientists to know it when they see it.

It is only too easy to criticize others for their ideas; perhaps we are guilty of making the same error as Wilson. We did not set out with the assertion that our favorite subject was the fulcrum of the gods. In our pursuit of understanding why humans do horrific things to each other, to other living things, and to themselves, love emerged as a powerful answer, for explaining human cruelty, avarice, and myopia, and also how we as a community should respond to these acts (DeValve, 2015). In the process of writing, it became clear that love offers far more heavy lifting for criminological theorizing than first anticipated. But again, we tend to view the rest of the world through our own disciplines. And why not, after all? Scientists choose what they study as a result of their own curiosities and capacities, and they remain in their discipline often because of genuine affection for particular questions despite an often arduous hazing process known as "post-graduate education." A passionate volcanologist will see consilience through geodynamic processes, and a cognitive psychologist may see consilience through the windows of perception. In the end, we leave it to you, gentle reader, to decide whether this version of consilience is compelling.

So what is this love, then, that promises such great capacity? No emotion, not even love, you may be thinking, is sufficient to reveal the nature of the universe. If you had that thought, you would be correct. Love as it is meant most often is mere affect, simply an emotion—hardly the firmament onto which to build a life or a vital social institution, let alone to build the edifice of human understanding. Certainly love thus understood is incapable of serving as the means whereby humans finally shed the shackles of greed, hatred, and fear. It turns out, however, that the error here lies not with the idea of love as foundation for social interaction and scientific knowledge. Let us say this as delicately as we are able: the error is ours, if we insist on the position that love is mere emotion. In *A Different Justice*, the sacred and secular scholarly landscape was reviewed in an effort to link human wisdom with the nature of love. The results may surprise you.

At the end of the first section of *A Different Justice*, it was concluded that love possesses several essential ingredients. Love is an art: it requires dedication, practice, sensitivity, and mastery. Love is understanding: the loved is known at a depth immeasurable though readily achievable. Love requires intentionality—deliberately leveraging the most precise and insightful understanding of needs and desires of the beloved. Love demands courage—not the courage to arm up and march toward the sound of guns, but a more profound courage to love with neither guarantee of return nor protection from heartbreak. No device or artifice offers protection from the withering pain of rejection, loss, or outright hostility. Love unites humanity as a whole even in the instance of love between two beloveds (e.g., mother and son; husband and wife; brother and sister; two strangers). To truly love another person is to love humanity in that person, and to see that person in every stranger one meets. Love often places the needs of others before the needs of the self. Love necessitates authenticity. No deception, no guile, not even the pleasure of knowing one has loved well can interpose itself in the loving process. True love does not consider the pleasure loving brings to the lover, nor whether the end sought in loving action is ever actually achieved. To love authentically means to seek with laser focus the actualization of the beloved without the presence of any other motive of any kind. Thus, love is joy and pain together, each in turn.

Ultimately we define love as: "the artlike, individualized, unconditional, aware, and end-less praxis, whereby a human or organization mindfully, assertively, and continuously labors for the actualization of another human being as an end in herself, without thought of return, without reliance upon authority, without fear, or possibility of cessation" (DeValve, 2015, p. 103). Love, unique among human capacities, is that power able to confront harm, suffering, and ignorance in order to transform them into insights, wisdom, and compassion. How we go about this process differs among the populace, even between the authors; however, we contend that love is knowledge-guided praxis, which seeks no name for itself, but instead only seeks the actualization of the beloved. It is the human capacity to risk one's body for the sake of someone else. It is the strength beyond strength, able to still the hands of the lover, enabling her to stand tall to face mortal danger. Love does not remove fear; though love can be analgesic and narcotic, to stand drugged before fear is to stand impotent. No, quite incredibly, love, while often an analgesic, allows us to stand firm and aware and smile in the grizzly teeth of fear. While most profess to understand the concept of love, the capacity to misunderstand what it means to truly love their fellow man is undeniably ubiquitous in societal groups, especially those involved in the criminal justice system.

In *A Different Justice*, it was argued that love must become the foundational and organizing principle for justice planning and action. If such a transition were to take place, not only would many of our existing institutional ills be diminished, the system would be a true "justice" system in the purest meaning of the word, bent on serving the needs of victims, offenders, and public servants. Additionally, Michael was able to craft a criminoetiological theory based on an understanding of love, capable not only of addressing crime but all harms, of force and fraud, humans perpetrate against each other, other sentient beings, and their own world. In this book, we will argue that love is not only the organizing principle missing from justice practice in America, but that *it is justice itself*, that it is the very substance of justice, something that we have sought since before Cain first killed Abel. Justice, then, is "the artlike, individualized, unconditional, aware, and end-less praxis, whereby a human or organization mindfully, assertively, and continuously labors for the actualization of another human being as an end in herself, without thought of return, without reliance upon authority, without fear, or possibility of cessation" (DeValve, 2015, p. 103). Regardless of whether you ascribe to the biblical story being fact or fiction, the account is the quintessential example of the need for justice as both a life was lost out of jealousy and redemption was never an option for the offender. In this book, we will examine several of the principal arguments regarding justice, and we aim to show that a reading from the perspective of love corrects their lacunae. Simply by replacing ideas like the Platonic "good" with "love" renders these arguments more potent and meaningful.

Our aim for this work is to offer a concise but defensively comprehensive review of the dialogues on justice and on crime causation (criminoetiology), illustrating key organizing concepts, problematic assumptions, and signal paradigm failures. Our purpose for this is to demonstrate beyond argument that what has been missing from both dialogues, what has caused consistent stubbing of toes frustrating the progress, and bumping of heads on empirical glass (concrete?) ceilings is that love as was described in *A Different Justice* (standing on the shoulders of giants) is the *desideratum summum bonum*, the most crucial missing part of the dialogues. There will be trimming and shaping in the making of a new justice paradigm; probably substantial portions of the criminological and justice canons will be swept from the cutting room floor when all is done. What will be gained in the bargain, however, will be well worth the trade.

Again, we have come to understand, without a shadow of a doubt, that justice *is* love. In fact, love as axle for human thought and inquiry unites not only thought about justice and thought about criminoetiology, but also thought about God, thought about nature, and the arts. It is both the means by which we inquire and the reason for the question in the first place. That thread to which Theseus clung was not superfluous. It is not his route to safety, but his route to supreme wisdom; it is his unbreakable bond, not only to loving and lovely Ariadne, but also to the Minotaur, to the labyrinth itself, to his own birth and eventual death, to you and to me, and to those who came before and after him. It is the thread of which Dr. King waxed poetic, with which the uniting garment of destiny is woven. It is consilience in the purest and most profound sense; it is the thing that gives all human life and human endeavor meaning. Love is the dark matter of humanity; without it, society would fly to pieces. The "us" that love makes possible is the only reason for science to exist in the first place.

Before we begin, though, we would like to make three observations. First and perhaps most crucially, the linking of justice and crime dialogues necessarily presupposes that what our social institutions do in the service of justice is related logically to the ends we seek. Such intentionality is most often not present, and when present, it is most often grossly misinformed or misled.

When twelve-year-old Polly Klaas was kidnapped from her bedroom and murdered by Richard Allen Davis in late 1993, many Americans began to clamor for stiffer penalties for violent offenders. The murder of an innocent child shocked the conscience of the nation as information regarding the horrific details of the crime came out at Davis's trial. At his sentencing, Davis reported that Klaas begged him not to "do me like my dad"; he sat with his cruel grin as his sentence was read, offering obscene gestures to the court. As grotesque as Davis's crimes were, public discourse, led by an irresponsible mass media, leapt at the chance to vent their disgust and anger toward Davis on other offenders; the venom was accompanied by the argument that had Davis been incarcerated for his previous felonies, he would not have had the chance to defile and destroy Polly. Therefore, if all multiple felons are locked away for extended periods, other crimes like Davis's can be prevented. As a result, the three-strikes law passed by the state legislature and was signed into law the next year. California's "three-strikes" sentencing law created aggressive sentencing enhancements for offenders convicted of second and third felonies. Penalties were doubled for second offenses, and an automatic life sentence was instituted for third felonies, no matter how trivial. This piece of legislation, enacted in 1994 and revised in 2012, would result in thousands of nonviolent criminals being placed in prison for life.

Although a horrific crime had been perpetrated, the observation regarding the incapacitation of Davis and other monstrous predators like him is a truism and offers no wisdom. It only makes us feel safer knowing predators, such as Davis, are behind bars. The strongest argument for the present state of the prisons in America is incapacitation: if an offender is behind bars, he cannot ravage the quiet countryside. Criminologists have been reporting for decades that crime, including violent crime, has been systematically decreasing since the mid-1990s, with only relatively small variances recently. In reality, the majority of prisoners in state and federal correctional facilities are not there for violent offenses. According to the Bureau of Justice Statistics (2015), the United States housed approximately 1.5 million individuals in state and federal prisons in 2014. Of that, approximately 53 percent of prisoners in state facilities were serving time for a violent crime; only 7 percent of the federal prison populations were convicted of a violent crime.

Moreover, the "monsters" that we envision filling these prisons, such as serial killers and child murderers, make up only a very small percentage of these crimes. We must recognize that the "monsters" that the law targets are extraordinarily rare and that the quiet countryside is far more often ravaged by its own occupants committing acts of intrafamily violence or nonviolent crimes than by any real "monsters." We inadvertently create a reality filled with our own worst nightmares by vilifying those who are not monsters but merely individuals, who made unwholesome decisions. Once we can humanize offenders (without having to justify the crime), we can see that the incapacitation model represents a wholesale abdication of our collective joint responsibilities to nurture and salve the offender, who is, in fact, another human being, no matter how deformed and miserable. In doing this, we may hope to ease the suffering and honor the humanity of those involved (offenders, victims, and families). However, incapacitation is not the path to healing. Although a small portion of those who offend require maintenance in a secure facility, the clear majority of the prison population poses little violent threat, and thus, incapacitation serves no purpose but to punish; redemption and reconciliation are not permissible in this injustice equation as incapacitation does not focus on returning individuals to the fold, but only maintaining the appearance of justice. Thus, simply warehousing offenders is ethically reprehensible and financially irresponsible: it provides little concrete benefit, and it costs taxpayers a fortune (see, e.g., Zimring, Hawkins, & Kamin, 2001).

During the 1990s, numerous states began to pass three-strikes or habitual offender laws. What most of the population did not realize was that nonviolent offenders were being sentenced to life in prison under these laws (American Civil Liberties Union, 2013). As time wore on, of course, the deleterious effects of the three-strikes law became clear. In 1995, Curtis Wilkerson was sentenced to life in prison for theft of a pair of plain socks worth $2.50 (Taibbi, 2013). Other individuals suffered similar fates over petty offenses like the theft of a slice of pizza. As heartbreaking accounts began to accumulate, so too did the pressure to reexamine the policy. In 2012, a sweeping revision of the law, including provisions for exceptions to specific crimes and for correcting some past injustices, was voted into law in dramatic fashion. This point is essential: not only was the original three-strikes law not the result of a considered and intentional process to revise the criminal law, its revision was just as unintentional and partly thought through. Both the three-strikes law and its revision were the result of a process that was at best semi-reasoned, but was initiated in the main by powerful emotions. That the law initially was bloodthirsty, and the 2012 revision seemed to seek a more moderate tone makes little if any real difference: despite the compassionate, wise, and herculean work of professor David Mills to change the law (Levine, 2014), both the original law and to some degree its revision are the result of affective, not deliberative, processes.

This haphazard and limbic policy process, coupled with the portrayed sense of perpetual and sacrosanct certainty, together have created a circumstance in which justice practice regularly fails. Even when the results are catastrophic, the system remains largely unchallenged, except in relatively rare circumstances. In those circumstances where justice organizations fail to the point where injustice becomes the norm, only the organizations themselves or individual actors are the focus of intervention, not the logic of the system or the ill-considered demands of the people. Justice practice fails because such miscarriages of justice are inevitable, even foreseeable at the outset, due to faulty theories of justice. Currently, justice is at best a transactional, brutal affair; it is little more than a price in discomfort and hurt we affix to an action, person, or thing. (In)Justice service is a partial, sclerotic, and differential thing, offering hollow gestures, cruel punishments, irresponsible theater, and empty promises. Instead of a mechanism that allows us to exact a price from the hide of others, justice must become the precious thing that each of us gives one another. The ideal justice system—the one our children deserve—is one founded on and operating in love. Justice is a tool whereby mankind's holy obligation to you and to every other human being is made manifest and meaningful. Justice, to be justice at all, must be a sacrament established in the principles of love (DeValve, 2017).

Second, none of us is a trained classicist, so we will apologize at the outset to those who are. Please, though, in critiquing our arguments to follow, though our arguments may not be as elegant or complete as yours, though they may overlook issues you may consider important, please consider what we say in light of the lived experience of justice for real humans. We will give short shrift to favorite thinkers, and our treatment of Hegel may contend for the most incomplete on record, we have made every effort to represent their ideas as authentically as we know how. We will not give the Greeks anything near the treatment in this work they deserve. The only argument that does not belong in opposition to our narrative for you, for it is the only one we have ever heard offered in counterpoise, is the impracticality of love as justice and as the engine for criminal justice. *Of course* love is practical. It is the *most* practical thing imaginable to see a beloved in the face of a stranger. Imagine sitting at a café with your significant other. Across the stairs from you, there sits a couple, dating or perhaps engaged. She eats gelato, probably stracciatella, he sips his coffee; they lean in toward each other, comfortable receiving the other's intense gazes, comfortable not talking. Sometimes their eyes pass each other, scanning the room, searching perhaps for something amusing to offer as gift to their beloved. It is the easiest thing to see that he sees his beloved like we see ours or you see yours, who might just be sitting across from you now as you read this; we become those people bound in love. On the far side of the café is a little girl in a princess costume. What she looks like is unimportant as she could be one of our daughters as we, the authors, all have daughters; they paraded in and out of shops, dressed in their best princess dresses, sung songs at the top of their lungs, and held daddy's hands while he looked at them with abiding and total love. We recall the feelings of love when we, along with our spouses, had similar experiences. That little girl *is* our little girl. Easy. It just takes doing. This is only to start, of course, but what a powerful place to begin!

Third, we think it is helpful to consider just how we theorize, mostly so that our theorizing here is not as subject to the errors of the past. More to the point, we would like to discuss among ourselves for a moment how it appears to us that we have built theories of crime causation: these theories that produce modest empirical support but have a limited value in terms of improving the lives of humans (e.g., Hall, 2012; see also Kubrin, Stucky, & Krohn, 2009). Of course, we cannot tell you how others do it, as we are simply not them. With that being said, we believe there is value in beginning from a place of transparency of criminoetiological thought on our part, and perhaps to assume our way bears some resemblance to the ways of others. Reconsidering how we theorize, of course, invites ontological reexamination of the foundations of criminology as well as the social science disciplines from which it takes its paradigmatic morphology. Just such reconsideration shall be required of us.

Fully recognizing that abstraction is, to a great extent, much the point regarding theory, it seems there is a tendency among criminoetiologists to think either in *excessively simplified* terms or in *overly convoluted* terms regarding crime and the people involved (Young, 2011). The achievement of theory often involves the creation of what one might call "avatars" (primarily but not exclusively in simplified theorizing) and etiological models (primarily but not exclusively in convoluted theorizing). Avatars are abstracted beings who live in the theorist's mind, and represent the actors in the ideal instance of a theory. We create for our theorizing prototypical offenders, victims, witnesses, system agents, and relevant others, and set them in motion according to theorized laws of human physics. These theorized laws that we witness at work in the play of avatars become the meat of our theories. In the case of Sutherland's learning theory, for instance, one can only conceive a fellow complete with a pack of dubious friends and pack of cigarettes rolled into his short sleeve, learning crime in the same way he might learn welding, learning techniques for committing crime, as well as a balance of definitions that favor crime. He learns these things from individuals who are significant to him, scilicet, his dubious buddies. Consider also the capacity to teach the concept of secondary deviance possessed by Riff, Diesel, and the rest of the triple-threat hoodlums who croon "Officer Krupke" in *West Side Story*. In the course of the song, they stand in as avatars for several criminological theories, including strain, labeling, and rational choice theories. Whether Sutherland or any other theorist actually composed theory through the use of mental avatars would be hard to discern, but to be certain, teaching theory is aided through the use of such avatars. It stands to reason, then, that if thinking about theory is so naturally draped over mental dress forms, it may well have been made there, too, even if only subconsciously.

The problem about theorizing using avatars or other ideal types is, simply, that humans are not avatars. Avatars, like Arthur Miller's miserable character, Willie Lowman, contain only a fraction of a fraction of the complexity possessed by any human. We hurt, we desire, we think, we change . . . in ways a character or mental formation simply cannot. Our theoretical ideal types are no more relevant to human harm than is a life-sized cardboard cutout of, say Liam Neeson, to Mr. Neeson himself. It should be no surprise, then, that we experience an empirical glass ceiling when it comes to explanatory power of the models we craft from them. Significantly, then, the empirical glass ceiling may be only partly due to our current level of empirical sophistication (Young, 2011). The chilling likelihood is that our near total inability to explain more than half of the variance in a dependent variable regardless of the variate we assemble is predominantly a function of the inadequacy of our theories, rather than merely the considerable inadequacy of most of our empirical approaches.

In terms of excessively convoluted models, criminologists may, and often do, find themselves prioritizing model attributes like elegance and integration over value for improving the lives of others, or even its relevance beyond narrowly tailored circumstances. The model becomes the end, in effect, rather than the means; model concepts become reified, just as the model itself is reified. Abstractions of abstractions become ends in themselves, rather than serving the ends of humanity. Research endeavors become something of a horse race of contesting criminological schools of thought (see, e.g., Hall, 2014, who shares this concern) over which school of thought enjoys the most empirical support. Uncritical use of multivariate statistical techniques facilitates this reification process to the point where many criminologists, in essence, spend their time running afield and seeking to catch farts in their multivariate butterfly nets.

These two tendencies have at least three consequences. First, theories often tend to be of limited real value because they tilt on abstract fields over fictional kingdoms. Theorizing in this fashion tends to dull the capacity of the criminological discipline to respond in robust and fertile fashion to the considerable and manifold harms committed by and against sentience today. As a result, criminology has remained rather isolated from other, more meaningful dialogues. Third, and perhaps most significantly, the use of avatars to theorize tends to have the effect of "otherizing" the harmer. This otherizing effect is itself a species of profound violence. In the end, those who should be concerned only with healing often end up perpetuating some of the most harmful and toxic ideas. Take, for instance, Wilson and Kelling's (1982) "broken windows theory," which postulated that serious crimes form as a result of the visible disorder associated with quality-of-life crimes. For decades, it was touted as an innovative tool in combating crime as "small" crimes were targeted to prevent "big" crimes from overtaking neighborhoods. While theoretically placing foot patrols in neighborhoods was a sound concept to reduce crime and create safer neighborhoods, broken windows assisted in an increase in the number of minority populations being arrested and incarcerated for nonserious crimes. Although the theory has long been criticized, recent empirical data determined that targeting quality-of-life crimes has no tangible impact on decreasing felonies. Instead, the increased focus on minor quality-of-life crimes has only led to overpolicing poor neighborhoods, especially those with high populations of black and Hispanic residents. The Department of Investigations of New York (2016) found that "precincts with higher proportions of black and Hispanic residents, males aged 15–20, and NYCHA residents had generally higher rates of quality-of-life enforcement" (37). While Kelling maintains that the broken windows theory has largely been misunderstood and its tenets misinterpreted, the effect remains the same. "Broken windows" only served to target specific populations, had a limited effect on the violent crime rate, and resulted in tremendous harm not only to the individuals affected but entire communities. Not only is criminology not as relevant as it should be as a result, it is actually guilty of causing considerable damage despite being the result of an attempt to serve.

And not everyone is as rosy about the future of criminology as we tend to be. Hall (2014) reports that movement from a focus on legalistic definitions of harms toward "zemiology" (a focus on the study of harm) was rejected by mock jury assembled at the British Society of Criminology in 2013. Hall rightly indicts this decision; we view it as indicative of a willingness actively to choose existing mediocrity and irrelevance over hard work toward creating a criminology that can have real relevance in improving the lives of all sentient beings. Let us be absolutely clear: any criminology that fails to take seriously its obligation to eradicate harm through transformation into wisdom is utterly and irredeemably worthless. It is, in point of fact, no criminology at all.

Whereas Hall and we agree about the state of the criminological endeavor (although again, we tend to be rather rosier about recent shifts toward increased fertility, wisdom, and relevance), and with the necessity of turning our collective attention to harm (zemiology), we differ somewhat with regard to the nature of what is broken, and therefore, what criminology must do next. He hopes, it seems, to recouple that which has come uncoupled—the business class no longer needs the consent of the working masses, except as consumers, and that only in limited fashion. Only when business elites can be made to be beholden in some fashion to the rest of us will we be able to reacquire true justice. Though at a distance, it bears some resemblance to a variance of strain theory, his is a most learned model that presupposes no meaningful realignment of social institutions or the exchanging of functional value sets for dysfunctional ones in the hearts of relevant actors. His model seems eminently more practical than ours on the surface. In fact, from our conversations it seems clear that we agree with each other right down the line, and differ perhaps most significantly in terms of the lenses we employ.

Yet it seems to us that because existing institutional arrangements vis-à-vis justice are wholly unsustainable, Hall's model likewise may be ever so slightly flawed. Our social ills come not from the particularities of a divorce between social classes, but from the suffering that comes from the existence of social classes in the first place. Whereas he takes as axiomatic the idea that the economy is the bedrock of human interaction, we reject this argument out of hand; the bedrock of human interaction is, for us, our ineluctable mutuality. Our social institutions, like the economy and the justice system, are of us, and not we of them. Therefore, no social institution can be foundational to who we are, any more than any tool can define its wielder. Although the health of an economy and the collective commitment to justice can be seen as barometers of the health of a people, the foundation of human interaction is our common humanity. As we will see in the first chapter, the ideas that provide the bedrock for a capitalistic economy are fundamentally and ineluctably fissured: they place the self at the center of the human world, which is perhaps the biggest lie anyone has ever told. When we fail to honor our mutuality, the institutions we create carry that lie forward; when we are in consonance with our mutuality, our social institutions thus constituted serve us well.

In the end, if our theorizing needs retheorizing and our empiricism offers only partial guidance, we are left with few dashboard gauges for the success of a given theory. Possibly the most powerful benchmark for measuring the quality of an ontological/etiological accounting of things is the ability of that idea to answer multiple questions in different areas of inquiry; a realigning of thinking, a reorganizing of knowledge, a reframing of questions so as to answer them is likely attendant to quality theory. The idea that justice is love does precisely this.

ASKING THE RIGHT QUESTION

Einstein said that if he had an hour to answer a question, he would devote the first fifty minutes to ascertaining the correct question. To more than a limited degree, criminology has been hobbled by the pursuit of a question that led in less-than-fruitful directions. From the first formal thought about why humans do harmful things up until the 1960s, with very few exceptions, the guiding question focused on the bandwidth of harmful action enumerated in the criminal law and looked for inspiration to the thought of a short handful of thinkers, most significantly Durkheim. The assumption, of course, is that the criminal law enjoys the unqualified support of all who live subject to it. There is a corollary, somewhat more sinister assumption, however, that those who violate the law are somehow different from those who do not violate the law; that science was equal to the task of discerning in what ways criminals differed from noncriminals. We refer, of course, to the corpus of work known as logical positivism, which is still the fashionable paradigm currently, judging from the content of most highly-regarded academic criminological journals. Failings of preceding paradigms point the way for new insights and approaches (see Kuhn, 1996). Spiritualism's failings were invitations to Cesare Beccaria and others to author a new paradigm with regard to crime. Subsequent failings such as those of the classical school created space for Lombroso and others to innovate. Now, positivism's chief failings loom ever larger even as banner journals continue to seek further works of empirical theory testing to fill their pages.

The classic definition of the field of criminology was given to us by Edwin Sutherland (& Cressey, 1978), and it is instructive to observe that current criminology textbooks (e.g., Bernard, Snipes, & Gerould, 2016; Lilly, Cullen, & Ball, 1995/2015) tend to avoid defining criminology at all, let alone radically differently from Sutherland's definition. He invites us to think of criminology in terms of three related but largely distinct sets of questions: questions about law-making, questions about law-breaking, and questions about the social response to law-breaking (Sutherland & Cressey, 1978). This tripartite definition, however, has outlived its usefulness. Basically, we need a different question. Before we can do this, we must briefly examine Sutherland's three discourses to understand their shortcomings relative to criminology today.

Sutherland and Cressey (1978) group together scholarship in "the sociology of the criminal law, which is an attempt at the systematic analysis of the conditions under which penal laws develop and also [an] explanation of variations in policies and procedures used in police departments and courts" (Sutherland & Cressey, 1978, p. 3). Here they are concerned with making space for the contemplation of the criminal law's characteristics: poltcality, specificity, uniformity, and sanction (Sutherland & Cressey, 1978, p. 4). Additionally, they emphasize the then-incipient sociology of criminal law as being necessary. Invoking Roscoe Pound's call for a study of "law in action," Sutherland and Cressey recognize four different theories regarding the origin of the criminal law. Three of these (torts, rational development, and the formalization of mores) take a consensus approach whereas the fourth assumes that criminal law arose as a result of conflict between interest groups (Sutherland & Cressey, 1978, pp. 9–11).

The second division they identify relates to work in the area of "the sociology of crime and social psychology of criminal behavior, which is an attempt at systematic analysis of the economic, political, and social conditions in which crime and criminality are either generated or prevented" (Sutherland and Cressey, 1978, p. 3). In a nutshell, this second division of effort deals with criminoetiology. They take some care in recognizing the complexity of the label "criminal"; such an animal is one who is reasonably suspected to have performed an act or specific omission that is proscribed by statute, the act or omission being detected and acted upon by state authorities. At the same time, they tip hats to those like Thorsten Sellin (1938), who would argue criminologists study all manner of conduct norms and their violation. Without fixed scientific definitions of behavior of all kinds, criminal and noncriminal, a science of criminology is impossible, according to Sellin. "Obviously legal definitions should not confine the work of criminologists," but "it is an error, however, to call noncriminal behavior [that resembles criminal behavior] *crime*, no matter how repulsive it may be" (Sutherland & Cressey, 1978, p. 23).

The third division represents work that focuses on "the sociology of punishment and correction, which is an attempt at systematic analysis of policies and procedures for reducing the incidence of crime" (Sutherland & Cressey, 1978, p. 3). The social response to law-breaking is, in the main, seen as synonymous with penology. Here our friend Cesare Beccaria, like Isaac Newton in the context of simple physical systems, reigns supreme still. Sutherland and Cressey recognize that although crime causes suffering, criminals suffer, too. They recognize that the suffering of criminals is essential to make the criminal law work, but that it is in the best interest of society to minimize the overall amount of suffering associated with the continuation of society.

Of course, it would be foolish to hold Sutherland and Cressey accountable for the current state of understanding regarding crime, and our critique of their triptych necessarily must not hinge on scientific currency. Instead, we argue, it was never a complete formulation from the beginning, though they may have been unaware of its shortcoming . . . again raising issues of currency. This is a tricky case to make, clearly. Again, no slight to these two great criminologists could ever be our intention. We are where we are because of them in no small measure. It must never be forgotten that theory is an expression of who we are as a species at a given point in time. Yet, it is worth considering the shortcomings of their framework they have given us, so that we might continue to move forward in the spirit of these two pioneers. Just as those who follow us after we are dust must be free to re-vision, we too are free to re-vision crime, harm, justice . . . ourselves.

Each of Sutherland and Cressey's three axes of criminological inquiry are defined as sociological in nature. Certainly much of criminology is derived from sociological roots; it is by no means merely a subset of sociology, even if some sociologists might prefer to see it that way. We are guilty of loving our discipline enough to see it as the nexus of all inquiry, much as Wilson does his own, but it is certain to say that criminology draws inspiration, content, and epistemic tools from psychology, biology, anthropology, religion, history, the humanities, and the arts. The same can be said for sociology with its many tendrils, but the sociology of religion is not a complete accounting of religion's influence in criminology. Perhaps there was a time when criminology was a subset of sociology. No longer.

One of the most obvious aspects of Sutherland and Cressey's framework is its marriage to legal definitions, both of actions and of people. Although they recognize the anatomical complexity of crime, to wit, that it is proscribed, codified, and detected behavior. They recognize the volatility and the relativity of the law across place and time, yet crime remains the overriding concern. Although it would be difficult to support with specific verbiage, it seems almost that the complexity of the phenomenon of crime, from law making, to law breaking, and to social response, is itself attractive. It is natural, perhaps, for scholars to be drawn to complexity; let's be honest . . . many of us prefer a formidable question to a straightforward one. It seems the complexity they saw at the time and were thus drawn to was the one they built into their framework. Time has revealed, however, that although the layers of complexity they witnessed surely exist, we now know that the rabbit hole goes much, much deeper. What behaviors are codified, which are not, and why, along with a host of other questions remain criminologically relevant and represent an area for fertile interdisciplinary dialogue with policy theorists and others. But there is far, far more to know. A new formulation of the definition of criminology would need to deal adequately, even if through an expanding of breadth, with this vast and seemingly expanding Gordian knot.

Some argue that the extant framework remains serviceable, mostly through implication. It is a valid endeavor, as Sellin observes, to contemplate non-criminal but harmful behavior because such an inquiry is implied by the invitation to study law making. The nature of the criminal's label, his experience as a criminal, are valid avenues of inquiry. They contemplate how long a criminal label should last and what that might mean for the offender. Still at the end of the day, it is clear that he is to be defined as one who has broken the law. No consensus assumption is necessary for Sutherland and Cressey, but the law and its environment is an object for sociological inquiry. Criminology is, according to Sutherland and Cressey, most succinctly described as the sociology of the criminal law and its surrounds. Clearly this is insufficient.

Yet Sutherland and Cressey give us a gift quite a bit mightier than their definitional triptych, a gift deserving of far greater appreciation: "The practical objective of criminology, supplementing the scientific or theoretical objective, is to reduce the amount of pain and suffering in the world" (Sutherland & Cressey, 1978, p. 24). One might be tempted to hear the utilitarian voices behind this sentiment, and thus take it as an abstract prescription toward maximizing pleasure. We don't. We see this statement as a charge and call to action. We would take it even a step further and say that the *primary* objective of criminology, *facilitated by* the scientific and theoretical endeavors, is to reduce the amount of pain and suffering in the world.

Given the shortcomings of Sutherland and Cressey's long-serving definition, it is time, we think, to offer it a noble retirement, while retaining parts that serve us still. Criminology as we understand it is the study of (a) the harm done by humans, and (b) the way the wider community responds to that harm. Humans harm themselves, other humans, other beings, as well as their environment (although upon closer inspection, we will find that these distinctions are of rather less value than one might think). Understanding human harm through aggression, greed, accident, industry, war, callousness . . . must necessarily be the single most consuming activity, in order to transform that understanding into the eradication of these darker facets of human existence. How we manage exchange, how we raise our children, how we settle international disputes, how we face humanitarian crises, and the like is of the very first priority and, in point of fact, is nothing less than the fundamental question of justice. Understanding the harm we do and how it can be transformed into wisdom is as profound an endeavor as understanding our place in the universe.

It turns out that both the law and sociology are incapable of fully tracing the shoreline of human suffering. Because the diverse vocabulary and contexts of human harm, because of the wide variety of beings subject to damage from human action, our attention must turn to the mechanisms in us that allow us to do harm, that bring us to actions that occlude our better angels. As humans have considerable range in our harming capacity, so too have humans developed a wide range of collective and individual responses to harm. Not all of these responses are equally noble or humanizing, of course. The relative capacity of different responses in different contexts, their mechanisms, the quality of their outcomes, shortcomings, blind spots, and particular strengths all are needed avenues of criminological inquiry. We argue for a criminology that bears very close resemblance to the idea of zemiology (Hall, 2012): one that approaches criminology through love.

The purpose of this assembling and recreation of criminological theory and justice thought to eliminate harm is not a simple process. Readers may be offended at our reconceptualization to use theory as a means to study the harms done by humans and the responses that we as a society have to those harms. Many may argue that we are examining crime through rose-colored glasses; quite the contrary is true. Having broken with the habit of viewing humanity only through the lens of the grotesque, we choose to see human beauty and nobility alongside humanity's grievous failings. We seek to author an idea of justice that embodies the very best of ourselves rather than one that can only respond to the worst of ourselves. In the coming chapters, we will discuss the principles of justice and the quest for achieving justice for ourselves and our progeny. We will examine the processes of selfism, punishment, possession, harm, and love though a justice lens. We will discuss justice and crime from the perspective of balance and exchange. We will talk about the roles of identity and of struggle in our more accomplished thinking about justice and crime. We will focus on specific criminological theories including classical theories, social disorganization theories, learning theory, social and self-control theories, anomie/strain theory, and control balance theory, and we will pay attention to thinkers like Nozick, Rawls, Camus, Levinas, and Buber. And along the way we will be joined by the occasional artist and musician. However, as noted, this book merges criminological theory with the ideas established in religious, philosophical, scientific, artistic, and political traditions to develop a holistic theory in which the harms of society may be addressed, presented at the end of chapter 5. Finally, we will discuss the successes of the justice system. It is our hope that by the end of the work, readers will understand, or at least consider the possibilities of the need for a theoretical paradigm in which justice is love.

One final thought we'd like to share with you before moving forward into the meat of the book. Folks who have read *A Different Justice* have observed its personal nature. Some have celebrated it and some have questioned it.

We expect some have criticized, even ridiculed it, if they haven't ignored it altogether. That's fine. Yes, it is personal. This work will also be personal. We believe in our cores that any criminology worth its salt is *necessarily* personal. It is our lot as criminologists to be scientific when being scientific serves truth, but to be human when being human serves humanity. We must be clear eyed and precise in one moment, and then wildly compassionate the next. It is often said in counseling circles that one cannot be part of the solution if one is part of the problem. And in counseling contexts, this is sound advice. For the criminologist, there is no lab in the sky. We are irrevocably part of the problem and part of the solution at the same time. And we must find a way to navigate between being lost to brokenness (including our own) and being lost to scientific detachment, for neither pole offers complete wisdom. As Martin Buber might say, this is the melancholy of humankind, and it is also its great joy.

Theorizing can do harm especially when it results in bad policy, but it can also bring us closer to actualization both as individuals and as a species. Thus, it is imperative that we reformulate the way we approach criminology, and in this we are intentionally rejecting Carlen's (2011) advice against evangelism. We recognize that loving justice may take time to be received well enough to drive research, policy, and further theorizing—more time than we may have. In the short term, we hope at least to encourage other young criminologists to approach criminology from a loving, personal perspective. If nothing but this comes from our writing, then we will have left this world a better place.

Part I

IMPOVERISHED THOUGHT ABOUT JUSTICE AND CRIME

As a subject of contemplation and debate, certainly justice is among the oldest and most substantively diverse, yet remains among the most contentious. Justice is relevant across the entire compass of human attention, relating right conduct to concrete distribution of social goods and sanctions. Few things that concern people are, in every way, justice irrelevant. Principles that guide how society responds to harmful ideas and actions apply as well to dating, food distribution, manufacturing, driving a car, finance, parenting, and music. The diversity of ideas about justice is probably in part a function of the breadth of its relevance. But this wide relevance offers a formidable challenge to the theorist who seeks to find common ground across all contexts, to find a theory capable of guiding all instances of a claim for justice to be done.

The quest for justice plays out daily in the criminal justice system of each of the many nations. Suffering of all stripes and sizes comes before courts, penalties great and small are assessed and levied, modified and suspended. Lives begin, end, and begin again in, through, and because of justice or its absence. The question of why harms come to be manifest as they are is a central component in the administration of justice. Except, of course, when it isn't. To a very real extent, herein lies at least part of The Problem with Justice Practice: speaking generally, it lacks intentionality, authenticity, vector, and coherence. Justice practice in America and elsewhere is akin to a leaky vessel adrift on the ocean. We attempt to fix leaks, bolting onto the weathered and world-weary hull patches, sometimes pulled from other parts of the ship. The patches often are local fixes; although they may help the instant problem, often they produce drag, or worse, create other leaks. But neither the purpose of the voyage nor the navigation of our wandering bark is intentional. Recent efforts to coordinate across jurisdictions (e.g., Klofas, Hipple, & McGarrell, 2010) are far from the same thing as intentionality. Desperately needed is a

Polaris, an intentional trajectory. We have become unshakably convinced, and we will argue here, that love is that Polaris for all matters of justice. It turns out that true north always points to home.

NOTA BENE

We could be accused of a lack of subtlety. Subtlety for its own sake is impractical and unsound; almost always truth is its own salve. We hope it is evident, though it bears emphasizing, that we intend no personal affront to any thinker discussed in this book. We will hold humans in the highest regard even as we challenge their ideas. To call theories of crime and theories of justice "impoverished" is not to call their authors stupid or their efforts valueless. But we have a task to do, one we think to be of the greatest import and urgency. So it is with the ardent hope that no harm come to any from our words that we have organized this work. At the same time, we feel the urgency of our task, also driven by human need, heavily upon us. Thus we have chosen to be direct and unambiguous with the normative assessments of the theories we discuss here. Indeed, doing so is essential to the overall narrative of the work.

ORGANIZATION OF THIS SECTION

This section will examine thinking in both justice and criminology that is, well, impoverished. We are calling them impoverished primarily because they appeal to the baser urges of the human psyche; they leverage anger and fear, they treat other sentient beings as means to ends, they simplify human decision making to the wingspan of a scale, or they compel some level of othering. Some of the ideas presented in these two chapters are themselves species of violence, whereas some merely fail fully to honor human nobility and beauty.

The "impoverished" moniker also indicates that they tend to be heir to a greater degree of contradiction, both logically and empirically. Here theories of justice and of crime are connected somewhat to each other, but the wisdom they bring is far from useful. It turns out that the failings of these theories tend to be understandable in terms of an overarching metanarrative; the considerable dehumanizing brokenness in Gottfredson and Hirschi's (1990) low self-control theory bears considerable resemblance to the brokenness in other theories of crime and of justice. And it is by highlighting this metanarrative that we are able to guide your eye to a more complete, noble, effective justice: love.

After these two chapters are behind us, these ideas will appear only ghost-like throughout the rest of the work. More significantly, once they are exorcised from our hearts and from our institutions, we as a species will be closer to actualization. The section that follows will present accomplished theories of crime and justice—theories less rife with contradiction and more fertile for the transformation of suffering into wisdom. Yet as fertile and noble as they are, they are incomplete in vital ways. We present them again with an eye to their commonality, and again, this commonality highlights why they are incomplete. In the last section, we will present a complete and unified theory of justice and of crime, the unification being possible because of the founding of both on love.

Chapter One

The Wrecking-Ball Sovereign Self

Aristotle tells us justice is about giving to each person what she is due: simple enough. Consider also St. Thomas Aquinas's words: "Justice is the habit by which a person renders each his due by a constant and perpetual will" (cf. Eitel, 2016, p. 269). The proverbial devil, of course, is in the details: how do we determine (it is we, the human collective, who have the primary voice in this determination, even if that determination is made through the decision making of an assigned agent) what is due to any one person in particular at any given time, particularly in contexts involving suffering and competing claims? We believe that we have both overthought and underthought this question, leading inexorably to a debate, which yields much heat, but rather little light. In this chapter, we will examine justice arguments and criminological theories that have in common the idea of the self as justification for the infliction of suffering on others.

These arguments, together something we might call "selfism," are, in our estimation, the least noble and most cowardly arguments among the canon, so it is fitting to dispense with them first. Disturbingly, there are many such arguments; too many for us to cover them all in a chapter. Some will get little space due in part to space limitations, whereas others will receive more careful attention in their coverage and refutation, mostly because they are more broadly representative and applicable to this analysis.

For our purposes, we will discuss two forms of selfism in theory. Both forms of selfism have two premises: one premise is held in common, whereas the other makes the two forms distinct. These two premises are related to views regarding the self in relation to others. The first premise is that the self is the legitimate center of the ethical and experiential universe; the self is holy and a manifestation of the "I." *My* needs come first, *my* desires are paramount, and *my* pain is a license to act in whatever fashion suits *me*: this is simply the focus on "my" needs and no one else's. More broadly, humans are seen to act (and in seeing them thus, such a view is ratified) from self-interest alone; the scope of interest does not reach beyond one's skin.

One of us has argued elsewhere (DeValve, 2015) that humans do what they do in general from a place of perceived self-enhancement, but that confusion about what is actually self-enhancing creates the space between loving or altruistic action and unwholesome and destructive action. Each of us is self, nor self and also not-only-self, precisely at the same time. The examined self reveals many truths about sentient existence that are not readily apparent: the boundary between you and me is increasingly difficult to perceive, and the distinction between the child and the woman she becomes is likewise hard to discern. Self is the vehicle whereby one can discover no-self, and in so doing, more fully sees self and the self's unity with all.

Most of us have contemplated our existence at some point in our lives. Is this consciousness all there is? Will my consciousness be recycled through rebirth? Is my energy doomed to wither, haunting the dark alleys of our days? Will my flame simply cease to be, its warmth spent utterly on the cold steel slab of the surgical suite? Will I leave my corporeal frame only to meet the face of God smiling like summer sun upon me? We have our own ideas, and in fact, many of us are closely wed to our own personal view. We the authors have our own beliefs, too. All of us, authors and readers alike, have speculated and hoped, stood tall and hid under our beds, prayed and cast bones; we have taken our fears to the stars, or perhaps to a spot in the ceiling through which God alone hears you. But lest we need a reminder, truth in doctrine (or in belief) is not necessarily truth. What we believe may or may not be beautiful, and in terms of what is correct, well, that's anyone's guess. What we *know*, however, is that we all share this time together, awake and aware. Strangers on opposite sides of the globe are closer to each other than our great-grandparents are to us; we share the present moment, we are brothers and sisters in sentience, in the now. What we *know* is that each self is a miracle, no matter how vile its actions, no matter how despised its mindset.

It is the confusion about what self is, and thus what self-interest truly means that creates for us what we are calling selfism. Selfism is something akin to the antithesis of the examined and enlightened self. Instead of an awareness of nonduality and oneness of all that is, selfism highlights and even nurtures the bright-line distinction between self and others. Self-interest is determined by what feels good, by simple pleasure-seeking and pain-avoidance behaviors. Being is simply being and nothing more. The self is reified; even if it exhibits changes over time, like aging, it is yet in some sense constant, discrete. Where for an enlightened self, the self is genetic for understanding the nuanced topography of need, selfist views are not so burdened with weighty contemplation. My needs reign, guiding my thought and action.

A central means for equipping selfism with the capacity to appear to be a meaningful philosophy is a blurring of the ethical and phenomenological universes. This blurring creates the illusion of a defensible ethical argument linking right conduct with selfish urges. My existence, and my separateness, together or separately, is justification for action. Further, the idea of separateness takes on a wholly new identity as its own end. Separateness in selfist thought is transmogrified into a perverted freedom (or set of freedoms), themselves devoid of attendant responsibilities. I act justly if I act to further either my existence or my independence, my freedom. The idea that my existence is a function of a wider unity is utterly alien to this ethical system.

The second principle that concerns us regarding selfism is the degree to which other beings may or may not be seen as mere means to the self's ends. Thus, *antagonistic selfism* places the self at the center of the universe and also views others as means to the self's ends. The adjective "antagonistic" was chosen for its connotation of actively setting one's self in opposition to others through one's action: others are seen to be the raw material for the self's needs, the foils for success, and the defensible targets of destructive action when the self is not properly honored. A flimsy scrim of love is hijacked by antagonistic selfism in the body of ethical egoism. At the very least, we do not have to worry about others' needs in the pursuit of our own. Antagonistic selfism creates the veneer of ethical defensibility over the spoiled selfishness of a naughty child. *Benign selfism* still places the self at the center of the universe, but in so doing, no active effort to use others as fodder for the achievement of one's aims is required; benign selfism worships one's own pleasure, but recognizes that others also may do the same, and have the same right to it. The self may be the center of one's ethics and ontology, but thought and action proceeding from the premise that others can be made into means to the self's ends is absent, or at most distantly present or highly unlikely. As we will see, some arguments about justice and crime share something akin to this position. In particular, we will examine the thought of Ayn Rand and Robert Nozick on the justice side, and Beccaria's thought and Merton's strain theory of crime. The pivotal difference between antagonistic selfism and benign selfism is the role of others in the selfist endeavor. Antagonistic selfism views others as means to the self's selfist ends; others can be used as one desires. Benign selfism recognizes that others are not defensibly used as means to selfist ends.

We must remember, though, that although theories of justice and theories of crime that come from a place where selfism's two premises are taken as axiomatic are impoverished in the sense that they diminish humans to the point of being little more than walking limbic systems, we should not conclude from this that such ideas are not without some appeal or even predictive value. Such ideas may be ignoble and cowardly, but at times, so are people. Again, we argue that theory writ large should speak both to human experience and human aspiration to the greatest degree possible; being is becoming, and theorizing about human nature invites us to pay homage to humans once and future. But our dismissal of selfist theories comes from more than mere idealism. To describe a simplistic and partial accounting of the human experience as if it were complete and invariant is irresponsibly reductionist and is, in point of fact, a species of violence. To be clear, violence need not be intended for it to be violent: authors may not have intended the harms they wrought with their theorizing, so no accusations of intentional harm should be understood as being leveled here. Harm exists nonetheless, and it is our ardent hope in this endeavor to bear witness to it, and then to help transform it into wisdom.

Antagonistic selfism equips its adherents with justification for putting the self before others, and in so doing, it allows us to treat others as means to selfish ends; benign selfism is nearly as permissive, though somewhat less dehumanizing, of both the selfish self and others in the way. Such reductionist and diminishing perspectives harm insofar as they are presented as fertile and broadly predictive. Without question, humans are far more than bundles of hungers, wandering the world in search of transitory surfeit. We can offer a far richer accounting of human harm and human justice than those predicated on an assumption that humans, lizardlike, travel on their stomachs. But the role of self in philosophical thought is storied indeed; it is often a starting point for inquiry—*cogito ergo sum*. At the least, it is motive or organizing principle for inquiry. For some, it is methodology. The self is the starting point for so much of our treasured ethical theorizing and a considerable portion of philosophy generally. Perhaps it is no accident that the intellectual working group that represented a flowering of American moral theorizing in the twentieth century and boasted such members as Dworkin, Rawls, Nozick, Walzer, and Nagle called itself the Society for Ethical and Legal Philosophy (SEL). It is useful for us to begin this experiment, as many others have begun their own, with the contemplation of self.

Such a beginning rapidly and perhaps necessarily turns to a contemplation of the nature of relationship between self and the rest of human society, and the rest of existence. A dialogue has continued across the generations debating whether we can most purely and usefully understand our existence as individuals primarily or as members of a community. Mighty thinkers have taken sides: individualists include giants like Aristotle, Mill, Emerson,

Camus, Locke, Thoreau, and Wilde; Tonnies, Durkheim, Etzioni, MacIntyre, Walzer, and Rawls all have strong communitarian leanings in their thought.

Now the likewise long-standing debate regarding the size of government is something of a wholly owned subsidiary debate of the communitarianism/individualism theme that ties this chapter together. Those who advocate for smaller government tend to be sympathetic to individualist ideas. Those who find a larger government more appealing tend to lean toward the communitarian side of the yard. The individualist/communitarian dialogue as well as the big-versus-small government dialogue will provide us themes for this chapter, helping to weave together the narrative and, for our children, at the end of this chapter we will resolve it, at least to our satisfaction.

ANTAGONISTIC SELFISM AND JUSTICE

Remains found not long ago under a Leicester parking lot, ironically marked with a seemingly random "R," have proven to be the lost remains of King Richard III. His bones were removed, and in that same hole, to compensate the loss, some myths about the man were buried. Shakespeare's Richard III richly deserved to be left under a parking lot and forgotten—he was a prick. But myth and fact often share little more than names, and poor Richard may have been no exception. Here we intend no ill toward the once-living man, defamed by the Bard likely in order to increase ticket sales. The poem we have, however, is powerful indeed, and as it turns out, traces perhaps the finest avatar of antagonistic selfism: as he cannot play the role of lover, he says in the very opening scene, because of his bent frame, he is "determined to prove a villain" (*Richard III*, I, 1); he is self-centered in the extreme, and he has no compunction about destroying any who stand in the way of achieving his selfish aims. We will not dwell with Richard long; our purpose is only to arrange an introduction to the principles of antagonistic selfism.

Above all, Richard wanted to be king. He had the bad fortune of being born into the correct family; however, his place in line for the throne made his accession unlikely . . . apart from catastrophe befalling King Edward's brother Clarence and Edward's two very young sons. After arrangements were made for quick conveyance of Clarence and the boys, poor Edward expired, and Richard had his miracle. Much is made in the play of his physical deformity mirroring his moral decrepitude, making that much odder a request he makes of Elizabeth. She, sister to elder Edward and now-cold Clarence, and mother to the poor dead boys, is approached by Richard (ever the romantic) to ask for her daughter's hand in marriage. Throughout the play, as intentionally despicable as he has been made to appear through his selfish decisions, he appeals to the audience for sympathy on a number of occasions, and is somewhat convincing in his self-serving rationalizations. But in Elizabeth, he has met his match. In a jewel scene in Shakespeare's canon (Act 4 scene 4), Richard and Elizabeth square off, and for the first time, really, Richard takes his lumps. Although he leaves the conversation somewhat worse for the wear, his reasoning is a gift for our purposes here.

Richard begins by trying to convince a grieving mother that he has such plans that any harm he'd done to her would be overwhelmed by the good he was planning. Of course, she buys none of his malarkey. What could you offer, she asks? Why, the advancement of your children, of course, he retorts. Do you mean advancement up the scaffold to be dispatched? No, he replies, *royal* advancement. The wrongs you suppose I did to you, he says, will be compensated for in my plan—I would make your daughter queen. And who, pray tell, she asks, would be her king? Why, me, of course, he replies.

Recovering, Elizabeth offers him something of a plan. Send to her two bloody hearts, she tells him, each stamped with the names of her two dead young brothers that you had killed. Then, to comfort her, send her your kerchief soaked in their blood. Nuance not being numbered among his gifts, ever-clever Richard sussed out that she was not *actually* providing sound advice. Sometimes men, he says, deal . . . unadvisedly. If I did it, I did it for her, you know. When I crush my adversaries and she is mine, he says, you will once again be mother to a king. A verbal tennis match ensues then between them; each of Richard's self-centered volleys is returned . . . with (E)nglish (if you pardon the pun), by Elizabeth. In the end, Elizabeth fools Richard, leading him to believe she will be "the attorney" of his love for her daughter. Instead, young Elizabeth marries Richard's rival, Richmond, the future King Henry VII, beloved by his people and by Shakespeare's audience.

Throughout the play, Richard rationalizes like he does in the above exchange, discarding people like cigarette butts, and appealing to the audience for their forbearance. His heart is as withered as his guilt-bent frame. By his own description—*and decision*—he is a villain, and does the office nobly.

Richard did not merely further his own ends at the point of a bayonet. His management style, such as it was, was founded on vengeance. To ensure Lord Stanley's allegiance in the inevitable battle, Richard held Lord Stanley's son's head as guarantee. When Stanley's allegiance to Richmond became clear, Richard orders Stanley's young son beheaded, even though nothing could be gained from the act, as Richard's regime was crumbling about him. Vengeance, it would seem, is a natural language, motivator, and justice framework for those who exhibit antagonistic selfism. Let us consider the justice vengeance gives.

Sorrow dogg'd by sorrow

Vengeance, an idea seemingly older than the sea, for many still reigns supreme in the court of justice. As an approach to achieving justice, it is the most obvious, most basic, and also most impoverished. In order to understand more completely that which we will eventually dismiss, we examine four significant iterations of it. We promise not to indulge in overtelling here, beyond a touch of poetic indulgence on our part. Each recounting has something different and fruitful to offer our conversation.

Greek Vengeance

First, let us consider another tale given to us by the Greeks. The setting: a royal party. Brother kings of Sparta (Menelaus) and Athens (Agamemnon) preside, with prince Paris of Troy and other notables in attendance. Paris fancies Menelaus's wife Helen and, on the pretext of a godly affront, he takes her with him as they depart for Troy. Outraged, eventually Menelaus convinces Agamemnon to wage war against the Trojans. En route, the stormy Aegean Sea roils; oracles tell Agamemnon that the only way to earn Zeus's blessing for his aggression is to sacrifice his daughter, Iphigenia. Agamemnon's choice is that the spoils of war were worth more to him than his daughter. Clytemnestra, Agamemnon's wife, saw things differently. After a decade-long war, won in the end at a horrible price, Agamemnon, with his concubine in tow, returned home to Clytemnestra. She hid her own lover and welcomed Agamemnon home, even preparing a bath for his weary bones. As he soaked, she sharpened her knife one final time, and then she gutted him like a rainbow trout.

Aeschylus portrays Clytemnestra's state of mind after delivering the agonal blow:

> I bid you to rejoice, if such you will:
> Rejoice or not, I vaunt and praise the deed,
> And well I ween, if seemly it could be,
> T'were not ill done to pour libations here,
> Justly—ay, more than justly—on his corpse
> Who filled his home with curses as with wine
> And thus returned to drain the cup he filled.
>
> (Aeschylus/Morshead et al., 1998, p. 89)

Standing over her husband's corpse, she makes no apologies, and even seeks to commemorate other dead—specifically her daughter—by pouring libations on his body as if he were already soil beneath her feet. Why be so monstrous toward her husband? True, he was a warmongering bastard who left her to manage the city in his absence (more to the point, to face the consequences of his own mismanagement and the displeasure of the populace over the ten-year war), but surely this sanguine stance is over the top. It would seem, though, Agamemnon had really slipped up: he put work before family. Put slightly differently, he killed his daughter in sacrifice to Artemis so his ships would enjoy fairer winds on their way to besiege and eventually rape Troy. Clytemnestra killed Agamemnon, even proudly, because she was delivering justice unto him at the tip of her blade. She rails against chorus members, who seem only too willing to condemn her, but were silent when Agamemnon found his daughter's life in balance to be less valuable than victory:

> Ye had no voice of old to launch such doom
> On him, my husband when he held as light
> My daughter's life as that of sheep or goat,
> One victim from the thronging fleecy fold!
> Yea, slew in sacrifice his child and mine,
> The well-loved issue of my travail-pangs,
> To lull and lay the gales that blew from Thrace.
> That deed of his, I say, that stain and shame
> Had rightly been atoned by banishment;
> But ye, who were then dumb, are stern to judge
> This deed of mine that doth affront your ears.
>
> (Aeschylus/Morshead et al., 1998, p. 90)

Had he stayed away her bloody deed would not be defensible, but his return necessitated that he be killed. All the more, the manner of his return deepened Clytemnestra's sense of injustice. Although she had taken a lover herself, his having indulged in concubines, even bringing one home as spoils of war, was all the more affront to the home they had made together. After some debate, the chorus begins to see things from Clytemnestra's perspective, and it is here where we can begin our conversation about the anatomy of vengeance. The chorus chants:

> Lo! Sin by sin and sorrow dogg'd by sorrow—
> And who the end can know?
> The slayer of to-day shall die to-morrow—
> The wage of wrong is woe.
> While time shall be, while Zeus in heaven is lord,
> His law is fixed and stern;
> On him that wrought shall vengeance be outpoured—
> The tides of doom return.
>
> (Aeschylus/Morshead et al., 1998, pp. 99–100)

The wage of wrong is woe: one gets what one deserves. As long as the heavens be ordered as they are, no other outcome than vengeance for wrong-doing reasonably can be expected; wrong rebounds to the wronger with the inexorableness and regularity of the tides. With such an ostensibly universal and natural physical law we might infer that, like with the Buddhist idea of karma, the obverse is true as well, that the former necessarily implies the latter: the fruits of generosity are prosperity. We do not hear any character in *Agamemnon* making such a case, however, even as counterpoint to and justification for vengeance. Of course, such a pregnant silence raises a rather disquieting point. Regardless of positive actions over the course of one's life, one cannot purchase one's way out of doom by repeated kindnesses; "none can wrench from off the home of sin" (Aeschylus/Morshead et al., 1998, p. 100). One cannot twist free of the grip of sin, even by doing good deeds or having done good deeds, or so one argument goes. Fate (in the body of the terrifying Erinyes) sets in motion dark deeds from dark deeds, only to be halted by preternatural intervention, if even then.

Later in Aeschylus's trilogy, Orestes will return to kill his mother for having killed his father. He then must flee from the Erinyes, only finding safety finally from his own dark deed (even though it was *commanded* by Apollo) at the bosom of Athena (the Erinyes are then transformed into Eumenides—"kindly ones"). Perhaps we should back up a moment. According to myth, the chain of horrors above was set in motion generations before by Orestes's grandfather (and interestingly, Tantalus's grandson) Atreus who, it would seem in revenge for his twin brother (Thyestes) sleeping with Atreus's wife, had all but one of Thyestes's children killed and fed to him (e.g., Havelock, 1978). Thyestes in return curses Atreus and his house, it would seem to considerable effect. It is worth noting that their grandfather Tantalus cooked and served his son, Pelops, at a banquet for the gods; only through divine intervention did Pelops become recorporealized, and eventually sire several children, including Atreus and Thyestes.

What are we to make of this? First, as was made clear already, Fate rules, unless it is shunted in its course by the might of Olympus. Fate cannot be escaped except under exceptional circumstances, and certainly not simply by being a good boy. Second, vengeance is the accepted means of responding to a harm done. Third, and as something a corollary of the first two points, Clytemnestra's sanguine acts (she killed Cassandra, Agamemnon's concubine, as well), as devoutly as she planned them, as richly as she savored them, and as brazenly as she proclaimed them, and as much as they condemned her to death at the hand of her son, were not her own. The pain that brought them forth, however, was hers alone in fullness, as was the price for them. But then, of course, Agamemnon's sacrifice of Iphigenia was not of his doing in the purest sense as it was the fulfillment of a curse inspired by his father. Each offense, aside from the initial offense (Thyestes's alleged adultery with Atreus's wife), was begotten by others, such that the doer of the dirty deed herself or himself is both guilty and innocent, precisely at the same moment. At least for Aeschylus, that Agamemnon was a consummate ass and unremitting bully mattered not; it would seem that were he to have had gentler virtues, the die was still cast, and his fate sealed. At least for Aeschylus, that Clytemnestra's tears were all the more bitter because of the person who took her daughter from her also mattered not, for *her* fate was sealed as well from before the beginning.

For Aeschylus's *Oresteia* trilogy, the two components of antagonistic selfism dance a koftos: killing another, even one's own daughter or husband, to further one's professional interests or to vent venom, is defensible. Indulging one's own base emotions through bloody tantrums, however, upsets a balance, and condemns one's descendants to make similar decisions of their own. Vengeance is a thing one *must* take, and from the hide of another, yet doing so seals one's own fate as victim of vengeance. Of course, the *Orestia* is a morality tale: crimes have nearly inescapable consequences. Tantalus paid for his horrific crime all on his own, with his perpetual temptation. Clytemnestra, however, marches apace to her doom, much like Pink Floyd's masked schoolchildren, tumbling in turn into a meat grinder. It is a doom known in advance by Aeschylus's original audience, and Aeschylus uses no devices aside from simple gravity to enhance the dramatic tension. It is a doom set in motion by others, by then long dead, but it is a doom she still seemed to author with her own hands. The lesson is not that we should not revenge, but that doing hurtful things sets in motion a natural process which results in one's own demise, along with the demise of innocent others, that doing destructive things assures that destructive things will be done to you. Vengeance is as rudimentary as water, air, fire, and earth. And like the elements, vengeance can only be diverted through the most herculean effort. The final battle is waged not by people, but by ideas: justice in the body of the Erinyes demands the blood of Orestes, tilts against equity, with Apollo and Zeus as advocates (Haigh, 1896). In the end, only mercy can triumph.

Vengeance in Shakespeare

Of course, the quintessential tale of vengeance is one of Shakespeare's most venerated works: *Hamlet*. Vengeance upon vengeance like threads in tapestry; Hamlet and Laertes as opposites tilt and tumble until those they love are dead, including themselves. Brooding Hamlet grieves his father the king's death until that grief is turned to smoldering fury when the king's ghost tells Hamlet he was murdered. The ghost charges Hamlet to help him by visiting revenge upon the murderer, Hamlet's usurper uncle, currently bedding Hamlet's mother Gertrude. Hamlet uses Polonius and his daughter Ophelia to further his plotting against his uncle, specifically to give the impression Hamlet is insane. An acting troupe is yet another tool in Hamlet's machinations; the play was the thing whereby he pricked the conscience of the king. But the king discovered Hamlet's ruse and sought to have a brother state dispatch him. Rosencrantz and Guildenstern, the messengers, were discovered and they themselves were dispatched instead as a result of Hamlet's vengeful craftwork. While telling Gertrude of the murder, Polonius overhears while hiding, but is accidentally killed by Hamlet. Laertes returns to seek vengeance against the king for the death of Polonius, *his* father. Meanwhile, Ophelia really does go mad as a result of Hamlet's ruse, and she drowns. Laertes, twice grieving, sets his sights on Hamlet, and poisons him with his foil during a fencing match. Claudius seeks to kill Hamlet with poison as well, but the poison ends up going to Hamlet's mother instead. Hamlet recovers Laertes's foil, wounds him fatally, then runs the king through just as the English embassy arrives.

Hamlet is unparalleled in its poetic power; so many quippy one-liners from the play have become part of parlance, and remain in common usage today. Characters, in particular Hamlet, question many aspects of their lives, even to the extent of challenging God's proscription against suicide. Never among all the musings the Bard offers us is the wisdom of vengeance meaningfully taken under scrutiny; only the still sword gathers its force against its adversary; it is silent only like a storm on the horizon is silent. Significantly, Hamlet even chooses to forego an opportunity to gut his uncle while his uncle kneels in prayer. To send him to heaven with God's forgiveness while Hamlet's father wallows in hell would be . . . the acme of injustice (Act III, scene iii). And in the end, the price of vengeance is only too clear: the royal blood of Denmark lies thick and dark, coagulating on the throne room floor.

Hamlet represents a mutual, unmitigated, and accelerating rush toward vengeance. Characters, most of all Hamlet himself, were richly contemplative, yet bent inexorably on uncritical vengeance. In these days, says Hamlet, "virtue itself of vice must pardon beg" (Act III, scene iv). The word "forgive" appears only three times in the play at all. The first appearance is when Claudius the usurper king on his knees begs to be forgiven for his act of murder. The second appearance occurs when Hamlet is confronting Gertrude with the foul murder of her first husband by her current husband. The final appearance comes at the very end of the play when Laertes, now mortally wounded by his own poisoned blade, asks Hamlet for forgiveness for killing him. Thus only one time is forgiveness requested without personal benefit at stake, and only once is forgiveness offered to another.

Again, the conclusion of this morality tale is the same as in Aeschylus's: vengeance may feel good, but it is far more expensive in the long run than it seems immediately. But we surmise there is more for us to learn here from *Hamlet*. Only at the end is there even a hint of remorse. Really only Laertes offers a heartfelt expression of legitimate remorse for having had his heart purchased wholesale by vengeance. Vengeance is not much seen as a choice, it is never questioned, but neither is it necessarily a force of nature as it is in Aeschylus's *Orestia*. Instead, vengeance leads gravitylike to oblivion for all who drink of the tainted cup.

One thing that makes both tales so compelling is that both casts contemplate and act without the merest inkling that there is anything toxic in their approach to justice. Vengeance as a value was uncritically accepted, vengeance as a course of action was unquestioned. Vengeance is seductive and worse, dangerously transparent, most of all to the seeker of vengeance. Vengeance gives the momentary rush of feeling rudimentarily akin to justice, but the rush is quickly gone, leaving an abyssal wound in its train. Vengeance is the heroin of justice.

Biblical Vengeance

Vengeance condoned from above was a familiar idea as well outside of the Aegean's salty embrace. A thousand miles east and somewhat less mythical, as the Israelites' years of nomadic living wound down, we are told, God told Moses to tell the Israelites to visit bloody vengeance upon the Midianites (Numbers 31:2). And they did, so it would seem. The Midianite men were killed, along with boys and any women who had slept with a man (Numbers 31:18). Their villages were razed, their livestock and valuables were taken and distributed among the Israelites. The girls who were kept alive were saved for themselves, presumably as wives, housemaids, concubines, or chattel. In essence, the Midianites were obliterated as a people. What could have precipitated such wrath?

Well, the Midianites were a nomadic people, like the Israelites had been for a time. At this point in time, though, the Israelites were quasisettled, in southern Palestine. Raiding skirmishes among nomadic tribes seem to have been somewhat commonplace, but in the particular case of the Midianites, the Israelis had some painful memories (Albright, 1915). It would seem, then, that the memory of harsh handling by the Midianites survived the Israelites' change in condition. Accompanying those difficult memories, of course, were dark machinations.

In the Bible, we are given yet another justification for the destruction of the Midianites: the Midianites were accused of tempting the Israelites into idol worship. The accusation seems ironic when we consider that the Midianites were also descendants of Abraham, and certain practices like circumcision were adopted by the Israelites from the Midianites. Even Yahweh himself was a Midianite god before he was proclaimed by Moses (Midianite, 2015). Regardless, the consequences for such a grievous spiritual error as being led to idolatry were potentially so severe other rules of conduct like the prohibition against killing were set aside for the sake of justice. Possibly. If we are to take accounts as we receive them to be tolerably accurate, in effect, we have before us two partial justifications for vengeance: they started it, and they made me do something bad.

Neither justification is satisfactory on its own, of course; leaning together they make something of an edifice ostensibly strong enough to bear the burden of the weighty acts suspended from them. It is difficult to determine to what degree simple sanguine vengeance was a buttress in this edifice, but what seems clear is that the destruction of the Midianites as a people was, in the eyes of the Israelites, a righteous albeit bloody act.

Events on Melos Go Ill . . .

With apologies, we return again to Greece for the last bit of the story. Please picture, if you will, the fateful conversation taking place on a green-gold hill, grass clinging to rocky soil. The Aegean is a deep blue-green almost too insistent and transfixing to accommodate a lazy scan of the beach; between earth and sea lies nestled the whitewashed and innocent city of Melos. A view of unsurpassed, resplendent beauty lies before the assembled party, nearly empyrean in cast. Capes dance over shining armor and snap in the littoral breeze. The city sits at the nexus of elements, seemingly ready to serve as mediator to the Gods. Our narrator, Thucydides, could not have been there to hear the dialogue, so like Thucydides, we shall indulge in a degree of poetic license.

The city fathers of Melos and a number of Athenian generals stand and share the vista as they talk of war and fate. The Peloponnesian War has ceased being a war of bluster and saber-rattling; it is the year 416 BCE, and the war is in full swing. Melos had had ties both to Athens and Sparta, but had pronounced its neutrality in the struggle. On the world stage, though, Melian neutrality is an implicit indictment of Athenian might, at least so argue the Athenian generals. As a naval power, island states within their reach should ally with Athens, so the logic goes, or Athens isn't as powerful as they claim to be.

The Melian fathers beg with the Athenians to see things another way: Melos can be your friend, they say, and still be neutral. Significantly, the Athenian generals argue that although in a perfect world, friendly neutrality could be the case, the requirements of realpolitik require them to impose the will of Athens on the poor people of Melos, even if doing so is less palatable than one might like. In fact, the Athenians argue, were roles reversed, if Mighty Melos was in a regional struggle with another major city state, and tiny Athens found itself downrange of Melos's security interests, surely the Melian generals would do precisely as the Athenian generals propose. The Athenian generals deliver the message they carried: state formally your allegiance with Athens or Athens with destroy you. After their efforts come to nothing, the Melian fathers shrug and say, "Do what you will."

A turquoise sea laps at the front steps of flat-roofed homes; boats bob in the harbor, hovering a surprising distance above their shadows. Yellow Pleistocene clay cliffs frame electric blue water. A trickle of crimson runoff meets the crystal blue, incongruous against white pavestone; all the men of Melos are slaughtered, the women and children captured and enslaved.

So where, you may ask, is the act of vengeance? The Athenians had no quarrel with the goodly people of Melos. The Melians did not in the end offer bloody justice upon the Athenians for their Herculean atrocity. The affront that makes events in Melos an act of vengeance was nothing more caustic than the Melians' insistence on their own sovereignty. They had the audacity to claim the right of self-determination, even in the face of the realpolitik needs of Athens. The Melians threatened Athenian sovereignty by callously asserting their own. For vengeance to be vengeance, the causative evil need not be objectively evil.

Or Else What Follows?

So what can we say about vengeance as a human technology? To begin, it seems to involve some retribution or paying back for a harm (Henberg, 1990), at least to the degree that retribution and vengeance share similar logic, the paying back occurs in the same or similar currency. Hamlet and Laertes sought to return like for like to those who are thought to have done harm. There is a simple, arithmetic shape to the process: what was done to me shall be visited upon the original doer. But then, of course, we have the "seminal" act of violence in Aeschylus's tale: Thyestes sleeps with Atreus's wife, Atreus kills and cooks Thyestes's children. There is something of a mismatch between adultery on one side, and murder and forced cannibalism on the other. Henberg has us think in terms of a constant currency in terms of retribution, but the wielder of vengeance is not always also as disposed to wield a clear eye. Still, the idea of a currency of exchange seems to be fitting where vengeance and retribution part company. With retribution, there is something of an appreciable balance in the exchange whereas vengeance offers no such structure. Retribution is, in essence, the repayment for one's misdeeds; however, the currency for vengeance seems only to involve pain.

Vengeance allows space for additional fees to be tacked onto the bill. Menelaus's wife leaves him for handsome Paris, and to Menelaus the logical thing to do is to amass his armies, to convince his brother to do the same, and to lay a decade-long bloody siege to a city innocent of any offense other than being Paris's home. No pretense whatsoever is made regarding scale.

The more pressing question in the end, however, is why: how is it that in return for harmful acts a victim or community seeks to answer the harm with harm, perhaps similar, but often sanguine. In a careful and erudite examination, Henberg (1990) argues that four types of solace can be derived from the misery of an offender. There is *metaphysical solace*, the sense that the universe maintains a balance, a kind of karmic equilibrium, within itself, almost like pH in a living cell. Perhaps if an attacker eludes us, we can draw comfort from the idea that he cannot elude God, and that what is beyond human reach is never beyond God's (e.g., Romans 12:19). Nature abhors when wrongs go unanswered, so the idea goes, just like it abhors a vacuum. It turns out that things are nothing close to that simple in actuality. Sometimes the universe (or God) needs a little help. After all, we *are* part of the universe, we *are* God's creations. The *solace of duty* comes from having delivered justice on behalf of balance. Clytemnestra celebrates her bloody deed, not only for herself, but for the balance she thinks it restores. Yet another type of solace can be found in Hamlet's example: he passed on the perfect chance to kill King Claudius so that Claudius would kick his heels at heaven and suffer the same metaphysical misery his victim knew. There is a type of solace, he says, that comes from refraining from doing that which would precipitate vengeance against one's self: *the solace of self-control.*

What might that justice look like? *Vindictive solace* gives substance to the pursuit; you get . . . what you gave. Like a turd mailed in a poorly addressed envelope, evil returns to the sender. The nature of the returning evil, however, is defined by the original act: there may be more pain or less, or precisely the amount thought to have been done, but the ugliness of the initiating act shapes the ugliness of the response, at least sometimes. Even the twisted brutality inflicted upon poor Robert Damiens, described in colorful detail at the beginning of Foucault's (1979) seminal treatment on punishment, follows this logic: he sought the death of the king; the king is France, and as France has many subjects, he deserves many deaths. Of course, they did the best they could to give him as many deaths as possible, torturing him for hours with hot pincers, molten lead, and wax before the four horses of his own personal apocalypse tore him to pieces.

So vengeance offers solace first to those who witness it, and also to the victim of the initial harm (note the priority). It may even offer some measure of comfort to the offender as well; once a harm is paid for, space may be created to rejoin the community more or less as an equal member. However, vengeance never seeks to reunite the offender with his or her victim. Vengeance is an appetite for punishment that is never satiated. Solace is only a partial answer as to why harm for harm offers comfort; from it we have something of a proximal understanding of vengeance's allure. Why vengeance offers solace is the next question. Almost invoking Mills (1959/2000), Henberg (1990) tells us that a careful and wide-ranging look at scripture, legislation, and literature from the Himalayas to the Adirondacks, from deep antiquity to today, would be necessary to provide a complete answer. He has done much of this for us, so our purpose will be to offer a far more cursory treatment. But the question remains: why is vengeance seemingly foundational, even something of a default setting, for our sense of justice, despite the oblivion it invites?

Put a slightly different but no less challenging way, Henberg asks his readers how we can be comfortable with the idea of repaying evil with evil if it is our intention to decrease the overall biomass of suffering in the world. His answer seems to hinge on the rich complexity of reasoning and emotional needs that can and have worked to justify or excuse vengeance, because his "tragic thesis" (Henberg, 1990, p. 7) is that some measure of retributive thought is inevitable for humans. "Alas," he tells us, the worlds where evil is answered with only forgiveness, where predation is extirpated "are ideals of subtraction that omit whole chunks of robust human experience. We can, in practice, no more rid ourselves of retributivism than we can escape suffering or cease searching for solace in the face of it" (Henberg, 1990, p. 8). We revenge, and sadly we regret that we have revenged, because doing so is just who we are.

Ah, but isn't that where wheels and carriage begin to part company? For Henberg, it seems evil is an objectively verifiable thing, something on which one may rest one's coffee mug. If vengeance makes any sense as an approach to justice, the causative harm must be regarded as such at the least by a nontrivial segment of the community, or, at the least, a Greek chorus. There is considerable breath behind the idea of evil's empirical certitude, not the least because of the way we tend to define evil. But most definitions of evil one might discover tend to rely on the power of synonyms and examples to convey a sense of the idea. The use of multiple synonyms can give the appearance of a nontautological definition when, in fact, it is hopelessly self-referential. Further, examples offer a sense of empirical clarity and agreement when, in fact, such agreement is at least culture-, context-, and time-variant. False certitude regarding the idea of evil occludes the fact that "evil" and "good" as constructs are meaningless. One can speak in terms of destructiveness, or of wholesomeness, as these ideas have some form of empirical relevance. We can discern that smoking tobacco is antithetical to one's long-term health, whereas sustaining a program involving a balanced diet and modest exercise is consonant with a long, happy life. Tobacco, however, is not itself evil, any more than spinach is, of its essence, good. The Melians understand this now only too well.

If evil is at most vaporous, it certainly seemed all too real for Clytemnestra, the last casualty of that war in miniature. If it is evil alone that differentiates vengeance from restoration, something of evil may well be solid enough from which to hang our hat. Earlier we mentioned destructiveness and wholesomeness as empirically sound alternatives in comparison. The comparisons between evil and destructiveness and good and wholesomeness are more fact than mere juxtapositions. Evil as an idea is a cowardly, mentally lazy cop-out. Labeling something as good or evil fails utterly to serve human ends, as not only does it imply that a thing's essence is immutable, it implies also that one need not take the time to examine the labeled and the process of affixing the label. Some things have a quasi-innate nature: a gun is designed to destroy (though it may destroy life or a paper target, depending on the wielder's intent), it can never create. A magnetic resonance imaging system seeks a view that can heal although it is possible that the knowledge gained from a scan could be put to nefarious use. Sentient beings, however, possess a true and overriding innateness: all sentient beings are innately and irrevocably beautiful and holy in themselves. Any conception of justice—any philosophy for that matter—that divides and creates camps based on cursory assessments of innate attributes fails to honor the divine beauty of each spark of sentience and is *at best* cheap and flimsy, and at worst, a special species of violence.

Now, not all thought on vengeance limits itself with torturing alone. The idea that ugly things might defensibly be inflicted on one who has not given rise to ugliness of her own, as we have seen in our examples of vengeance, is far from new, and it has a related principle in modern penal thought. General deterrence in its purest form makes no assumption that a guilty party be the one who receives unpleasantness in return for wrongdoing. General deterrence seeks only to convey the cost to the community for wrongdoing of its members; it is a theater of cruelty of a sort. Something bad was done by a member of the community, something bad must be done to the community. The punishment need only make the threat of punishment credible (von Hirsch, 1976). Consider, for example, the plight of the poor Melians. More modern versions of general deterrence have connected the instrumental suffering imposed and the individual thought to be responsible for the offense of interest, but no such connection should be presupposed.

The idea of fate-doomed vengeance receives mixed reviews today. In Euripides's telling of the Agamemnon/Clytemnestra/Orestes myth, he is careful to highlight the distasteful unfairness of it all: Apollo's ordinance is cheap for himself, whereas the impact on mortals is truly grievous (Henberg, 1990).

Generally, we think of punishment in terms of deservedness on the basis of one's own actions. We see punishment as being appropriate, in a retributive sense, according to the seriousness of one's actions, which is itself a function of two things: the damage one causes, and the degree to which one acted willfully in the causing of the damage (see, e.g., Sebba, 1984; von Hirsch, 1976). The damage one does, and the intentionality with which one does it, are clumsy barometers when used as primary indicia for how a community should respond to harm. As we shall see in later chapters, merely turning our gaze from harm done to the divinity of harmer and harmed alike, retuning our thinking from emphasizing disorder to honoring beauty represents the single most profound evolution in justice thought since the first act of vengeance.

In his own seminal work on punishment and the law, Newman (2008) argues that Herbert Spencer and Jean Piaget both in their own ways first pinned the human moral sense to the harshness of life. The slings and arrows of outrageous fortune, and the bloody consequences therefrom, seem to have predisposed humans to responding to unpleasantness in kind. A storm destroys a primitive shelter; food scarcity bleaches nutrition, and eventually life itself, from a prehistoric child. Perhaps naturally, those who suffered hardships sought answers to a question nearly identical to the one we are asking now: "Why do bad things happen?" With fists clenched and shaken skyward, flanked by shouts sharpened to pierce the clouds, no answer comes. Meaning is sought from the noise, and whether it is there or not, it is found. Metaphysical solace is perhaps one consequence of the pursuit of meaning that chases hard on the heels of hardship.

There is a fatal flaw to this argument as well. It turns out that we in the contemporary Global North do not live with the fear of destruction, deprivation, or predation. Certainly there *are* those in the Global North who do (to our interminable shame), as of course much of the Global South knows such fear only too well (again, to our unremitting humiliation). Yet it is not those who know bodily such horrors that concern us for, if the argument (which we might call the "naturalistic punishment" argument) is to be believed, they should be the most vociferous advocates for vengeance. In fact, it seems the "Haves" of the world are far more likely to advocate for vengeance than the "Have-Nots." The relatively settled Israelites without compassion put the sword to the wandering Midianites, and the scholarly young regent Hamlet gave his last breath to see his duplicitous uncle undone. Indeed, it was the very might and majesty of Athens that compelled their hand against the defenseless Melians. The reliance upon the state of "primitive" humanity to justify the most cowardly and ineffectual approach to justice by the privileged elite in fact illustrates precisely who is primitive in actuality. We wonder if they enjoy the irony.

Returning to Henberg's four types of solace, it would seem he has given short shrift to a vital aspect of solace. When he speaks of metaphysical solace, he refers to "the comfort implicit in perceiving a larger order and assimilating ourselves to it" (Henberg, 1990, p. 4). But he continues, acknowledging the possibility of merit, but emphasizing the solace that comes from the notion that our aggressor will get his later on, either on earth or in heaven. Metaphysical solace is the consolation of the powerless, says Henberg.

A different kind of metaphysical solace is possible, however; something like the obverse of Henberg's: if we manage to stay clear of things that are proscribed and to do the things we should do, if we eat our vegetables and stay away from pool halls and fast women, we hope to have some measure of agency over the likelihood of our suffering. Historically, there has been considerable appeal to idea that desert and harm, like merit and reward, are causally coupled (see, e.g., Kelsen, 1941). As we have seen already, the Greeks understood the relationship between actions and consequences to be natural, elemental, and even magnetic. Gods themselves were subject to it, as gravity tugs on kings and jesters alike. Iron filings do not debate the relative nobility of one magnet over another; they respond from within themselves simply according to power. The idea that deservedness and suffering, along with merit and reward, follow in causal lock-step is seductive and salving.

Salving, perhaps, but consider: restorative justice scholarship tends to think itself to be something of a breed apart, even a cut above; vengeance seen from a restorative justice perspective is impoverished and unedifying. This assessment is fair enough, yet restorative justice and vengeance are conjoined twins, differing only in the means used to craft redress. Both vengeance and restoration are retrospective in nature and seek to marry the community response to harm to the nature of the harm imposed. In both vengeance and restoration, the harmer gives of herself a measure of suffering, a pound of flesh if you will, in an attempt to facilitate the recovery of the harmed. Surely, in restorative practices, we ask questions about helping victims recover, how to catalyze healing, whereas an avenger seeks wisdom on how to harm with precision and effectiveness, and this difference ends up creating vastly different outcomes. Additionally, the pound of flesh is employed differently in vengeance than it is for restoration. For the latter, it is an act of contrition ideally, or an act of repayment at the least, whereas for the former it is its own bloody justification.

The significance of vengeance and restoration living so close together, separated only by a few numbers of their address, is not that restorative justice approaches are impoverished for their kinship to vengeance (as restoration may be "impoverished" in a very wholesome and beautiful way). The crucial point for us is that the metaphysical marriage of desert and harm is a fiction;

that *we* make the difference between cruelty and healing though our choices and our actions. If good and evil are meaningless, desert, in the end, would have only a ghost for a bride. With no justification for harm in turn for harm, the mask falls away, and we see vengeance as it really is: wanton cruelty in a judge's robe. Karma is indeed a pleasant myth, but humans fashion meaning through a very manual, very mutual, if only quasi-reasoned process. The true beauty of the oneness of all sentience is that there is no faceless force guiding clumsy notions of good and evil according to desert: when wholesome things happen to those who cultivate wholeness in others *it is the result of intentional and purposive action by other sentient beings,* even if that action happens at a metaphysical level. Indra's net is vast indeed, and inescapable, yet it has no room for mythological creatures.

One final possibility exists for vengeance to retain anything close to viability. We will have to squint rather aggressively, but let us consider briefly Kant's thinking regarding punishment. He is an advocate of *lex talionis*, and retribution is, as we have seen, something of a cousin of vengeance (though differences have been noted). If retribution can be salvaged, however, perhaps a hope remains for vengeance, and it would seem that if anyone can save retribution, it would be humanist Kant.

Kant's advocacy of retribution is derivative from his idea of the categorical imperative (Potter, 1998). A harm done creates an unconditional and unalterable requirement, itself rooted in the principle of universalism, on the part of the harmer. The requirement created is to receive unto one's self what was done, in the nearest terms possible, as what one did to another. Universalism both creates the requirement for retributive punishment and limits it; the harm in response must be of equal proportion to the harm done, or else the principle of universalism is violated, up to and including death. In Kant's view, any moral principle must be paired by some incentive (Potter, 1998), as inner motivation is insufficient always to influence behavior. Kant's own elegant imagery in this regard is evocative of Newton's Third Law (Potter, 1998), and thus takes on the raiment of cold and constant physics.

Where Kant runs into trouble, though, is with the goal of punishment. Potter argues that for Kant, punishment seeks to protect everyone's rights through deterrence. If Potter is correct, Kant has a problem. Certainly specific deterrence might be defensible; *lex talionis* would communicate to the harmer the inappropriateness of his action in literal terms, and even offer him the respect of a moral actor in doing so. After all, only a moral actor can choose to act immorally. To punish in this case is to reaffirm the humanity of the harmer, at least partially. But if the interest is to assure the rights of others, if the punishment conversation has any audience beyond the harmer, then the punished person necessarily becomes the means to a larger end, to wit, general deterrence, and thus punishment would violate the categorical imperative. In actuality, the only possible value of punishment is that it can establish some sense of having paid for a harm done. Otherwise, punishment is suffering inflicted on others at a distance for our enjoyment: it is pornography. More precise means of payment exist, more effective means of ennobling harmers are available, as we shall see later in this work.

There is one other problem. Vengeance assumes, in more than a couple of ways, actually, that human actors act fully rationally. In essence, it is assumed that humans act rationally, meaning that they calculate the costs and benefits of their potential choices for action before they act. As a result of such consideration, if a human chooses to harm another for their own personal gain, it is assumed that the harmer considered nonharmful actions first, and chose the course of action that involved harming another. The rational man assumption is a common assumption among thinkers from the Enlightenment through the middle of the twentieth century. It turns out, however, that the assumption is a fatally poor one. Kelly (2009), for instance, argues that in order to justify retributive punishment, the individuals we punish must necessarily have the moral capacity to *understand* harmless conduct, and *choose* harmful conduct over harmless conduct. In essence, retributive punishment, at least from a strict liability framework, assumes full human rationality. Such an assumption implies that humans know all possible options for action, and all possible consequences deriving from each option. We are not, it turns out, omniscient. Humans are no more capable of true rationality than they are of unaided, self-powered flight.

Conclusion

As a framework for justice, vengeance is without doubt ancient and manifest, as few of the characters we met earlier ever questioned its inevitability. It is also irredeemably stupid. Even Laertes, himself poisoned with eyes now opened to the need for forgiveness, still endorses running the usurper king through as Hamlet's last corporeal act. Catastrophe fills the room, the dead and dying Danish elite lay cast about like cordwood. The marriage between vengeance and self-destruction now finally fully clear, and still Laertes blesses one last act of vengeance.

Vengeance begins with an appeal to the idea of exchange, a kind of sanguine transaction, but very quickly it outstrips the framework of "fair" exchange as taxes and fees of suffering for suffering quickly multiply. Interest becomes compounded, and the debt can never be repaid. At first, vengeance may wear the raiment of *talion*, but it is not long before the disguise is seen for what it is. We tend to think, as Locke seems to think, that the likeliest reason for the ratcheting up of the penalty demanded in response to harm is that it is the harmed who does the appraising. Assessing a fair exchange of suffering is almost impossible. Even if we would not condone it, squaring off against the Midianites, we can at least understand; if the Israelites felt as if they had been done wrong by another community, expressing displeasure is defensible. Destroying them utterly is rather more than "heavy-handed," and does not mete out anything that resembles justice.

In any event, vengeance is the clearest example of antagonistic selfism, and thus deserves to be banished forever from the field of justice action. Vengeance operates from a cowardly and feeble, if at times convincing, lie: the self is enthroned at the center of all, and that any action that pleases, or that furthers the self is defensible, regardless of the harm done to others. There is no justification robust enough to countenance the destruction of sentience, so there is no condemnation vociferous enough to adequately denounce vengeance as a justice paradigm. Least of all would such a justification find footing in selfishness.

CONTROL THEORIES: ANTAGONISTIC SELFISM AND IMPOVERISHED CRIMINOETIOLOGY

When we move from the contemplation of how individual wrongdoing should be addressed communally to the natural questions regarding why the wrongdoing happened in the first place, vengeance (as the most direct iteration of antagonistic selfism) might be defensible as a community response under only two circumstances: either the harmer acted through a willful, fully rational process, or the harmer's actions are the result of a natural propensity on the part of the harmer or the harmed. Vengeance in response to a harm done rationally seeks to offer *talion*: like harm for like harm, like intent for like intent—retribution. Vengeance as a response to harm resulting from a harmer's propensity is somewhat less direct in nature. Against a harmer who harms from her propensity we inflict vengeance, or at the least retribution, as Henberg observes, in order to restore order, to reaffirm the gravitational center of the community, to do God's work. It may seem cruel to ravage one who harms because of a condition beyond her control, but such harming is necessitated by a larger order: she may not be deserving on her own, but her suffering brings metaphysical order, even if we cannot see how directly.

Clearly vengeance in the context of theories that assume harm to be the result of failed social connections (e.g., Shaw, 1930; Shaw, McKay, & McDonald, 1938; Shaw & Moore, 1931) makes no sense. Vengeance shatters bonds; it cannot hope to rebuild them. Likewise, if one assumes harm to be the result of learned behavior (e.g., Akers, 2013; Sutherland & Cressey, 1978), vengeance is a poor means of achieving any constructive ends. The tyrant who teaches through violence should not be surprised when its citizens prove themselves to be apt pupils in revolt (Foucault, 1979). "When lenity and cruelty play for a kingdom," Shakespeare's (2017) King Henry V tells us after hanging his childhood friend in punishment for pillaging a French sanctuary, "the gentler gamester is the soonest winner" (*Henry V*, III, vi).

From the accounts of vengeance above, we see both rationality and propensity play for their respective kingdoms. For Aeschylus as well as for Shakespeare, rationality and innateness seem to coexist: Unaware that her decision to murder Agamemnon was preordained by the actions of her in-laws, Clytemnestra is certain her actions are her own. They are, and they are not. Hamlet's decisions are fully intentional, and although he contemplates practically every other sector of his humanity, he neglects to question, even remotely, whether the vengeance begged for by his father's ghost is in the best interest of the kingdom. Because it was requested by the dead, it is sacrosanct, even if in the end it only adds to their number.

For the Israelites, in the decision to destroy the Midianites again we can see both rationality and some form of a propensity argument at work. From a rational perspective, if the Midianites "started it," it would seem clear that the Israelites well and truly sought to finish it. In terms of the propensity argument, it is difficult to discern precisely how the Midianites were perceived by the Israelites at the time, but it stands to reason that as the Midianites remained nomadic at the time of their destruction, in the minds of the Israelites, they remained the Midianites of old: skirmishing rivals and tempters into idolatry. The destruction of the Midianites was really as much about destroying the Other precisely because of their nomadic and heretical nature.

There are criminological theories that live with this misfit marriage between opportunity and propensity. Gottfredson and Hirschi's "general theory" is one of the most heavily researched theories in the canon of criminological thought despite the flimsy logic that almost holds it together. We will discuss Gottfredson and Hirschi's general theory below. As a result of these examinations, we anticipate hurt feelings on the part of those who offered and those who support it. We want to be absolutely clear: such harm is the furthest from our intention. We offer only love, honor, and gratitude to the authors of these ideas and to their followers. The ideas themselves, however, shall not benefit from our affection. Indeed, the only violence we might ever condone is violence toward a violent idea.

Low Self-Control: A "General" Theory

The criminological theory offered by Gottfredson and Hirshi (1990) referred to most often as "low self-control" or "LSC" theory argues that a propensity, usually formed by one's eighth year of life, predisposes one to crime. Such a propensity seems to be the result of being ineffectively reared as a child.

When an individual with a low self-control propensity (one who was not monitored for wrongdoing, and punished when wrongdoing occurred) then comes across a circumstance that offers the opportunity for crime, that individual's ability to restrain herself fails and, like an immuno-compromised patient exposed to a nasty cold virus, crime happens. Two criminogenic mechanisms concern us, then, regarding LSC: the nature of the compromised propensity, initially called criminality, and the nature of offenders' responses to perceived opportunity. Opportunity requires little of us conceptually, so let us turn our attention to the idea of propensity.

Self-Control Propensity

What, then, is the nature of this propensity? Gottfredson and Hirschi take foremost as a point of departure the thinking of Jeremy Bentham, which is natural, as the theory bears some natural resemblance to classical theoretical arguments. Bentham's thought seeks to account for crime in terms of a weighing of costs and benefits for an offender. Bentham's balancing act will receive quite a bit more attention in the next chapter, but like Bentham, Gottfredson and Hirschi see something of a consideration of benefits as relevant. A common element among behaviors related to crime, as well as some forms of noncrime, they tell us, is the immediacy of benefit, rewarding short-range thinking. It is this tendency toward short-range thinking that is at the heart of LSC's idea of criminality. Where Bentham and other classical criminologists took for granted the presence of rational thought regarding choices to offend, and assumed no particular propensities beyond that capacity for full rationality (again, a huge and fatal assumption), Gottfredson and Hirschi emphasize the tendency to think in the short term about benefits, to prioritize immediate and pleasurable feedback, like engaging in risky behaviors (1990; Hirschi & Gottfredson, 1993). And indeed, it seems possible that an individualized risk preference may exist. Dopaminergic drugs have been shown to manipulate the perceptions of benefits and costs, *but only relative to a baseline trait level* of risk preferences (Norbury, Manohar, Rogers, & Husain, 2013). Specifically, Gottfredson and Hirschi specify six semi-overlapping elements, or axes of a low self-control propensity: immediate gratification, ease or simplicity, risk or thrilling nature, few long-term benefits, little planning, and harm to a victim (1990, p. 89). These six elements represent the manifestations of low self-control in individuals.

Critique of LSC

It turns out, though, that these six elements may not have any *causative* link to crime per se. For example, evidence exists (Righetti, Finkenauer, & Finkel, 2012) that low self-control may be as useful for predicting altruistic behavior as it is at predicting destructive behavior. Not a particularly auspicious start to things.

Of course, the longest-standing critique of self-control theory is the tautology complaint (Akers, 1991; see also Hirschi & Gottfredson. 2000). Generally speaking, a tautology is a statement that is meaninglessly provable in all circumstances, sometimes as a result of self-referential definitions, sometimes because the equality it asserts is merely a function of the meanings ascribed to the juxtaposed terms. "All cars are automobiles" would be an example of a tautology, as it is absolutely true, but only by virtue of definition, and thus utterly useless. Another example of a tautology, one that bears closer resemblance to the problematic theorizing in LSC, is the familiar parental command to "behave yourself." Now, any time one behaves, one is behaving very much like one's self unless, of course, one is adopting someone else's behavior. If Tammy is not mimicking Groucho Marx, say, or Michael is not doing his superlative impression of Steve Buscemi, merely by behaving one is behaving fully *like myself.* This, of course, is not what is intended by the exhortation. To "behave one's self" means to adhere to a set of behavioral norms specified in advance by the exhorting parent. These behavioral norms themselves find root in moral principles espoused and taught by the parent. "Behave yourself" means to "behave as I have shown you." For the command to make any sense, reference to an altogether separate set of ideas fully independent of "yourself" is necessary.

Akers (1991) observed that LSC was a tautology, as it identified the predictor concepts (scilicet, the six elements of low self-control propensity) by examining attributes of offenders, and then deriving a theory based on what was observed. The theory's central conception of criminal propensity, an idea that seeks to explain crime, is derived merely by examining assertions about those who are "criminal" and the "criminal" acts they commit, and then defining this explanatory construct on the basis of the constructs it finds. For instance, crimes, according Gottfredson and Hirschi, involve short-term benefits. Therefore the people who commit them (scilicet, criminals) have the attribute of preferring short-term benefits over longer-term benefits. Perhaps their words show it best: "Criminal acts provide *immediate* gratification of desires. A major characteristic of people with low self-control is therefore a tendency to respond to tangible stimuli in the immediate environment, to have a concrete 'here and now' orientation" (Gottfredson & Hirschi, 1990, p. 89). Setting aside the deeply problematic premise, the conclusion evidences simple circular logic. More than merely falsely provable, this loop is just bad theorizing.

But there is more. According to the theory, individuals who have criminoetiologically relevant low self-control should also exhibit similar (to wit, immediate-reward, risky, selfish) noncriminal behavior. To some, such a capacity is a considerable strength of the theory: it is thus not merely a theory of crime, but a theory of behavior more generally, explaining both crime and certain kinds of noncrime (Gottfredson & Hirschi, 1990, pp. 92–94). And in all honesty, we tend to agree that this attribute is perhaps its most attractive feature. Here's the rub: the measurement of low self-control is performed through a series of questions that ask if respondents exhibit impulsive, easy, risky, physical, or selfish behavior, or if they often experience impulsive, easy, risky, physical, selfish, or angry preferences, ideations, or emotional states, many of which are noncrimes. The standard instrument used for much of the empirical testing of low self-control theory employs the Grasmick and colleagues' twenty-four-item scale, or a modification thereof (Grasmick, Tittle, Bursick, & Arneklev, 1993). Questions address both attitudes and behaviors in this instrument; if attitudes and ideation alone were the focus, again, space might exist for an argument in favor of a logical break in the tautology. Unfortunately, Gottfredson and Hirschi have expressed a *preference* for *behavioral* measures for barometers of low self-control (Gottfredson & Hirschi, 1993; see also Delisi, Hochstetler, Higgins, Beaver, & Graeve, 2008). It should be no surprise that questions which ask about shortsighted, risky, selfish, and myopic noncrime behaviors would correlate positively with self-reported shortsighted, risky, selfish, and myopic criminal behaviors. Conceptually, this is not pulling a rabbit from a hat: the magician merely presented his audience with a rabbit while mumbling something about a fedora.

One might be inclined to argue, as Gottfredson and Hirschi do (Hirschi & Gottfredson, 2000), that a tautological flaw is fatal up until the point where it isn't, up to the point where empirical evidence bears it out. If the theory is supported in empirical tests, it matters little if the theory is self-referential. It may be crazy. It is right. After all, Wittgenstein (1922/2007) argued that only contingent propositions, statements which had demonstrable observational truth, could be called truly nontautological. Wittgenstein might well get Gottfredson and Hirschi off the tautological hook. And again, the idea of low self-control has received considerable empirical attention since its introduction. Just to begin, low self-control has been found to be predictive of a wide variety of offending, including delinquency among Hispanic youth in the United States (e.g., Vera & Moon, 2013) and among Korean youth in South Korea (Yun, Kim, & Kwon 2015); fraud (Holtfreter, Reisig, Piquero, & Piquero, 2010); violence (in a nationally representative sample, Larson, Vaughn, Salas-Wright, & Delisi, 2015; and among youths in Turkey, Ozbay, & Koksoy, 2009); violent victimization (Higgins, Jennings, Tewksbury, & Gibson, 2009); school bullying (Moon & Alarid, 2015); police deviance (Donner & Jennings, 2014); movie pirating (Higgins, Fell, & Wilson, 2007); and noncompliant behavior while incarcerated (Delisi et al., 2008).

Unfortunately, despite the authors' claims regarding the success of LSC in empirical tests, its results are impressive only in comparison to even worse performance of other theories in the dubious tilting field of contemporary quantitative social scientific empiricism. The measure of empirical success with most statistical models is the probability of Type I error (or the probability of a falsely rejecting the null hypothesis). The standard normally used for a sufficiently unlikely outcome is something that happens only 5 percent of the time or less ($p \leq .05$), or one randomly occurring outcome in twenty. Such a measure, of course, has nothing whatsoever to do with substantive meaningfulness; it speaks only to the likelihood of an effect or difference occurring by chance (see, e.g., Ziliak & McCloskey, 2013). The assumption, of course, is that improbable events are likely the result of something aside from natural variance. More crucially, most studies of *any* theory, even those like LSC that tend to perform best in empirical tests, have not and likely cannot meaningfully attribute more than 37 percent of observed variance in key dependent variables (e.g., "deviance" or "crime") (Weisburd & Piquiero, 2008). For example, Vazsonyi and Belliston (2007) found that in a very large cross-cultural and international sample, LSC could account for no more than between 25 and 36 percent of the variance in deviance. Michael's friend Chris Donner and his coauthor (Donner & Jennings, 2014) properly find support for their hypotheses related to LSC and police officer misconduct, though their able research at best could attribute a 23 percent increase in the odds of misconduct (verbal abuse, specifically) as a result of officer low self-control. Another reading of their findings offers a different hypothesis altogether: one rather potent explanatory force for misconduct in their data was sex. It turns out that according to their findings, it might be of far greater value to hire women as police officers than it would be to measure and hire officers based on their levels of self-control. In comparison, results indicate that simply being male created a 48 percent increase in the odds of an internal affairs investigation, and a 339 percent increase in the odds of physical abuse complaints. Likewise in another able piece of research performed by another of our friends, Leanne Alarid and her colleague found statistically significant but operationally tiny prediction for bullying behavior from measures of low self-control (Moon & Alarid, 2015). Higgins et al. (2007) found unlikely but operationally small relationships between low self-control, delinquent peers, and movie piracy. Self-control among South Korean youth (Yun et al., 2015) could account for only about 9 percent of the variance in delinquent behavior. Among Saudi Arabian youth, measured low self-control and substance abuse had no relationship at all (Beaver, Al-Ghamdi, Kobeisy, Alqurashi, Schwartz, Connolly, & Gajos, 2015).

One argument to be made regarding the weakness of empirical findings regarding low self-control is that the instrumentation used to measure it is suboptimal. In the first, and still standard, measure of low self-control, Grasmick and colleagues (1993) examined twenty-four items for their factor loadings. If the items were a valid fit for the construct, and the theory was sound, the twenty-four items should produce one factor, with all items loading onto it. That's not what happened. Five factors had eigenvalues greater than 1.5, and three had eigenvalues in excess of 2.0. The conclusion: low self-control, either as measured or as conceived, is rather more variegated than portrayed by Gottfredson and Hirschi. In the end, the Grasmick et al. instrument—again the standard instrument for measuring low self-control—could not do better than explaining a fraction (about 26 percent) of the variance in measured force and fraud.

If we were to be clear-eyed about the evidence in relation to the claims made by self-control theory, in fact there is scarce evidence for low self-control as it is defined by Gottfredson and Hirschi being a discrete and articulable phenomenon in human experience (Grasmick et al., 1993; Weisburd & Piquero, 2008) that has more than a minor influence on harmful behavior (e.g., Moon & Alarid, 2015; Higgins et al., 2007). Evidence has found small influences on harmful behavior from measured low self-control, but the creature the theory describes seems to be almost as rare as the Yeti.

Curiously, LSC purports to be a general theory, covering the entire human compass of force and fraud, yet its acolytes celebrate as success the meager results of studies that find only a fraction of force and fraud to be attributable to it. But part of the problem is related to choices made by studies performed which sought to find evidence for LSC. As we have seen, often the considerable majority of the phenomenon of interest—crime—is left wholly unaccounted for by even the most lauded theoretical models. It is easy to chalk up such catastrophic failure to the natural variation in the substance of interest, to wit, humanity. Such a concession emphasizes methodological shortcomings. Although despite the confidence some have in it (e.g., Gottfredson, 2013) methodological problems are many and profound to be sure, the real failing is in the comic-strip theorizing. Setting aside the bent reasoning, LSC theory seems to posit the existence of a creature with a propensity for harming others in his own dimly understood interest. In point of fact, what studies have done is to look for the traits identified by theory in the wider population. It is unclear whether the theory depicts a discernible being as such—a roaming limbic system—or whether it seeks to identify a level of propensity for low self-control in the wider community. In the latter case, the evidence is thin at best; the evidence for the former is wholly nonexistent. Either the creature specified by LSC has never been sought, or he has never been found, in either case the error lies not primarily with those who have looked for it, but much more with the theorists who initiated the hunt and anointed the tools of the search (Hirschi & Gottfredson, 1993).

And in fairness, both methodological and theoretical failings are the result of a deeper epistemic misapprehension that traces its roots to Western modernism. Specifically, modernists assert that to know something is to be able to articulate it atomistically, to have the understanding sufficient to remove it surgically from the world and to articulate it mechanistically under laboratory conditions. More tragically, to know means to grasp and hold, to penetrate and manipulate. There are parts of the human world where to hold is to know, but it is a type of illness to insist on encircling and violating that which we seek. Often, the greatest knowledge comes from releasing, from quests inward as much as outward colonization of the experiential universe. It is well understood that many quantitative social scientific methodologies borrow faulty logic from the natural sciences, and thus create a false sense of knowledge. But it is clearly also the case that much nomothetic theorizing makes a similar error in its struggle to be test-friendly.

One might be struck as we have been, when reading the primary exposition of the theory in the 1990 book, as much by the nature of the conversation than anything else. Instead of close analyses of ideas in order to divine some manner of wisdom from them, the authors seem intent on building an argument in the same fashion as one might build a model with an erector set. There seems to be rather more interest in building a theory that is different from other theories, than a theory that offers meaningful insight into human suffering. The authors seemed concerned with selecting constructs to include or leave out according to which empirical hurdles concerned them most, rather than seeking truth and trying to understand how what is believed to be known sheds light on the nature of the human condition. Writing around inconvenient empiricism is meaningfully different from seeking to theorize with the assistance of empirical insights. In short, LSC is a theory about the human condition made in a theory lab instead of where humans are; it is a theory which directs our gaze toward a rare, probably psychologically or organically damaged person who, we are told, is responsible for all force and all fraud, despite considerable evidence to the contrary.

Low Self-Control and Antagonistic Selfism

So what claim on our attention might such a paltry and threadbare theory hope to make? An answer seems to come from the links between self-control theory and antagonistic selfism, of which there are at least four. One link involves the nature of the theory avatar created by self-control theory. Another link is related to the ontological nature of the phenomenon it seeks to describe. Yet another bears on the policy implications of the theory. The last link we will highlight is concerned with the role of criminological theory in creating a more sane and humane world.

The low self-control avatar, the homunculus over which is draped the raiment of ill-considered, impulsive and self-centered propensity, is a clear example of one who would exhibit antagonistic selfism often, were he to take corporeal form. The archetypal low self-control offender puts his own interests before all, and he does not care who is hurt in the furtherance of his self-serving aims. Given an opportunity, using another human as a means to his own end only makes sense to him. Given an opportunity, vengeance seems like a very, very good idea.

An altogether separate question is whether or not such a creature exists. It seems clear from the exposition of the theory that tracing the outline of a living being was not the aim of the theorists. And it strains credulity well beyond failing to argue that low self-control explains all human force and fraud in all contexts. Instead as we have mentioned already, they sought to ascribe, to combine, to choose among alternatives, and thus to cobble together a theory that is predictive of force and fraud using contemporary social scientific methods. This shift in purpose is no small shortcoming and has come at a dear price.

The current state of criminological evidence is not sufficient to indicate whether the low self-control avatar is a living, breathing being. What evidence we have, despite its considerable volume, can only speak to the *occasional* influence of proxy measures of low self-control on harmful behavior *en masse*. It is certain, though, that there are many individuals alive today who live with the propensity for impulsive, self-serving, unskilled, thrilling behavior: children. Most kids under the age of eighteen exhibit precisely these behaviors. During World War II, the United States Army Air Force sought young men as pilots, because once they reached the age of twenty, they tended to recognize their mortal danger and thus take fewer risks (e.g., Keegan, 1989). But as self-control theory is concerned with *stable* propensities for impulsiveness, selfishness, thrill-seeking at others' expense, then our attention must turn to those who either do not or cannot utilize their neocortex sufficiently, and thus who live life ruled by their limbic system. Such creatures are few indeed relative to the human population, those who will not or cannot understand some semblance of delayed gratification, planning, or nobility in another person, but it seems clear they exist. Even these few unlucky characters who move through the world like horny teenagers do, on occasion, do wholesome things as well as unwholesome things (see, e.g., Pedneault & Beauregard, 2014). They may even plan something worthwhile, like a wedding or a funeral. They drive to work, they shop, they hug their children. What Gottfredson and Hirschi have done, perhaps without intending to do so, is to combine symptoms of phenomena like ADHD, fetal alcohol syndrome, pervasive developmental disorder, and other similar conditions into an irresponsible conglomerate model of force/fraud causation. Those individuals who exhibit the criminal propensity Gottfredson and Hirschi describe are few, but they are far more diverse than Gottfredson and Hirschi appreciate, and they are hurting.

And this point raises our second connection between self-control theory and antagonistic selfism: if self-control theory describes a real creature, one is left to contemplate the social obligation to them. If creatures with perpetually low self-control cause a significant amount of crime, then deterrence makes no sense. The policy options that exist for handling such offenders are few: find treatments for their propensity, incapacitate them until they become too frail to pose a meaningful threat, or destroy them utterly. Gottfredson and Hirschi offer little hope for a treatment, and incapacitation is an expensive proposition indeed. The last option has some appeal, particularly among those who also function from an antagonistic selfist perspective. Vengeance, or worse, simple utile extermination, is the most logical course, if Gottfredson and Hirschi were fully correct.

If such creatures do *not* exist as such, at the least not as such before the creation of the theory, one is left to consider the degree to which the idea itself, of archetypal offenders with greasy hair and greasy spine moving from urge to urge, blithely myopic and selfish, is deeply othering and thus constitutes a special species of harm. It seems to us that the ideas as constituted in the exposition (1990) dress simple prejudice in the robes of austere science. Only Gottfredson and Hirschi can know, and even they may not, but the degree to which this theory itself is a demonization of those labeled "criminal" is the degree to which it is itself a species of violence. If it was an effort to theorize in order to create empiricism-friendly theory, it is both force and fraud; if it was an authentic effort at theorizing a human experience, it is merely fraud.

Concluding Note: "Price Tag" Vengeance

Recently, four Israeli teens were convicted of arson in the "price-tag" burning of a Palestinian-owned café (Magnezi, 2015). In other words, the four teens decided to burn down a Palestinian café in retaliation for having their own hangout burned down, despite the fact that the teens, who planned the attack well in advance, knew for certain that the Palestinian owner of the café they torched had nothing to do with the destruction of their hangout. Such convictions are rather rare, it turns out; most price tag attacks go unanswered. The Anti-Defamation League (2015), who *are* concerned about price-tag attacks, reports that since 2008 a large number of attacks (probably in the hundreds) have been carried out by fundamentalist Israeli settlers against Israeli Arab, Palestinian, and Christian people and property as well as Israeli security forces in reprisal for action against illegal settlement activity. Revenge is both motive and defense for these attacks; although many Israeli leaders have spoken out vociferously against them, the number of price-tag attacks continues to rise.

Price-tag violence might be dismissed as the ravings of a small enclave of people, brought together by a common insanity, except for the power and extent of influence of the idea that gives their violent attacks meaning. Although the judge for the four youths was not swayed by the defense attorney's argument, the claim made by the defense deserves our attention. The defense argued that, as the act was an act of revenge, it was not, in fact, a crime. The duty to provide a zealous defense notwithstanding, the defense argued in essence that revenge is settled Jewish law, as embodied in the "an-eye-for-an-eye" teaching (*lex talionis*, which we will discuss at length in the next chapter). If there is anything at all more than mere legal defense to this claim, and we believe there is, revenge is not only the purview of ancient Greeks, Israelites, or tilting Danes. Vengeance remains, at least in the eyes of a considerable number of humans, a legitimate model, and possibly even the default model, for holding others to account for wrongdoing.

And indeed, were we to use current scientific methods and validated instruments in order to examine youths involved in price-tag attacks in Israel, we have every confidence that many would exhibit a degree of low self-control. It is also clear that such low self-control is at most a proximate construct in relation to the harm they do. The particulars of the harms may be related to the existence of a type of innate propensity which, when given an opportunity, finds itself setting a fire, defacing a vehicle, or bedeviling a child. It is not low self-control, however, that gives the fire meaning, or set the fire of righteous fury in their breasts; without these flames, no harm would have resulted.

It is the duty of scientists to be able to examine empirical results, not only in the context in which they were intended, but also in wider epistemic terms. The number of studies that offer support for a theory—any theory—is not itself the final measure of its grip on Truth. There is, in short, no scoreboard.

But like justice generally, when meaningful outcomes have been in short supply, where the things that count cannot be counted, we find ways of counting things that can be counted, and reforming our questions and our methods so that those countable things begin to count. And then we proceed to forget that we had been compromising all along.

BENIGN SELFISM

At this point it seems clear that harm for harm as a meaningful community response is rife with logical brokenness. It transforms broken humans into billboards advertising communal hegemony. It otherizes and dehumanizes through violence heaped upon violence. It is plagued by allegations of inequality and racism. It is the very last thing from sanity. In a similar fashion, Gottfredson and Hirschi's LSC theory, also logically damaged, creates the perception of an ineradicable taint in "criminals": that they are selfish, uncaring, predatory, myopic pleasure-seekers without a shred of nobility. Whether the authors intended such a taint to be dehumanizing or not is, in the end, immaterial, for the result is undeniable. Criminals are othered and dehumanized by a theory that justifies violence heaped upon violence. Not all impoverished theories of justice and of crime are so destructive as those that embrace antagonistic selfism. Indeed, there may be views where selfism offers something fruitful, even edifying, to our understanding of human suffering. At the least, a benign selfism is not wantonly destructive. Here we will examine a few systems of justice thought and criminology that are founded on a benign selfism.

BENIGN SELFISM AND JUSTICE

The Pripyat night was cool and quiet. A wintry chill could still be felt against spring's promise in the small hours before dawn. A little before 1:30 in the morning on April 26, 1986, the night was pierced by two explosions. There is disagreement about the nature of the second explosion, but the first—smaller—one blasted the massive lid of Chernobyl's Reactor 4 from its resting place and set it vertical. Over the course of the next hours, workers gradually grasped the scale of the damage and the danger. First responders were sent in to pump water into the reactor, thought perhaps to be still intact. They were dead within days from acute radiation poisoning having received their lethal shares in less than a minute. The fire crews arrived to contain the fire, and found themselves kicking around bits of graphite and nuclear fuel. Still, they fought the blazes within the reactor building. Many were dead within days. Helicopter pilots who flew over the smoldering ruin of Reactor 4 to drop sand, clay, and boron also received deadly doses of radiation. Cleanup workers in shielded clothing ("liquidators"), roughly two hundred thousand of them, were limited to four minutes of work per day due to the extremely high radiation. Many received several decades-worth of radiation exposure relative to natural background radiation (about twenty thousand received something to the tune of 250 millisieverts). Although some may have been unsure at first as to the danger, none could claim ignorance after the first days (World Nuclear Association, 2016).

Soon, attention turned to long-term containment of radioactive isotopes like strontium-90 and contaminated dust and water. It was decided to construct a concrete and metal encasing structure, called "the sarcophagus," around the damaged portion of the plant. Before such a structure could be contemplated, the risk of a massive steam explosion from superheated water in the bubbler chambers below the reactor had to be managed. Miners from across the Soviet Union were invited to come to the aid of the Motherland by digging a long tunnel under the stricken reactor, in order to allow intervention (either to drain the dangerously irradiated water, to pump liquid nitrogen into the soil below, or to fill the voids with concrete). They came by the trainload.

From first response to control to long-term staff (other parts of the plant operated until 2000) to suppression, in all more than half a million workers placed themselves in mortal danger for the sake of others (World Nuclear Association, 2016). Even more workers are today laboring to create a more permanent containment structure, currently slated to be in place by the end of 2017 (World Nuclear Association, 2016). Events such as the Chernobyl experience will pose a considerable difficulty for us. Well, not for us, exactly, but for those we will contemplate in this section. Specifically, we will examine the arguments of Ayn Rand and Robert Nozick as the embodiment of benign selfism in justice.

Objectivism

For a philosophy to be, well, a philosophy, it needs to possess a few attributes. One of the most important attributes is that it must be internally consistent. In the main, Objectivism is just that, but a philosophy must also rise to critique. Alas, Objectivism utterly fails to do that even though proponents such as Rand claim the philosophy to be truth. Rand did not countenance debate, especially in later years. It would be difficult to argue she was a philosopher at all, as debate and dialogue are our most consistent habit. But it is not our intention to diminish her here; being a philosopher is not necessarily a thing to wish on a friend. Instead, Rand's thought has an altogether different value for us, one that we will enlarge on after treating it.

Because Objectivism lives on the margins of being a defensible system of thought, for our purposes, we will give it something of a head start. For that head start, we can think of no one more able than Simone de Beauvoir. Of course, de Beauvoir and Rand would not necessarily have been best of friends (Champagne & Gladstein, 2015), and we do not intend to imply that they shared a common philosophy. Far from it. Rather, we intend to highlight that they shared an era—a singularly brutal one—admittedly from somewhat different perspectives, but given the time period when both thinkers lived, both have ample reason to be something short of chipper. One cannot escape having been changed by the bloody tempest of World War II Europe; how any given thinker copes with the wholesale cheapening of life resulting from such insanity is a function of the orientation of her deepest spirit. Here, we believe, these two people differed most significantly.

To understand Rand's purpose, we can put de Beauvoir's lovely prose to work for us. We hear de Beauvoir here providing some words that Rand could have never found, but almost certainly would have intended. As a "sovereign and unique subject amidst a universe of objects" (de Beauvoir, 1976, p. 7), each of us is privileged to the point of poverty. We are rich in awareness, to the point that we are aware that each of us is "nothing more than an individual in the collectivity on which [we depend]" (de Beauvoir, 1976, p. 7). Each of us "has the incomparable taste in his mouth of his own life, and yet each feels himself more insignificant than an insect within the immense collective whose limits are one with the earth's" (de Beauvoir, 1976, p. 9).

If we take de Beauvoir's imagery as starting point, Rand's intentions regarding the creation of an objective ethic for mankind are entirely not without merit. Indeed, some of her statements could be confused with those made by the Dalai Lama or Martin Luther King Jr., if excised from context. Her arguments, however, along with her conclusions are more than a little goofy. They offer perhaps the most high-profile apology for selfishness available to us currently.

For her aim, Rand perceives the need to skewer altruism as a viable ethical model for human relations. Unfortunately for her, she fails altogether in this, having instead chosen to tilt with a truly pitiful straw adversary. "Altruism" she claims, "declares that any action taken for the benefit of others is good, and any action taken for one's own benefit is evil" (Rand, 1964, p. viii). She supposes the dictator who slaughters innocents for the benefit of the nation would receive the altruist's blessing; she argues that a young man cannot but conclude that in an altruistic society, morality is his mortal enemy. Altruism, supposedly, provides no space for the self-respecting individual, and instead mandates that each individual be ready to self-immolate when doing so is in the collective best interest.

Of course this is a comically imprecise estimation of altruism; clearly agapic love includes the self within its compass. Kierkegaard's (2009) formulation of the Divine Command to love others and self, for example, makes clear that one is to love others as self, and self as others; thus both equally and totally. Indeed, the Divine Command requires each of us to *self-actualize*, to bring one's God-given gifts to fullest capacity, just as we do the same for those in our reach. Altruism makes no categorical command to self-immolate at another's whim. Catching fish is easy when they're belly-up in a barrel. But let's continue.

Now an objective human ethic is an aim worthy of pursuing. Rand dismisses the millennia of thought on ethics since Aristotle as being subjective, emotional, and impulsive. Instead a human ethic needs to be founded on objective criteria, on things that make us human. First, of course, we are alive. Life—our life to be exact—is the only thing "that makes the concept of 'Value' possible" (Rand, 1964, p. 16). The goal of action is life, thus the standard of value for any action by an organism is the degree to which it protects its life. Things that protect an organism's life are thus "good"; things that damage or end an organism's life are "evil." The central goal for an organism is life; life is the only end in itself. As good and evil comport with an organism's life, pleasure and pain are the biological rudiments of the assessment of good and evil. Rand is careful to point out, though, that pleasure is not an end in itself, as some pleasurable things are not rationally related to life. Chocolate is pleasurable, but it cannot suffice as the main course for every meal, or health will suffer.

It is necessary to understand that Rand's selfishness is not carte blanche. That other thing that makes us human, rationality, is the means whereby we secure our life (as we do not have claws or venom or instinct). We have to choose to use it, however, or we cease to be human, either in terms of being subhuman (e.g., criminals) or we die. When we act according to pleasure in irrational ways, like when we harm others, we become subhuman and we embrace destruction, primarily our own. If we fail to use our rationality altogether, we run the risk of failing to rise to the challenges life faces, and we may die. We may die before our time anyway, of course, but when we use our rationality, we give our own life every possible chance. We may be able to ask for forgiveness, but we are not capable of escaping the consequences of our irrational action or inaction.

Rationality crucially limits the scope of action; "The Objectivist ethic holds that *human* good does not require human sacrifices and cannot be achieved by the sacrifice of anyone to anyone. It holds that the *rational* interests of men do not clash" (Rand, 1964, p. 34). My life may be an end in itself, but I cannot defensively use another human as a means to my end. Consider her words here: "To love is to value. Only a rationally selfish man, a man of *self-esteem*, is capable of love—because he is the only man capable of holding firm, consistent, uncompromising, unbetrayed values." If one is equating "rationally selfish" with "having self-esteem" then the argument is a strong one indeed. Certainly, individuals without adequate self-esteem can love, it is likely their love is impoverished by their own lack of self-love. Rand's ideas dwell in uncomfortable proximity, it would seem, to ideas we have celebrated elsewhere. John Galt, Rand's protagonist in *Atlas Shrugged*, shouts soliloquys that might garner more than a few nods in agreement. Yet at the end of the day, Rand has completely missed the ball with regard to creating a human ethic.

Justice in Objectivism

As we take Rand, justice for her is rooted in two principles: the sovereign self and rationality. Regarding the self, it is manifestly evident that what I have made for my survival—all of it—is mine and cannot be taken from me justly. My life is license to act as needed within the bounds of rationality. This is akin to Nozick's (1974) assertion that what is rightfully mine is rightfully mine by virtue of just acquisition, or by just transfer from someone who is entitled to hold (and presumably but not explicitly entitled to transfer) the item of interest. The second principle, rationality, again requires that predicate volition: my life is an end in itself and rationality is my means of assuring my survival, *but I must choose intentionally* to be rational, I must opt for survival *qua* human. If I choose irrationality, say, by predating on other humans for my own survival, I have ceased to be fully human: "the men who attempt to survive, not by means of reason but by means of force, are attempting to survive by the method of animals. . . . Such looters may achieve their goals for the range of a moment, at the price of destruction: the destruction of their victims and their own. As evidence, I offer you any criminal or any dictatorship" (Rand, 1964, pp. 25–26). In terms of how a community should respond to harm done by a human, one might infer from Rand's wording here that anything goes. In his discourse with other humans, once a person has chosen the "method of animals" he may be treated as such by the community. His life, therefore, is no longer an end it itself; he would have no more dignity than an animal on an industrial farm, queued up to become an ingredient in chili.

The dialogue regarding justice has featured a vector of debate related to individualism and communitarianism. Sandel, McIntyre, Taylor, and others advocate for the view that human well-being is best understood and most surely secured through the community. Individualist arguments, in contrast, like those of Nozick, Rand, Beccaria, and others, tend to emphasize the interests and inherent rights of individual humans. In terms of a social contract reading, communitarian arguments tend to emphasize community members and their obligations to the wider community. In rough terms, the amount of their individual rights they cede to the collective "bank account" is relatively large, and thus the resulting government is relatively large and, one might assume, capable. Individualists advocate for a tiny contribution from each individual to the collective government's "bank account" of authority; the resulting government will tend to be small, even inept. An Objectivist justice system would be a relatively anemic thing to start with. The criminal court, such as it would be, would find itself concerned with determining the rationality of an individual's actions; even if deeds were in violation of criminal code, something like jury nullification would exist to protect rational humans from irrational criminal sanction. Such a justice system would live forever on the verge of being irrelevant.

Critique of Objectivism

Rand is guilty of a rather common error. She, like so many esteemed thinkers including de Beauvoir and one of our favorites, Erich Fromm (e.g., 2006), irresponsibly extrapolates information about the differences between humans and other nonhuman animals. Humans, unique among animals Rand tells us, must volitionally use their rationality in order to survive. Only humans, then, exist intentionally. The degree that nonhuman animals are self-aware is the degree to which her argument is specious. It turns out that higher animals, like chimpanzees, cetaceans, and crows, probably possess a considerable level of self-awareness, even empathy. For example, chimpanzees exhibit contagious yawning behavior, much like humans; contagious yawning is thought to be linked to robust self-awareness and empathy (Anderson, Myowa-Yamakoshi, & Matsuzawa, 2004). "Man is the only living species that has the power to act as his own destroyer" (Rand, 1964, p. 24). Not so. Cetaceans in particular exist intentionally, as each breath is a volitional act. At least two dolphins are thought to have committed suicide—by drowning—after their exciting careers as show animals came to inglorious ends (Greenwood, 2014). Kathy, one of several dolphins that portrayed "Flipper" on the television series, purportedly swam to her former trainer's arms, looked her in the eyes, and simply stopped breathing. It seems living is quite a bit more volitional for cetaceans than it is for us humans.

Our rationality is supposed to be the means whereby we as humans live. We use our faculties to wrest from our environment safety, food, and shelter. Everything we have, we create. Therefore, everything we create is ours. Very well, but it seems to us that she has committed a simple yet monumental error here as well. It seems to us she has confused "Man" with "man." Humankind ("Man") creates its survival from its environment, without a doubt. But no one "man" can be said to have wrestled nature into submission on his own. Whether Rand likes it or not, humans require other humans from even before birth, throughout the arc of their days. We are social animals. We fail to thrive without loving touch. We have neurochemicals that respond to skin-on-skin contact. As hunter-gatherers we hunted in packs. We achieve greatness when we work together. There's just no "I" in "Team," Ayn. The very gift she holds up as being emblematic of our humanity, our rationality, leads us to join arms and to be stronger together. The pages of the Chernobyl story are illuminated with the sacrifices of an army of individuals. First responders entered irradiated areas to combat fires; pilots flew dangerous missions over the reactor, thousands volunteered to dig under the reactor in order to prevent a larger cataclysm. And this is not a one-time event; over and over, we see images of human beings throughout history risking their lives for strangers regardless of national origin, religion, color, gender, or sexual orientation. Rand might argue she can explain such sacrifice, but she cannot. We give of ourselves, even unto death, because doing so is at times rational. We plan for the future together, storing goods in anticipation of a long winter because sometimes doing so is rational. We work together, dividing labor by capacity and skill because sometimes doing so is rational. But we do these things for far grander reasons than their rationality. Rand has crafted a myth of the sovereignty of the individual from the strength of the community as raw material, and she has done so with little more than the imprecise use of the Shift key.

Rand gives us an able iteration of benign selfism, yet this formulation falls apart almost immediately upon inspection. Although Objectivism appears to make some cogent points, one need not scrutinize it carefully to see clearly its fatal flaws, covered over by a thin plaster of rationality stretched far too thinly. It, like any argument that seeks to found itself on the idea of inherent rights of a person without reference to the wider community of persons, is doomed to fail. Rights are created and honored in community. To assert a right against nature, to argue with the cold or with a bull shark, claiming that one has a right to live is utter foolishness. Humans have innate beauty and nobility, and we agree with Rand that humans exist as ends in themselves (although we argue that all humans, even those she dismisses as subhuman by their deeds, are equally beautiful and noble). Indeed, it is the innate divine flame in each of us that compels us to write, so that we as a wider community remember to honor that flame, especially when that flame is hardest to see. To claim we owe, or that we are owed, is to imply that we owe or are owed thus in relation to others (e.g., Taylor, 1992). We can argue about what rights a community owes each individual (as Nozick does), what responsibilities are attendant to those rights, and even whether rights claiming is an appropriate forum for the distribution of social goods (as Weil does), but it is certain that the existence of rights implies the existence of a community, and of social goods held collectively by that community. "What each person gets, he gets from others who give to him in exchange for something, or as a gift" (Nozick, 1992, p. 137). This, it seems, she forgets.

Rand's thought, as ham-fisted, desiccated, and barren as it is, has some value. We must first recognize that it is not a philosophy, as it is utterly bereft of wisdom. Instead it is a characterization of one in need of love. Her thought can serve something of a diagnostic purpose: if Objectivism is appealing to someone, we have insights as to where she hurts, the degree and nature of her confusion, and can begin to act to nurture her back to health and clarity. Rand's ideas are in themselves a cry for help, and we should not demonize her for her toxic arguments any more than we should demonize someone for being febrile. Instead, we are called to recognize the pain behind the things she says, and be moved to compassion for her.

Robert Nozick and Benign Selfism

Our initial inclination was to leave Objectivism out altogether, as treating it as a system of thought is to misuse it. Sunlight is the best sanitizer, though, and showing it for what it is has considerable value for diminishing its misuse as a philosophy, and transforming it into its wiser use as a tool for more wisely loving others. Of course, by using Objectivism alone here, we would expose ourselves to a legitimate critique: we would have done what Rand did with altruism: she chose a vacuous straw man description of her adversary idea; if we allow Objectivism to stand in as the representative of benign selfism, we will have addressed only the feeblest iteration of individualist thought. A far more robust and careful treatment of what we view as selfism is provided by Robert Nozick.

Nozick begins in much the same way as Beccaria, with the social contract, and in what seems a similar fashion (though in greater detail), comes to the same conclusion about the state. He walks his readers through a process of comparison which in the end justifies the state of nature as a sound starting point for justifying the state. Like Beccaria, he argues the state that results from a contract view should be minimal. Nozick, however, works out the math regarding how robust a state must be in order to be minimally viable and meaningfully distinct from private protective agencies. He asks first whether we need a state at all. Like Rand, he founds his argument on individual interest; individuals will seek to protect their shelter, their tools, their reproductive partner, and resulting offspring. As such protection is both common among humans and best done collectively, small groups of humans are inevitable. Groups of groups also begin to be advantageous for much the same reason—to avoid being compelled by bigger groups. At some point protective agencies form, alliances in common interest. As conditions require incrementally more ceding of freedom to the group, a threshold is crossed and a "minimal state" exists. Such an entity offers protections from predation and the establishment of inviolable claims against the state and its members (i.e., rights), but it also levies excises on members in the form of ceded freedom (e.g., states claim a monopoly on the legitimization of the use of force). Thus, the state is formed from the invisible hand of individual interest, and any redistributive attributes, like mutual protection, must be justified on some other grounds than the redistribution itself.

Nozick is concerned with honoring the separateness of individuals, and as a result, he treats our perceived separateness by arguing that "no moral balancing act can take place among us" (Nozick, 1974, p. 33). He also sees the use of what he calls side constraints as being emblematic of our separateness. It is this separateness that is both central to the success of the invisible hand engine behind the minimal state, and is also the logical fissure that brings the model into rubble.

The state is constrained by the inviolable sovereign rights of its many masters (Nozick, 1974). Neither the state nor any proto-state institution may violate an individual's rights of freedom of action and association (Nozick's first primary claim). The only constraint upon an individual's freedom is the like, freedom of others. Almost a corollary of the first is Nozick's second argument: the state has no moral principles of its own that are not in some way derivative of the natural and inviolable rights of its many members. Merely because it is an entity representing collective interest does not mean that it inherits the capacity to accrue rights. Silly rabbit, rights are for people.

Nozick's third main principle is most instructive regarding the state he envisions, and is a special case of the second argument: there is no moral reason to ameliorate human suffering due to inequality (Nozick, 1974, p. xiii). No collective end can be seen as sufficiently robust to successfully challenge individual rights of action and association. Possession is legitimate, according to Nozick, if what I have I either created or was given by someone who had legitimate ownership. If what I have or what I make is of greater value than that had or made by another, the individual with proportionately more value is not beholden to correct the imbalance made by another's inferior possessions or workmanship. Further, the state cannot compel me to give what is mine to another to correct an inequity of distribution not only because no one can impinge upon my freedom of action, and not only because there is no inequity in fact (as I either made or was given things of greater value), but also because the state in particular cannot make *any* moral claims of its own whatsoever.

In his turn to distributive justice, Nozick invites us to consider famed basketball star Wilt Chamberlain. If Chamberlain's mastery on the basketball court can provide him the necessary leverage to convince team owners to give him a large portion of every ticket sold, and assuming they, looking out for themselves, agree, is he not entitled to that money? The owners are satisfied with their shares, and presumably the fans are pleased with their choice. Certainly, Wilt Chamberlain is pleased with the windfall of cash that would emerge as a result of this negotiation. How could this not be justice? Nozick's point regarding Chamberlain is "that no end-state principle or distributional patterned principle of justice can be continually realized without continuous interference with people's lives" (Nozick, 1974, p. 163). If goods are to be transferred to others in order to correct inequities, such goods transfer must out of necessity be counter to one's desires. If that transfer were a function of one's desire, one would have redistributed them accordingly already. The logic in this is that I must be free to dispense what I have according to my choice. If in that distribution, more goes to persons A and B who make good things, and none goes to person C who does not, no justification can be made for impinging upon my resources to correct this imbalance. Nozick summarizes himself in a slogan: "*From each as they choose, to each as they are chosen*" (emphasis in original, Nozick, 1974, p. 160).

Critique of Nozick

One common critique is that his rights foundation is shaky to say the least, and is acknowledged to be thus, really right away. In his *preface* he makes clear that the book will not contain a "precise theory of the moral basis of individual rights" (Nozick, 1974, p. xxiv), though he is concerned with how those rights work through an invisible-hand system to create and guide the minimal state. Nozick's entire formulation is imprimatur, a guarantee on the idea of the inviolability of individual rights. If we cannot take his formulation as providing for us a defensible and coherent model of those individual rights and if we cannot specify the nature of those rights in some detail, Nozick's entire formulation is questionable. Is it sufficient merely to speak in terms of freedom of action and association? It seems reasonable to say that more is required, considering how so much rides on the idea of individual rights.

We also challenge Nozick in his concern to honor the separateness of each individual. To be sure, his desire to honor separateness comes from a nobler place than does similar sentiment in Rand. Nevertheless, such separateness is an illusion as we have seen already, and as we will see in greater detail later on in this critique. Nozick's Wilt Chamberlain transaction would appear irrefutable; if you accept the beginning premise as just, and if you accept the process of its creation as also just, you must inevitably accept the outcomes—all of them ad infinitum—as just. Cohen (2011) presumes a paradox is intended here; if you would challenge the justness of the end point of the transaction, presumably then your favorite egalitarian principle is itself paradoxical. The paradox, however, evaporates if we hold it to be possible that what is just at the beginning and what is just at the end may refer to different kinds of justice. Different principles or concerns, in other words, may apply at different points in the process. We may argue, for example, that although Wilt Chamberlain is a masterful basketball player and that he deserves to be rewarded for his skills entertaining crowds of fans, our social priority is that a nontrivial portion of collective treasure be allocated such that schoolteachers can be compensated handsomely for the fearsome responsibility they carry and that schools enjoy an embarrassment of riches for their mostly uncompensated work. There is no paradox of distributional justice to hold that although Wilt Chamberlain deserves compensation for his skills, schools should not want, and no child should go to bed hungry. Examining the outcome merely in terms of the process ignores the broader social context within which the transaction occurs. Just like with the proportionate reserve system in the United States, one who saves large amounts of money virtually guarantees others will not have enough.

Consider another example, our own answer to Wilt Chamberlain. One of the authors is a musician. Let's assume that his spouse and he have worked out an arrangement where one-eighth of the family budget is to go to strings, speakers, parts, and perhaps a new instrument on occasion. Then let's say the family gets a considerable raise in income resulting from a promotion or a new job. The share that is allocated for music, the one-eighth, has increased in total amount. It turns out, however, our child needs braces. Would we say it was unjust to sacrifice some of the portion allocated for music to be reallocated for braces? The premise was just, and the process for implementing it was just. The child was a preexisting commitment, even if the braces are new. It seems clear that most would argue that insisting on retaining the same budget fraction for a hobby would be selfish. Admittedly, the money for the braces could come from other portions of the budget, of course, like family entertainment or food; however, would this be just or egalitarian? Of course not. Not contributing to the braces fund from the music fund would be unjust, precisely because there are other concerns, other claims to be considered beyond legitimate distribution through legitimate processes. We argue that among such claims, manifest and paramount, is need.

Conclusion

Two models of justice, both proclaiming the individual as sovereign and thus constructing a set of relations for others from the basic and sacrosanct rights of the individual, are before us. Rights are the focus of both authors; rights inviolable and natural, springing from the free body. Freedom to do as one chooses, to be as one desires, is the central organizing principle for both Rand and Nozick. In both cases, the individual looms so large that little room exists for the rest of us. With all the talk of rights, little room is left for contemplation of attendant responsibilities. Of course with each right claimed there is at least one attendant responsibility. If it is one's natural right to own a gun, it is one's natural responsibility to use it in a fashion that does not destroy life except as one fully intends (to wit, hunting, self-defense). If it is one's natural right to speak one's mind, it is one's natural responsibility to consider the harm one's words can inflict, and to realize that some form of social response may result from harm one does with one's words. To be sure, for

Nozick at least, one's natural rights are limited by the presence of others in a minimal way; my right to swing my fist ends where your nose begins. We must consider, however, that when we become selfish and focus only on our own rights, we often trample on others before we realize our mistake. Rather than community being our focus, it is our own selfish needs, or as we often term them, rights that are paramount. This is nothing like the contemplation of responsibilities owed to the wider community in exchange for rights claiming, and no such contemplation occurs for either Rand or Nozick. Such a failing is, in our view, fatal.

Consider a quote purported to have been offered by Papa John's CEO, John Schnatter: "If our business is successful and achieves excessive profits, we're under no obligation to share that with our workers." We were unable to identify where or when this was said or if in fact he actually said it, and indeed it seems to be something of an urban myth. What is no myth is his palatial Kentucky home and his two other residences. Equally clear is his feeling about his deservedness of wealth: "When you have built a $3 billion company out of a broom closet, I think you are entitled to a nice house" (Wolfson, 2013). His founding the business was just, and the processes through which he amassed a fortune were also just. Therefore, according to Nozick, no legitimate claims can be made on him to contribute to the healthcare needs of his employees. If you are left dry, or more likely perhaps disgusted by this argument, it is helpful to remember its source.

BENIGN SELFISM AND THEORIES OF CRIME

Often criminal behavior is self-interested to some degree, and many theories of crime, including a number not discussed here, operate at least implicitly from the assumption that a nontrivial portion of crime is in some way selfish behavior. We are often guilty of impending too much significance on first inclinations, nomothetic accounts, generic examples, and in this, these many theories fall woefully short of full potential value. The avatars that inspire them are cartoonesque or otherwise incomplete, and as a result, theories perform poorly in empirical contexts. Although we recognize fully the value of theories that offer nomothetic accounts of social phenomena, we likewise recognize that theories that offer nothing more than nomothetic, legalistic explanatory accounts offer limited value toward understanding the infinitely complex human and society as a whole.

It is true that theory is charged with accounting for what is; we are to understand unwholesome, toxic, prurient behavior, which oftentimes is ill-considered, thinly inspired, and poorly executed. Theory should, in short, follow the shoreline of the known. But what we know is not or cannot be limited to what is discovered through published scholarly empirical projects alone. Criminologists are called to see with their whole being, not merely crime as we already know, and not even merely harm and suffering, but also the entire tapestry of sentience in its transcendent fullness even as it moves and pulses, borealis-like all, around us.

The systems of thought we present in this chapter and elsewhere fall quite a bit short of this ideal, yet they enjoy a considerable amount of respect and influence in criminological dialogues. In common, they share some form of a prioritization of the self, either in terms of the assumptions they make about human motivation evidenced in the avatars they engineer for our use, or perhaps more subtly, with regard to the nature of social structures that create criminogenic environments. As examples of benign selfism, these theories are similar also in that they do not promote self at the expense of others. But without further ado. . . .

Beccaria

Cesare Beccaria Bonesana is one of those thinkers claimed by several disciplines. Legal scholars count him among their number, as do political scientists, and as should students of public administration. His work modeling mathematically the relationship between tariffs and smuggling secures his *bona fides* as an economist. And his focus on crime and punishment is sound justification for regarding him a criminologist. Unfortunately, this wide-ranging relevance may have contributed to Harcourt's cogent point that Beccaria's seminal book, *On Crimes and Punishments* (1764), is "much cited but little read" (Harcourt, 2013, p. 2). His prominence in the latter half of his days among us would be easy to overstate, but less so his influence. To be sure, Bentham, Voltaire, and Thomas Jefferson all admired Beccaria's work, sometimes to the point of immodesty. Today, Beccaria's respected visage stares down at his eponymous piazza in his hometown of Milan; a somewhat grander Piazza Cesare Beccaria, containing the gate of Florence's old medieval walls, lies just over a kilometer almost due east of the Duomo. Despite the rapid rise of his small book, *Dei delitti e delle penne* (*On Crimes and Punishments*), he did not fare well among the conceited philosophers of Paris, and after a time teaching in Milan, he took a job as a civil servant, which he held until his death. Although it would be an exaggeration to say he died in obscurity, no deathbed accounts exist of his passing like those of Voltaire, and in fact his passing was little noted at the time (Beccaria, 1986).

Of course Beccaria is known in the context of criminology for his single (and singular) work, mentioned earlier. Little more than a pamphlet on steroids, its diminutive size belies its significance. Its influence is appreciable even today. Contemporary critics like Foucault perhaps do not have sufficient appreciation for the radically progressive nature of Beccaria's arguments, for the potential peril he placed himself in from raging, tyrannical rulers and the condemnation of the Catholic Church; his work was published anonymously at first. What ideas could possibly be so dangerous?

On Crimes and Punishments was far more a treatise on behalf of humanism than it was an apology for governmental authority. Beccaria's core interest was to reform what justice system existed from being little more than a tool for personal whim for the aristocracy into a system of mutual accountability toward generating the greatest amount of happiness possible for everyone. Central to this effort for Beccaria was that justice be egalitarian. The law should apply to all alike, regardless of station or duty. Kings and serfs alike should be equal before the law, as they are bound together in a common self-interested endeavor. Moreover, sovereigns are not the arbiters of justice they supposed themselves to be heretofore. Kings do not have unfettered right to punish as they see fit. How he gets here and, even more important, what justice means for him require our careful attention.

Beccaria begins with the social contract assumption: people give up certain natural liberties, and in return, they are bestowed certain protection by the government enabling them to form a secure and civilized society. Central to his logic, he argues that the rights individuals cede to the collective are minimal; we give only enough to incentivize others to defend it. Anything more than the minimal rights-ceding is tyranny (and if Beccaria rails against anything, it is tyranny). To his social contract, however, he adds a healthy helping of utilitarianism. Utilitarians, like Bentham, thought little of the social contract—he called it "nonsense upon stilts" (Harcourt, 2013, p. 6), so at least for his time, his theoretical model raised more than a few eyebrows. But Beccaria's aim was the maximization of social welfare, and the social contract was a useful basis for creating certain obligations and rights carried by each person, whether she be sovereign or serf, toward that end. In this way, Beccaria merged seamlessly two relatively odd philosophical bedfellows.

Crime and Social Response in Beccaria

According to Beccaria, crime is the result of a rational act comparing costs and benefits of the proscribed deed. Like water always pursues the lowest place to rest, we pursue self-interest. For Beccaria, it strained credulity that one would rationally commit a crime outside of a framework that incentivized it, though "it is impossible to prevent all disorders in the universal strife of human passions" (Beccaria, 1986, p. 14). His paper on tariff levels sought to penalize smuggling to the point that it was disincentivized, but also that fines added maximally to the princes' pockets (Harcourt, 2013). The criminal law and the penalties for its breach should be made absolutely crystal clear; if laws were crafted properly, this clarity coupled with the incentive structure the laws create consonant with the *minimam imperium* model of the social contract should diminish crime to the point where one could drown it, as they say, in a bathtub. If laws are imprecise, they belie the Swiss precision of the "Invisible Legislator," who set in motion a perfect mechanism of intercourse among all sentience (Beccaria, 1986, p. 15), and may even create the very thing they seek to prevent.

In terms of punishment, the social contract Beccaria employs is relevant here as well: as no one cedes all of their rights (least of all their right to live) to the sovereign, there are concrete limits on the sovereign's right to punish. The only defensible reasons for punishment are to deter the offender from reoffending (specific deterrence), and to deter others from following his example in the first place (general deterrence). "The purpose of punishments is not to torment and afflict a sentient being or to undo a crime which has already been committed" (Beccaria, 1986, p. 23). Beccaria leaves no space for vengeance or even, in many cases, retribution. Neither does he leave space for restoration, however. Punishment or, as Beccaria calls it, "political obstacles" (Beccaria, 1986, p. 14) should strike a mathematically precise balance between the needs of the sovereign and the interests of each citizen. One iota of punishment more than is necessary to deter crime is tyrannous. The only proper measure of punishment is the harm done to the nation. Offender status, his intentions, and the gravity of the event all are superfluous to establishing punishment.

Rather than allowing punishment to be meted out on the whims of unrestrained judicial power, Beccaria's central tenet asserts that punishment should be certain and follow close on the heels of a determination of guilt. Certitude does the heavy lifting in Beccaria's model: "one of the greatest checks on crime is not the cruelty of punishments but their inevitability" (Beccaria, 1986, p. 46). But celerity is yet vital "because it spares the criminal the useless and cruel torments of uncertainty" (Beccaria, 1986, p. 36). Unlike some who invoke Beccaria today, he sought to minimize the suffering of sentient beings, including criminals, in the name of justice.

It is instructive, however, particularly in the current endeavor to consider what Beccaria intends by the term "justice." "By 'justice,' moreover, we do not mean anything but the bond necessary to hold private interests together. Without it, they would dissolve into the earlier state of incompatibility" (Beccaria, 1986, p. 9). Justice, then, is little more than the weak gravity that holds together the *di minimis* collective sharing of rights that is Beccaria's enfeebled social contract. There is, to be sure, not much there. He continues, lest he be unclear: "One must beware of attaching the idea of something real to this word 'justice,' as though it were a physical force or a being that actually exists" (Beccaria, 1986, p. 9). He pays brief homage to the idea of a divine justice apart from this world as an afterthought, but it is far from sufficiently robust to support a more fertile reading of justice. For Beccaria, then, justice is nothing more than the force that keeps us committed to a state, sovereign, a body of law—in essence, justice for Beccaria is rational self-interest. Justice is to be pursued, but perhaps like a bad joke, one never actually gets it in the end. Certainly, it is not a thing that can be denied someone because it is not a thing at all. He worries that we will be tempted into reifying justice into a goal, a commodity to be distributed, perhaps even a proto-sovereign.

As Milquetoast-esque as Beccaria's idea of justice is, if we were to squint, it would bear notable resemblance to a far mightier casting of justice. We can fully agree that justice is that thing which binds us together as a community, as a family, as a species. It is not self-interest, though self-interest is served. And it is not predicated on making private interests stickier, though it does bind us together against the force of the centrifuge.

Critique of Beccaria

Beccaria's thought is fully susceptible to the standard challenges against rationalism, which we have presented already, and his concept of justice is anemic to the point of uselessness. In addition, though, there is something of a logical tension in Beccaria's thinking with regard to the size of government. Beccaria argues for a government of limited size; in fact, Beccaria's government would be the smallest iteration of something recognizable as government, not unlike Nozick's. Had he and Jefferson had the benefit of instant communication, Beccaria likely would have counseled the incipient United States to stick with the Articles of Confederation, or perhaps even to scale back the federal unit. Yet his reliance on certainty and celerity of punishment would require considerable governmental resources. It is unclear to us how he would resolve this tension, but our assumption is that he would argue for increasing government as needed to allow for certainty and celerity to be possible, thus ensuring a large government, in particular, an executive branch of considerable size.

As influential as Beccaria's thought has been, as humanistic and noble as are his innovative ideas, rationalist theories of crime come woefully short of useful. As we shall see later on, even neo-classical models with their circumcised rationality, despite their appeal, offer overly simplistic and impoverished criminoetiological accounts. Let us turn to just such theory now, in part as development of our themes, and in part as added critique. More problematically, Beccaria, as well as other classicists, failed to take into account the individual circumstances of offenders, especially those who are less equal within the eyes of the law. In so doing, he focused on the act rather than looking at the individual, who is oftentimes not entirely rational in his or her actions. By denying that judges should look at the act solely as the means for imparting justice, it eliminated the humanity from decisions. Thus, justice remains a myth for those who are considered "other" as they can never achieve the promises of the social contract.

Routine Activities

Before we begin here, a point of order is necessary. Often, routine activities theory is grouped with theories discussed in the next chapter. In common these theories share some measure of a rationality assumption. We find it fruitful, however, while recognizing their rationality kinship, to treat routine activities theory apart from its rationalist cousins, here in the context of self-ism. The reasons—and benefits—we hope soon shall be clear.

Cohen and Felson (1979) begin with a concern about the somewhat disconcerting increase in crime occurring at the time despite improvements in conditions then thought to cause crime. The authors concluded that the leap in crime was a function of a shift in routine activities over the course of the previous years that has led to an increased spacio-temporal interaction of three social "earthly" (Felson, 1987) elements: motivated offenders, suitable targets, and a lack of capable guardians (Cohen & Felson, 1979, p. 589). Normal activity, like going to work, to the store, to the nightclub, where different people meet and interact, creates the raw materials for crime to occur. Moreover, shifts in activity including women entering the workforce, increased travel for vacations, and changes in demographic patterns all combine to create an increase in crime when none was expected.

The mechanism for this increase in "direct-contact predatory violations" is the accidental spatio-temporal collision of the three key ingredients: offender, target, and guardianless environment. In the same way as we can understand fire being the intentional or accidental interaction of fuel, ignition source, and oxygen, crime is the product of the human chemical reaction that results from the interaction in space and time of target, offender, and guardianless environment.

Unsurprisingly given their emphasis on environment, Cohen and Felson draw inspiration from the ecological school of Shaw, McKay, and colleagues (see, e.g., Miller, 2013), and they emphasize that the analogy drawn between human experience and the competition among species in the natural realm is not merely figurative. Lives hang in the balance, Cohen and Felson remind us, and they hinge on the accrual of goods, often through swift and fierce collision. Sounding strikingly Nozickian, in order to increase their chances offenders will cooperate with each other. "As offenders cooperate to increase their efficiency at predatory violations and as potential victims organize their resistance to these violations, both groups apply the symbiotic principle to improve their sustenance position" (Cohen & Felson, 1979, p. 590). Simple self-interest again rules the day.

We can see then that there is in routine activities theory another version of Adams's and Nozick's unseen hand guiding the incidence of attempted direct-contact predation, as well as social response to predation attempts. When and where target and offender meet, if the environment is suitable, crime happens. Eventually, targets discover mutual action is advantageous; soon after, offenders organize themselves into wolfpacks of greater efficiency. Targets might then seek to create some kind of gendarmerie to stand in the gap between targets and offenders; thus routine activities theory and the unseen hand work together to predict the eventual creation of the police. Alternately, conditions may arise that reward individual predators' initiative. Convergences and divergences through the ebb and flow of normal activity in time and space thus drive the nature and prevalence of predatory crime, according to Cohen and Felson. Felson develops this in later writing (e.g., Felson, 1987) where he seeks to link individual events to larger trends. He argues "the study of crime is the study of accidents" (Felson, 1987, p. 914); a robber sets out to rob, but is foiled by a target inexpertly chosen; a couple went out dancing but ended up by sleeping in a doorway. Together such accidents taken together across the range of actors create structural phenomena that can be seen and measured. He refers to this principle as "systematic accident." "Although the fox finds each hare one by one, the ecologist knows that the fox population varies with the hare population on which it feeds" (Felson, 1987, p. 914). The unseen hand strikes again.

It is worthy to note for current purposes that the theory is almost totally acognitive with regard to the criminogenic mechanism (e.g., Pedneault & Beauregard, 2014); aside from avatar actors behaving almost solely according to short-term interests, crime happens when an offender wants something he sees, and in that context thinks he can wrest it from a victim. Ordering from a restaurant menu exhibits more cognitive steam than does the commission of a crime for the routine activities avatar offender. It would be difficult to portray a more selfish being, or a more simplistic understanding of human behavior, than this. Like most classical theories, critics have long noted that an inherent problem in this simplistic theory is that it does not address individual-level characteristics; however, the real problem with routine activities theory lies in realizing that it is more about the behavior of the victim rather than offender.

As a result, we end up blaming victims for their behavior rather than looking at why an offender really commits a crime.

Merton's Strain and Modes of Adaptation

It seems fair to say that among twentieth-century criminologists, few names bend more knees than Robert Merton's. His, a career that spanned nearly six decades, is the stuff of legend. His formative intellectual environment included figures like George Sarton, Alfred Whitehead, George Simpson, Vladimir Sorokin, and Talcott Parsons. He gave us theories of the middle range, the self-fulfilling prophecy, sociological ambivalence, and a deepened structural functionalism, inter alia.

It is not in our nature to genuflect, but Merton truly made sociology more fertile. Moreover, it is not our aim to imply that Merton employed jaundiced or prejudicial thinking regarding the beings about whom he theorized. Like many philosophers and academics, he is without doubt a product of his privilege, and such privilege can blind us at times to our common humanity. We intend no scathing critique of Merton. Indeed, among the theorists and thinkers discussed in this chapter, Merton stands head and shoulders above them all in terms of influence, breadth of source, and humanist wisdom. At most, it can be said that his formal style and his consensus-fueled functionalist assumption set may have colored his view in some regards. But it seems clear that his explanation of criminal and similar behavior is appropriately discussed in the context of benign selfism, as we shall soon see.

In classic functionalist style, Merton begins by asking after the "social structures [that] exert a definite pressure upon certain persons in the society to engage in nonconformist behavior rather than conformist conduct" (Merton, 1996, p. 132). He is clear in his assumption that it is social structures, and not attributes of offenders themselves, that are responsible for nonconformist harm. The structures toward which he gestures are socially agreed-upon goals, and the socially approved means to be used in the achievement of those goals. Societies will differ both in terms of the substantive goals and means to which they offer imprimatur, but also in terms of the degree of differential emphasis on goals or means. A society that emphasizes goal achievement, but offers less emotional valence for adherence to specified means tends to create what Durkheim called anomie. It is this disjunction between the societal goals and means to achieve these goals that seems to result in the chaos inherent in the self. Winning, or getting yours, is more important than how it is gotten. Of course, such a society bears striking resemblance to the state of nature that offered Nozick and Rand their starting points. Such a world is driven by selfishness, and indeed would be best seen as antagonistically selfish. Merton holds up contemporary America as an example of such a goal-driven, means-poor society. We are a society obsessed with pathological materialism in which the goals we pursue are laden in selfish desires; selflessness and altruistic reasoning become subservient to the material wants that are reified by capitalism.

Merton turns then to a consideration of individual adaptation strategies. Every sociology and criminology text presents them as he did, in terms of their acceptance or rejection of cultural goals and institutionalized means: conformity, innovation, ritualism, retreatism, and rebellion. The conformist adopts both goals and means according to social expectations and from a deviance perspective is, for Merton, uninteresting. The innovator, however, concerns us greatly. Those drawn powerfully to goals often are willing to engage in risky behaviors, and this willingness to do so is part of the problem as individual needs and the focus on the self become more important than community or even family. It is conceivable that many will be drawn to find the inside line on winning. For anyone who has seen the film *Days of Thunder* or is a NASCAR fan, the idea that winning is everything is not uncommon; remember, rubbin' is racin' and it is okay to push the lines even if it not always socially acceptable (e.g., legitimate). Quoting Veblen, Merton draws on the notion of what is considered legitimate: "It is not easy in any given case—indeed it is at times impossible until the courts have spoken—to say whether it is an instance of praiseworthy salesmanship or penitentiary offense" (Merton, 1996, p. 140). Of course, in the context of white-collar crime, such marginal and even clearly illegal actions occur, and Merton cites evidence that the scale of such behavior is probably far in excess of what was thought to be the case at the time. In lower economic classes, far greater is the pressure to innovate, as few chances for advancement exist. Coupled with the wide social emphasis on advancement and money, means other than those sanctioned by society are inevitably chosen by some. Organized crime is one such set of means; Al Capone represents an illegitimate success story, an underclass entrepreneur. While he was able to engage in a business enterprise, albeit an illegal one, his self-serving nature led to the death of innocent people. Ironically, murder and the engagement in organized crime did not result in imprisonment, but simple tax evasion did.

The ritualist accepts the means, but has undergone a downgrading of goals. The ritualist recognizes he will never get ahead, yet he continues to adhere to socially approved means for making a living. Arthur Miller's Willy Loman is the quintessential ritualist. The protagonist in Miller's *Death of a Salesman* creates a fantasy world in which he tries to escape from the blue-collar reality in which he has become immersed. Merton sees such an adaptation as not being a "social problem," though it represents a departure from the American model. Such an adaptation represents for Merton a personal exit from the stressors of striving for advancement. Merton expects to find ritualist adaptation in the lower-middle class from which there is no escape. Willy and the rest of the lower class are inextricably bound by chains made by others, but secured by their own hands.

The retreatism adaptation is, Merton concludes, least common. Retreatists are in society, Merton says, but not of it. They occupy the fringe of society, described as part of it "only in a fictional sense" (Merton, 1996, p. 148). Clumsily, he includes in this category "artists, pariahs, outcasts, vagrants, tramps, chronic drunkards, and drug addicts" (Merton, 1996, p. 148). Both socially approved goals and institutional means have been deeply imbibed by such individuals, Merton argues, but that the goals are wholly out of reach and approved means are wholly ineffective. This adaptation is an expression of defeat, of hopelessness, and of despair. One cannot achieve set goals through legitimate means, and one cannot employ illegitimate means because of internal constraints. Such an adaptation is roundly, publicly, and disparagingly proscribed by the society. "Nonproductive liabilities," such as crack moms and welfare queens, represent a collective drag on society as they are considered collectively to be the result of private, individualized decisions. Again, here we go blaming those who are often victims of society.

In something of a parallel, though representing a more systematic and collectivized adaptation, rebellion represents a wholesale alienation resulting in rejection of both goals and institutionalized means, and the collective creation of a replacement system of goals and means. Merton is careful to distinguish rebellion as he intends from *ressentiment*; invoking Max Scheler, Merton clarifies that while ressentiment involves a powerful but diffuse and perpetual sense of anger, envy, hostility, coupled with an impotence in terms of the capacity to express that nest of toxic emotions, ressentiment is not rebellion. Though rebellion may draw on an extant reservoir or ressentiment, the rebellion adaptation represents "a genuine transvaluation" (Merton, 1996, p. 150), a complete and consistent new social narrative, including new myths to accompany new goals and new means.

This tension between ends and their differential achievability acts to diminish the gravity of social proscriptions generally; innovation, retreatism, and rebellion are to be found primarily in the lower social classes, where social goals focused on advancement and the accrual of wealth are simply untenable. The imperfect alignment of goals and means generates anomie, predictability is diminished, and the degree of chaos increases. Although Merton would hold out the possibility that some measure of nonconformist behavior is socially functional, the degree to which it wore down mores and social norms is the degree to which it is socially toxic.

Critique of Merton's Anomie and Modes of Adaptation

Consensus plays a central role in Merton's thought, even if he is not actively assuming a given set of mores or norms is itself to be preferred. Mores and their codified counterparts, the law, stand unchallenged and marmoreal, and indeed are to be protected from erosion by anomie, itself the result of too much dysfunctional adaptation. The consensus assumption, of course, represents a form of tyranny; to assume that the law is representative of society's best interests is to state therefore that those who find themselves irrevocably outside the compass of capacity are, in essence, superfluous; at most they are means to a larger social end.

The avatars portrayed by Merton for each of his modes of adaptation are, in essence, self-centered creatures driven uncritically by the goals and means defined for them. The innovator is the selfish person par excellence, rejecting limitations on his means to achieve wealth and success (at least in America). Ritualists and retreatists both detune the goals/means clockwork by adopting lesser goals or by rejecting the calculus as a whole. They are perhaps selfish also, but also maybe untalented to the point that, as in Nozick, no duty is owed them in recompense for their poverty. To be sure, rebels represent something of an exception in that they strike off and create a wholly new narrative of their own, but in this they represent something of a particular challenge to the society in that they are actively and directly wearing away the consensus on which norms are founded; rebels, even when justified, bring anomie in their wake. Merton's model of nonconformist criminal and harmful behavior, being a function of distemper between socially approved goals and institutionalized means, simplifies human decision making to a grotesque degree, even if that simplification has some intuitive appeal to some. Whereas, to his credit, Merton makes no link to rationality in the goals/means process he identifies, and whereas he himself keeps at arm's length the normative trap of overidentifying with either the offender or the offended society, the five avatars he fashions for us are paper-moon and cardboard-sea versions of humanity. Certainly we do not recognize ourselves in these avatars beyond a passing familiarity; why should we suspect Merton saw himself in them?

There is an ever-so-slight othering at play in Merton; it exists in uncomfortable tension with his assertions about social conditions being criminogenic. Just as he liberates the human from fault, his crimes still happen over there somewhere, clearly not where we are approaching criminology from, as we understand criminology to be deeply personal. Even if crime is similar to other noncriminal behaviors (itself an important insight), and even though it may be functional in some regard, it remains something to which society must respond with punishment. Functionalism presupposes a degree of consensus of social approbation and proscription; what is illegal is illegal for a sound reason. Systematic violation of the law may provide something of a function, say, like advancing thinking about social responsibility, but the result of such influence would only be a new consensus. It seems clear that Merton was not necessarily embracing consensus per se; he was far too interested in an objective analysis to condone or sanction. Still consensus, rigid though it may be, is the vertebrae that hold his account vertical.

Selfism of both kinds lives and dies on the fulcrum of the human heart; we bring into being the world we perceive, fear, or desire through our thoughts and crucially our decision and actions. The awareness that retribution and restoration share an apartment wall is a reminder, warning, and fete: the inescapable reality of our interbeing is not of our creation, but the relationships we have, the communities we build, the societies we sustain *are*. We make our families, our marriages, our organizations, and the rest with our decisions and actions. These institutions are made in our image when they are made and continued, honoring our interbeing; they are lies and confidence schemes when they are not.

CONCLUSION

Putting self first, living life through the lens of my wants, my pain, my perspective, creates a false impression, a funhouse mirror of reality. In this unnatural existence, we see false distinctions, false walls. We perceive ourselves as separate beings from the rest of humanity and sentient nature. Things can get so distorted in that mirror, our own pain and pleasure can appear so large that it becomes impossible to see beyond them. At such a point using others as means to serve my ends makes sense. Clytemnestra, Hamlet, and Shakespeare's Richard III all were such creatures, themselves akin to the avatars of criminological theory. All of them, even from what we know about them are but shades of real humans in terms of the complexity they carry, and thus were made to bear their suffering obviously for the sake of the narrative. Had they been real people, it would be instructive to contemplate how it was that they had come to be so confused, so bloated that they could not see anything but themselves. The Israelites *were* real people, and *did indeed* come from a long history of suffering. From such suffering, their leaders may have concluded that their survival itself justified any bloody acts performed in order to secure it. "They started it" might be a sufficiently sound license to justify obliterating a people, given what they had been through.

The capacity to view others as means to one's ends, even when selfishness guides thinking, is still not a natural view; it helps immensely to alter the quality of one's vision, and the funhouse mirror obliges. At the least, others can appear as cardboard cutout abstractions of humans, each as disposable as a Starbucks cup. A symptom of rather deeper illness is not to see others clearly at all. Richard III was only vaguely able to discern that Elizabeth's sanguine strategy for winning her daughter's heart was insincere. Luckily for Elizabeth, he didn't get the sarcastic barb, or she might have tasted Richard's wrath herself. In order to mimic the person lost to himself bemused by his own machinations, Shakespeare gave him a tin ear with which to miss Elizabeth's sarcasm. Clytemnestra treated her still-warm husband's corpse like it was already dust; medically speaking he might still have been alive, and he might well have felt the sting of alcohol in his wounds and perceived the warm wine mixing with his own blood beneath him.

Hamlet had his suffering, in nature similar to that of Clytemnestra (both were royal, but lost someone beloved by them). But Hamlet lived under his own form of a divine command. Vengeance for him was not an option simply because his father's ghost, the beloved dead king, charged him with achieving it. Ophelia, an object of his affection, now became a means to his end. Were things different, they might be together and happy. One day, she would be queen; one day she would be mother to his children. Ah, but there's nothing for it; such is his circumstance as she was simply a powerful tool for proving his madness.

But then there are the Athenians. They did not have a history of suffering the way the Israelites, Richard, Clytemnestra, and Hamlet did. No, instead they had their war and they rationalized their way into an injury that did not exist. And they were very, even grotesquely, real. The Melians' autonomy was clear silent testimony to Athenian weakness, because any island nation would swear allegiance to Athens out of sheer fear, if Athens were indeed as powerful as it thought itself to be.

Ah, and there's that old yarn rationality again. Gottfredson and Hirschi relied on it, as did Rand, Nozick, and Beccaria. Among the systems of thought reviewed here, really, only Merton's stands clear of being walloped by the rationality train. Rationality and propensity living together in an *Odd Couple*–esque setting as portrayed by Gottfredson and Hirschi (1990) does not offer protection. Such irresponsible theorizing not only damages the quality of the theory it produces, but undermines the endeavor of theory creation more generally. The garment does not even fit well on the form, let alone offer some sense of how it might drape on a human. It traded hyper-abstraction for attempted breadth, but achieved neither. On balance, we are poorer as a species for LSC ever having been taken seriously.

To be fair, perhaps even overly so, selfism as we have discussed it here has its earliest roots in thought that, at one time, was noble and liberating.

Enlightenment thinking sought to shatter the shackles of doctrinaire oppression, celebrating the freedom and capacity of the human spirit. It would seem, however, that we have only partly taken their meaning. Where Voltaire practically intones about human nobility, in Andrews Sisters–like tight harmony, Montesquieu also sings, but also offers many careful cautions about the need for limits on power. We would contend that such limitations are a natural outgrowth of an awareness and celebration of the mutual accountability that accompanies the enthroning of love at the center of the policy universe.

The quality of an idea is measurable in terms of the number of debates it settles, the scale of those debates, the influence they have had on thinkers. We have spent time with communitarian and individualist arguments about the nature of human existence. One might be forgiven at this point for assuming that we are sympathetic to communitarian arguments. We have used communitarian logic to indict individualist claims. We do not, however, think of ourselves as a communitarian, nor is love as it has been portrayed a communitarian phenomenon alone. It is true that love binds us together, spouse and stranger, across the fabric of humanity and sentience, a fabric dyed many wondrous colors. Love is the dark matter of humanity; it holds us together when by rights society should spin into oblivion, hurling sparks to die in the icy dark.

But we are not simply members of a collective; your divine flame does not simply unite you and us across the miles and years, it is the marrow of your beauty, your holy individuality. Rand and Nozick were not wrong to celebrate the sentient individual. Far from it. Where they failed was in not seeing how an individual's power is maximized. The truest and most bountiful individualism is possible only through the loving action of the community. Our fullest actualization is possible only because we belong to each other, and act accordingly. Only through love, the support of a community, the nurturance of family, the wisdom of parents, the tenderness of a spouse, the stalwartness of a sibling, can any one being actualize. Humans organize because we are capable of doing more together, as we have said. Michael's uncle built skyscrapers for a living. He worked with city government, with unions, with other companies, with the mob, with thousands of workers, together to change the New York City skyline three times. Only together could they hope to succeed. One of the most challenging (and most beautiful) things humans can ever do, far more challenging than raising steel, is to raise a human to her fullest capacity. Only together is this possible. And so we give of ourselves to each other, and in so doing, without expecting it, we ourselves are lifted up.

The age-old debate regarding communitarianism and individualism is, in the end, of little value. We as individuals are possible only through the community, but only when love is the organizing principle of both the individual and of the community. With the addition of fertile and wise love, the debate about communitarianism or individualism falls away; it is sound and fury, signifying nothing (DeValve, 2015). We are inescapably interconnected, yet we are capable of rising to our full actualization through love. Love gently but utterly destroys the wrecking ball sovereign self, while at the same time preserves the dignity of the individual and the pregnancy of the community.

The fact that Rand, Nozick, and Beccaria all began from similar ontological myths should not be taken to indicate that they were operating under similar motives. For all three, the sovereignty of the individual was the starting point for their reasoning. For Beccaria, of course, this was revolutionary. His individualism was a scathing critique of the capricious regent then so common across Europe's exploited expanse. In Nozick's hands, what begins as a bold proclamation against tyranny ends up creating a tyranny of a different kind. For Rand, her celebration of the individual is nothing more than a celebration of selfish desire. In both cases, the unseen hand is best left unseen; it is unmitigated greed, the penultimate grotesqueness of the human psyche.

As we wind up here, we recognize we are beholden to you to deliver something of a resolution regarding ideal government size. Unfortunately, the answer we have may not be as specific as you might prefer. We cannot offer you a measured and detailed answer; an estimate of the ideal government size in grams. Quite frankly, such an estimate should be viewed with a jaundiced eye, no matter who offered it. Still, an answer can be found if we consider a few key points. First, from Kierkegaard's Divine Command and its sacred analog, it is clear that the core, foundational purpose of government is the facilitation of the actualization of each sentient being within its compass. It is also clear from the foregoing that the actualization of each sentient being is not defined in terms of selfishness, individualism. This does not mean that only community interests define how an individual's talents are to be developed. It becomes very easy to overmanage the contemplation of the amount of one's talent which should be redirected back to the state. Such an overcontemplation was a major contributor to Communist failings. In point of fact, we would posit something of another unseen hand: as we truly actualize, we are naturally drawn to give of ourselves, not out of some sense of guilt or broken duty, but from joy.

If we have a clear foundational purpose for government, then the proper size of government is dictated by the size of the community, the scale of their suffering, and the challenges faced in transforming that suffering. Government, then, may shrink and grow as needed to meet the actualizational challenges of the community it serves. It is a means composed of ends. Never forget that a government is a tool. It is a human tool, made of people giving of themselves for the betterment of others, but it is an instrument, and when that instrument needs adjustment, it is to be adjusted.

In the final analysis, it is not selfishness that binds us as a community. We are not merely amygdalae with legs, searching for a fast buck and a cheap fuck. What unites us as a community, and in turn makes us fertile, fecund, and effective individuals, is love. Often, we do horrific things to ourselves, to each other, and to our world; the reasons for our horrific actions as well as our more pedestrian bummers are far more nuanced, contextual, involved, and convoluted than any existing theory recognizes, even when one considers the purpose of theory being the creation of nomothetic explanations of harmfulness. One can be sure that fast bucks and cheap fucks are sought, but the whys behind them, as well as the whys behind choices of college, spouse, career, car, friends, books, actions . . . are nothing like a simple appetite demanding sating. If it can be gainsaid that trees are simple stimulus-response systems, that they are in the practice of making friends with other trees (Wohlleben, 2015), then criminology has much to learn from them.

Failing to understand harm, even thoughtless, unplanned harm without recognizing it in the context of the blinding human beauty of the harmer is perhaps the single biggest sin of criminology. We have sought to demonstrate the regal might of a symphony orchestra by focusing our attention on the timpani drum. It is time for criminology to be forever rid of its caricatures, for in the end they teach us little.

Chapter Two

Theories of Balance and Exchange

One can almost watch it turn colder. We sit and watch, Michael and his beloved, as the sun grows steadily paler; leaves now with legs to roam tumble with their newfound freedom. Summer cedes to autumn with grace, without the fight one would expect from such a warrior. In time, patient autumn will give its gentle blessing to the icy cheek of winter. Spring will unfurl her coy smile bud by delicate bud, and in her turn will hand the mace of office once again to soldier summer. Nature observes in itself balance and symmetry, and nature rejoices. Balance and rhythm are nature's bosom against which we press ourselves at every occasion. The unexpected, the chaotic, the cacophonous arrhythmia that sometimes seems to envelop us is the habitat of shades and strigoi; here there be dragons.

For many of those who have contemplated human harm, order and balance have been both the state sought and the means thought to affect it. For many of those who have contemplated justice, balance has been a consistent theme. From Empedocles's elements and Aristotle's golden mean to Bentham's utility and Rawls's fairness, the weighting and averaging of polar opposites has been the arithmetic of wisdom. Like a statistical mean, oftentimes, it stands in the gap for a guess, but the balancing acts we will discuss here have proven as guesses to be disappointing, even destructive.

And like a statistical mean, misdirection can be purchased easily with error. Balance perhaps easily conceived is often notoriously difficult to maintain. Often, it means holding pitch against dissonance without resolution, finding and holding a path no more generous than a razor's width against tidal pulls, dancing a bark between Scylla and Charybdis in gale conditions at low tide. As we have already said it is not a settled thing, at least as far as we can tell, that balance is necessarily synonymous with justice; the scales of justice are not always even. It may well be hard to achieve, and for some, often not worth the pains of achieving it.

Now that's a dicey thing, is it not? Of all possible firmament where we might find agreement regarding justice, surely fairness seems the friendliest of acres. Some aspects of fairness and exchange are so familiar and ingrained in us as to be fully transparent to most. We concede that, at times, fairness can be just-ish. But just as confidently, we assert that justice is not synonymous with fairness. What is more, to equate the two is deeply problematic, and again, can lead to deep injustice, even violence.

In this chapter, we will contemplate several systems of thought which have in common some sense of balancing, some pursuit of exchange or transaction model for understanding how justice might be achieved or how crime might occur or be addressed by the wider community. We have contemplated retribution and *lex talionis* already in the previous chapter, and we will here finish the job we started on them. But as balance and exchange are ostensibly so robust, we will be spoiled for choice regarding which other thought systems we examine.

Before we launch into our discussion, let us first contemplate an idea, relevant to both justice and crime. The idea requires close examination and its disassembly will provide some of the spare parts needed for the rest of our task in this chapter. The idea to which we refer is the idea of punishment.

PUNISHMENT

There is a precocious toddler across from Michael at the coffee shop. She is angelic, but with a laser focus. They sell gelato here, and she knows it. She wants to go downstairs and get some. He cannot blame her . . . it is a warm day, and they have knee-slappingly, jaw-gapingly good gelato. Worse, the adults with whom she sits are obviously boring. After a moment, she conjures the magical phrase, each syllable offered with care: "I will be right back." At first the incantation does not have the desired effect, so her tone changes. Beginning almost as a question, she offers her talisman with increasing assertiveness: "I . . . *will be* right back?!" She rises and moves carefully but with purpose to the curving metal stairs, treacherous for any toddler. Her mother repeats the command for the girl to return to her table, even as the girl edges closer to the stairs, repeating "I'll be right back," now in a tone almost like Elvis presenting his "federal-agent-at-large" badge. Mom stands. The child freezes and for nearly three thundering seconds the two remain frozen, eyes locked on each other. The little girl breaks the stand-off; she squeals and returns quickly to the table and her mother's side. What was it that the girl understood? What had filled those three seconds in the world of that little girl, and what was the nature of the force that drove her to give up her dream of gelato? What had transpired between them, unseen to we who looked on, to explain the contents of the wordless conversation?

Punishment has very different connotation for the three authors as Michael was born and raised in the north, Beth hails from Wisconsin, and Tammy is, and forever will be, a southerner; however, we can all agree on the inherent problems associated with punishment, especially that of the physical nature. While corporal punishment is used in all areas of the United States, inhabitants in the southern part of the United States seem to embrace this type of corrective behavior as the norm. Since moving to the south, Michael has been exposed to the practice of "picking a switch." While he and his Yankee friends also knew the occasional sting of corporal punishment as kids, he is struck (. . . if you'll pardon the expression) by the psychological weirdness that "picking a switch" invites. According to accounts, a child is told to pick a switch when corporal punishment is in the unavoidable and very short-term future. The child is directed to go outside and find a branch of a bush or tree to pick, with which the adult will strike the child. For Michael, someone who has not experienced this, it is difficult to contemplate how this practice is anything aside from brutal and cruel, yet many people have emerged apparently unscathed from homes where picking a switch was a practice, Tammy included. Although Tammy and others may have survived, the fear in those moments of choosing the tool with which you were about to be beaten was every bit as terrifying as the physical beating, and often left more scars than the literal one. Now Tammy can laugh as she talks with us about how she and her siblings were punished as children; however, she can still hear her mother screaming "I'm going to beat you until the blood runs right down your legs" before the whoopin' to come.

Sometimes the repeated sting of a green stick is insufficient, even when administered to clarify every syllable of the parental explanation. Sometimes more severe measures are necessary. Without having directed the necessary scrutiny, one might be forgiven for viewing the parental continuum of punishments as being seamlessly integrated into the state's continuum of punishments; where one leaves off, ostensibly the other takes over without hiccup. So intentional and careful a system *we do not have*. Forgiven indeed, however; after a careful historical and psychological inquiry, Newman (2008) claims that punishment is such an agreed-upon thing that the only thing requiring justification is the distribution of punishment. Similarly, Von Hirsch (1976) along with an enviable blue-ribbon panel, including Erving Goffman, Alan Dershowitz, and David Rothman, indeed the very cream of penological academia at the time, concluded that sufficient evidence simply did not exist regarding the kinds of things that worked to rehabilitate offenders. Therefore, regrettably, the only defensible justification for punishment is retribution. *Please note: after careful review, the criminological cream of the crop simply shrugged and offered their blessing to retribution.* In general terms, *whether we can* punish is so settled as to be transparent; *who*, *when*, and indeed *how* we punish are the questions that remain. The question of whether each of us is legitimately punishable hinges only on our relative deservedness; no space exists to contemplate the idea that punishment as a collective social response to harm is a usurpation of power (DeValve, 2017a), and in any event is grotesquely dysfunctional. This lack of space for questioning the dehumanizing nature of punishment is itself dehumanizing.

Newman (2008) goes on to observe that the vast majority of us have been punished corporally (e.g., spanking, the switch . . .), have punished someone corporally (e.g., a child), or both, yet many feel as if physical punishment, like caning or whipping, is a morally unacceptable alternative for punishing individuals convicted of criminal offenses. This shift in emphases is particularly telling, we think. Tammy's children and Beth and Michael's daughter have at times responded powerfully to incentivization, but sometimes it doesn't work, and as a result, a form of what might be called punishment rather than a reward system has had to be implemented. Although Kinsey has never been spanked or struck in any way, she lost unfettered access to her iPad for a time because she was not turning in homework (because it was the thing distracting her from completing her assigned tasks). Though it is worth considering whether such a condition was processed by her as punishment or merely as a clearing of her attention space as Kinsey's parental committee intended, the intervention worked—she began turning her work in, and on time. Tammy has employed incentivization and the taking away of possessions, she has on occasion spanked her children even though she is well-versed in the literature noting corporal punishment as an ineffective punishment tool; she has also found it to be ineffective as spanking her children did not have any long-term results. While this physical act may be rationalized in the moment (and may have made her feel better in the short term), hindsight always proves to show a more effective manner in which the situation could have been handled.

As our children grow, however, and as they advance relative to Kohlberg's moral reasoning schema, different approaches to guiding their behavior become rather more effective. One of the perpetual challenges of being a loving parent is the provision of guidance in a manner best suited to the needs of one's child. For those who use corporal punishment, as children grow punishment often becomes less corporal in nature, and in time less common at all. In contemporary thought, generally we think of corporal punishment as a thing to offer to children.

But corporal punishment is a thing thought perhaps to be too cruel to offer to adults in exchange for their wrongdoing, at least so it would seem, at least at the level thought to be effective for adults. To be sure, adult corporal punishment tends to be extreme: whips and bamboo canes remove layers of skin in strips, and the scars are deep enough never to go away. But it is not the scars themselves that make the punishment; the experience has to hurt enough to be memorable. The belief that the damage done to a child with a switch does not include a physical scar is irrelevant, for a scar is raised nonetheless. It is the pain of the strike, coupled with the betrayal of trust that accompanies the blows, that together comprise the anatomy of this particular punishment. Small children are rarely worldly enough to realize that the pain they feel does not correlate to permanent damage. Generally speaking the evidence is consistent regarding corporal punishment for children: corporal punishments for children is directly linked to a lifetime prevalence of psychiatric disorders (e.g., MacMillan, Boyle, Wong, Duku, Fleming, & Walsh, 1999), externalized behavior later in the developmental arc (e.g., Benjet & Kazdin, 2003; MacKenzie, Nicklas, Brooks-Gunn, & Waldfogel, 2014), symptoms of depression (e.g., Christie-Mizell, Pryor, & Grossman, 2008), and impaired cognitive development (Straus & Paschall, 2009) among other things (e.g., Gershoff & Grogan-Kaylor, 2016). Still, the vast majority of parents in the United States report spanking their child at least mildly (Lansford, Wager, Bates, Pettit, & Dodge, 2012). To be sure, children emerge from homes where corporal punishment is common and live normal lives. But when in a nationally representative sample more than 90 percent of respondents report having spanked their two to four year old in the previous two weeks (Straus & Paschall, 2009), it is difficult to hold the normative state up as being anything like ideal.

Moskos (2011) invites us to consider whether we might prefer to receive a couple of lashes with a split bamboo cane for each year of our sentence instead of going to prison. In *In Defense of Flogging*, Moskos asks if it is the case that we ourselves might well prefer flogging or whipping in place of a stretch in prison, why would we not offer it to others as a policy option? But perhaps our contemplation of Moskos's bargain is not fully clear-headed. Choosing a brief flogging over years of separation from family makes some sense, even to the point where the damage done by the flogging might require hospitalization: prison time can have . . . supplemental . . . punitive consequences. Rates of infection from communicable diseases like tuberculosis and hepatitis are considerably greater in prison (see, e.g., Schmit, Wansaula, Pratt, Price, & Langer, 2017); rape and forced consensual homosexuality is far from uncommon (see, e.g., Beck, 2016). Missing from the contemplation, however, is that fundamental question of what is thought to arise from the flogging, aside from blood and torn flesh. The question of flogging over prison does not place before us whether punishment makes sense in the first place. Perhaps we should consider what punishment seeks to do.

When criminologists and their students contemplate the purposes of punishment, often we blast out a conditioned list of ends: incapacitation (both general and specific) (Zimring & Hawkins, 1997), retribution, deterrence (both general and specific), rehabilitation, and sometimes restoration. Critical criminologists like us might, with sufficient snark, add reclamation or some other -ation word, but the current set of -ations is best understood in relation to the vocabulary of punishments in common use today: community supervision and time in a secure facility, either jail or prison. Each of these purposes has its apologists and detractors as well as policy iterations, often with a mixed bag of partial successes and less-than-successes. Of these, only retribution and a narrowly read version of incapacitation can claim anything like relatively reliable results. Prisons can succeed at separating a set of individuals from opportunities to do harm in the wider community, though it is relatively poor at separating individuals from similar opportunities within institutions. Likewise, they inflict a clear measure of harm in exchange for harm, though today the measure of harm doled out is less a function of a precise *lex talionis* and more often weighed in terms of the seriousness of the harm and whether the harmer has harmed before. None of these aims, including the ones that sort of work, are terribly meaningful, however, and debates regarding which aim has the most empirical support end up sounding suspiciously like conversations about angels dancing on the head of a pin.

There is, Newman (2008) tells us, a natural etiology for our idea of punishment. The earliest humans tended to impute intentionality and instrumentality to harsh environmental conditions, if for no other reason than to help make sense of the world. Crop devastation or family decimation are perhaps more easily taken on board by early humans if they are given instrumental meaning. What is more, if the source of nature's wrath can be determined, a degree of agency can be reclaimed by those early humans subject to it. Crops were destroyed because we have been willful and obdurate children—we did something wrong. Consider the biblical story of Job as reinforcing the natural etiology for the justification of punishment. Job was a man who had it all: wealth, land, family, and faith. As a result of nothing more than a mere bet between God and Satan, not his own doing, Job lost everything except his faith. However, in a moment of weakness, he asks God to explain why all this happened and why man is allowed to suffer. Coming to Job in a "whirlwind" (e.g., the devastating tornado), God chastises Job for his questioning, and only when Job relents and understands that God is in control and can reward and punish at will does God seemingly restore all that Job once had. Appeasing an affronted god may require more than the usual ceremony, more than the usual sacrifice, but it is a thing we can undertake.

So the human idea of punishment, at least according to Newman, grew out of a need among early humans to impose a kind of human ontological order on the natural world. Powerlessness before a tornado might well make one wish for a god to be turning the turbine. Otherwise, the human confronts an inhuman and insensate megalosaur far beyond human capacity to deflect or prevent, and utterly deaf to the pleas of those crushed to dust in its wild and wandering rampage. And we think it would be premature to claim that we have moved wholly beyond a degree of need for such an explanation for harms. For many, the question still dwells before us, insufficiently answered: "why do bad things happen to good people?" Religions make and lose membership on how doctrine provides an answer to this question. After the recent loss of a loved one, our faith buoys us up on just such answers . . . or it does not. And in this function alone religion demonstrates value. But if the idea of punishment is the result of a need to cope with human frailty, clearly it is an idea that can be dispensed with once need is gone. Further, of course, if it is a need-filling idea, it is not itself as foundational as we take it to be, nor indeed as foundational as we think Newman intended it to appear. If we were to use King James–esque terminology, as Newman might well prefer, "God created nature to please himself. God created Man to rule nature. Man created punishment to help him cope with his office." If punishment is merely a tool, this observation alone liberates us utterly from it. Punishment is a means, and as such it can be reforged or even discarded to be forgotten. That it has seemed to serve well at times is insufficient, for when a tool shows its fissures or it becomes clear that it has not worked optimally all along, the time to retire it has come.

Let us consider punishment from a different angle, one that does not presume a state or some weird contract arrangement. Newman (2008) examines several means of execution used by precursors of Western culture as we know it today: stoning, breaking at the wheel, burning, burial alive, drowning, hanging, beheading, quartering. Four different frameworks, which he calls "theories" (along with a few elaborations), are employed in the effort to explain why the punishments were employed. In no particular order, Newman speaks of sacrifice theory, apotropaic theory, reflection theory, and honor theory. In simplest terms, respectively, punishment can take the form of one being sacrificed, say, to a god; it can be administered in such a fashion as to ward off evil; it can be rendered such that it represents a mirror image of the offending act; or it can be imposed in order to reclaim someone's honor. A wheel with nine spokes, thought of as a symbol for good, was used to crush the bones of the doer of evil; in literal Manichean collision between symbols,

Evil was broken by Good. In Roman culture, a person who committed certain crimes was thought to have acted against the *polis*, and thus was embracing the way of animals. Such a person might find himself tied into a burlap bag, with his presumably preferred company of wild and toothy beasts, and perhaps cast into a river.

The key point for us here is that punishment was in some way instrumental. Harm done by the community to a guilty party had a purpose, just like nature's destruction was imbued with purpose to make it comprehensible. Human punishment thus mirrored the imputed instrumentality of natural disasters, but early on added the additional layer of instrumentality relating the specifics of the punishment itself to the ends sought.

In contemporary criminal justice, punishment remains of course, but merely as a fact. Punishment has been denuded of any meaningfulness, and thus, without our ever having realized it, we have bleached it of any justification. Community supervision and long-term incarceration may involve forms of need-related interventions, but these are ancillary to the purpose of punishment and its central mechanism: surveillance and control. As we saw in the previous chapter, we in the United States have moved away from all but the most seemingly humane means of executing, ostensibly because we as a community embrace capital punishment for its incapacitation value. There are a number of voices who have advocated for a return to emphasizing a degree of reflection in capital punishment (though, presumably, not all the way down the punishment continuum), they are relatively few and far from credible. Today we punish in the most sanitized and generic ways possible; punishment no longer carries anything like the intentionality it used to. The trend toward humanizing punishment has been synonymous with the removal of the logic of punishment. If it is insane to use the bones of a burglar to repair his victim's home (and it is), and if it is likewise insane to brand someone according to the nature of her crime (and it is as well), then the very thing that has been thought to make punishment useful—its use of injury to convey a message—has been forever lost to it. And by having moved to a penal model where punishment is rendered fully generic such that it consists of the *fact* of surveillance and control, or of the *fact* of death, we have thus admitted that punishment itself is fully meaningless and without value.

Punishment and Balance

Well of course it is meaningless, or rather relatively meaningless. Punishment is, at least for our purposes, a human thing. After all, it may well have arisen from humans wresting meaning from nature. We know a great deal about social construction; punishment only has the meaning we as humans give it.

We are free to shape and reshape punishment's meaning and value according to our need and desire. The concept of social construction bears passing resemblance to the Buddhist idea of "emptiness"; and with emptiness, all things are possible. At a minimum, our insights about ourselves, into things we have forgotten so easily, free us now to rethink how, why, and indeed whether we should punish.

Common among some of Newman's (2008) theories is the idea that punishment addresses some form of imbalance: punishment restores an injustice, reaffirms a value, offers antithesis to toxic thesis. The heretic is burned in the purifying flame, and thus we are cleansed to receive God's forgiveness for allowing heresy to exist at all. The wheel, symbol of good, is victorious over evil. In Hammurabi's code, I must donate my bones to close the hole I made in the wall of your home.

Few took the logic of balance to a higher art than did Jeremy Bentham. Now we will spend considerably more time with him later in this chapter, but Bentham is the patron saint of seekers of balance, and thus must be invoked here. An act can be assessed, so says Bentham (1948), in rather simple terms. We might think of it thus:

$$\sum_{\mu}\sum_{x}(V_{pl} + V_{pa} + F_{pl} + F_{pa})$$

Where, beginning with any one individual impacted by the act, V_{pl} represents the value of initial pleasure from the act, and V_{pa} represents the value of initial pain from that act. Considered in the weighting of pleasure and pain values are the intensity, duration, certainty, and propinquity (nearness) of the pleasure or pain. F_{pl} and F_{pa} refer respectively to the fecundity, or the likelihood of a given experience being followed by a similar sensation (or interesting experience, in Bentham's terms). The sum, Σ_x, is derived for the first individual, and assessed for its pleasure/pain (or good/evil, for pleasure is *only* good, and pain is *only* evil (Bentham, 1948, e.g., p. 102) balance. Then the same procedure is undertaken for each individual impacted by the act, and summed, Σ_μ.

As "the business of government is to promote the happiness of society, by punishing and rewarding" (Bentham, 1948, p. 70), this felicific calculus can be used to tune punishment in such a way as to deter rational evil. All that would be necessary is to be certain that the pleasures gained from any given act are outweighed by the pain of punishment it would yield: punishment thus strikes a balance that not only carries the indignation of the community, but also aims to deter future mischief. Bentham recognized that his calculus placed considerable demands on the legislature; working out likely balances, including fecundities for nefariousness, and punishments is a daunting undertaking. Nevertheless, Bentham's goal of achieving a true science of legislation (e.g., Mitchell, 1918) depended on it.

In fact, punishment is incapable of bringing balance to anything, mostly because what it brings is only suffering. Suffering in kind does not restore a balance, as we have seen already. As the classic saying goes, "two wrongs do not equal a right." The idea that by suffering we make atonement for our wrongdoing is dependent on the idea that a bill must be paid, a score settled. Somehow it seems inconceivable that one who harmed would not also experience some form of harm in return. Perhaps, the harm done represents some form of benefit to the harmer, or perhaps, there is some more ethereal sense of a need to make atonement. But atonement is an impoverished form of accountability even when the atonement is self-imposed and for a more nebulous, numinous benefit. Far more meaningful than suffering for harm done is the opportunity to help heal the victim; doing so legitimately rebuilds trust and repairs relationships, where suffering for atonement merely desiccates dialogue and embattles hearts. Regarding deterrence, we will speak a little more below, but what is known is that the balance Bentham sought to strike was a balance struck in vain; deterrence among humans is far more nuanced a thing than a simple weighting of yummy and nasty. Punishment and balance are things wholly apart from justice, and any apparent relationship is mere illusion, or is itself an expression of a need altogether different from what seems obvious.

Punishment and Exchange

Punishment is like rain. Precipitation as a cleansing force is at best symbolic, but the water that falls ("the rain is falling" is redundant: if it were not falling it would not be rain) cleanses and makes new, does it not? Being hit or locked up is itself unrelated to the initial harm done, but the suffering it cultivates seems to possess a cleansing capacity in the eyes of some. It is inflicted suffering that seeks to purge from us the taint of our misdeeds. It washes away the sin for which it has been imposed. The suffering represents a payment of a kind in exchange for the initial harm. Something was gained, ostensibly, in the initiating harm; something must be offered up in exchange. Capital exchange is a model so engrained in contemporary world views that projecting it upon the amorphous question of justice is only natural. Christians honor the broken body of Jesus; he served as the Great Human Scapegoat, carrying in his suffering taint that was not his, but was borne by him for everyone else. Payment in full has been made.

Harm does not translate handily to the modality of exchange, even if it has appeared to do so for millennia. Harm offered in response to harm is verily the definition of insanity. Suffering washes nothing from us, in fact, except perhaps our dignity. The literal analogy is instructive: no careful parent seeks to remove grass stains from his child's clothes by rubbing grass on the knees of the child who tackled him. Into the lives of those who suffer, we need not introduce more misery. One might forget about one's toothache for a time if one smashes one's thumb with a hammer, but neither tooth nor thumb nor owner of both fares well in the end. Indeed, were we to contemplate the model we have so uncritically accepted for so long, punishment offers a price tag for pleasure: if we seek something for ourselves, we need only be willing to accept the punishment for it. As we will see later on in this chapter, Bentham addresses just this problem. But what is not addressed by Bentham is the creation of a parallel economy; one can pay for what one wants in money or in pain. The two economies are not insulated from each other, of course; money is understandable as a manifestation of past pain (e.g., work done). Still, money and suffering are meaningfully distinct phenomena.

Lex Talionis

God is generous indeed. He provided his son, Marduk, to rule over the land. And Marduk gave us a set of laws in order to help us work through what is just after harm has been done. Hammurabi, beloved of Bel, is the lawbringer, the vessel for Bel's wisdom. The Code he gave us presents details regarding how we are to respond to all manner of misdeeds, including murder, theft, fraud, even economic crime. He also provided fair prices for services, so that such things would not lead to discord. The physician's fee for a mended arm is five shekels. Half a mina is due to the owner of a garden's tree felled without his permission; two-thirds of the produce of a garden are to go to the gardener, whereas the remaining third belongs to he who was given the task of working the garden; a robber caught shall be put to death.

In Hammurabi's code is also something of a relativistic principle, a sliding scale for penalties dependent upon the harm done. Correcting for the social status of those involved, the price of an eye taken is an eye. This principle became known as *lex talionis*, or the law of the talion, meaning precise equality of compensation for harm. It seems clear that Mosaic law reflects either Mesopotamian law or reflects a common influence, and as one might conclude from the Latin name for it, *lex talionis* found its way into Roman law as well.

Such an elegant model; the logic is impeccable, of course: although a given codex might offer guidance in foreseen circumstances, instances where the unforeseen may arise still must be spoken to, and the *lex talionis* provides a guiding principle for just such circumstances. When it was first offered, *lex talionis* was a progressive idea, limiting the price for suffering, the cost for wrongdoing. Problems arose, though, from the literal nature of the principle; as a solution, Roman law provided for delicts, or fines paid set relative to the value of a talion penalty. *Lex talionis* continued to enjoy influence in the Latin, and then the Christian spheres of influence. The "truces of God" in German parts of Europe tended to include the *lex talionis* as a mechanism for securing the peace of God within communities (Schild, 1981).

We might be tempted to assume that current penalties for wrongdoing are yet another abstraction of the *lex talionis*. Such a conclusion would be misguided, of course. The logic between harm and social response has dissolved largely because of the dysfunctional nature (in relation to reducing recidivism) of all we have tried heretofore (DeValve, 2015). *Lex talionis* was replaced by penitence in the middle of the nineteenth century, and penitence as then conceived was shown to be valueless only a generation later. Again, today, no coherent narrative binds criminoetiology to social action in response to crime.

Conclusion

As a practice, punishment—for the purpose of harm of any kind, for anyone—belongs on the Heap of Very Bad Ideas. Punishment through fear and violence purges nothing; it does not ennoble or offer recompense. It is tantamount to taking an individual with pneumonia and intentionally infecting him with MRSA. Punishment is about as dumb an idea as humans have conceived, perhaps beaten out for the title of Dumbest Idea Ever by the idea of "war." Too often, punishment is nothing more or less than suffering imposed upon someone for the benefit of a community. People often confuse discipline or justice intervention with punishment. Justice intervention is corrective behavior acting out of a desire to remedy wrongs and instill humanity; some behavior demands an intervening agent as they are often harmful to others. Punishment, however, is a selfish, cowardly, and despicable act which dehumanizes the punisher in concert with the punished. Punishment is instrumental violence which seeks to communicate a message: it is a close cousin of terrorism. Each of us has been disciplined; however, many of us have experienced its negative counterpart. Each of us knows that little is learned from the process of punishment; from picking a switch one learns far more about botany than about morality. The great mystery regarding punishment is that it is so transparently accepted by so many, despite what seems like an obvious and fatal illogic to it.

For us, though, at the back side of this conversation on punishment, we might recognize two key points, closely related to the etiology-action divorce discussed in *A Different Justice*. Punishment is taken as a foundational practice in the pursuit of justice. It comes complete with a list of half-baked rationalizations and justifications linking it to justice, some thought by some to be related to the very roots of the human idea of punishment. None of these rationalizations or justifications withstand examination, however. None can be seen as actually furthering any idea of justice that itself is meaningful beyond even modest scrutiny. Are there times when we cannot avoid sanctioning those who violate the social order? Of course . . . we recognize that there is a small segment of the population that will author harm prolifically; granting them a pass to do so would further victimize those which they have harmed along with themselves; however, dehumanizing these individuals and losing our humanity at the same time fails to embrace justice. Punishment and justice are not equivalent sides of the same coin, and in fact, they counter one another. However, like a frustrated parent, sometimes, we are desperate and do not have an easy solution to the problem at hand, but intentionally "picking a switch" and not considering one's options will ultimately punish us all.

The lesson we must take from this as we move forward is that we must be very careful and deeply deliberate about what we understand to be the purpose of any intervention we make in the lives of humans in the furtherance of justice. Dysfunction regarding punishment has only underscored the point Mill (1993) makes with regard to how far we have come regarding the human understanding of justice—almost nowhere.

As punishment seems so clearly useful, as it seems able to restore balance or to operate transactionally, we see yet another lesson we must take in: where justice is love, need is the focus of action. Where need is the focus, there is necessarily a moveable framework for responding to harm. Interventions on behalf of those who harm and those who hurt necessarily must consider the nature of their need concomitantly with more absolute principles, but in order to be effective and thus legitimate, all interventions must depend from the armature of human need.

UTILITARIANISM AND RATIONAL CHOICE

Don't just take it from us, though. Consider Bentham's own words: "But all punishment is mischief: all punishment in itself is evil. If it ought at all to be admitted, it ought only to be admitted in as far as it promises to exclude some greater evil" (Bentham, 1948, p. 170). Continuing, he argues that punishment must not be inflicted in cases where it is groundless, inefficacious, too expensive, or needless. Further, it must be deemed worthwhile to attempt to prevent the mischief in question. If it is worthwhile, prevention is the first aim, doing a smaller harm is the second aim, limiting the mischief is the third aim, and doing whatever is done as cheaply as possible is the fourth. "*The value of the punishment must not be less in any case than what is sufficient to outweigh that of the profit of the offence*" (Bentham, 1948, p. 179, emphasis in original). As he made clear in the foregoing as well as in his agreement with Beccaria, the punishment also must not be more to great excess than the profit of the offense would be, as any amount of superfluous punishment would be tyranny. It is only at the knife's edge, that balancing point between deterrence and tyranny, only there is punishment to be seen as efficacious. Echoing Beccaria, if it is wasteful or if it is not worthwhile, it is tyranny. The anticipated punishment must be just enough (but not too much) to outweigh the anticipated profit from the crime; such precision Bentham requires of his legislators.

Like with Rand, altruism throws Bentham a curveball, or so it would seem. I do something for my child that is expensive to me, but pleasurable to her. Just today Kinsey and Michael painted her model rocket. Skilled with a paintbrush far beyond anything Michael will ever manage, she is only just learning to use a spray can. It turns out, however, her tender skill did not dissuade her from energetically emptying the can of paint not only on her rocket, but also on one corner of our deck, and on her father. In the dull glow of Michael's laptop, as he writes these words his hands can be seen still to have a flattering greenish hue. An event like this would wreck the pretty math. Not so, Bentham says: we have simply apprehended "pleasure" incorrectly. In fact, says Bentham, Michael derives pleasure from being painted green to the wrists by his daughter, because her happiness is a far greater pleasure than having hands of a more humdrum color. But is this discerning, or is this merely intellectual gymnastics to avoid being pinned down in error? Asserting *a priori* that all human activity is explainable through the felicific calculus, and that apparent variations from the theoretical premise are merely errors of empirical grasp seems, well, a little Barnumesque. This way to the egress.

With the advantage of more than two and a quarter centuries, though, we can see rather plainly that punishment almost always meets one of Bentham's criterion as "unmeet for punishment" and is thus indefensible on its face, even rendered so by one of its most authoritative technicians. The walk along the knife's edge is not merely a fool's errand; in fact, today there is no knife at all. Bentham sought to be remembered as the Newton of Morality (Mitchell, 1918), setting out his felicific equation and its constituent parts with mathematical precision, and applying his calculus favorably in a variety of human contexts. It was his precision, in fact, that made him special among his contemporaries, as utilitarianism had been the dominant ethical framework in England for more than a generation (Mitchell, 1918) when Bentham wrote

The Principles of Morals and Legislation. He did not create utilitarianism; he simply took it to its logical limits and colored in the whole scheme. In the end, of course, the very thing that made him stand out in his time is today largely ignored; much of his blueprint for legislation and even criminoetiology is at best a curious academic cul-de-sac, and no more. His felicific calculus remains, and as it remains it would have been articulable by many of his contemporaries, if only in a more generalized way.

Bentham as a character was and remains still somewhat larger than life, and his posthumous eccentricities only add color to the palate. Unifying his desire to offer the moral world its Newton in the body of himself and his eccentric and grandiloquent persona, Karl Marx immortalized Bentham thus: "in no time and in no country has the most homespun commonplace ever strutted about in so self-satisfied a way" (Geis, 1955, p. 160). Both visionary and prick, in order for us to use Bentham's thought properly, it remains for us to decide in what ratio these two qualities lived side by side in him.

Bounded Rationality

The rational assumption in its purest form holds no water, but rumors of its death have been greatly exaggerated. There are a number of criminological formulations (e.g., Cornish & Clarke, 1987; Felson, 1987; Gottfredson & Hirschi, 1990; Stafford & Warr, 1993) which share a rational actor as part of their premises, though the sketch of that actor is rather less of a caricature than it is for Bentham.

In what has become something of a series of seminal works, Herbert Simon (1945/1997; 1946; 1947) took a mighty whack at the authoritative thought in the area of administration. From the founding of the discipline by Woodrow Wilson in the last days of the nineteenth century up until then, the predominant pursuit of thinkers in administration had been to discover principles, flawless and unerring fluted-marble-column ideas that would bear the weight of the new science. Simon, in essence, informed the emperor of his nakedness, deflating the pomp and grandeur with a few simple observations. First, he pointed out that the principles of administration accepted and prized by scholars, like that efficiency is increased by task specialization and limiting span of control, were nothing more than proverbs or adages, with practically no scientific, generalizable value. Second, he dispatched the Rational Man, and from the spare parts assembled and introduced the Administrative Man. He offered the painfully simple observation that because humans are mortal, temporal beings, we suffer from a noted inability to perceive all possible options and all possible consequences of each action into the far future. Because of our decidedly un-godlike understanding of options for and consequences of action, no human is capable of pure rationality. Instead, he argued, humans operate from a rational calculus, but within an environment of limited, or bounded, understanding. Simon called this trait bounded rationality.

Now there is more than one lesson for us to consider here if we are paying attention. The obvious one is that the assumption of purely rational functioning of humans, really in any context, is one we should studiously avoid. This first lesson will be fodder for the conversation that follows, but it is fair, we think, for us to take a very brief pause to observe something that should give anyone interested in theorizing about humans more than a tiny shudder. Woodrow Wilson, racism and sexism aside, was a smart man, as were many of his contemporaries in the study of administration. They issued forth what would become a fertile, practical, and nuanced, if clumsy, and sometimes bastardized and purloined, discipline. For so many smart people to have committed so glaring and simple an oversight in their theorizing as to forget the mortality of human beings is more than a little disconcerting. Groupthink, social construction, and other social psychological limiting forces aside, surely it need not have taken half a century for someone to figure things out. The second lesson, one coequal in importance with the first, but applicable more generally, is the need for any theorist to be attentive to the assumptions they make. Assumptions are necessary at some level, of course, in any social theorizing endeavor. One way to step in shit with assumptions is to accept uncritically the assumptions of others as a matter of course. We think we have done reasonably well there thus far, but consider this an invitation for you, kind reader, to help us. It is also a point of critique for the following conversation.

Simon's simple observations provided the opportunity for something of a renaissance of rational choice criminological theorizing, albeit forty years later. In a seminal article, Cornish and Clarke (1987) examine the phenomenon of crime displacement from a revivified rational choice perspective. Crime displacement, of course, necessarily implies a decision-making process, and probably one that weighs costs of an act against its payoffs. Still, it is a limited or bounded rationality (Cornish & Clarke, 2005) at work, and at times can be, well, impoverished.

More than merely bounding rationality is necessary, though, to make rational choice even close to watertight, and Cornish and Clarke are ready with a plan. Specifically, they observe that multiple decision points, and decision processes, are at work in any instance of a criminal act. The decision to engage in criminal behavior (involvement decisions), for example, is likely to be procedurally different from the decision to deepen the criminal enterprise in order to escape detection when plans fall apart (event decisions) (Cornish & Clarke, 2005). A crime is chosen, it is assumed, for specific reasons. An offender considers costs and benefits as he apprehends them at a given moment, and in the space where offense (with its unique characteristics, like exposure and reward) and offender (with his unique characteristics, like valence for an appetite, skill, awareness) interact, a specific crime is chosen in order to fulfill the offender's needs. These offense characteristics that channel offender decision making, or the decision making of an entire class of offenders, are called "choice-structuring characteristics" (Cornish & Clarke, 1987, p. 935). And this space where these characteristics are at play allows latitude for controlling participation in those activities, channeling offender behavior through incentivization. For example, by increasing the risk of detection of one form of gambling, say, by ramping up visible police presence at one venue, provided the remunerative components are comparable, those intent on committing a gambling crime will go where the likelihood of detection is smaller.

Involvement decision making has three stages: initiation, habituation, and desistance. Event decisions, apparently less temporally aligned, include everything from preparation to target selection, to doing the deed itself and to the means of escape (Cornish & Clarke, 2005, p. 19). Crime is purposive; involvement decisions are deliberate, considered things, so they say. Involvement implies the existence of some need and the connection between that need and crime as a likely means of meeting it. Desistence does not mean the need is gone, but that the matrix of offense and offender characteristics no longer favors crime commission: given what knowledge the choice-maker has, given the needs he has, the inducements that exist, the relative risk, the consequences of apprehension, the choice to commit crime no longer makes sense.

Cornish and Clarke (1987) highlight gambling, suicide, and car theft in West Germany as examples of displaced offending resulting from changes in situational conditions: car theft was displaced to older cars when all new cars had ignition locks installed; betting shops, lotteries, and numbers games were compared by gamblers for their relative "action"; the detoxification of gas led to a nontrivial drop in suicides in Britain. Sounding more than a little like Robert Merton, they observe that in some cases where both legal and illegal avenues to need meeting may exist, like with drunk driving, it is likely that "criminal behavior will usually be contemplated only after legitimate means have been foreclosed or rejected" (Cornish & Clarke, 1987, p. 938). As rational choice theory offers explanation regarding the choice of particular crimes, it is a theory of crime. As it also offers something of an accounting of the criminal career, it is a theory of criminality (Cornish & Clarke, 2005). A theoretical model with such a dual capacity without doubt is a more robust accounting of human activity than a theoretical model that has no such dual capacity.

But any theoretical model must be judged by other things before its elegance can be considered. Cornish and Clarke have given us a theoretical model of crime that offers two key enhancements. First, it recognizes the limited capacity of humans to act rationally. Second, it pays homage to the complexity of the decision process involved in the commission of many crimes. As valuable as these improvements are relative to the pure rationality of Bentham present in every human action, even as a nomothetic narrative, rational choice theory remains a marginal accounting of human thought and action. In our view it has three primary weaknesses. First, bounded rationality still assumes rational decision making of actors, only in a context of limited information. Cornish and Clarke recognize the humanity of the criminal, and they honor the human as a decision-making machine. Where the model fails is in the assumption that cost-benefit comparisons are the only (charitably, perhaps, the primary) calculus humans use in making decisions. Here Cornish and Clarke made a species of the same error that Simon corrected in 1947 when he introduced the idea of bounded rationality: they adopted an assumption (of course only they know if they did so without thought, though no evidence of relevant contemplation exists in the written record to our knowledge). Specifically, and ironically, it seems they adopted the cost-benefit calculus assumption from Simon, the very fellow who obliterated the rational man assumption in the first place.

The evidence, though, seems to speak for itself, does it not? Displacement seems to go further than merely implying rational decision making. Indeed so; it would be foolish to argue that humans never use cost-benefit thinking in the process of decision making. Of course we do. The error arises when we assume that we all use rationality, or that we use rationality all the time, or that rationality for me is the same as it is for you (see, e.g., Bouffard, 2007; Bouffard, Bry, Smith, & Bry, 2008). What Tammy contemplates in the process of evaluating a given behavior may well be very different from what Beth evaluates when contemplating the same behavior. Oftentimes, the events we think of as criminal are, for a variety of reasons, nuanced and emotionally charged events. Even holding apart deeper interactions relative to precipitation, which themselves can attenuate the capacity for cool and rationed thought, there can be copious amounts of excitement, fear, and anger. Bounded rationality aside, our decider, the neo-cortex, can be rather easily shorted out of the decision-making process by our limbic systems, in precisely these very times: contexts of fear, excitement, and anger. Decisions regarding involvement as well as those related to the events themselves are all subject to affective states (DeHaan & Vos, 2003), even limbic hijacking (e.g., Goleman, 1996). It is difficult, to say the least, to believe that most humans under the conditions related to many crimes, like, say, the fear of detection, are capable of remaining clear-headed and able to discern cost and benefit, even if limited in scope.

If the theory is, like other theories, nomothetic by design, what does it matter if bounded rationality is only sometimes an apt description of human deciding? If it is only generally applicable to human decision making vis-à-vis crime, it has value. Fair enough, but there are two closely related problems that stem from the rational choice accounting. First, the idea that harm was undertaken rationally invites more than just deterrent endeavors, it invites vengeance—punishment, which we have already seen to be both unethical and ineffective. Second, the imprecision of the model makes social response to crime deeply problematic. Even assuming that cost and benefit decision structuring would be meaningfully possible for a nontrivial portion of criminal offending, with regard to any one particular case of criminal decision making, we are not (and shall never be) capable of discerning precisely to what degree cost-benefit calculi played a role in the commission of the crime. Appearances can be deceiving; what appears to be the result of bounded rationality may be the result of other nonrational decision processes, like fear, impulse, or habit energy. Social responses to crime that are yoked to rationality, presuming of course they are even marginally effective, therefore, cannot hope to find their mark in any reliable way (see, e.g., Kelly, 2009).

The second major failing of rational choice theory is related to the crime specificity assumption of the theory. Again, it is assumed that specific crimes are undertaken for specific reasons. Just as it is odd to assume crime occurs by the stochastic, lucky-loo interaction of target, offender, and protectorate, it is equally impoverished to assume that crime is an action specifically undertaken, driven by need. Like any human behavior motive is deeply complex, even inscrutable at times. To conceptualize human decision making as always purposive is to remove the classic reason for climbing Mt. Everest: because it is there. To see human action as always deliberate or always knee-jerk is to obliterate broad swaths of art.

The third failing that concerns us is the rational choice emphasis on crime. It has already been treated in detail (e.g., DeValve, 2015; Quinney, 1970; Young, 2011), so it need not be enlarged upon here, but crime as a construct is no more than a detected act or omission that was a contravention of a criminal codex. Criminal behavior is just like any other noncriminal human behavior, save for the potential consequences and the social proscription attendant to it. And again, treating crime as a discrete human phenomenon operates under the assumption of the consensus of the law, which is an assumption that should be dismissed out of hand. The concern with crime as a reified thing represents a grotesque oversight and fatal flaw.

At a distance, one might argue that Michael's criminological theory (DeValve, 2015) bears an uncomfortable resemblance to rational choice assertions, and in particular with regard to the dynamic of offender need driving decision making. Perhaps, but upon closer inspection, one can see the differences are considerable. First, Michael's criminoetiology of love does not rely on cost-benefit decision making. In fact, it makes no assumptions about the mechanisms used in deciding, as mechanisms (a) vary (meaning rationality is not the only means of reasoning); (b) are sometimes amalgams (meaning any decision is both assessed and emotively justified); and (c) are of decidedly less importance than the ideas that feed and guide them (e.g., DeValve, 2015). Self-interest is a theme held in common, but again, where Cornish and Clarke seem to assume self-interest is understood, or at least is discernible, Michael does not. Indeed, central to Michael's theory is that although individuals act on the basis of perceived self-interest, often they misapprehend at some level what is in their best interest as a result of greed, aversion, or ignorance. Perceived self-interest may be only dimly grasped at any given time by anyone, whether they are engaged in criminal activity or not. Truest self-interest is objectively discernible; it is found in loving others around us to, even beyond, the limits of our capacity. In this regard, then, love offers us insights that are applicable not only to actions that happen to be proscribed by law, but also actions that are not; from the mundane to the majestic, from the destructive to the altruistic.

BALANCE AND EXCHANGE IN THEORIES OF JUSTICE

We, humanity we mean, deserve at least an occasional detached, wry smile for our folly. So easily do our best intentions go careening madly off the rails, the yield being bizarre, even grotesque mishap. Popular media is not without its colorful vocabulary of adjectives for President Trump, including "a traffic cone soaked in raw sewage," offered by Trevor Noah. From such images, and from conversations powered by them, we can expect no truth, no wisdom to emerge capable of healing the broken hearts that bracket them. Political partisanship creates layers of hollow meaning that results in pointless conflict. No party can claim hands that are all too clean. Meaning machines, humans think and converse in symbolic terms, and the images we craft can have considerable impact on understanding, even to the point where candidates find more purchase on polls trading aggressive images more than substantive critiques.

Yet it is most often with the best of intentions that we turn metaphors into battering rams, ploughshares into swords. Even if we fail to understand how anything like wholesome intentions could possibly be present behind someone's eyes, something like good intentions are likely present in some way; our vision is so easily clouded by fear, ignorance, clamoring. And symbols can with ease take us far afield of truth. Lindsay and Michael were again at their favorite café during an open-mic poetry evening not long ago when one of the poets presented us a handful of lapel pins: they were in the shape of a Christian cross, but the American flag colors filled in the area of the pins. For anyone who purports to be a student of the US Constitution, such a symbol should raise deep concern, as it seems to be a direct affront to the establishment clause, and an indirect affront to the free exercise clause, of the First Amendment. Judging from his poetry, however, he seemed to be in possession of considerable patriotic zeal.

So it is with many of our symbols: we hold them high for the feelings they stir, but we fail to recognize their acroamatic dysfunctions. Take, for example, Themis. She is the begowned and blindfolded woman equipped with scale and sword who graces so many American courtrooms. Her accoutrements are intentional, of course, and speak directly to the nature of the institution of American justice. Just so, they tell much of the tale of its dysfunctionality.

The scales in Themis's hand represent balance, a fair weighing of claims against each other. The blindfold is to remind us that in her deciding regarding competing claims, Themis is blind to extralegal differences. Finally, the sword reminds us of the state's sovereign power to punish. An altogether different reading of the symbolic troika seems more apt given recent events, however. One could take the scales to be emblematic of the ability of the wealthy to purchase justice (merchants often used scales to regulate exchange); the sword seems indicative of the coercive modality of justice currently in place; and the blindfold reveals the callous and uncaring nature of the consequences of state action.

Themis has not always been so portrayed in fact. The scales are one of two common objects in her reach, but not so the sword or the blindfold. The sword may be borrowed from Themis's Egyptian colleague Ma'at; Ma'at had no scales as Themis had no sword traditionally, and neither was blindfolded. We (meaning Tammy, Beth, and Michael) are unsure precisely when the sword and blindfold were added to Themis's kit, but we doubt not that the modification was done with the very best of intentions. Tragically, though, they replaced the mightiest bit of Themis's gear, and created untold confusion about the truest nature of justice. Historically, Themis was depicted with a scale and/or a *cornucopia*, symbol of bounty. As we will see in time, the cornucopia is a far more apt symbol for justice than is the scale or the sword. And indeed as we will discover, we will want Themis to lose that blindfold and show us her incredible hazel eyes just as soon as she can.

The failings of current justice practice aside, the idea of justice as balance seems to be the idea sought in the portrayal of Themis with scales. The ideas of justice that follow have at their core some sense of balance or weighing consistent with what one might take to be Themis's counsel. Treating all such ideas is not possible in the current context; the ideas chosen have had and continue to enjoy considerable influence over contemporary thought. This chapter and this section of the book will conclude with a critique of the idea of justice as being founded in balance or in weighting. We understand that dispensing with the idea of justice as balance will be a hard sell for many, and in the end many will cling to the idea even after our argument is proffered. After all, where else but in fairness can we be sure to find justice? In time, perhaps generations from now, balance, fairness, and weighing as metaphors for justice finally will lose their cache and respectfully be mothballed. We have no doubt that time will come, though.

The Social Contract

We have spent time with the idea of the social contract already, in our conversation about Rand and Nozick. Central to our argument in this book is the idea that a noncontract collectivism not only is possible, but is in fact optimal as a foundation for government (but specifically vis-à-vis justice). In the last section of this book, we will craft just such a collectivist model, but as the social contract is so securely ensconced in current Western thought, it behooves us, it seems, to treat it in depth on its own, even at the risk of recovering some ground.

We should show some reverence in our courses, however; the social contract represents more than a milestone in human thought about human government. As an idea it is richly and proudly very much of its time, the social contract had important use. Legitimacy is basic human currency, more basic than, well, . . . currency. Every human government that has ever existed has sought it, and those that exist today seek it still. According to legend, Arthur, King of the Britons, was graced by the Lady of the Lake to wield a sword, Excalibur. The legend wielded great romantic power, if not citable authority for England's kings, up through the reign of Henry VIII and beyond. Apparently and contrary to popular sentiment, one can indeed establish legitimate government on the basis of having had a watery tart pelt you with scimitars . . . at least for a time.

One of the few practical uses of the philosopher is to send her to seek for narratives that ratify a particular government or governmental model. The kings Aquinas described in *De Regno* proved to be elusive beasts, and in time the idea of God-constituted regents lost its cache. The regent no longer stood in as God's mouthpiece on earth. If, for Enlightenment audiences, neither God nor ownership nor being pelted with glaives by a lady bather offer a believable narrative for the existence of royalty, some other narrative for government legitimacy was necessary. Some narrative, some generalizable and believable accounting of who we are relative to each other is necessary to replace feudal religio-hegemonic accounts. The social contract provides something of an entry-level model for legitimizing governance in a land with a million and more sovereigns, but in so doing it tells each of us who we are. Of course, there may still remain a regent, but the authority of that regent no longer rests with the person himself, but with the office of regent; the same is true of other institutions like a congress, diet, or politburo: power no longer emanates from a person but from an office, whether that office be king or congressperson. Such an arrangement is called socio-political conventionalism (e.g., Chwaszcza, 2013).

In simplest terms, the social contract idea is the claim that government is the result of a deliberate, rational central ceding of individual rights to a recipient agent, thus ordained to act in the interest of the community. So simple an assertion as this is deceptively complex in fact. It turns out there are two main schools of thought regarding the social contract, though the schools overlap and possess a rather generous rattle and hum between them. We will treat them only very generally here. There is so much rattle in the distinction between contractarianism and contractualism in fact that the distinction seems to have remarkably little value. When we reach the most currently relevant treatment of the social contract (that of John Rawls), the distinction will have practically no value at all.

Contractarianism, rooted in Hobbes's formulation, assumes that people are self-interested and rational beings who have decided to pool their energies and resources, and it is this rational self-interest that acts to function as the firmament of legitimate government. Within the contractarian camp there are considerable differences, of course. Several of the contractarian models differ from each other methodologically (see, e.g., Chwaszcza, 2013). Others differ in scale. For example, Hobbes's project is Cecil B. DeMille–esque in scale: the natural state of human existence would be one of mutual warmaking; total freedom is synonymous with total warfare. Hobbes's driving concern was sociopolitical order in a time of great domestic discord (Rawls, 2001). His contract, then, seeks to find firmest footing in the nature of the human condition and the need for, well, a kind of mutuality. His contract is the rational result of the recognition that in order to assure my continued survival, I can contract with you and others, ceding some of my natural rights to the collective, and thereby gain safety and more. Ostensibly, there is quite a bit more to be gained than lost in this transaction, as I secure not only certain property-related guarantees from the collective, I secure my own neck. Locke's concern is narrower in scope. Members of the landed gentry rationally recognize their common interest, and thus contract together in order to make civil government, but contractual arrangements like this are not the only relations among humans one can articulate (Gauthier, 1977).

The second school of thought, contractualism, looks not to Hobbes or Rousseau but to Kant; we are categorically bound to live by certain identifiable moral principles, given to ourselves by virtue of our reasoning (e.g., Richardson, 2016), and good government embodies those principles in its relations with each person. The contractual project is something of an extension of universalism; agreements are arrived at among equals, paying homage to the moral principles that help make collective living possible. Generally, principles identified are principles to which no one is likely to object; one seeks to make one's actions defensible to the wider community (e.g., Ashford and Mulligan, 2012). The contract that results is an agreement made in furtherance of the endeavor of living by these principles.

For both contractarians and contractualists there are normative concerns regarding the contract, though normative claims may be differentially derived, or they may play different roles in evaluating the contract's potency, but injustice is not tolerated by either formulation. For contractarians, "sociopolitical obligations and inequalities are justified only to the extent that they can be conceived of deriving from individual agreement" (Chwaszcza, 2013, p. 6). For contractualists like Rawls, inequalities are defensible only when they are consistent with the best possible arrangement for the most unfortunate. When indefensible inequalities exist, the contract is in breach and the government has defaulted on its trust.

Critique of the Social Contract

As legitimacy is the name of the game, if such a contract can in fact be said to exist, there should be some form of empirical evidence of an intentional ceding of rights at the founding of past or current governments, at least according to Hume. Locke was concerned, in fact, about what seemed to be a lack of historical examples of a social contract (Brownsey, 1978); no intentional ceding of rights to a leviathan seemed to be in evidence. The Magna Carta worked the other way of course, as it granted rights, really in dual form: it created duties of public agents, and it created expectations for how one should expect to be handled by the law. Really only nations established after Locke's and Hobbes's works can claim anything like a formal, intentional contract making of any kind, and the US Constitution is perhaps the purest example. But if, as Hume charges, all of us who are born free are naturally free of allegiances, and that no empirical examples can be found before the idea itself came to be, if the social contract is the cornerstone of legitimate government, the most charitable take on things is that no government founded before 1689 is legitimate.

Thus arises what is known as the justificatory problem: contract arrangements create justification for government action in its own interest. In the absence of formal contracting, one might defensibly ask why he must abide by laws that constrain his freedom. By what justification can a state impose its will upon individuals if that government is without legitimacy in the first place? The two main schools of thought differ in how they deal with the justificatory problem. Contractarians, again taken very loosely, address the justificatory problem, again, through rationality: it is rational to obey law rooted in consensus. Even if no formal contracting process can be said to exist, it can be inferred by the freedom of community members to stay or leave; members can be said to vote for the contract with their feet (Ashford & Mulligan, 2012). The justificatory problem is resolved for contractualists through the meeting (or not) of the compulsory moral demands that rule human collective life.

Neither solution to the justificatory problem is satisfactory, however, for such high stakes. Either a government is thought to be sovereign because there is a consensus that ordains it (which we can safely assume to be a fiction, as Hume does), or it is sovereign because, in essence, it acts right. Clearly, the latter suffers from a rather considerable temporal order problem; a government could only justify itself at the outset on the basis of something like a credit line of credibility. The former suffers from its foundation on one of Grimm's thinnest yarns.

We might, as Chwaszcza (2013) does, slice things a little differently. She treats contract thinkers in terms of methodology; she speaks of ideal constructivism, and includes Hobbes and Kant in this pile. Hobbes's assumptions of rationality (again, including complete knowledge and understanding of choice consequences) would certainly qualify as an ideal condition. Now Kant might just have something to help us here. It is a key point helping us unravel the social contract narrative and to build its replacement. Kant, she reminds us, views social institutions as "mere thought entities" (his words), or "normative fictions" (her words) (Chwaszcza, 2013, p. 5). Kant's conclusion, she points out, is to require of us a more abstract analysis of the contract than might be inferred from conversation about inequalities just above. We will, as Hume does, pass on that invitation for now, and look more concretely at the legitimacy of contract apologies for current government, though we will consider in the last chapters what Kant's insight truly makes possible. If social institutions are normative fictions and thought entities, then to exist in concrete form, there would need to be a degree of consensus about what they stand for, what they are to do, how they are to do it, their limits, and so forth (see, e.g., Gauthier, 1977). We might also assume that there was some form of *a priori*, normatively managed rights bank account. Because without such an *a priori* creation, from a contractualist perspective, adherence to normative principles, like those of Rawls, becomes the guiding measure of legitimacy. All of this is rather bad news: either the social contract is a fabrication, or scarce few human governments have ever been even close to legitimate, and among those that did in fact have a formal contract-making stage, the contractualist concerns loom quite large.

If we read closely, in fact no formal contract making is strictly required by contract theorizing. The lack of a contract signing in history does not necessarily tank contract thinking (of course, by extension, the existence of a formal contract signing at a beginning point in a nation's history does not absolutely bind future generations to the same contract). The social contract is a metaphor; it intends to speak to the nature, not the cause, of the relationships among people in a society (Gauthier, 1977). We are to understand the contract as hypothetical: we are to engage with each other, and social institutions with us, as if a contract existed.

But to say the contract is a metaphor, to say its core argument is that we should act toward each other *as if* a contract existed (Gauthier, 1977), is merely to say that our institutions have obligations to each of us, that we have obligations to each other, and to ourselves. Surely such a metaphor is unnecessary. Further, if the contract is merely hypothetical, so is its force, and if so, when a government or system of social institutions is thought to act in contravention of the desires or interests of a significant portion of the community (and of course what "significant" means is open to wide interpretation—one might even argue that a single person constitutes a "significant" portion), then arrangements, hypothetical or not, are in breach. Currently in the news as we write this book is the 2016 Democratic National Convention (DNC), and the WikiLeaks revelation that high-level functionaries in the DNC worked actively to torpedo Bernie Sanders's campaign. The ashes of the Republican National Convention still cool in Cleveland; by all accounts the Republican Party seems finally to have imploded under its unsustainable policies and fear-mongering personalities (imploded their way to victory, so it would seem). The reverberations of Alton Sterling's and Philando Castile's deaths have faded only somewhat, and the potential for ISIS-affiliated attacks in Europe continues. The consequences of America's failed foreign (e.g., warmaking and exceptionalism) and domestic (e.g., racist justice practices, antidemocratic machinations) policies are coming fast and thick. If it can ever be said that the United States had enjoyed a formal contract-making stage that contract, hypothetical or not, most certainly is in full breach. Either there was a contract that is not voided by the government's actions, or no such contract existed at all. A new civil rights era is fully upon us, one that promises (or threatens) paradigmatic changes to the contract, if not its total obliteration.

Generally, social contract thinking had fallen out of vogue among many philosophers after Kant, until it was given new life by John Rawls. Today, the social contract as a narrative seems to enjoy traction in contemporary thought (Gauthier, 1977 speaks to this), at the least among students in our classrooms. The social contract has a certain appeal when considered uncritically, but as we have shown it does not bear close scrutiny, at least as conceived previous to the twentieth century, and especially now at what seems to be the end of an era.

John Rawls

As we did with Merton, so too must we do with Rawls. It would be unfair in the extreme to call Rawls's thought impoverished. Without question, Rawls stands among the most esteemed thinkers of humanity. Aspects of his thought are discussed here not because his work is in any way impoverished, but because of the nature of his argument that, though elegant and wise, is flawed in its foundations. His is a beautiful edifice, somewhat built on sand: transactionalism. Rawls's thought is transactionalist in nature; his contract model assumes that actors behind a veil of ignorance, in possession only of rational economic self-interest will transact a fair distribution of social goods, or at least any inequalities that result are in the best interest of all, and are consonant with the well-being of the least well off among them. And although Rawls writes with force, compassion, and wisdom, his emphasis on the practical and on transactional metaphors weakens his system in our estimation. It seems useful first to consider why so obviously compassionate and powerful a thinker might be drawn to model justice in transactional terms. We will not engage in a detailed examination of Rawls's biography, as such a subject as Rawls's life deserves a far more noble treatment than we can give it here.

John Rawls's life was one of privilege, but it was also marked by heartbreak. As a child, two of his three brothers died from illnesses they contracted from him (diphtheria and pneumonia), and as an infantry soldier in World War II, he witnessed the capriciousness of death (Richardson, 2016). One can envision Rawls as living with a measure of survivor's guilt. His thought seems possessed by a degree of contempt for the slings and arrows of outrageous fortune.

"Hell," says Oliver Stone's character Chris Taylor, "is the impossibility of reason." Like so many of his generation, his thinking bears the scars of living through World War II. Great minds like Rawls's and Paul Tillich's (Tillich was a fellow university professor at Harvard with Rawls, and one might argue that neither's faith in God survived the tempest) are naturally vexed by living through the insanity of total war (Tillich lived through two world wars). Rawls had been influenced by Wittgenstein's students like Norman Malcolm, so an eschewing of the metaphysical seems natural. Faced with an affront to humanity of colossal proportions, then, Rawls grappled with the question—what the institutions that work to create a just society might be like—with the equivalent of one hand (his spiritual one) tied behind his back. Transactionalism was the currency in middle-twentieth-century America, thus it makes sense that Rawls would seek to offer his critiques of American society (Richardson, 2016) in terms that might be understood in that framework. It is poetic, perhaps, that one of our chief critiques of Rawls's thought might well have been a function of his decision to be heard.

The first transactionalist vector in Rawls's thought, as we indicated, was his reanimation of the social contract, though in a contractualist style. In fairness, he did so precisely to euthanize an even clunkier transactional approach: utilitarianism. Critique of utilitarian thought is insufficient to pronounce it dead; like head lice or acid reflux, utilitarianism continues to crop up. In order to end the influence of utilitarian arguments, Rawls reasoned, a viable alternative must be offered, and to this task Rawls gave himself fully.

Each of us exists in a space influenced by the gravity of social institutions. They guide our chances, our expectations for life, and the likelihood of actuality achieving full possibility. Whether on our car or not, we all have our bumper stickers, proclaiming bands, ideas, alma mater, and Bill Murray. But bumper stickers and window decals say more than where one went to school or what one values. They point directly to the institutions to which we owe the actualization of our possibility. We are what we are in no small measure because of the social institutions that shaped us. But like a face-blind man in a mirror we ask with more than a little disconcert, who exactly are we?

There is a fishing lodge not far north of the US/Canada border. It sits snug against Gananaque Lake, a picturesque scar carved out of the felsic gneiss. Bare rock faces and moraines are common furniture; trees still scratch at the surfaces of bedrock for footing. Michael's father and several of his more "unsavory" friends (in fact, these men are some of the most noble and beautiful people Michael has had the privilege of knowing) have gone to this place for the past decade or so. The bass hit hard when they're hungry and the perch nibble contemplatively. Here, things seem clearer, like the glacial meltwater that feeds the lake before wandering south to the St. Lawrence River and so out to the Gulf of St. Lawrence and the North Atlantic. There is a gentle edge to the place, something of a cold and kind reality; ideas are fine and all, but ideas don't power your boat, fill your stomach, or protect you from the numbing cold to come. Death is bare like the gneiss that juts, but it is cool to the touch like the mild water. Again, humans make meaning for our own use like we make food, and as significantly so for our survival. Here, meaning stands off from existence in sharp relief. It seems to, at least. Here, then, how we are may seem to be the purest answer as to who we are. But just as clear, though, is the insight that although meaning and existence stand off as discernibly different things, that maybe some truth about *who* we are lies in *how* we are in such a place as this, so too is it the case that we can make our existence in light of what we honor, what we stand for. Life's continuation for one being requires life's end for another, but the *manner* in which we exist within the latitude given us by nature is fully a function of what we want to be, who we strive to be. Such a striving being is us in the truest sense, at least so we argue.

Who we are. Hobbes and Rawls are not alone in pursuing this question, of course, but their answers are at the core of their social contract narratives. Both men sought to find that creature by stripping away the veneer of civility, the trappings of pedestrian politeness. What are we without our French press coffees and felt hats to tip smartly to passersby? What is our nature when we haven't got to worry about political correctness? Are we "screaming cantaloupes," caricatures of selfism and xenophobia? Are we even sufficiently monolithic as a species to be a *we* in this regard at all? It is this undiluted and uncompromised entity, if it exists, with whom both Hobbes and Rawls seek an audience. And both of them write from the pictures they captured; both interrogate the blurry images from their trail cameras, taking measurements, trying to stare the beast in the eye, seeking its deeper secrets. The search is something of a fool's errand, though. Like Bigfoot, the entity they seek is *actually* blurry as the joke goes. The creature is alive, yes, but because so it is alive in another way as well. It is alive and thus it is changing, and most often changing because of the search for it itself. What they see when they scan their screens in the dark is their own biases and predilections, their own monster within, though as face-blind as their clients, they do not recognize themselves in the reflection. To seek self requires of us not to seek self, but merely to seek. Otherwise, we risk mistaking our scars for our natural features.

Hobbes looked to earliest humanity for guidance as to where to place his trail camera. What he found was a rather sweaty, panicked, twitching hungry ghost of a human. Wide-eyed and stooped, Hobbes's creature greets life with tight lips and set jaw, ready to spring away from predator or after prey. Happiness is a stranger, fleeting if occurring at all, but probably simple and sating; the deep slake of cool water on a hot day, the comfort of a full larder space from a recent kill, the relative safety of a campfire. But the poetic simplicity of Hobbes's creature reveals his imprecision: humans are the result of collective living. We did not emerge from the most total of wars into a community. We are the result of community; community is something we co-create, but just as surely we are co-created by it. For years after birth we are not viable as beings without the active and knowing nurturance of a number of adult humans. Husbandry and agriculture, again collective activities, offered the fats and proteins needed to develop a more sophisticated brain. Bipedal locomotion allowed not only for the advantage of initiative in combat against predators, it freed arms for carrying young. Fine dexterity and opposable thumbs also became possible with bipedalism, which gave rise to tool specialization, and eventually thus to skill specialization (again, sustainable only when individuals lived in communities). From at least *Homo Habilus* onward, at least small communities were the default social arrangement for primates. In the end, then, Hobbes's trail camera caught lonely Bigfoot: a dude in a fur suit.

Rawls, on the other hand, fixed his trail camera elsewhere. Instead of metaphorical history, his setting was an even more abstract and remote clearing. Rawls reasoned that interested parties could assess relative claims on goods from a place of interested unawareness. Like the state of nature and the contract justified by it, the original position is hypothetical, as is the contract it presupposes. It exists behind a veil of ignorance, and it assumes that people will act rationally in the traditional economic sense (Rawls, 1997, p. 14). In this original position, two people acting in their own rational self-interest will arrive at a distribution of goods between them that is consistent with the well-being of the least well situated as a result of that distribution. In other words, that distribution might be equal, or any distributional inequalities would be to the benefit of all, and consonant with the well-being of the least well off. Interestingly, the ethical principle relied upon here is actually no principle whatsoever; it is assumed that no *a priori* ethical system will be used by either actor. They enter the original position without any preconceived notions or knowledge about who they will be, beggar or rich man, in the world to which they will go. As a result, Rawls argues, accidental fortunes or misfortunes will tend to correct themselves by virtue of simple fairness. Rawls observes, though, that like other contract models, his model (which he calls justice as fairness) can be challenged at two levels. One can critique the abstract state, his original position and "the problem of choice proposed there" (Rawls, 1997, p. 15), or one can zing the propositional system, the principles for distribution that emerge from behind the veil.

The strength of Rawls's model is that it assumes nothing; just bring yourself as they say. All the hard work has already been done. In the original position, without a sense of who we will be in the end, acting from simple economic rationality we will either distribute things evenly or distribute things such that the least well situated has needs met, and indeed inequalities are in some way in his best interest, even if he loses out on some of the goods distributed. The strength of Rawls's model is also its weakness; it seeks to challenge utilitarianism in the abstract, and unfairness in the guise of greed and selfism more directly, and although it succeeds superbly in this task (it is remarkable, really, how elegant and benevolent rational choice can be), to do so it must sacrifice a significant portion of human capacity. Rawls's own trail camera may have captured part of a real beast, but it snapped the shutter late, missing the coolest and most revealing parts. Rawls's rationalism is rendered gentle in the original position, but it is not the truer gentleness that flourishes in the human heart, that is the basic duration of the homeless shelter, the leitmotiv of nurturance. It is not a mighty kindness. It is dramatically instructive that selfism is obliterated so completely so easily; no skills were needed, no bravery was required. Ah, but skill we have in plentitude; and bravery beyond reckoning is ours for the asking. How much more might we do, then, than merely this, merely what Rawls allows? He has his reasons, we think, for ignoring the best parts of us in his effort to diminish the worst parts of us. The fact remains that he did; as noble a creature as Rawls describes, we are justified in leaving his side saying we are yet better than this.

BALANCE AND EXCHANGE IN OTHER CRIMINOLOGICAL THEORIES

Vast swaths of three continents lay in smoldering, fetid ruin. Jewel cities once the pride of their children still held smoldering bodies in their shattered embrace. The Nuremburg Tribunals had been plodding on for four months and had another eight to go. The hectic scramble for "appropriated" art and German scientists like Werner Von Braun that marked the last days of World War II had cooled with the seasons; winter lay like a fresh corpse on Europe. The Soldiers of the West and the Russian Bear had squeezed Nazi Germany like in a vice until there was nothing recognizable left but ashes and tears. The armies pushing Germany into oblivion from both sides now had met in the middle. Two vast armies, blooded and razor-honed, now stood toe to toe in Battlefield Europe. It was in this setting that George Kennan sent his famous (1946) telegram that set diplomatic thinking regarding Soviet Russia, and indeed the thinking of many about things more generally.

Collision was inevitable, Kennan reasoned, between Russia and the West, not because socialist and capitalist nations were natural enemies (indeed they are not, he argued), but because of the natural insecurity to which Russian people are inclined (resulting from environmental and social conditions). Russian insecurity encourages illogical, truculent, prestige-seeking behavior on the part of the Soviets; they will reason that their security necessarily requires Western capitalist nations be diminished in power. If no *modus vivendi* is possible between the West and the Soviet bloc, an effective defensive diplomatic strategy is necessary in order to protect not only our interests, but our very continuation. Kennan's suggestions for policy, however, did not have the same sway as did his analysis. The Russians obtained plans for a nuclear device and the wall went up. From then on until 1989, conversations were held through barbed wire, over barricades, or on dedicated red phones. The Soviets understood force, Kennan said. Short of open conflict, then, the only logical means for countering the Soviet threat was to face their force with an equal or greater force potential. Mutually assured destruction justified the amassing of vast destructive might, set to glare at its own opposite across a human fault line.

As armies stared down gunsights at each other and engaged in proxy wars, the Cold War was also fought in technological terms, principally in aerospace competition. Sputnik's three months in orbit marked the formal commencement of the space race. German ballistic missiles and knowhow were retasked to create viable launch vehicles. Successful designs as well involved precise calculations of centers of gravity and thrust, themselves delicate and high-stakes dances among mighty forces, always spinning millimeters from catastrophe. Increasing successes demanding increasing scale; Sputnik's R-7 was about half the size of the mighty Saturn V, and produced less than five percent of the Saturn V's thrust.

The Cold War was so profound a part of life for those living in those times that it should be little surprise that the idea of a balancing of forces, like those on the ground and those en route to the moon, would figure prominently in how theorists living then theorized. Kurt Lewin, gone before his time, envisioned organizational change (1951) in terms of a struggle between two opposing dynamic forces. Sutherland's differential association and Tittle's control balance, discussed later, also certainly qualify.

Here we will examine two criminoetiological theories that employ some form of balancing mechanism in order to account for someone's decision to do harm. That the theories themselves qualify as impoverished is not to be held against their authors who, notwithstanding the following, stand tall among criminologists.

Differential Association

Everything changed Chicago and Chicago changed everything. Edwin Sutherland's father could remember a time when Chicago was a modest city on a lake, but by the end of the nineteenth century, it was the second most populous city in the nation. It practically leapt from Lake Michigan's muddy margins, and from its courses flowed many of the raw materials with which to manufacture the West. In many ways, the "Second City" was America in miniature: like wisps and mosquitos trapped in amber, all of what was good about us, and all that was bad, is embedded in Chicago. A Midwestern morality play unfolded with Chicago doing service as the nation's Globe Theater; organized temperance and organized vice tilted for national attention and for the national conscience; capital and industry grappled with socialist and populist movements, helping to define industrial relations for the extent of the twentieth century. Chicago's becoming offers crucial insights to America's—and criminology's—being today.

Like Krakatoa's roar, six hundred miles was hardly sufficient to muffle Chicago's thunder from Sutherland's early life; Young Edwin's father sheltered in his fundamentalist certainty. For Edwin and his siblings, the crack of parental discipline only occasionally drown out other more distal noises (Gaylord & Galliher, 1988). As the middle child, it seems he did not suffer as grievously as his siblings, though he was witness to their suffering. It was natural, perhaps, that in his criminology, he would be driven in part by a sense of others' suffering.

Sutherland's sociology descended from his disaffection with its limited capacity, even impotence in the face of inequity's consequences. During his time studying sociology in Chicago, he became disaffected with what he saw in the incipient discipline. Though he came under the influence of both Thomas and Henderson while in Chicago, his sociology was neither the fully abstract sociology of Thomas, nor the ecclesiastical sociology of Henderson. Sutherland sought an objectively scientific sociology, with both stout theoretical frameworks and sound empiricism, but one that would affect the lives of real people. In his later years in Chicago, he came under the influence of Hoxie, a political scientist and student of political economy. In the end, then everything changed Sutherland and Sutherland changed everything.

There was yet one more influence that would give rise to Sutherland's most vaunted achievement: differential association. The years after graduation would not be bereft of irony.

Finding Differential Association

Purpose drove it, and a very particular form of empiricism gave it raw material. It is reasonable, then, to contemplate both the *why* and the *what* that led to differential association, as it turns out, in that order. The theory of differential association was something of a formative thing in Sutherland's hands for a time; it is helpful, we think, to draw out that timeline in some detail. The 1934 (second) edition of *Principles* "contained an inchoate—yet discernible—version of differential association theory" (Gaylord & Galliher, 1988, p. 111). As the events recounted below, occurring between 1934 and 1939, differential association, perhaps the most significant criminological theory of the twentieth century, grew from embryo to viability.

In 1928, Sutherland took over as acting chair of the Department of Sociology at the University of Minnesota. His time there was short, as he left soon after for New York to do research for one of Rockefeller's philanthropic projects, the Bureau of Social Hygiene (Gaylord & Galliher, 1988). As if fate had intervened, the Bureau would play a rather larger role in his work than he could have realized at the time. One of the two projects on which he was hired to work was a feasibility study for an institute for criminology. He did not participate in it, though the report from those who did do the study changed criminology fundamentally. After his time with the Bureau, Sutherland left the comforts of secure funding for an untenured position . . . back in Chicago. And it was while in Chicago, doing the work of a tenure-seeking scholar, that he found his blessed servitude.

After Sutherland's departure, the contemplation of an institute for criminology had continued at the Bureau, seemingly without Sutherland's hand. The result reverberates still, though relatively few recognize it as such. The Michael–Adler report (e.g., Laub, 2006), written by Jerome Michael (an attorney) and Mortimer Adler (a philosopher), absolutely skewered criminological research as being futile, in large part because of the scientific incompetence of criminologists. It recommended a bifurcated discipline structure, with criminology focusing on crimino*etiology*, and criminal justice concerning itself with system processes, legal issues, administration, and the like. Furthermore, it recommended that any institute of criminology be staffed by philosophers, physicists . . . and, almost begrudgingly, one criminologist, preferably who had not yet been tainted by having done any criminological research.

Sutherland was incensed at first, and offered a stiff defense of criminology and its practitioners. Later, he would concede that points made about criminological futility, particularly that no formal hypotheses existed in the field, were not completely off the mark. Even if Michael and Adler had been unfair in their judgment of *criminologists*, some of the points made about criminology withstood scrutiny. In later writings, he clarified that he had crafted differential association as a formal theoretical hypothesis for criminology, largely in response to the Michael–Adler critique. Thus the *why*.

Now as things would have it, work begun in Minnesota, but formalized while in Chicago, proved sufficiently fertile to drape limbs and lungs around his ideas regarding crime causation. In *The Professional Thief*, we meet Broadway Jones, a man with decades of experience in his profession. Sutherland gives him a pseudonym, though, in the proud tradition of "Brent Snackwell." As was somewhat common among Chicago School acolytes, "Chic Conwell" (Jones) actually writes much of the work; Sutherland provides some insights in the footnotes and in the last two chapters, but the book is basically Jones, and edited (and illuminated) by Sutherland. In Jones's words, we come to understand the world of the professional thief: he is just that—a professional. His profession has a clear set of goals (gathering money in relative safety); the professional thief has a particular body of knowledge and a practiced set of skills that he must learn; he has a community of colleagues and a coherent code of ethics among them. He is obliged to work with those of other professions (like fixers and attorneys) in particular ways. It is in Jones's account that we can see the outline of differential association emerging . . . the *what*.

Donald Cressey took on the responsibility of carrying editing *Principles* well into the latter part of the century; here we will examine the 1947 fourth edition and the tenth edition (1978) by Sutherland and Cressey, now renamed *Criminology*. As was stated already, differential association experienced considerable growth in print in its development toward what we understand today. One key shift in the theory is that early iterations, in *The Professional Thief*, "he conceived of differential association in terms of contacts and interactions with persons and *not* networks of learning experiences" (Gaylord & Galliher, 1988, p. 112, emphasis in original). Such a conception seems only natural in that context, and an expansion from people to networks also makes sense in the context of writing grand theory.

Another change for Sutherland is in relation to his advocacy for a multiple-factor theory. Early on, he had been receptive to multiple-factor theories (Gaylord & Galliher, 1988), the articulation of a coherent and empirically falsifiable sociological theory seems to have changed all that. Although the 1947 edition of *Principles*, the last one he edited before his death in 1950, contains chapters on race and nativity, families and crime, social institutions, psychopathology, cultural areas and crime, and social institutions and crime, "these traits and conditions are taken as a point of departure for the discussion, and the fact that they appear in this chapter does not necessarily mean that they are believed to be important causes of crime or that any associations they may have with criminality are explained by physical or physiological process rather than by social processes" (Sutherland, 1947, p. 82).

He spoke of two types of explanations of criminal behavior, what we might call proximal and distal: mechanistic (proximal) explanations account for events occurring at the moment, whereas historical/genetic (distal) explanations contribute explanations related to history of a thing. He is clear that both kinds of explanations are needed in criminology; differential association deals in both, but such an assertion near the very beginning of the book (1947; and retained though developed in the 1978 edition) leaves the door more than ajar for contributions from a wide field of influences. From this point, he moves into a series of assertions, well known to students of criminology.

Crime is learned. It is "learned in interaction with persons in a process of communication" (Sutherland, 1947, p. 6). The lion's share of the learning regarding criminal behavior "occurs within intimate personal groups" (Sutherland, 1947, p. 6). The things that are learned include not only the techniques needed to commit the crime, but also "the specific direction of motives, drives, rationalizations, and attitudes" (Sutherland, 1947, p. 6). These motives and drives take the form of "definitions of the legal codes as favorable or unfavorable" (Sutherland, 1947, p. 6). At the heart of the theory is a balancing scale; delinquency results when a person has adopted more unfavorable definitions of the legal codes relative to the number of favorable definitions of the legal codes. The associations among persons that in turn give rise to definitions vary in terms of "frequency, duration, priority, and intensity" (Sutherland, 1947, p. 6). The learning process for crime is just like the learning process for anything else. Finally, although crime "is an expression of general needs and values, it is not explained by those general needs and values" (Sutherland, 1947, p. 6) as the same needs and values drive noncriminal behavior. Thus, differential association maintains delinquency is learned like any other behavior, in large part through interactions with significant others in social networks, each varying according to frequency, duration, priority, and intensity. The student learns not only skills but also the psychological software that allows for the application of the skills. A nontrivial part of that human software is related to the social rightness or wrongness of crime, which takes the form of definitions of criminal behavior as being acceptable or not. Even though criminal behavior is related to needs and values, it is not caused by those needs and values; it occurs (over noncriminal behavior) from a person having on balance more definitions in favor of crime's acceptability.

Differential association is intended to explain crime from an individual perspective; it offers an accounting of how a person might engage in crime. From the perspective of crime rates, however, the theory scales up somewhat: "The postulate on which this theory is based, regardless of the name, is that crime is rooted in the social organization and is an expression of that social organization" (Sutherland, 1947, p. 8). Communities can be organized for or against criminal behavior, though most communities are organized for both. Thus, "differential group organization as an explanation of variations in crime rates is consistent with the differential association theory of the processes by which persons become criminals" (Sutherland & Cressey, 1978, p. 83), as any crime rate "is a summary statement of the number of persons in the group who commit crimes and the frequency with which they commit crimes" (Sutherland, 1947, p. 9).

Cressey is careful to keep differential association verbatim from the 1947 edition, as he says, because "the theory is still being analyzed, criticized, and extended. It would be inappropriate to modify the statement in such a way that research work of a number of persons would be undermined" (Sutherland & Cressey, 1978, p. 83). While much of this research has been supportive, there remain limitations to this landmark theory.

Critique of Differential Association

One can see why Michael and Adler might have been squeamish about criminological research methods of the time; Sutherland's method for *The Professional Thief* might be summed up succinctly: "I handed him a pencil and tablet and bade him write." It would not be a stretch to assume that a practiced con artist might take the opportunity to cast himself in a light more favorable than one he had enjoyed previously. At the very least, one might question the shelf life of Conwell's observations and thus Sutherland's conclusions (e.g., Vasoli & Terzola, 1974). Sutherland did not intend *The Professional Thief* as an etiological model, but it seems as if he himself may have put it to that use in the fashioning of differential association. Clifford Shaw's book, *Brothers in Crime* (Shaw, McKay, & McDonald, 1938), seems also to have a significant influence on how Sutherland envisioned crime (Jones, 1986), but two things seem clear to us: first, Sutherland's exploratory method for *The Professional Thief* left more than a few loose bolts in the portrayal it produced, etiologically speaking; and second, that at least the silhouette and gait of differential association bear a striking resemblance to Chic Conwell's.

But we should not neglect to observe that in offering critique of differential association, Sutherland's most grievous error (and perhaps greatest kindness) was to leave key terms only vaguely defined (e.g., Tittle, Burke, & Jackson, 1986). It is both error and blessing in the sense that the concepts left unclear have generated rich debate, which in turn has produced numerous theoretical offspring. Indeed, much of traditional criminological thought today can trace a root at least to differential association. Because there is space to contest the nature of concepts from which Sutherland fashioned his theory, critique and even empirical support are negotiated things, with plenty of rattle and hum for even the most enthusiastic adventure seeker. An invitation to fruitful disagreement and creative empiricism, along with the ensuing corpus of social theory, are Sutherland's last gifts to us.

The most pointed and perhaps classic critique of differential association theory was offered by Kornhauser (1978). For her, Sutherland's theory offers "no *sociological* variables, only constants" (p. 189, emphasis in original). Social organization, she says, does not vary; "it is never more or less effective in its capacity to support culture" (p. 189). The definitions on which Sutherland hangs his hat are standard units; they stack up like bricks on one side or another of a scale, never themselves being worth more than their mass. The content of values may indeed vary, but their etiology is lost in the ether. Anyway, their impact on people is standardized, so etiology almost would not matter. People are passive recipients of the social organization(s) in which they live and move, and once a balance of definitions is set, their behavior is totally and solely a function of that definitional balance. Behavior and cultural values, thus, are one and the same; likewise culture and social organization are one and the same. Transitively, then, behavior is social organization.

Pretty clearly, Kornhauser's critique begins from a rather gross simplification of Sutherland's ideas, undertaken possibly in order to shoehorn differential association into her cultural deviance category (1978). In any event, as Matsueda (1988) cogently observes, Kornhauser's critique is of little use for its creation of a straw man to skewer. Kornhauser argues that cultural deviance assumes humans to be bereft of a human nature, that they are rather more than merely blank slates, but in fact are fully and passively manipulable (Kornhauser, 1978, p. 34; see also Matsueda, 1988, p. 290). It also assumes, she asserts, that there is an infinite variety of potential cultural or subcultural norms or values. Taking these two claims together, humans are thus docile and homogeneous entities, each poured from a mold, onto which the mark of subculture is struck. Cultures work equally on us, and we, merely mirrors, simply reflect cultural values and norms. Sutherland's nuanced thinking about crime bears scarce resemblance to Kornhauser's caricature; here we meet the straw man. Matsueda's rejoinder to Kornhauser's critique is sound. The edifice Sutherland creates begins with an individual level of explanation, and then works upward to increasingly wider social levels. She "confuses the statement of an abstract generalization with the statement of concrete conditions that can be explained by the generalization" (Matsueda, 1988, p. 292). To us, it seems that Kornhauser has viewed differential association through the wrong end of the telescope.

Nevertheless, Kornhauser's reading has its adherents, too. Matsueda and Barbara Costello end up having something of an exchange (e.g., Matsueda, 1997; and then Costello, 1998) regarding differential association. In particular, Costello (1998) shows that defenders of differential association seem somewhat squirrelly regarding the meaning of "normative" or "cultural" in the theory. Matsueda (1982, p. 489) argues, "crime is rooted in normative conflict," but if that's the case then subcultural norms should be seen as causes of crime (Costello, 1998, p. 86). It would seem that Matsueda wants both to have his cake and eat it. And Matsueda is not alone, Costello (1998) asserts. Sutherland's acolytes refer repeatedly to a normative or cultural dimension within differential association, but insist that such a dimension is not where Sutherland hangs his etiological hat.

It turns out that some clarity can be found later in Sutherland's (1947) text, specifically in his section on "behavioral systems." Here Sutherland illustrates both how they are related to criminal behavior and yet not themselves causative of individual acts of crime. The behavioral system that is baseball offers shape to the activity we call baseball, while not itself explaining why any one person practices their swing or their split-finger fastball. Consider also his example of the professional thief (again, Conwell-as-author presents himself): professional thieves are a subset of those who engage in stealing (itself a rather volatile and happenstance set at its margins). Professional thieves are a more distinct group, with particular techniques, skills, mindsets, an esprit de corps, as well as rules and practices that bolster the boundary between themselves and others ("rule number one: don't snitch"). "They have a high status among other thieves and in the political and criminal underworld in general. They have differential association in the sense that they associate with each other and not, on the same basis, with outsiders, and also in the sense that they select their colleagues" (Sutherland, 1947, p. 222). "Professional thieves have their groupways of behavior for the principle situations which confront them in their criminal activities. Consequently professional theft is a behavioral system" (Sutherland, 1947, p. 222). Participating in the behavioral system is not itself criminal, though it is related to criminal outcomes; for long-term success as a pickpocket in an urban setting like Chicago, the behavioral system "professional theft" is necessary, though it is not sufficient. It is where the individual dynamics of differential association scale up to sociological explanations that difficulty arises. Again it seems to us as if Sutherland's normative/value critics have forgotten where Sutherland began to knit; because of individuals' differential association and the learning that occurs as a result, many individuals' associations taken together contribute to group culture and organization, and the crime that results from it (Sutherland, 1947, p. 9).

The Gluecks' "birds of a feather" critique (e.g., Bernard, Snipes, and Gerould, 2016, pp. 191–92), leveled in their book *Unraveling Juvenile Delinquency*, in essence observes that Sutherland's idea confuses cause and effect: social relations don't cause people to do criminal things, instead like-minded people tend to associate with each other (or, crime causes social relations). Recent evidence indicates, though, that there is at least some credibility to Sutherland's ordering of things. For example, Walters (2015) found that a model where "peer delinquency" preceded "criminal thinking" was more statistically viable than a model where these terms were reversed.

There is an argument, however, derivative of Kornhauser's charges that does seem to have some sticking power. If a culture's definition set tends to be excessively in favor of crime, whatever the behavior reason, it is likely to cease being a crime eventually. That culture, if it has sufficient access to the criminal code to alter it, will work to make certain that those behaviors otherwise thought to be criminal likely will be decriminalized. But as Kornhauser shows by quoting him, Sutherland recognizes this issue himself (Kornhauser, 1978, p. 190).

Another point to be made, one stemming from Sutherland's aforementioned and famed vagueness, deals with the mechanisms whereby the sociocultural patterns, against crime or favoring it, render themselves as definitions within a given individual (see, e.g., Merton, 1997). Considerable thought has gone into examining these mechanisms. DeFleur and Quinney (1966) offered the observation that then-current thought on learning, to wit operant conditioning, filled the gap admirably. More recently, anomie (e.g., Merton, 1997) and social bonding (e.g., Church, Wharton, & Taylor, 2009) theories, among others, have been used to offer integrated etiological narratives of crime. None are truly satisfying narratives, however.

There are many reformulations and nuanced examinations of differential association in the academic literature, invited, of course by the blurriness of Sutherland's formulation. One, already mentioned by DeFleur and Quinney (1966), can only be described as beautiful; few works today exist that are as useful and also as lovely as this. Other formulations, like that of Tittle, Burke, and Jackson (1986), seem to raise more questions than they answer. And there are scores of empirical treatments of differential association; recently, Walters (2015) examined the order of theoretical constructs and general offending for juveniles, whereas other studies examined more crime-specific dynamics of the theory. Zaloznaya (2012), for example, examined more crime bribe-taking behavior among professors at Ukranian universities; Gray and colleagues (2015) treated marijuana use in a sample of juveniles involved in drug courts. Many dozens of empirical examinations of differential association have been published. It is not our aim to recount them here. What does deserve mention is that despite the considerable social scientific attention directed at it, differential association as offered by Sutherland near the middle of last century has neither been meaningfully refuted nor meaningfully revised such that Sutherland's formulation, now seventy-odd years old, remains the definitive model.

Critiques of differential association have found navigable space because of Sutherland's noted lack of clarity regarding key concepts; conversations in the literature have foundered somewhat on the meaning of terms and speculation regarding mechanisms. In the end, though, the creative space made by Sutherland's vagueness has not been used as fruitfully as we might hope. Instead of that space being employed for creative empiricism or debate about the nature of human existence, much of the work has sought elusive truth in theoretical nuance; as a result it ends up sounding, again, rather more like arguments about how many angels can dance on a pin's head. These analyses, we feel, offer us little in the way of understanding humanity in order to liberate it.

If we examine Sutherland's work as a whole, even grouping it with the work of other fruits of the Chicago School, we might easily be encouraged and disheartened, almost simultaneously. It seems unquestionable that the Chicago sociologists were motivated by the suffering they saw; whether it be ecological arguments regarding urban change, Shaw's *Jack Roller*, Sutherland's *Thief*, or any of the many offerings they gave us, they were motivated to understand the brokenness they saw, at the very least from something like pity if not authentic compassion. They wore out shoe leather and got their pants scuffed. Today, most criminology happens in comfortable chairs in climate-controlled offices on sterile computers. Only perhaps Jeff Ferrell and a handful of others might find themselves submitting bills to their home universities for clothing ripped while doing research. The conceptions of the vast and grotesque problems with which the Chicago School students grappled were simplistic and flawed, it is certain, but we must credit Chicago Schoolers with getting at least this much right: they followed the suffering.

So where did they run aground? They followed the suffering, yes, but to a degree, their thinking was defined by it, and not by its amelioration. The abstractions they offered were more descriptions of the wounded they encountered, rather than medicine with which to treat them. But it may well be that one must stare horrified and dumbstruck into a sucking chest wound before one has legs to learn how to intervene in order to heal it. We do not fault any of the Chicago School thinkers for their incipient theorizing regarding harm. Indeed, we celebrate it even as we here recognize its incipience. They described the brokenness they saw; Sutherland in particular offered elegant and pregnant theory regarding that brokenness. His, we argue, was a first crack at the task of understanding as such the tsunami of suffering that was (and is) Chicago; as such it deserves the place of honor it enjoys currently. That it was incomplete is no failure, any more than a future sprinter's first awkward steps are failure for their tenuousness. Differential association is a theory to be celebrated for its insights and even more for its spirit. We must then set out on the task of earning an even more complete understanding of the suffering it describes in order to eradicate that suffering.

Perhaps the clearest example of the attenuated usefulness of differential association's use in application to the lived human experience is the balancing mechanism at the heart of the theory. To our knowledge, no one has questioned this mechanism in particular, and indeed it seems as if it has enjoyed some empirical support. To us, though, the idea of a simple weight scale comparing two piles of definitions as being predictive regarding one's involvement in criminal behavior systems is overly simplistic relative to the magnificent, vibrant, vast, bewitching, and inscrutable capacity of the human being. What is more, Sutherland's thought is in other ways wonderfully nuanced and subtle, to the degree to which one might well wonder whether Sutherland came to the question of competing claims on the soul of a person, and simply punted, opting for a simple preponderance of definitions. It was intended, we understand, to be only a sketch, a stick-figure rendering of one curve of humanity's shape. Unfortunately, it would seem as if most users of differential association, both theorists and crafters of studies, either forgot the abstract nature of differential association, eventually becoming content with threadbare nomothetic theorizing and anemic empirical findings, or honestly felt humans were just that simple.

The potential for the latter to be the case should serve as stark reminder of the value of an intensely personal criminology. It is all too easy for criminologists to construct theory regarding what harm humans *over there* do. Theorizing at arm's length, holding the theorist and her subject apart as if they share different constituent elements is dishonest, dehumanizing, and deeply dangerous. It is even a species of violence to craft social theory from a distant, uninvolved, and superordinate perspective. As noble as their efforts were, the Chicago School thinkers tended to regard their subjects as meaningfully different from themselves, even if that difference was no longer thought to be the criminogenic force it had once been by previous generations of criminologists. For all their concern, and despite their desire to address the suffering they saw, as a result of simplistic abstraction and theorizing from social distance, the theories of the Chicago School and Sutherland's differential association in particular also did some harm. Whether they did more harm than good is difficult to say, though we tend to think not. It is not our aim to take a firm stand on that particular point, however, as such a position is meaningful only in the fullness of time. It remains for us to take up their mantle, learn from their mistakes, and begin again the dogged pursuit of suffering, this time never to relent until our quarry is brought to ground.

Control Balance

We are certain that the vast majority of our readers are familiar with the story of "Goldilocks and the Three Bears." Either your parents read this classic to you as a child or perhaps you read it to your children. We have read this bedtime story and the many current iterations of this children's book to our own kids over the past few years. Regardless of how the story is told (e.g., an old woman or a young girl), what is repeated over and over is the notion that things must be balanced for "Goldilocks" to be happy. Things can neither be too hot nor too cold; too hard nor too soft; they must be "just right." Now, the concept of balance is a precarious one in this story. If you consider the story in a literal fashion, our antagonist is simply looking for things to possess; these things for Goldilocks must be perfect and equally balanced; however, as criminologists, we see a deeper meaning here. Goldilocks was, perhaps, looking to find balance in her own life as she was willing to engage in deviant acts to acquire control.

We all know how the story ends, Goldilocks, the deviant, is found by the inhabitants of the home she has feloniously entered, the Three Bears, and is chased out, screaming for her life. Goldilocks leaves the house in terror. In the modern version, her fleeing into the woods is the end of the story, but is it really? Once deviance is detected, do we as a society just accept it and move on? Obviously not, as we have over seven million US citizens under the control of the criminal justice system. We, as a society, demand that punishments be doled out based on the transgressions of offenders; however, in the case of Goldilocks, the true end of the story eludes us. Goldilocks does not appear to take any responsibility for her behavior even though she illegally entered another's dwelling resulting in the theft (predation) and destruction of another's personal property (defiance). As social scientists (and parents), we really want to know why a young girl was out wandering in the forest all alone looking for food and shelter and why that child was willing to engage in delinquency to fulfill her needs.

This, however, is in part not the point of this story. The point was that this wayward youth in an attempt to find balance seemingly committed a crime without remorse (or retribution). While we are in no way excusing her criminality, we are curious as to why she exhibited this delinquent behavior. Was Goldilocks simply looking for food and shelter or were her transgressions intentional? Could it be that someone without was acting against a repressive society in defiance, as will be discussed momentarily? The story ends with her running away in fear from some rather angry bears, but like Paul Harvey, we really want to know the "rest of the story." Perhaps, she could have returned, offered compensation, and made amends for the physical damage she caused. Then again, that might result in her being incarcerated; the bears, as the landowning class, have power while she does not. So maybe it was best that she ran away, never to return, and simply focused on tending her wounded pride. In reality, the consequences could have been dire as she might have not only been held accountable under the law but could have also been lunch rather than simply stealing it. While many may argue that she knew that her transgressions were wrong, we must consider that those without may not always consider the consequences of their behavior.

Sometimes, good people make bad decisions, especially those who have little control (or too much) over their lives. What factors, however, influence individuals to make certain decisions on how they react to suppressive or humiliating responses regardless of whether blame can be directly attributed to their behavior is what we must consider.

While you may chuckle at the use of the story of Goldilocks to illustrate how those without often respond to a lack of control, we consider this analogy consistent with Tittle's explanation (2004) of responding to humiliation; he uses the example of a professor humiliating a student in class to illustrate the reaction to humiliation. Without question, Tittle acknowledges that when an individual is humiliated, she has the ability to respond in a number of ways. Most will act in an acceptable manner and conform to society, especially when there is a distinguishable power differential; however, some may respond in deviant ways depending on the amount of control (e.g., power, wealth, or status) they possess. Some may even resort to engaging in "a decadent lifestyle" in which they shed the controlling bonds of a conformist society, drop out of school, and act in a manner that is impulsive, thereby disregarding the needs of anyone other than him/herself. There are those who might even respond in an aggressive manner (e.g., predation or exploitation) and retaliate directly or indirectly against the offending party. This option may be unlikely for those with little power as the consequences of engaging in such behavior may be more demeaning than the original act. How does one overcome not only the stigma of being arrested for a crime but possibly worse, having to call one's mother from jail? Sometimes, they don't.

According to Tittle (1995), individual responses are a result of the balance between overcoming one's sense of humiliation weighed against the probability that negative consequences will arise for committing such acts. Those who possess wealth and power are more likely to have control, and as a result, these individuals are not likely to face the consequences of someone with less power. These individuals, therefore, are often emboldened to contemplate deviant behavior without fear of reprisal. As Tittle maintains, a student from an influential family may have a vastly different response than the poor student attending college on scholarship. As such, degradation is a possibility especially when one has less power than another individual or group as retaliation with the intent to harm the offending person is unlikely. Those without relative control may have to simply "suck it up" rather than retaliate. Yes, we know that Goldilocks was an offending party, but she was also a child, who simply could not control herself. Not much is known about the child; however, in *The Uses of Enchantment* (Bettelheim, 1976), Goldilocks is described as poor, yet beautiful. In essence, the only positive trait she possessed was her golden locks. While it is not the intention to discuss the psychological description presented by Bettelheim, we do recognize the moral tale is a means to instruct children on the benefits of respecting property rights. Although individuals should not touch, take, or destroy another's property, we wonder if the story might have ended differently if the antagonist was the child of a wealthy landowner (e.g., a bear cub). If we adhere to Tittle's "control balance theory," we believe control balance would argue that those who have more control may not be faced with such fear of punishment.

Control Balance Theory

Control balance (Tittle, 1995; revised 2004) formally came about shortly after the end of the Cold War, but from the primary treatment of the theory it is clear that it was cultivated over the course of several years during the Cold War détente and "glasnost" periods. It is not a theory developed overnight; it bears the mark of a theory developed carefully, navigating the space around logical sandbars and down empirically dredged channels. It is an integrated theory that draws on its predecessors; deterrence/rational choice, strain, social control, and social learning theories, in an attempt to explain a general theory of crime and deviance. This comprehensive theory attempts to explain criminality and noncriminal forms of deviance based on a ratio (Paternoster & Bachman, 2001). Thus, at the center of the theory is a control balance ratio that, controlling for situational and predispositional factors, is thought to be predictive of crime.

In *Control Balance*, Charles Tittle presents an integrated general theory to account for all forms of deviance. Borrowing foundational and conceptual elements from notable theories, the basic premise of control balance theory maintains that the amount of control an individual can exercise is determined by the probability of deviance in which one is likely to engage as well as the type of deviance involved (Tittle, 1995). While all behaviors can be considered deviant, all individuals, however, do not engage in deviant acts as those in positions of power deem these behaviors acceptable within mainstream society. It is not that those who "conform" to acceptable societal norms are not aware of and do not consider engaging in deviance, but they choose to accept pre-established societal rules (Tittle, 1995). Deviance or behavior that is viewed as unacceptable not only elicits a negative societal response but is also a reaction to the excessive control of others. As "control is a central concept in conformity" (see Piquero & Hickman, 1999, p. 320), those who have an equal ratio between the control to which they are subject and the control that they can exercise conform to the societal norms. In contrast, it is the operating outside of the acceptable norms that results in being identified as deviant. Control balance theory holds that "the amount of control in which one is subject relative to the amount of control one can exercise determines the probability of deviance occurring as well as the type of deviance likely to occur" (Tittle, 1995, p. 135). Control is, in essence, based on the degree to which outside actors or surrounding social agents limit an individual's behavior and the outside actors' ability to escape these controls and control others.

Control imbalances can be separated into two distinct categories: "control deficits" and "control surpluses." Control deficits occur when the control that an individual can exercise is exceeded by the amount of control to which he is subject. As noted by Tittle (1995), being controlled or experiencing control does not inherently indicate the total prevention of behavioral motivations and goal achievements, but "the extent that full realization of desires and impulses are limited by other people's abilities (whether exercised or not) to help, or reward, or hinder, or punish, or by the physical and social arrangements" (p. 143). Basically, control must be just right; not too hot, not too cold or in the case of Tittle, not too deficit, not too surplus. As Tittle (1995) notes, when there is an imbalance between these two principles, nonconforming behavior may result as control deficits and control surpluses are inexplicably linked to deviance.

Being controlled or "experiencing" control may result in repressive forms of deviance, which consists of predation, defiance, and submission, in an attempt to achieve control balance; the greater the extent of the deficit, the greater the likelihood an individual will engage in repressive deviance. These "forms of repressive deviance help individuals escape control deficits in an effort to return the control balance ratio to equilibrium, if only temporar[ily]" (Piquero & Hickman, 1999, p. 320). Of the three, as noted by Tittle, predation is the most serious as laws have been established to prevent many of these types of deviant acts by labeling them as criminal. Unacceptable behaviors involving direct physical violence (e.g., homicide, assault, and sexual assault), manipulation (e.g. fraud, sexual harassment, and parental use of guilt), and property extraction (e.g., theft, robbery, and other property crimes) are considered predation. Engaging in such behaviors often results in punitive action by the criminal justice system. A second type of repressive deviance involves challenging conventional norms while avoiding serious harm upon the target. As defined by Tittle (1995), defiance occurs when "the individual perpetrator expresses contempt for, or hostility toward, a norm, a set of norms, or to the individual, group, or organization with which that norm is associated" (p. 138). Examples of defiance include curfew violations, vandalism, status restrictions, and political protests. These acts, while not overtly harmful, often seek to challenge authority, thus resulting in societal responses intended to control the behavior. Submission is the final and seemingly the least serious of repressive deviance. While direct harm is not necessarily involved, this repressive type is defined as "passive, unthinking, slavish obedience to the expectations, commands, or anticipated desires of others" (Tittle, 1995, p. 139). Examples included helping to repress others (e.g., concentration camps), allowing oneself to be physically abused or humiliated, or simply not questioning authority (e.g., slavery). Albeit indirect and not always eliciting a criminal justice reaction as sometimes those in power are the one's eliciting this behavior, submission still results in harm; it is simply more covert. Submission, as a result, allows complete authority to be given to another with consideration of the consequences for oneself or another (Tittle, 1995).

In contrast, those with a control surplus or those who exercise control over others are more likely to engage in autonomous deviance in an attempt to extend their control over others. Extending control results in autonomous forms of deviance, consisting of exploitation, plunder, and decadence, in an attempt to maintain or extend the control surplus. While control surpluses enable individuals (often through organizations) to seek more control, this need for more power offsets the balance. Sir Ferdinand Dalberg-Acton in his assessment that "power tends to corrupt, and absolute power corrupts absolutely" would have inevitably been a fan of control balance as those who have power are always looking for ways to extend their control thus resulting in further disequilibrium (again, if only temporarily) (Piquero & Hickman, 1999). Exploitation, while considered an autonomous form of deviance, is an indirect act of predation. As defined by Tittle (1995), exploitation is when "the individual or group, as exploiter, uses others as intermediaries, or uses structural/organizational arrangements to coerce, manipulate, or extract property from individuals or groups to benefit the exploiter without regard for the desires or welfare of the exploited (p. 138); third parties may also be responsible for exploitative actions. This form of indirect predation involves endangering workers, corporate price fixing, contract killings, and personal use of religious contributions. While considered more tolerable than predation, this form of autonomous deviance is still considered publicly unacceptable even though it often warrants limited intervention by the criminal justice system. When legal intervention is necessitated by the public, individuals or groups are often deemed not responsible as a result of the inherent manipulation of the legislative and legal processes by those who have a control surplus. While exploitative acts are often ignored, plunder or acts in which "individuals purse their own ends with little awareness or regard for much else" are regarded by most as intolerable and often labeled as evil (Tittle, 1995, p. 139). Examples of plunder include corporate pollution, attempted racial and ethnic genocide, and the destruction of forests and animals. Victimization may not be intended, but it is often a by-product of selfish actions as a result of a "poorly developed social conscience" (Tittle, 1995). The aristocracy, other governing bodies, and corporations have been associated with such actions.

While control ratio is the major condition for control balance theory, other conditions must also come together for deviance to occur: "(1) a predisposition toward being motivated for deviance, (2) situational provocations that remind a person of a control imbalance, (3) the transformation of predisposition into actual motivation for deviance, (4) opportunity for deviant response, and (5) the absence or relative weakness of constraint, so that the mental process of control balancing will result in perceived gain in control" (Tittle, 2004, p. 317). It is when these conditions come together with a control imbalance that deviance will occur.

Critique of Control Balance Theory

Tittle's attempt to create a general theory of deviance has received at least partial support; however, as with any theory, especially one that attempts to explain deviance across all levels, criticism and the problems inherent in developing such a theory are inevitable. From the beginning, critics such as Savelsberg (1996) pointed out the major flaws to this expansive integrated theory. Savelsberg argued that the Achilles heel of control balance theory lies in defining deviance, as his definition often refers to the reaction to deviance rather than the actual act. This, while important in such theories as social interactionism/labeling, fails to consider the behavioral aspect of engaging in deviance as a result of surpluses and deficits. Further critiques based upon demographic distributions address the widespread concern for the theory as inconsistencies in interpretation bring question to the validity of the proposed theory. Jensen (1999), with regard to an oversimplification of the use of gender to explain differences in deviance, questioned the evidence on which the theory was based. In this instance, Tittle made certain assumptions regarding deviant typologies regarding gender when self-report data was not consistent with his assumptions. Additionally, as noted by Jensen, gender ratios in "theft, violence, and vandalism vary by seriousness but the typology of types of deviance is superfluous to that observation since the measures of specific category types either fail to vary as expected or vary contrary to the expectations" (Jensen, 1999, p. 342). To Tittle's credit, he would later acknowledge the problems inherent in using individual characteristics such as femaleness as a proxy measure.

John Braithwaite's 1999 review in *Theoretical Criminology* is perhaps the most comprehensive critique of control balance theory. Braithwaite criticizes the theory on several fronts: power imbalances, the concept of humiliation, the failure of linking types of deviance with levels of a control surplus, structural differences, and the failure to address foundational implications. It is, however, the issue of power imbalances that, from our standpoint, causes the most concern for the theory. As noted by Braithwaite (1997), Tittle is in some way constructing an argument on the premise of "power corrupts," but his intent is unclear, as his argument is convoluted in some places; he seems to say that those with control surpluses seem to want balance. In reality, those with power seek not only to maintain that power but to extend it. Admittedly, Tittle tries to backtrack in his analysis, but it is unclear whether he is truly striving for balance. As Braithwaite notes, the most horrific crimes in history are explained by the pursuit of power; this thirst for power has never been quenched by balance. Hitler's appetite for world domination would never have been satiated as he would have always wanted more. But isn't that what powerful people do? Why are we surprised when the cat eats the canary? . . . Isn't it just his nature? Mankind is supposed to be different; however, we are not. Rarely do we search for balance in a world of haves and have nots. We may purport the ideas of equality established with the founding of our country. But what happens when the systems that are in place to protect us actually serve as a means of maintaining imbalance?

Braithwaite does not go far enough in his critique of power imbalances as the structural systems established to protect and punish are often founded on the idea of imbalances. Punishment is a precarious idea. While we agree that it is necessary to punish the rule violator for a crime, the punishments far exceed the actual sentence by creating a control deficit. Simply, the more control the system exerts, the greater deficit those who come into contact with the system will have. The "system" may seem big but when examined under a microscope, this singular entity is made up of a billion parts acting not only in the interest of the system, but the self. Because the criminal justice system is inherently made up of people with their own biases and desires to obtain power, this excessive control by an organization will create an imbalance in which it and the people working within the institution have a surplus, and those who are being sanctioned by the system experience control deficit. While mainstream society is concerned with the repressive responses by those who are deemed deviant, it is the actors who collectively make up the system in which we are most concerned and seem to be glossed over by Tittle. Take, for instance, the shooting of Michael Brown in Ferguson, Missouri. While a tragic event, all around, the divisiveness over fault in this case has created an impassible wall between the two warring camps: one holds the shooting as valid while one does not. While the loss of this young life was tragic, it is so easy to get bogged down with the idea that this was simply about Michael Brown . . . it was so much more. Darren Wilson, a white police officer who was exonerated twice for the shooting, was serving to "protect" a primarily black community; this is the norm in our country. Most likely, he brought his own biases to the job regardless of his personal belief that he was there to protect the public. What we cannot deny is that these biases are multiplied with every citizen interaction. Whether it is reality or not, officers are taught that every interaction could be their last, especially when dealing with a "dangerous population." Now, this in itself does not necessarily create a power surplus even though unquestionably the badge gives officers power over others. But, when we look deeper, we see an impoverished community that was victim to a criminal justice system, plagued by police violence, inordinate fines, and a court system that was inherently biased against its constituents. Darren Wilson was a single actor working within a system designed to maintain a control surplus; those living within the Ferguson community were designated to have control deficits. Thus, an "us" versus "them" mentality was established. Neither Brown nor Wilson were saints, even though both have been exalted and villainized. Both were flawed individuals with their own biases and faults, but when those who have a deficit come up against those serving a system with a control surplus, the powerful will always win. This shooting sadly ended the life of a young man and ruined the career of another. While attention was brought to the issue of biases (corruption) within the criminal justice system for a brief period, the system remains relatively unchanged . . . and the systematic power surplus remains.

While Tittle's original work received noted criticism, a number of works have supported (in part) Tittle's integrated theory (Baron, 2010; Baron & Forde, 2007; Fox, Nobles, & Lane, 2014; Delisi & Hochstetler, 2002; Hickman & Piquero, 2001; Piquero & Hickman, 1999; Piquero, Leeper, & Piquero, 2006), so maybe we shouldn't be so hard on him as social structure does fail to consider the individual. We all forget this even in the best of times. Tests of control balance theory have found that both control deficits and control balances, regardless of being characterized as repressive or autonomous, have been associated with deviance. For instance, Piquero and Hickman (1999) found mixed results for their test of Tittle's work. Both control surpluses and control deficits were found to significantly predict predation and defiance. Studies have also been supportive when examining victimization; general and predative victimization increased as control imbalances intensified (Piquero & Hickman, 2003). Recently, Fox, Nobles, and Lane (2014) found similar results to preceding studies; however, interactive effects of control balance and self-control indicate that those with control surpluses are more likely to commit a variety of crimes. Tittle would reformulate control balance theory in 2004 in an attempt to answer many of the criticisms of his original theory. In this revision, Tittle replaces repressive and autonomous deviance with the concept of "control balance desirability." Control balance's desirability of deviance examines how effective deviant acts are at improving one's control imbalance ratio. According to this theoretical reformulation, deviance that is successfully completed with little involvement by the actor will likely result in an improvement to the control imbalance. Little, however, is known about how this revision has impacted the theory empirically. So, we are left again with some hypothesizing (and a little testing), but questions about how this theory really impacts the individual, one who has been subject to inequality, desperation, trauma, and all the -isms (racism, classism, sexism, etc.), remains vague especially when we consider that the playing field in which individuals are judged is not equal but unbalanced.

CONCLUSION

John Rawls and Charles Tittle walk into a bar. No, that's not the beginning of a joke, although it is fun to imagine them knocking back a few and chalking up a few pool cues. Given the foregoing, it stands to reason that they would be concerned with making sure neither one of them got too drunk or paid too exorbitant a bar tab relative to the other. Pool balls click and roll over felt, trailing a faint sibilance. The jukebox thumps out a Boston tune (John had the quarters) as Charles, chalky cue stick resting on the back of his thumb joint, his fingers straight, forming an aqueduct, makes his shot. Clicks and cursing shortly follow.

No, the bar to which we refer is not a place for strong drink and wanton ribaldry. It is the bar that their elegant and praiseworthy ideas cannot clear. Both assume balance between (or within) claimants produces something of an ideal state. And again, after all, why not? We exist in a state of perpetual balance after all, not only metabolically but also barometrically. Submerge us in water too far too quickly and ears rupture. Drag us up from the depths too quickly and gas bubbles form in our blood. Take us to the edge of space without protective gear and our blood quite literally boils. We are beings of balance.

But with regard to the more complicated aspects of our being, aspects beyond endocrine production and relative pressure, balance is not so much a harder thing to achieve than a thing whose fruits do not justify the effort to gather. Rawls and Tittle seem to assume that, in a state of static fairness, a human will be less likely, perhaps even incapable, of harming. For Tittle, of course, harms done are an attempt to achieve stasis or to achieve . . . all the things. Rawls assumes that the reasoning out of goods distribution done while in a detached state of equality will produce a maximally just arrangement of goods. And they may both be narrowly correct, at least insofar as their claims go. Abstract conditions might produce some measure of real fairness, and an individual in a place of control balance might well be less likely to commit crime, even given something of an opportunity and a propensity toward crime.

The thing is, we do not live life on the razor's edge. We, humans, are not to be found in such a place as Rawls describes, and even in death we are never as bland as the creature living at the bottom of Tittle's parabola. We may pass through such places, and even tarry, appreciating the scenery, but humans live in the louder, greasier places. More to the point, we move in between balance and imbalance, consonance and cacophony, not because we are made to (although that is certainly true), but because we *want* to. Perhaps there is a mistaking of the place of silence within each of us for the preferred state of our being. Meditation reveals our vast silent place within, but it is not necessarily desirable to live in silence. We may find truth about ourselves in silence, but we find ourselves not in stasis but in movement. We are not defined by how we are in balance and static stillness, but how we think and act in between the tempest and the respite.

Days before his death from cholera, Peter Illich Tchaikovsky conducted the premier of his sixth and final symphony, with its mistranslated moniker: *Pathetique*. The last movement, the Adagio lamentoso, stands in sharp contrast to the toe-tapping, chin-lifting Allegro molto vivace that precedes it. The Adagio drags balefully, strings inhaling achingly in choir, brass and winds cutting metallically through the lamentation like a coroner's slab. The movement sits at the very end of a life lived between blinding beauty and withering depression. Just like his life and ours, the *Pathetique* walks between Allegro molto vivace and Adagio lamentoso, with every melodic tension and release in between.

The Adagio lamentoso is so familiar to us, so inescapably human, precisely because we recognize it as we recognize the tracing of our own shadow as we walk. We ourselves know tension, and know resolution, and then a new tension again. Tchaikovsky lived that path between joy and sadness, between ecstatic beauty and death's rot, between creation and frustration. And it was his having worked in a crappy job before going to a conservatory, his knowing the sting of failure and the blush of success that makes the Adagio lamentoso possible. Rather, that he walked thus just as we did makes us able to recognize ourselves in his masterwork. We do not thrive in stasis. We die there.

Similarly, exchange, balance's cousin, does little for us with regard to justice or crime. Economic exchanges have become so commonplace in our landscape that it only seems reasonable to apply the logic elsewhere. In point of fact, however, there are places where exchange makes utterly no sense. What price would one put on the health of one's child? Rushing a sick child to the emergency room in hair-brained panic, one might well sign over one's mortgage for the comfort of knowing she or he will be alright. Payment for healing seems utterly cruel, for what price is fair in exchange for a loved one? Likewise, punishment as an exchange for wrongs is as dumb as a sack full of left shoes. Exchange in the context of healing and of justice is the wrong framework. In such contexts, need must guide.

Balance and exchange have guided thought on justice and on crime, but because they have guided them in directions away from where living humans are, they have not found each other in order to create a unified narrative that unites them. We are not beings of balance, and justice is not to be found through exchanging harm for harm. In order to bring together the dialogues on justice and on crime, dialogues about why people do harmful things and what we as a society should do about such events, we must find a wholly different framework.

Part II

ACCOMPLISHED THEORIES OF JUSTICE AND CRIME

To say that Richard Bach likes flying is an understatement. He also seems to honor the reluctant messiah in his writings. Michael's dad for a time knew reluctance, too, and in relation to flight. In 1968, a brand new music teacher was minted, complete with thundering velvet hand. His number had come up, though, and he could not secure a teaching deferment. Now he is as brave a man as there ever has been, of course; he abhorred violence then, and still does. He refused a commission as a B-52 navigator and enlisted in the United States Air Force where he would pilot, with consummate skill, a big grey desk. During his time flying his desk stateside, Bach's book *Jonathan Livingston Seagull* was published. He relished the book enough to retain a copy long into his son's adulthood. A reluctant messiah seagull who adored flight, and a reluctant soldier who would not fly for death's purpose: one a fictional bird, another a living man, for a moment they shared a synchrony of rhythm, harmonizing across the ether, more alike than different. The nature of their harmony was the delicate interplay of key forces which will be the focus of this section.

Jonathan Livingston was not like other gulls. He was not driven by materialistic concerns. He didn't regale the fisherman with a squawking jeremiad as he hovered; he didn't chase trawlers for scraps. He didn't tilt with other gulls for bits of chum or water-logged bread. He spent his free time learning to fly. Strike that: he spent *nearly all* of his time mastering flight. In particular, he loved speed. For a time he struggled, seemingly limited by his frail, graceless gull body, until he had a flash of insight. Soon he was achieving terminal velocity dives and fancy aerobatics. His flock found his behavior to be disconcerting to say the least, and given the merest provocation, they excommunicated him. They excommunicated him for his folly of flight. He had listened to himself, he had followed his heart, and though he lost his flock and family, through striving he transcended his identity and found himself. As we will see, though, that's far from the end of the story.

Fair enough: we admit that the labels we have given these two two-chapter sections are, well, somewhat charged. "Impoverished" as a moniker is rarely a flattering nickname, even in the former Soviet Bloc. The "Impoverished" and "Accomplished" labels serve a vital purpose for us, however. We should not, for example, conclude that criminoetiological theories discussed in the "Accomplished" section are necessarily more criminoetiologically sound. In fact, there is great wisdom in the "Impoverished" arguments, as we have shown. Lest we forget, the three big schools of thought in mainstream American criminology today, learning, strain, and control, all descend directly from the noble and compassion-rich Chicago School.

Arguments about which is a subset of which, whether theory integration is impossible due to conflicting "basic assumptions," like those regarding the "fundamental nature of humanity," are specious. It would be no trick to weave a fully integrated theoretical narrative from strain, learning, and control. No trick and no point; taken together, the understanding regarding human harm offered by the three schools is partial, conditional. No, the status of "Impoverished" or "Accomplished" has to do with the nature of the ideas in the sections relative to the understanding of the human condition, and thus toward achieving our goal of a unification of thought regarding justice and crime. "Impoverished" theories of justice and crime tend to drape themselves over misshapen avatars, like fabric over a broken dress form. The fabric may be velvet or rags but stitched into garments they fit no one well. Impoverished theories, then, are impoverished for their avatars. Likewise, accomplished thought deserves the title because we might recognize others, even ourselves, in the silhouettes cut by the avatars used by their dressmakers. They are accomplished, yes, though they are not in fact completely on the mark with regard to the most authentic garment that should concern us. And because they are more similar to us, thought about justice and about crime tend to begin to mesh together better. We will assemble our own garment in chapter 5, as well as a full integration of thought about justice and love. It will not be perfect, but it will be an authentic effort, and we hope it will represent a step forward toward deeper wisdom.

The criminoetiological theories that properly belong under the "traditional" umbra seek to offer nomothetic accountings for crime's causes, and in this there is no sin. Yet in this there is fault, perhaps. It cannot be gainsaid that taken as a whole, the biomass of empirical interrogation of the traditional criminoetiological theories has come up short of producing a fertile understanding of human nature in relation to harm. Nomothetic models require stripped-down, aerodynamic avatars. Such homunculi, however, bear scant resemblance to the folly-prone, noble, debauched, enigmatic, and ever-changing sophomore that is the human being. We have been told this often before by luminaries like Jock Young, Hal Pepinsky, Richard Quinney, and others. Nomothetic theorizing fails because general laws are of very limited value when dealing with human beings. If we hope ever to have meaningful thought about human harm, we must take seriously wise critique and authentically connect with humans as they are. Such a connection does not itself necessitate idiographic explanations of crime, either. In actuality, love requires of us an entirely different reason for theorizing (DeValve, 2015).

In actuality, we should view these two chapters, one dealing with identity, one dealing with striving, as being something of an arc moving and gesturing to the denouement, the unity we reveal in chapter 5. Examining identity and then struggle will offer us key insights necessary for the ontological project that our unity necessarily requires of us. As we will see, choice and meaning will play central roles in how we understand identity and how we struggle, and will contribute directly to the possibility of reconciliation for each of us from each of us. Jonathan Livingston's choices in the face of struggle led him not only to a truer meaning of freedom, but to the possibility of true freedom of others of his community. In like fashion, Michael's father's choices in the context of struggle freed not only himself from the yoke of violence, but also taught his family the meaning of selflessness in defense of true freedom.

Now it should be observed that in terms of thought regarding justice, several of the sources on which we will rely may not be what one might consider traditional arguments about justice. Justice claims from Camus, for example, are not the usual fare in textbooks, and we recognize that, though neither do we claim originality in this regard. In terms of justice thought, then, though familiar authors will join us, the works examined in this section were chosen for their merit, their accomplished nature, and not for their traditional place at the table.

So, dear reader, it might be best if, having understood that we seek to privilege the thought featured here for its use in building our edifice, you should pour a favorite beverage and get cozy. While you're up, though, take a moment to carefully fold any expectations you may have, and place them carefully in the dustbin. That's fine. Take your time. We will wait.

Chapter Three

Identity, Justice, and Crime

As with most any character portrayed by a thespian or presented in a piece of masterful fiction, their personae are carefully crafted and finely tuned to react with their intended reagents, and to create the desired result in us; it is a chemistry of its own kind, but whose substances never seem to touch in order to produce the resulting compounds, now coursing through us at heart speed.

In an episode of *Off Camera with Sam Jones*, Robert Downey Jr. spoke at length about his process for acting; he articulated how his practice varied wildly across projects. For some projects, he fretted every detail, but for others he simply made sure to be on time, tan, rested, and ready. His character in *Chaplin* received months of lavish attention, whereas other characters received, well, the hotel equivalent of a free continental breakfast. In between, he observed, here there be dragons; the grey waters are the most treacherous. What seemed to indicate to him the proper preparation model was context; portraying Charlie Chaplin necessarily required precision, as the man himself personified it. Other roles would need to rely upon inspiration more than perspiration. Yet even in this there is space for models to lose their cohesion; Michael's grandfather reminded him often "perfectionism in practice, pragmatism in performance." All creators, regardless of the field, are aware of the need to hone the craft. This careful and constant preparation is what musicians call the "woodshed," but when the show starts, technique almost necessarily must fall away for the music to emerge. Perhaps Robert Downey Jr. felt the need to think technically while rendering Charlie Chaplin, but speaking for at least a sample of musicians, the more one thinks technically while making music, the more mechanical and unmusical that music is. Simply, what works for one, does not always work for another, but technicality cannot simply replace the love one expresses through his craft.

Like the thespian and the musician, each of us refines our own craft of being and navigating among other humans; we find muses, we steal great ideas, we even rehearse our characters before presenting them to the wider human audience. Some aspects of these characters are intentional and affected, some aspects are just who we are. Some aspects are carefully rehearsed to imitate another, some are flame and farts. The purpose of the characters or avatars we offer to others is not necessarily all that different from those we meet in movies, TV, or in literature. Characters, both our own and professionally made ones, are meaning mules. Like the examples in this book, they have a mission, a goal, a point to get across to the reader.

Consider a rich bit of wisdom Michael received, which he attributes to his father, one that deepens the identity challenge: each living being responds to the collective balance of suffering that she confronts daily according to the gifts she has. Often, though, we do this while in full costume, and Kabuki masks are not known for the wide fields of vision they afford. If we are to contemplate the corpus of human suffering and harm, including that subset thereof which we call crime, then it is incumbent upon us to understand first how the characters we have crafted might move true to character through the stage space in response to that suffering and harm. We must tend an intimate sense of how our masks alter and occlude our vision, both yours and ours. And we must also be aware that sometimes this distorted vision may cause us to be able to view our audience and actors with a sense of purpose, but prohibits us from seeing what is closest to us, the harm that we create in our own lives. Thus, if we care enough to invest in true justice, then we must grapple with identity, understood in isolation and in social context, and be deeply cognizant of the individual, including ourselves, who is merely acting his or her part on the universal stage.

It is easy to condemn the offender, but understanding the "why" is much more difficult, especially when we are looking for justice. If we truly understood our fellow man, the characters on the stage of life, we, criminologists, might just put ourselves out of a job. And, while we will discuss identity, such a task as tracing the footprint of identity on crime and justice would require a book far more voluminous than this one. Instead, kind reader, we invite your participation; we will offer our tracings, and in your critique we ask for you to provide your own. In such a fashion are movements made. Here below, then, we shall contemplate ideas about justice and crime that deal with identity in some way. They are deemed accomplished by us for the very reason that they seek an authentic fit for their avatars to the human frame in order to understand the human experience in relation to harm and justice.

IDENTITY AND THE STUDY OF CRIME

The steering wheel is comfortably warm in Michael's hands even as the wind whips cool across the open window. He chases the sun on the sun's birthday;

the cool air is sharply clean. The annual arboreal orgy remains a thing of the future . . . there is almost no pollen whatsoever . . . so today breath is painless. He is alive intentionally, and intentionally does he live this here, this now.

It is a question worth asking whether it makes sense to sacrifice moments like this to the task of writing empirical scientific articles in the field of criminology. It seems likely some rather well-regarded thinkers (e.g., Young, 2011) have asked this question and answered in the negative. Books about birds and ox herding seem like they are something else entirely, an escape from the droll drudgery of positivist social sciences into something altogether different and unrelated. They are an escape of a kind, but that does not mean they are not criminology. What they are, if we are to name them, may be somewhat trickier.

Ah, yes . . . the name. A rose by any other one, after all, right? Perhaps, but if programs for American Society of Criminology conferences from the past decade are any indication, the number of flavors of criminology has proliferated considerably. Note has been made of the proliferation of what one might call "brand-name" criminologies (Carlen, 2011): public criminology, cultural criminology, and critical criminology; to which we might add narrative criminology, queer criminology, newsmaking criminology, revolutionary criminology, and even quantum holographic criminology. A number of these discourses offer something of value; they may represent new takes on the problems that face criminology generally, they may come with a new empirical toolbox, or at least they may specify preferred empirical technologies, and they may give voice to the suffering of marginalized communities, bearing witness to misunderstood suffering, and thus making possible the truest and most sacramental criminology. Then again, they may be little more than incompetent criminology in new form (Carlen, 2011). But what does this proliferation of "brand-name" criminologies, or "identity" criminologies, actually mean for criminology?

In something of a departure, we will consider these brand-name criminologies as a phenomenon. Content of their arguments will play a limited role here; as at least one of the above will be discussed in greater detail in the next chapter, in the end we shall not be appreciably poorer for a turn here to the wider discourse and its vitality. We will then examine labeling theory as a thought stream related to identity, and examine it in much the same way we have contemplated other theories here.

Brand Name or Identity Criminologies

What are we to understand about ourselves that individual identity plays so big a role in how we live our lives and how we interpret and assess the lives of others? Today, perhaps more than ever in a human world full of information, we seem adrift in an ocean of shattered meaning bobbing with the current, seahorse-like, unable to power ourselves much less raise a ripple. Identity may seem something of a floatation device, a life raft of meaning and connection afloat in a vast meaninglessness. "I am Huguenot" is thought to mean something; it asserts the I as one to be recognized while it welds one to others: it proclaims a separateness while it binds us in common experience or cause. Identity has the dual action of proclaiming self as relevant and portraying self as part of a particular community. One might almost hear Camus's style here in his talk about the rebel; the proclamation of separateness is actually a ratification of the collective as central to one's being.

It is with this idea of identity's dual action in mind that we begin a contemplation of a . . . dynamic, trend, subgenre . . . something . . . in criminological theory that others have noted and it seems to deserve some, well, some intentionality. There has been a proliferation of what we have taken to calling "identity criminology." Carlen (2013) refers to a similar phenomenon by the name "brand-name criminology." Although not precisely the same thing, Carlen's phenomenon is sufficiently proximal to what we refer to that her critiques of brand name criminology point as sharply at identity criminology.

Mesearch

In a recent conversation with colleagues over sack lunches, Michael raised a concern he had had about a tendency among some criminologists to generate publications from what was either beloved by them, or to build a criminological identity around one aspect of their own identity. Has the pressure to produce creative published scholarship driven some academics to rent out space in their own personal comfort zones? If so it is fair to wonder which institution, academia or the hobby space/"man cave," is encumbered by the encroachment. "Me-search," as Michael likes to refer to it, is all about turning what is supposed to be sound inquiry into studies that often offer little insight into the nature of humanity. "I can publish articles on this topic because it is fun" or "This subject interests me because it is about me." Somehow such a thing felt disingenuous, even somewhat compromised in terms of its usefulness.

Of course, "mesearch" is wholly different from examining a thing enjoyed or an identity for the wisdom it can produce. Whereas, for example, queer criminology would lack validity were it done only by cis heterosexual scholars, whereas clearly there are times when introspection is profoundly frightening and of evident value to social research, and whereas there is truly rich and wise scholarship in queer criminology, there also seems to be work (or at least the possibility of work) that is convenient, even self-indulgent "maritime studies" (contemplations of one's "navel"). The same seems to be true of other criminologies structured around identity: conservative criminology, revolutionary criminology, African American criminology, cultural criminology, and many others. (It is worth noting that there is currently no coherent, discernible Native American criminology as such; doubtless such a discourse would be of inestimable value.) Criminology, it would seem, can be newsmaking, peacemaking, constitutive, narrative, and even holographic. We, along with many of our criminologist friends, study comic books, video games, and television series: things they and we loved before coming to criminology. In each case, the studies have offered compelling insights into what we understand justice to mean, but is there something disingenuous, something self-indulgent about turning one's own hobby or identity into the subject of one's scholarship? (We do not hold ourselves apart from the possibility of being "mesearchers" as much of our own passions are aligned with our personal interests and our subjective view of the world; Tammy, who likes to fancy herself a cultural criminologist, still struggles with its relevance.)

Let us provide something of a partial answer here, but it is one that raises another question specifically: what is the purpose of identity criminologies? Of course these particular dialogues have value. Specifically, we are thinking of Kishonna Gray's (2014) wonderful study of racist and gendered violence in the Xbox Live space, and Cary Adkinson's (Adkinson, 2008; Vollum & Adkinson, 2003) fertile study of justice themes in Spider-Man comic books. Criminology is a deeply personal and formative discourse. Rather, certain sectors of the criminological discourse honor and value personal and creative contemplations of the nature of justice, of ourselves, of suffering, and how we might respond as a community to suffering revealed to us. These studies in particular give us rich humus with which to work. At the same time, because we in our discipline are left to police ourselves and each other with regard to legitimacy, it is fully defensible to ask after the legitimacy of what we call mesearch, and not merely because of self-indulgent appearances. And if we can identify fruitful identity/brand-name scholarship from mesearch (and discourage the latter), it is defensible to contemplate how best to cook and eat it.

As is the case with many things, value depends upon purpose. If we assume that the purpose of all scholarship is to create objective knowledge, then indeed identity or brand-name criminology is inherently self-indulgent claptrap. Fortunately, such an assumption has outlived its welcome in many corners of social science. As things are, there is more than ample room in criminology for exploration; it is becoming increasingly clear that the search for standard answers to most criminological questions is a fool's errand, that although Truth exists, the path to it is to be found in tiny truths (e.g., DeValve & Brightman,

2018), borne in each moment between two people, each with their suites of claims, of sufferings, of strengths, of vulnerabilities, and the rest. In such a search for Truth, individual voices become as good as gold, provided they are authentic in nature. Instead of an atomized and reductionist view of humanity taken by logical positivism, identity/brand criminologies cleave, but cleave along the grain. Done well they invite a voice giving, a bearing of witness to suffering that cannot help but be transformative for the sharer and audience alike. Such a capacity grants to wider criminology a power it has craved but too infrequently sought: the capacity to facilitate human healing.

Central to the value, then, of an identity criminology is its authenticity. One tricky thing about authenticity, though, is that it is most precisely appraised by the seeker herself. Only the author of a line of scholarship can say for sure whether that scholarship exists in order to transform ignorance into wisdom or if it is an easy means of amassing fodder for publications. To be sure, those of us who read and teach and use works of identity criminology can and must assess them as we receive them, but it could never be our office to proclaim them invalid. It would be a dangerous thing, say, for Michael (a cisgender heterosexual white male) to deride as inauthentic Unnever and Gabiddon's (2011) theory of African American offending. He can critique it from empirical, logical, and conceptual angles, and even cite critiques of those who do have some standing to impugn its authenticity. We might take issue with logic or construct, but before we do, we have an overriding duty simply to listen. Just as an aside, this duty to listen first and with great care is the same as the duty we have to listen to women and men when they report being victims of sexual violence, whether that violence is rooted in power and privilege or not. There will be time to talk about helping survivors find their hearts again, but close in the shadow of Harvey Weinstein's and others' actions, talk of compassion and forgiveness is yet another species of violence. That time will come, but it is not now. Indeed, it could be a most noble contribution of criminology/zemiology to help guide national dialogues in circumstances like this.

This care to which each authentic identity criminology is due brings forth yet another concern for both author and audience: intentionality. Evident in the foregoing, the intent of both the author and her audience deeply matters. Authenticity, of course, is a direct function of intentionality; social scientists seek to understand the human world more fully, and to share and apply that understanding for the betterment of humanity. Intentionality can go awry in a number of ways, of course. The scholar who studies his subject *because* he need only roll out of bed to be in the midst of his setting does no one any favors save himself. The same scholar rolling out of bed into meaningful suffering and authentically seeking wisdom among what she finds is the truest scholar. There is also the pressure to create for one's self . . . an identity.

Almost anyone who reads this understands the pressure not only to publish works in scholarly journals, but also to create for one's self a brand. Some of us contemplate identity, then, in order to create an identity, and it is worthwhile to understand the possibility for disingenuousness this creates. To be the "victim lady," "pop-culture woman," or "that love dude" is appealing to the academic; to be known is welcome, but to be known *for* something is useful, even lucrative.

The reader who carries a bias against the author and his identity cannot be available to listen deeply to what the author seeks to share. Both author and reader must agree to the meeting; they both must come prepared to perform their respective roles in trust and with skill (the new cleavage does not remove the obligation to rigor for the author—indeed, likely it redoubles it). For the author, there must be an honest intention to understand self and offer self, regardless of findings, to the wider community. Likewise, there must be an honest intention to accept the gift of grace from the author, to pose critique with respect and gratitude for the message and the author. If authenticity and intentionality be our companions, what, then, is there to fear?

For purposes of assessment, then, we might frame critique according to authenticity and intentionality; authenticity of *content or claims*, and the intentionality of the *author and critic*. Now not all identity criminologies are crafted so as to offer insights into oppression or suffering. Perhaps in place of a particular suffering being reported, an identity criminology (perhaps more properly a brand-name criminology, in Carlen's terms) represents a particular treasured insight. Adherents gather among fluted columns carrying vaulted gothic arches, priest and acolyte alike, around a flame entombed in cloistered granite. The light is tended lovingly, and shared according to dogma. With regard to this core message, the duty to listen deeply is different. This is not to say the duty to listen is not present, but it is not as pressing, and it does not enjoy the same insulation from direct critique enjoyed by those who have built a criminology around the bearing of witness to harm.

It seems, then, we can craft an analytical framework for creating identity criminologies as well as critiquing the creations of others. In the creation process, wholesome intention is essential. The author must be at all points concerned about honoring Truth; it stands to reason, then, that something of a parallel to Satyagraha serves well: some process of purification is recommended. We understand that the word "purification" might raise concerns for some. What we mean by the term is the achievement of mental, spiritual, and methodological clarity of purpose. Although one of us advocates strongly for meditation, other contemplative practices can work as well. Even a simple process of self-querying in order to discover purpose, intended result, and the legitimacy of method can help ensure an authentic effort. Second, a

Satyagraha-esque *discipline* is required in order to ensure that authenticity, once secured, is not lost. Truth must be . . . and remain . . . Polaris; what might be found in a journey such as this may be disquieting, occasionally even horrific beyond description, but Truth is its own salve. Third, method must be as transparent and tightly reasoned as possible, while allowing for flexibility for adaptation to unforeseen circumstances. Method and results may be deeply intermingled. Honoring these requirements in the creation of an identity criminology will make the offering of greater utility for the criminological community.

In terms of the critique of a work of identity criminology, we can discern some clear requirements. First, both in terms of order and priority, it is crucial that the critic attempt to identify the presence of an authentic voice of suffering. If such a voice is discernible, it is incumbent upon one to listen. Simply listen. The critic may have an honest response to that voice after hearing it carefully, but first one is duty bound to listen with the greatest of care. Importantly, whether or not the author intends a bearing of witness to suffering does not matter; intentionality is not a requirement for the bearing of witness. Only authenticity is required here. When critiquing a brand-name criminology, again the requirement to listen is meaningfully different, as no harm is being proffered per se. The second requirement for the critic is to be transparent to self and others about the intent of the critical effort. Is the critique soundly criminological or merely political? Similarly, the critic must do her best to discern the purpose of the work: what does it seek to do? If its purpose is to bear witness alone, time will come when the clarity, completeness and veracity of the claims are to be considered, but only after authenticity and truth intention seem evident. Contemplation of result and method can then follow. Authenticity of content and author intentionality oriented toward Truth must be found for such works to pass scrutiny. Critiques of identity or brand name criminologies that honor these requirements will be of greater value to the discipline as a whole.

Carlen's Critique

Let us pause briefly to contemplate the critique of "brand-name criminologies" offered by Pat Carlen (2011). Although she offers some useful insights, in the end (quite literally) we are left to wonder after the point of her exercise.

She is careful to observe that she has something of an affection for at least one of the three camps (critical, cultural, and public criminologies) that she critiques, as well as important arguments of the other two. She has written things that likely qualify as falling in the critical criminology camp, she says, and indeed she points out with no small sense of irony that in the United Kingdom, it may even be the case that critical criminology is the dominant narrative. Regarding cultural and public criminologies, she offers at times affection for some of the ideas they claim as their own, though she finds those ideas to be not so definitively belonging to those camps alone. Cultural criminology's emphasis on "meaning, representation and power in the contested construction of crime" (Carlen, 2011, p. 98, cited from Ferrell, Hayward, & Young, 2008, p. 2) is something for which she has great affection. "However, given that the centrality of meaning, representation and power has been a taken-for-granted assumption in academic criminology since at least the 1960s" (Carlen, 2011, p. 99), she is challenged to discern why a new label is necessary for it now. Public intellectuals, she adds, properly have taken up vexing problems of crime, but proponents of the "attempted institutionalization of public criminology . . . conflate their personal morality/politics with a scientific art form . . . and then by labeling the whole bundle as public criminology are overly prescriptive about what type of intellectual work may contribute to this latest rebranding of academic criminology" (Carlen, 2011, p. 99).

But her organizing "beef" with these criminologies deals with the tendency of some thinkers in these camps to proselytize. Evangelicals, she says, are more concerned about how criminologists *are* as moral actors than what they *do* as social scientists. Evangelists are oppositional, and define themselves in such a manner, but are rarely creative, inviting others to occupy newly razed ground in order to collaboratively rebuild. Maligning the old paradigm, rebottling wine, and (ironically) silencing alternative voices are the habits of the evangelist. She chafes at the tendency of some criminologists who inhabit these three tents (critical, cultural, and public criminologies) to offer evangelistic arguments for their particular criminological worldview, ultimately, instead of just doing the type of criminology they value. If the chapter had a fitting sub-subtitle, it might be one borrowed from Nike: "Just Do It."

Fair enough. But to be sure somewhere between the human need for a rigorous exchange of ideas and the contrived and disingenuous requirement for academics to publish *something* so as to have a lengthy CV, or perhaps to be known for something, there is some value in openly contemplating a particular bandwidth of criminological thought, like meaning, and giving that contemplation a name. It might even make sense to encourage, even to recruit others to do the same. But to what end? Again we argue one should think about the authenticity of the claims and the intention of the authors and determine the merit of the dialogue accordingly.

Let us talk more about old and new, though, and about art. Carlen seems concerned that evangelists are not authentically producing new ideas; as she says, reinventing wheels. Yet her own assumptions pose for herself something of a challenge. In setting up her understanding of academic criminology as a scientific art, she takes as axiomatic that "it is in the discovery and creation of the New out of the *bricolage* of the Old that criminology becomes an art form" (Carlen, 2011, p. 97). Criminology is artlike because it allows creative space within a rule set: use only bits of the old to make the new. Of course Levi-Strauss (1966) posits that brilliance is possible when crafting the New from shards of the Old. Musicians in the West operate within a set of rules: twelve tones represent the palate of colors with which they can work; they are cautioned against contrary motion, against voices (except the bass) leaping more than a perfect interval. Yet musicians break these rules regularly; they bend notes dangerously, they invoke the Devil when they write parallel perfect intervals, and high voices leap and duck without the merest regard for safety. They know about the rules, even if subconsciously, when they break them. And some musicians even go further, utilizing noninstruments or inventing new frameworks for themselves. Some music is derived solely via mathematical algorithm and is not heard even in the composer's head until first performed. Polymetric music, twelve-tone music, and polytonality are all examples of challenges to traditional musical rules. Of course, they operate within a wider set of boundaries, perhaps using Western scales, meters, instruments, and idioms, and this is Carlen's point.

Here is where we run into some difficulty with the analogy. It is tempting to observe the parallel constraints placed on music and on criminology; both have their natural boundaries. But consider then the challenge facing music. As Levi-Strauss observes, bricolage can allow for brilliance; indeed all Western music is derived from the creative arrangement of twelve tones and their several octaves. Yet often musicians strain at the leash; some borrow instruments or ideas from other cultures, whereas some seek to invent through alternative tunings and harmonization. If the analogy were a direct one, we would be reinventing music not with the twelve tones that gave creative space for Taverner, Stravinsky, Duke Ellington, and Stone Temple Pilots, but *only* with the idea palate provided by the band REM. Mainstream criminology does indeed provide bricolage, but of a narrow handful of thinkers, most notably Durkheim, lensed through the Chicago School.

There is another issue with her sense of artfulness. Art is more than a sandbox, although it can be that as well. We tend to prefer Fromm's (2006) formulation of art. One of the authors has spent a nontrivial portion of his life in a practice room setting; from this vantage another reality becomes clear. Music heightens its moment by heightening each listener. The musician understands this, and she understands that the heightening of others is a thing achieved at a high price, but it is a price she pays gladly, away from the audience's gaze. The artist masters theory as well as practice; she knows what is known, and what is not; she is dedicated in her bones to the amassing of understanding of her genre and the deepening of her technical capacity; she is disciplined in practice in order to discover and impart the tidal movement of the soul that is art's natural power. The sandbox may exist, but it is least of all concerns once music is the aim; indeed it disappears altogether in the moment of performance. To define music (and other art) by the rules that make it is akin to defining one's child by the chores and bedtimes he must keep. Derrida (2001) reminds us that if borrowing from heritage is bricolage, we are all bricoleur.

Although same-sex love has been part of the human landscape since the beginning of humanity (and indeed exists in many nonhuman species, so most likely predates humanity by a million years or more), a scientific understanding of harm from the vantage of one who belongs to the historically marginalized gay community is a thing *altogether* new. Indeed, a scientific understanding of harm from the vantage of indigenous Americans, themselves victims of a near-genocide engineered by the United States, *has yet to exist*.

So what have we learned? Well, for one thing, identity plays a major role in latter-day criminological discourse: criminology has done rather more than breach the fourth wall, as evidenced by the broken bricks scattered at our feet. As the wider narrative of this book intends to demonstrate, there is something of a natural turning toward a wiser and thus gentler iteration of human justice, the vector of which is only too clear while the fruition of that journey lies as yet beyond our view. In no small way this turn from experience-distant, positivistic, and iatrogenic theorizing and empiricism finds at the least encouragement in the contemplation of identity and suffering. We must be cautious, however, and recognize that identity's contemplation grants identity, and in so doing, can dilute the insights about identity that might otherwise have been possible.

In the final analysis, then, the mere existence of a set of criminological subgenres, and the tomblike quiet in other corners of the discourse (Native American criminology) points to the need to assert self or identity into the wider criminological narrative. The cynic might frame it as an inevitable post-modernist turn in a discipline marked by irresponsible peregrinations, but such a typification would be grossly unfair. We take it to be a planting of seed in heretofore barren soil. It is something of a banner-planting effort as well—it is an assertion: we are here, and we have voices that matter. Even if that is all mesearch ever produces, it has some value. What makes it really work, though, is the *intention* of its authors to create as *authentic* a rendering of their subject as possible. And we laugh, because it is in this book and a number of scientific journals, books, and reviews that we, criminologists, like to critique, without concern for intention. If you have been reading closely, you will see our intent is not malicious as some others has been, but to bend the dialogue about the true effectiveness of these theories. Perhaps no theory or set of perspectives has been so criticized as "labeling" theory. While there are unquestionable flaws with the perspective, it cannot be denied that the intent is real and the value to human discourse is immeasurable.

Labeling Theory

When Tammy and her husband received the call that they had been matched with a potential adoption placement through the foster care system, they were overjoyed; however, their excitement was quickly replaced with apprehension as one of the children, Gracelynn (age four), had some noted behavioral issues as she had been previously diagnosed with Reactive Attachment Disorder (RAD). In case you are not familiar with RAD, it is a condition in which children have not developed healthy attachment relationships; these children often experience severe behavioral and emotional issues as a result of neglect in their early formative years. RAD has commonly been associated with children being adopted out of Russia and Eastern Europe, but children in our own foster care system have also been diagnosed in rare instances. Tammy, always being the optimist, was undeterred, and she and her husband decided to meet the children. Instantly, both knew that the diagnosis was incorrect. A child that was described as being detached, disruptive, and destructive was found to be full of laughter, and affection was definitely not an issue. From day one, they were "all in" as the love they felt for this child was immeasurable; however, the child they saw was not the child that the system or the foster parents described at all.

Now, this doesn't mean that all of those working in the foster care system who encountered her felt this way and that Gracelynn was not difficult; she was. She acted out and had her fair share of temper tantrums, but that is par for the course for most four year olds, especially a child who had been in foster care for over two years, was on her third placement, and had a history of abuse and neglect. Gracelynn was often described as "bad" by social workers, mental health professionals, and foster parents. Needless to say, Gracelynn was blamed for all the issues that occurred within her foster care placement. If things got broken, food was eaten (without permission), arguments started . . . it was Gracelynn who was at fault. The previous foster parents even accused the four-year-old girl of peeing on the floor intentionally; it never occurred to them that she might be sleepwalking and inadvertently peeing on the floor as she consumed an excessive amount of caffeinated products and potty training was not a priority prior to being placed in foster care. Even in therapy, Gracelynn was viewed as the problem. And, as a result, Gracelynn viewed herself as the problem and defined herself as "bad." She identified with the label that was placed on her without question. When confronted, her reactions would intensify, tantrums would increase, and she would literally try to show you how bad she could be. Correcting the behavior and undoing the harms done by the reactions of others would take a lot of patience and love, and sometimes this was not easy.

Unlike many foster care placements, this story has a happy ending. As of the writing of this book, Gracelynn, who was adopted within six months of being placed with Tammy and her husband, is currently in third grade, an avid reader, loves school, participates in a myriad of extracurricular activities, and laughs and loves like no other. She has the biggest heart and sometimes an even bigger attitude, but that may be more of a result of socialization from her mother than a personality flaw. So what does this have to do with criminology? Why does this story matter? After all, the story is just a personal account of one of the authors.

When we think of crime and delinquency, we often place blame on the individual, and we identify the offending party with prejudicial conclusions. Is it just the individual's behavior that matters? We would argue with a resounding "NO!" But isn't that what we do? Society often points out those who have deviated from acceptable behavior, and without considering the circumstances and the reasons for acting as such, we define them as "bad." Some may argue that it is up to the actor to correct their unacceptable behavior; however, this may not be so easy when everyone around you sees you in a negative light. Wouldn't this affect how you viewed yourself regardless of whether you were a four-year-old foster kid or a sixteen-year-old juvenile delinquent? For some, it is definitely a possibility that being labeled "deviant" may actually shape who they will become.

When examining labeling theory, we cannot simply point to one scholar as we have with other criminological works as numerous sociological theorists (e.g., Lemert, Becker, Schur) along with contemporary criminological theories (e.g., Matsueda, Braithwaite) have created, modified, and expanded the concept. While many may argue about the propositions and limitations of the theory, and if the theory is really a theory at all, what we do know is that labeling has had a major impact on how social reactions are viewed as influencing criminality.

Similar to other criminological theories (e.g., social control), labeling/social reaction theories address the failure of socialization and how these negative interactions help form who one becomes. Rather than asking why (or why not) individuals commit deviant acts and/or linking them to the failure to bond to society, labeling theorists approach deviance and criminality from the perspective that deviance does not originate from the individual act alone but as a reaction to the act by society (see Akers, Sellers, & Jennings, 2016; Lanier & Henry, 2010 for a concise review of the perspective). Simply, one's social environment defines what is labeled as criminal. It is how others characterize an individual as a result of the behavior rather than the actual consequences that shape our behavior and lead one to self-identify in a negative manner.

Labeling theory's causal argument stems from the symbolic interactionist perspective that a person will develop a deviant self-concept if others perceive one's behavior to be deviant (Schur, 1971). Since deviance is not inherent in a person, labeling is the process in which others respond to the behavior, which, in itself, establishes deviance. It is, in essence, the reaction to the reaction. Many would argue that our actions define how people react to us, and the notion that their reactions create and enhance deviance is incomprehensible. But, have you ever thought back to your own youth and the behaviors in which you engaged? Would you be sitting where you are if your youthful behaviors had gone detected? Now, some of you may be Pollyanna-like youth and would never have considered engaging in behaviors deemed inappropriate; however, many of us, including the authors, were not as dedicated to societal rules and logic. Miraculously, many of us did not get caught engaging in child's play, and evolved into rule-following, productive citizens . . . for the most part. However, this does not change the fact that we were delinquent, but simply the fact that we were not labeled. As noted by Becker (1963), many individuals commit deviant acts, but if the behavior goes unnoticed, this "secret deviant" remains accepted by society. Many of us can relate to this concept of the secret deviant as we engaged in delinquent behaviors (e.g., alcohol and drug use) without detection. Even if we escaped formal sanctions, what would those informal social control agents have thought of us if our hidden self had been known? Would Tammy have still been allowed to be a teacher's assistant in high school if it was known that she often smoked weed before boarding the school bus? Who knows? But it is worth considering from a labeling perspective. According to labeling theorists, if an individual is perceived as deviant, whether the individual is "falsely accused" or truly a "pure deviant," she becomes labeled by society (Becker, 1963). This sanctioning may result from official or unofficial social control agents (Matsueda, 1992). While labeling often begins informally, it may expand or occur in tandem with formal social control sanctions. Once an individual comes into contact with the criminal justice system, the identity of the offender will change significantly. The individual has been singled out negatively by both formal and informal agents, thereby forcing the offender to reconsider his/her identity or self-concept. Thus, as a result, the offender will self-identify as deviant and the behavior will not only continue but will possibly escalate.

Because the identification of the self is a key element in labeling, it is important that we acknowledge symbolic interactionism, the foundation from which the theory originates, before we delve too deeply into the theory. The basic premise of labeling can be traced to the works of Emile Durkheim and Max Weber. Durkheim (1997) maintained, "some people are criminals because a collective definition is attached to them, not because of any intrinsic quality of the acts they engage in" (Traub & Little, 1994, p. 289). Similarly, Weber argued that individuals act based on their interpretations of what occurs around them. It is, however, the works of Cooley, Mead, and Tannenbaum that brought life to symbolic interactionism. Inherent in symbolic interactionism is the idea that a person's identity, self-concept, and beliefs are "seen as existing only in the context of society—acting, reacting, and changing in social interaction with others" (Ritzer, 1992). Although an individual's experiences may influence his perception, it is often the interactions with others that influence the individual's reality. As a result, subjective meanings are given credibility over truth as our ideas and attitudes are socially constructed through our interpretations with others. Stemming from the works of Cooley (1902/1964) and Mead (1934), the idea of self-concept emerged as a means to examine the "self" as a social process. Cooley argued that our self-concept is simply a reflection of other's perceptions of us, "the looking-glass self." Simply put, we become what we determine others perceive us to be. Like Cooley, Mead, as noted, maintained that "the self" was merely a social construct holding that the self is a dichotomous process divided between the "I" and the "Me."

Whereas individuals have the ability to construct images of the self and lead others to believe this is reality, others often respond to the constructed "Me" thereby affecting the "I," which in turn, leads individuals to make objects out of themselves. According to Matsueda (1992), this concept of the self is an amalgamation of how others actually see an individual (actual appraisals), how an individual perceives others as seeing him (reflected appraisals), and how an individual sees himself (self-appraisals). While Cooley and Mead established the idea of the self, it was Tannenbaum's analysis (1938) of conflicts in urban neighborhoods that truly established the foundation for "labeling theory." Tannenbaum (1938) argued that as a result of minor rule breaking, interactions with social control agents may impact the identity of those being sanctioned. He warned against involvement by the criminal justice system as punishments may transform minor offenders into career criminals. The intent of the punishment may have been to suppress behavior, but instead the deviant becomes what he is accused of rather than conforming to society. Attempts to correct the behavior by calling and labeling someone deviant may actually backfire and have the opposite effect of what was intended.

The first dramatization of "evil" that separates the child out of his group for specialized treatment plays a greater role in making the criminal perhaps than any other experience. . . . He has been tagged anew and a hitherto nonexistent identity has precipitated out of him. The process of making the criminal, therefore, is a process of tagging, defining, identifying, segregating, describing, emphasizing, making conscious and self-conscious; it becomes a way of stimulating, suggesting, emphasizing, and evoking the very traits that are critiqued. The person becomes the thing he is described as being (Tannenbaum, 1938, p. 19).

Rather than the act, in itself, being considered evil, others transfer this concept to the person, thus defining the individual as evil (Lanier & Henry, 2010; Traub & Little, 1994). It is in this process that the labeled person becomes stigmatized as deviant (Goffman, 1963) and is likely to adopt this new self-identity as his own and may perhaps become more deviant as a result of being labeled as such.

Becker (1963) maintained that "treating a person as though he were generally rather than specifically deviant produces a self-fulfilling prophecy" (34). A label, albeit untrue, can become accepted by those who are willing to embrace it. Once an individual has embraced this false definition of himself, the person will cause this newly constructed designation to become reality. By embracing the self-fulfilling prophecy, societal perception of the "deviant" individual will be substantiated by the behaviors that follow. Sadly, many labeled individuals are identified incorrectly as an act may be defined as deviant, not an individual. Society makes assumptions about the deviant that may not be accurate, which leads to a negative reaction by the labeled individual. This stereotyping behavior reinforces the belief that one is criminal, resulting in the self-fulfilling prophecy in which an individual will recidivate (engaging in further criminal behavior). Simply, "their reactions have the power to set in motion the processes that evoke the very behavior that was anticipated, that transform an offender into the very type of criminal that was feared" (Lilly, Cullen, & Ball, 1995/2015, p. 118).

Edwin Lemert (1951) coined the term "primary deviance" to explain spontaneous and sporadic rule violations. Since these behaviors are typically transitory and not stable, they do not impact an individual's self-concept or ability to engage in mainstream social roles (Scheff, 1966; Traub & Little, 1994). As noted, however, by Becker, deviant behaviors are not intentionally deviant and the commission of a nonconforming act is typically the first step in deviant careers. In many instances, these nonconforming acts are committed by individuals who have no intention of committing a deviant or criminal act; they are simply unaware that the behavior is unacceptable. Many who will become labeled deviant are often ignorant about what constitutes deviance because they belong to a different subculture than that of mainstream society. Or, in certain instances, such as alcohol abuse, many engage in behaviors that are not considered deviant until "they are organized subjectively and transformed into active roles and become the criteria for assigning status" (Lemert, 1951, p. 75). Individuals in the early stages of deviance will often rationalize their behavior as a temporary deviation from the norm, or will go as far to perceive their actions as acceptable within society. As the saying goes, "boys will be boys." This failure to conceive one's self as deviant allows the individual to avoid shaping his/her life around the label of deviant (Lemert, 1951). Once these behaviors can no longer be rationalized and cross the boundary into unacceptable behavior, the individual becomes labeled deviant. Secondary deviance, behavior that results after one's primary deviance has been identified and reacted to by social control agents, does not occur instantaneously, but rather through a sequence of interactions beginning with primary deviance and ending ultimately with the acceptance of a deviant social status (Lemert, 1951).

Secondary deviance occurs through a process of reinforcing actions between social control agents and the identified person until the individual takes on the deviant identity. With each act of primary deviance, societal reaction heightens, causing the labeled individual to be stigmatized through "name calling, labeling, and stereotyping" (Lemert, 1951, p. 76). These individuals are placed in a deviant role and are prohibited from resuming their normal role in society. This "deviance amplification" (Young, 1971) produces the very deviance that social control agents attempted to prevent, causing not only a self-fulfilling prophecy but a continuation and possible increase in criminality. Simply put, individuals labeled as deviant engage in additional deviant behaviors due to their newly assigned status; this deviant self-identity becomes their "master status" (Hughes, 1945).

In mainstream society, the master status of an individual is often based on variables such as sex, race, religion, and/or type of employment. Based upon this master status, certain assumptions regarding auxiliary traits, secondary characteristics of an individual based upon a constructed idea of the master status, are made regarding an individual. For instance, a doctor (master status) has historically been expected to be white, male, upper-middle class, and Protestant (auxiliary traits) simply based on the perception of the profession as one's master status (Hughes, 1945).

Even though it is not always the situation, we often harbor these traditional definitions of what someone is based upon their designated master status. When an individual's master and auxiliary statuses do not coincide, their acceptance into certain areas of society may become blocked since specified traits such as race automatically carry negative connotations (Hughes, 1945). As with race, those who become labeled deviant are defined above everything else as such. When individuals, whether actual or perceived, stray from the mainstream, they are assigned this deviant status. Becker (1963) argued that to become labeled a criminal an individual simply has to commit a single offense. With this modification of the labeled individual's "public identity," this deviant classification becomes the principal label; all other traits become subordinate, and this designated identification proves to be more important than other traits with which the offender was previously associated (Becker, 1963). "Phone calls are not returned, invitations to social engagements are not extended, friends suddenly no longer can find time to meet, and intimate relationships terminate" (Lilly, Cullen, & Ball, 1995, p. 119). For a single act of rule breaking, one is now defined as deviant.

Labeling theorists argue that those who had been imprisoned had the greatest difficulty in changing their master status since ties to conventional society are broken. Once an individual has been labeled as criminal, previous relationships, both personal and professional, are severed (Lilly, Cullen, & Ball, 1995). Individuals who have been convicted of a felony are prohibited from holding certain positions since criminal records are considered a deterrent in hiring. Because criminal history often has a greater influence on job attainment than an individual's experience or education level, criminal history becomes the master status while experience and educational level become subordinate. With a master status of "criminal," employers are unwilling to place them in positions of trust, resulting in offenders being relegated to low-income positions. On a positive note, the recent move to "ban the box" has garnered nationwide support with companies such as Target Corporation removing criminal history questions from employment applications. Hold the applause . . . before we start congratulating ourselves for living in such a progressive society, we must recognize that assigning individuals a deviant master status is far from over. Individuals who are convicted of a single drug offense are prohibited from obtaining federal financial aid to attend college, sometimes indefinitely, thereby prohibiting these individuals from attending university as it is not financially feasible. Additionally, those who have been arrested and/or convicted of a criminal act are required to report these experiences on college applications, which may result in being denied admission. Since these individuals are blocked from their professional goals, they are prohibited from changing their master status because those without college educations are usually regulated to working in low-income jobs. As a result, deviants may return to criminal activity as it remains the most viable option for existence as the labeling process has limited or completely restricted the individual from engaging in legitimate activities. "Ban the box" may have granted access to legitimate opportunities, but success is relative, and statistics indicate that those with a college degree are more likely to make more money over the long term. Thus, rather than allow "deviants" to transform this negative status, social control agents including universities help ensure a deviant population remains. So, can one really ever escape a criminal history when social control agencies promote the labeling process?

Rule Making and the Establishment of a Deviant Class

According to Becker (1963), "social groups create deviance by making the rules whose infraction constitutes deviance, and by applying those rules to particular people and labeling them as outsiders" (9). This shift of causality from the individual to society is important as those in control determine what is considered deviant behavior. Erikson (1964) determined that deviance is not inherent within our society, but rather an inferred property bestowed upon it. Deviance is only defined as such because members of society have designated these particular behaviors as such. Although social constructionism is ubiquitous throughout society, it is perhaps most prevalent in the application of law. As normative laws are framed around societal values, rules are specific in nature to ensure that the exact purpose of the rule (and no other) results from the rule. The problem in the creation of law is that normativeness is subject to those in power who are able to create the rules based on their own interests. Simply, rules are made, and at a later date the justification is found based on some societal value (Becker, 1963). Becker would use the term "moral entrepreneurs" to describe the rule makers as the creation of the rules was an initiative to shape the law based upon the rule maker's definition of right or wrong.

Gusfield (1963) found that when the "moral entrepreneurs'" own social status and way of life is secure, it is easy to label another as deviant especially when the behavior of another challenges the beliefs of conventional society and/or the reformer; punishment must result. Because society is constructed and separated based upon specific characteristics such as race, class, gender, educational level, etc., those in the less powerful groups are more likely to be labeled as deviant. In order to benefit the powerful, social control agents must find the means to rally the mainstream audience against what is considered offensive behavior. By discovering, defining, and labeling an individual's behavior different from the "average" citizen, those in power are able to persuade the collective to pass legislation criminalizing this behavior.

Criminalizing behavior previously deemed acceptable is not a new concept. Take for instance the governmental efforts to criminalize marijuana. As Becker (1963) clearly detailed in his book, *Outsiders: Studies in the Sociology of Deviance*, social control agents were able to create a moral panic based on information fabricated by the federal government and lacking scientific integrity. As a result, marijuana was deemed a "dangerous" drug and characterized as a "gateway" to other drugs. Until the late 1930s, cannabis was unregulated by the federal government; however, due to the drug being associated with minority populations, Harry Anslinger, the first commissioner of the Federal Bureau of Narcotics, was able to expand the reach of the FBN by launching a national scare to ensure that marijuana would become as demonized as cocaine and heroin. Using fictionalized portrayals regarding the violence associated with marijuana use, Anslinger was able to link the drug to psychosis, violent crime, and criminal populations. As a result, the propaganda created by Anslinger was a key factor in the establishment of the Marijuana Tax Act of 1937, thereby criminalizing nonmedical marijuana use. Behavior that was once legal was now deemed illegal, and those participating in such behaviors were labeled as part of the deviant class (Becker, 1963). This acceptance of marijuana as a dangerous drug by mainstream society would continue throughout the next several decades. While attempts to decriminalize marijuana possession have been occurring since the 1970s, it was not until California's passing of the first medical marijuana legislation that states began to call for reform and the end to targeting and labeling those who engaged in marijuana use. Currently, twenty-nine states and the District of Columbia have passed legislation legalizing marijuana use in some form. While the majority of the states have enacted medical marijuana legislation, eight states along with the nation's capital have legalized marijuana for recreational purposes. There is growing support for the legalization of marijuana and as of 2016, approximately 60 percent of the population has reported being in favor of legalizing marijuana for recreational purposes (Gallup, 2016).

Some areas of the country (e.g., the south), however, continue to support prohibition, and since federal law prohibits doctors from actually writing a prescription for marijuana, the drug remains classified as a Schedule 1 drug at the federal level. The Rohrabachar-Farr Amendment (2014) does, however, prohibit the Justice Department from using federal funds to prevent states from "implementing their own state laws that authorize the use, distribution, possession or cultivation of medical marijuana." Although the Obama administration was tolerant of states passing marijuana reform, the federal government failed to legalize marijuana even though the bias associated with marijuana prosecutions were clearly noted. In an interview, President Obama admitted his use of marijuana up until adulthood, and while he would not encourage his own children to engage in such behaviors, he clearly pointed out that the dangerousness of marijuana was unfounded, and the labeling and sanctions for those engaging in such behaviors was often disproportionate. As noted by the former president, "Middle-class kids don't get locked up for smoking pot, poor kids do . . . and African-American kids and Latino kids are more likely to be poor . . . we should not be locking up kids or individual users for long stretches of jail time when some of the folks who are writing the laws have probably done the same thing . . . it's important for society not to have a situation in which a large portion of people have at one time or another broken the law and only a select few get punished" (Remnick, 2014). Sadly, the newly appointed Attorney General Jeff Sessions has indicated that he plans to target states that have passed marijuana reform and has asked Congress to undo the federal medical marijuana protections previously established. It appears as if we have gone full circle and the moral crusade to target and label individuals as deviant as in the Anslinger era has returned. As we already know, this is not the solution. The "war on drugs" is largely responsible for the expansion of the prison-industrial complex (e.g., Christie, 2000). Those who have been the "victims" of such legislation have been labeled resulting in a criminal master status. And, if you are to buy into the labeling perspective, once a deviant, always a deviant.

Critique of Labeling Theory

Although labeling theory became popular during the 1960s and 1970s with academics and practitioners alike, this trendy practice began to lose its acceptance among many criminologists. The earliest critiques of labeling objected to the idea that the theory failed to explain why people engage in primary deviance and why some continuously engage in unacceptable behaviors more than others (see Akers, Sellers, & Jennings, 2016). Gibbs (1966), Hirschi and Selvin (1967), and Tittle (1975) argued that the theory failed to account for the causal connection of the reaction to deviance and causality could not be determined. Although labeling theorists admitted that definitional issues surrounding labeling were problematic (see Schur, 1971) and that the initial deviant act was not a product of the labeling process, they continued to disregard the outside variables responsible for the individual's behavior after the labeling process began. Hence, labeling theorists ignored the initial behavior of the individual and overemphasized the behavior after the labeled individual became the focus of the system. As noted by Akers (2013), many labeling theorists assume that an individual's behavior is not as important as the actual person. Although there have been injustices against individuals, most deviants are labeled as such based upon their actions; therefore, the labeling process is not arbitrary but is appropriately placed on those individuals who have violated societal rules. Citizens are not arrested unless the police have probable cause to do so, and the courts are not likely to convict an innocent person (Akers, 2013). Labeling makes it out as if "people go about minding their own business, and then—'wham' bad society comes along and slaps them with a stigmatized label" (Akers, 1967, p. 46). Many offenders become immersed in criminal behavior prior to coming into contact with the criminal justice system. Mankoff (1971) held that deviant careers can and do occur without the deviant being publicly labeled. If deviance is a product of public labeling, why do some engage in criminal careers without being publicly labeled? As noted, Becker (1963) acknowledged the existence of "secret deviants." While the behavior may not be formally acknowledged, some deviant identities are actively sought regardless of being labeled (e.g. gang involvement).

Traditional theorists were not the only ones to criticize the perspective. Many critical theorists argue that labeling has not adequately addressed the social constructionism created by a capitalist society (see, e.g., Liazos, 1972) to confront crimes against humanity (e.g., poverty, racism, sexism, exploitation). While these criticisms are warranted, many labeling theorists do consider the labeling perspective in the context of social structure (Akers, Sellers, & Jennings, 2016), albeit in a more limited approach. According to Tittle (1994), the theory may be flawed, but it provides a deeper explanation of the link to crime and our structural system more than many of our other simple theories. It may fall short in details, but "it theorizes a sequence of consequences—blocked opportunity, likely association with others also labeled, crisis of self, transformation of self-identity, and finally additional deviance—all interacting in reciprocal networks" (Tittle, 1994, p. 49).

Critiques of labeling theory have led criminologists to rethink their views toward the perspective. While many of these critiques have been sound, others have been answered. Although labeling has historically been criticized for its lack of empirical support, contemporary labeling theorists have suggested that it is too early to dismiss societal reaction as irrelevant to crime causation (Paternoster & Iovanni, 1989). Contemporary supporters of labeling have moved away from viewing labeling as deviance causation and have begun to emphasize the need to identify how the labeling process occurs (Akers 2013). Palmara, Cullen, and Gersten (1986) found that official intervention increased delinquency in juveniles. Felson (1992) also found support that juveniles subjected to stressful life events were likely to be led to act out. Rather than focus on organized social control agents, much of the "new" supporting data has been based on the analysis of informal sanctions (Bartusch & Matsueda, 1996; Matsueda, 1992) and negative self-image (Al-Talib & Griffin, 1994). Perhaps the most salient research in the area has been that conducted by Matsueda and colleagues. This research notes the importance of informal labeling theory in which parents, neighbors, teachers, and peers acted as informal social control agents against inappropriate juvenile behavior. Matsueda argues that delinquency is significantly affected by the "reflected appraisals of others" or, simply, how one perceives others as seeing them. While these labels are not official sanctions, informal social control agents designate the offending youth as "bad" resulting in negative self-appraisals. Simply the youth is now likely to see himself as the "rule violator" as the coupling of actual and reflected appraisal led the juvenile to embrace this conception of himself as delinquent. It is in this manner that these negative appraisals lead to secondary deviance (see Bartusch & Matsueda, 1996; Heimer & Matsueda, 1994; Matsueda, 1992).

Thus, we come full circle to where we began this analysis. We told you that Gracelynn had a happy ending. The labeling she experienced as a child ceased with her adoption, but what happens when that labeling continues, especially for children who have experienced high levels of trauma in early childhood? In the United States alone, there are over four hundred thousand youths residing in foster care annually (Child Welfare Information Gateway, 2017). While over half of these youths will be reunited with their families and approximately one-fourth will be eligible for adoption, there are thousands of children who will remain in the foster care system until aging out. Many will become justice involved as juveniles, and later as adults; mental health issues as scars will become manifest and drugs will serve as self-medication. Between 9 and 29 percent of foster care youth are involved in the criminal justice system (Goldstein, 2012). These crossover youths "act out" due to a history of abuse and neglect, multiple foster placements, and the realization that their lives will remain in a transitional and temporary status; however, equally concerning is the notion that these children are "bad" and thus unable to be placed in a permanent home. Again, we reiterate that the informal and formal labeling processes by social control agents and community members contribute to this behavior. Why would anyone not engage in delinquent behavior when acts that are often uncontrollable and not the fault of a youth is deemed as intentional and a sign of future criminality?

The foremost reformulation of the labeling perspective stems from John Braithwaite's (1989) *Crime, Shame, and Reintegration*. Braithwaite looks at the stigmatizing labels as an indirect cause of deviant behavior. Consistent with labeling theory, stigmatization is responsible for an increase in criminal behavior; however, unlike labeling theorists, Braithwaite draws upon traditional criminological theories to expand and give credence to his reformulation of labeling. This stigmatization effect is at the heart of labeling, but Braithwaite is able to integrate aspects of subcultural, social control, differential association, and learning theories to explain the process in which individuals become involved in criminal careers. Braithwaite (1989) argues that there are varying consequences in sanctioning delinquent behavior; that sanctioning is dependent on the type of societal reaction, formal and/or informal. As a result of norm violations, social control agencies, family members, and other informal members of the community attempt to control the offending individual through community and legal sanctions. It is through the process of "shaming," which Braithwaite (1989) defines as "all social processes of expressing disapproval which have the intention or effect of invoking remorse in the person being shamed and/or condemnation by others who become aware of the shaming" (p. 100). Although shaming does not have to be inordinately punitive to produce the desired effect, the outcome may remain the same. Punishment is inflicted and a moralistic aspect is incorporated as well. While all shaming expresses disapproval, it comes in two very distinct forms: reintegrative and disintegrative. It is here that we get closer to more fully recognizing how the reaction to crime may influence criminal behavior.

Reintegrative shaming attempts to reintegrate the offender back into the community while removing the stigmatizing label from the individuals. Shaming that is reintegrative emphasizes the bonds of respect and love by eliminating displeasure with forgiveness rather than focusing on and amplifying the deviant act (Braithwaite, 1989). In essence, it is here that we recognize that it is appropriate to acknowledge that a wrong has been committed and to sanction the offending party for such behavior. But rather than labeling the person as "bad," the community, both informally and formally, allows for a return to the acceptable social order (Braithwaite, 1989). The problem that we see, however, is that society is more prone to continue to condemn past behaviors rather than to reconcile the offender with the community. Throughout this process of "disintegrative shaming," an idea consistent with traditional labeling, we simply stigmatize a person, forcing the individual into a class of outcasts and further establishing the deviant identity as the offender's master status without any attempts to reconcile the offending party with the community (Braithwaite, 1989).

Like labeling theorists, we would argue that this reaction is a key element in establishing the career criminal, but it is Braithwaite's concept of reintegration that we are most interested in as it establishes the foundation for restorative justice. It is this framework of approaching punishment through love rather than malice and fear that intrigues us the most and establishes a foundation for our own work. As the major premise of Braithwaite's theory is founded in the Christian tradition of hating the sin and not the sinner, we find societal acceptance of blame and stigmatization to be contradictory to the founding principles of our nation and the idea of reintegrating offenders back into the fold. Whether you are of the Christian faith or not, the reality is there is a disconnect between mainstream rhetoric of politicians, voters, and even our religious leaders when it comes to punishment and the forgiveness of sins. As a "Christian nation," shouldn't we be more focused on healing the sick and broken than punishing them? Or is this only reserved for those who seek redemption on the televised alter in front of a jam-packed megachurch complete with a million viewers at home?

Conclusion

Gracelynn is a good kid. She loves her mommy and does well in school. But, sometimes, she is still haunted by the memory of her past. The trauma experienced, even though she cannot often verbalize or does not even remember why she is afraid, creeps in resulting in tears, clinginess, and acting out over some event that just happened to trigger a memory. She cannot clearly recount specifics, but she has discussed vague instances of possible physical and sexual violence. As much as she has grown into her own identity, Tammy still fears who she will become. She is all too familiar with the literature on victimization, revictimization, polyvictimization, and the self-harm that is associated with this. But again, she is one of faith believing that love really can conquer all. If one were to seek to make a process whereby the innocence of childhood and the love of a mother could be overridden by violence, we might all be in trouble. Tragically, the world is filled with individuals who have been harmed, but still, they persist. They survive not simply alone in a bubble, but in a world filled with emotion, a world filled with both fear and love. And it is in the process of exposure that we figure out who we are. Often, it takes some of us longer than others. Identity does not simply surround the self, but it is influenced by our and others' experiences, hopes, dreams, successes, and even failures. It is, for us humans, co-created. Those who know success are not self-centered, even though at times they may exhibit these characteristics. No one is. Every one of us is shaped by those who have crossed our paths, good and bad, and each of us owes something to someone. For Michael, he owes more than he can ever hope to repay to his parents, his beloved, his daughter, his friends, and his colleges. The same goes for Tammy and Beth. Life is not always easy, but the identity we take on in our co-creation remains a stark reminder that we are in each other's care. When we fail to recognize our divine responsibility to each other, we lose ourselves, suffering results, and injustice often prevails.

JUSTICE AND IDENTITY

The awareness of our co-creation may begin as insight, but insight alone may not be enough. An epistrophe (DeValve, 2017b), a turning in thought and behavior leading to a praxis-like process where further insight follows reflection-informed action, is necessary. Though it seems like something of a long-shot, in fact, such an epistrophe is akin to rolling downhill. If we are co-created, clearly then we are inextricably connected to each other in ways that are both obvious and hidden (and one lives life accordingly). While we are individuals, we are also part of the collective; not the "Borg Collective," but in a way in which we love, share, and identify with one another based on our experiences and our humanity. If we are truly bound to each other in such an intimate, personal, and total way, that means we have an obligation to belong to each other publicly through our social institutions. The responsibility such mutual belonging creates is both a blessed burden and a new kind of freedom, far more potent than the trivial kind associated with having no obligations (but being fettered to everything). That trivial, inauthentic freedom is an illusion; the sense of choice is in fact nothing more than freedom to choose the nature of one's servitude, to pick which of our many fetters we will privilege with our attention. We are, as a result, our brother's keeper, responsible for not just our own identity but the identity of others. It is in the intentional discovery of our bonds to each other that we can begin to shed our shackles and find true freedom.

In this section, we will contemplate justice, but from the place of a collective identity that has known profound injustice, rather than simply examining the theoretical. We will first contemplate the nature of anti-Semitism because, as Hannah Arendt says so powerfully below, attempts to understand and explain anti-Semitism are only natural for anyone who seeks to assert that the human world possesses more than a modicum of sanity. We will follow our contemplation of anti-Semitism with the thought of two post-Holocaust Jewish thinkers, both of whom have retained strong Hebraic influences in their own thought. Given context, it is our hope you will be as moved by their arguments as we were putting this work together.

Anti-Semitism

Hatred and distrust of immigrants, despite the recent history of terrorism being predominantly white, male, and Christian, is wholly unreasoned and unreasonable. It is sickening and heartbreaking. It may also be a reason to hope for a wiser future. It has fallen to our generation to take on the work left undone by previous civil rights efforts: the reclaiming of individual hearts from burrowing hate. Only overt hate allows for a clear target for action. It is harrowing work, staring into the icy, inky dark of a hateful heart, but the possibility of freeing someone from her self-made shackles is more than worth it.

In order to understand hate, then, we have taken to the contemplation of a particular hate that has fascinated us for some time: anti-Semitism. The unreasonableness of anti-Semitism is surpassed only by its indescribably bloody history. As Hannah Arendt so wonderfully puts it, the "discrepancies between cause and effect outrage our common sense. . . . Compared with the events themselves, all explanations of anti-Semitism look as if they had been hastily and hazardously contrived, to cover up an issue which so gravely threatens our sense of proportion and our hope for sanity" (Arendt, 1979, p. 3).

But anti-Semitism is not properly understood as an idea, Sartre (1995) says. It does not enjoy even the meager protections afforded an idea, like "the right of free opinion" (Sartre, 1995, p. 10). It is a passion; it is a provocationless feeling, and thus is mostly impervious to facts. The sense that Jews possess some negative quality is fully apart from the actuality of such possession.

More to the point, however, Sartre's examples make clear that anti-Semitic feelings and sentiments are self-serving. They work to serve some narrative the anti-Semite requires served. Perhaps blaming Jews for corrupting institutions makes personal failure more tolerable. Perhaps portraying Jews as having loathsome and nefarious qualities makes the confrontation of one's own loathsomeness more tenable. Whether Shylock was representative of other Jews in Venice is immaterial; almost certainly he was not. His attributes and actions justify the distaste for him the audience shares with the protagonist . . . because that distaste serves a need. For Shakespeare, of course, it serves to make a villain. Anti-Semitism is an attitude of hate that seems in some way salving for he who carries it (DeValve, 2015), even to the point of necessity: "If the Jew did not exist, the anti-Semite would invent him" (Sartre, 1995, p. 13). That sense of salving, of course, is a noxious lie, and the simple words offered by the anti-Semite do damage, grenadelike, to all around, whether they recognize it or not.

Anti-Semitism is a choice one makes in order to elevate one's self, though the perception of elevation is a false one. It appears to serve one's end, even if subconsciously. It is, crucially, a choice, "free and total . . . a comprehensive attitude" (Sartre, 1995, p. 17) not only toward Jews alone, but toward humanity and all its creations. It is both affect and worldview, sense and orientation. "If the anti-Semite is impervious to reason and experience, it is not because his conviction is strong. Rather his conviction is strong because he has chosen first of all to be impervious" (Sartre, 1995, p. 20). It is a choice made that the chooser at some level recognizes to be ludicrous, but its absurdity and toxicity is immaterial, and may even work to redouble his commitment to that choice. With this choice of accepting a hating but personally analgesic-but-toxic worldview, the anti-Semite has chosen to be monstrous. The absurdity, though, is not only a function of exogenous facts scrupulously denied, it is also an absurdity of a wholesale rejection of self-knowledge. The anti-Semite chooses affect over wisdom; he *knows* better, but chooses instead to weave a lie to help him *feel* better without cause. Ironically, though, the darker aspects of the self, though denied by himself are written in scarlet on his sleeve by his anti-Semitic acts. Sartre speaks of a fishmonger who handed over two Jewish competitors to the Nazis. In other respects, we are told, the fishmonger was an upstanding sort, but Sartre will have none of this. The fishmonger may never assault his wife or bugger the neighbor's beagle, but he "cannot have our conception of humanity" (Sartre, 1995, p. 21). We might challenge Sartre's last statement here, which is somewhat akin to a proto-criminoetiological assertion, though he has turned our attention where it needs to go.

For Sartre, the degradation of the Jew and her people is done to raise the anti-Semite, but not too terribly far. The anti-Semite hates the Jew but fears himself being singular, being unique or exceptional in either direction. Anti-Semitism is a thing for the crowd, a celebration of mediocrity, a psalm for the Prosaic. Inexplicably, both genius and devilishness are Jewish traits, both at the very same time, and again the absurdity of the argument means nothing. The anti-Semite thus chooses hate over fear, specifically fears of being free and being alone. He embraces the crowd and at the same time makes the crowd his crown and staff. "To this end . . . the Jew is absolutely necessary" (Sartre, 1995, p. 28).

But why is *the Jew* necessary? Of all the world's peoples, of all the communities that have been, why is the Jew marked for hate? We are likely to have a far easier time understanding what being tormented feels like than understanding why "the Jew" is so palatable a target. Sartre (1995) posits that one of the intended meanings of Kafka's novel *The Trial* might be to convey a sense of the tractionless innocence of the Jews, the sense of absurd torment despite efforts to comply with meaninglessness. Ever reasonable and ever reasoning, the protagonist Josef K works to free himself from a snare he can sense only vaguely, until at last he is murdered like a dog on a pile of rocks.

In order to formulate something close to an answer for the question "why the Jews," it is necessary to turn to historical accounts, not in order to find something like Jewish guilt, but instead for something akin to a reasonable explanation for unreasoned hate. We will return to Sartre after, but when we see him again we will be in possession of something like an understanding of the why of anti-Semitism.

A Historic Turn

It will not be our aim to present an entire history of anti-Semitism here, but merely to trace its roots sufficiently to derive some understanding of the confusion, fear, and pain that gives rise to anti-Semitism. Contemplating this particular hate will grant us insight into the relationship between justice and identity; it can help us understand our duty as criminologists and as humans to both honor and transcend identity for purposes of other-actualization. As we pointed out in the first chapter, we take the defining role of criminology to be the contemplation of suffering, both cause and effect, in order to transform it into wisdom toward the eradication of suffering. Human suffering may never cease, though it may diminish; that suffering may never end does not degrade or cheapen the task of criminology. As long as there is suffering, there is healing to do, and something to learn about ourselves in the bargain.

Early History. The historical treatment offered by Arendt upon which we will rely most heavily does not treat events before the Renaissance. She pins the growth of anti-Semitism and its full and bloody blossoming in the twentieth century in part on the rise and fall of the nation-state, and the role Jews played therein. We will join her later, then. First, we need to wind back the clock.

A number of sources posit that the earliest likely source of anti-Semitic sentiments was related to a breach of ancient protocol: conquered peoples were expected to convert to the faith of the conquerors (Anti-Defamation League, 2013; Goldstein, 2012). The Jews of Israel, the northern Jewish kingdom, which was conquered by the Assyrians in 721 BCE, may have assimilated into the conquering culture (Goldstein, 2012), but the Jews of Judea conquered by the Babylonians just under a quarter-millennium later refused, and clung to their faith in their god. The resulting diaspora created for the Jews a circumstance that would both define and haunt their identity for millennia. They would be culturally and religiously distinct yet politically homeless. In the centuries before the nation state, such a status carried some risks, though the Jews were far from alone in their homelessness. Still, their statelessness coupled with their unwillingness to accept an imposed religion put them at odds with others.

Alexandria, Egypt, at the turn of the epoch was a world city even by today's standards. An Egyptian city founded by Greeks, now part of the Roman Empire, it held a library that was one of the seven ancient wonders. Scholars from all over the world came to Alexandria to study. Jews comprised a significant plurality in the city, and were as much a part of its life and governance as any group. They enjoyed a variance from Rome regarding the worship of the emperor. Tensions between Jews and Egyptians grew over religious rights (Egyptians did not enjoy the same emperor-worship variance as the Jews did). Further, the Jewish narrative regarding the pharoahs and their servitude tended to rankle Egyptian sensibilities (Goldstein, 2012). Greeks also had odds with Alexandrian Jews, as the Greeks felt they should be in power. Around 38 CE conditions arose such that the Roman governor Aulus Flaccus, insecure with his standing with the new emperor Caligula, permitted anti-Jewish demonstrations to escalate into violence. The Greeks were primarily after control of the city, and were not seeking to run the Jews out of the city (Goldstein 2012). After Caligula's death, the emperor Claudius worked to restore order, but even after harsh words Jews, Greeks and Egyptians continued to vie with each other for control.

Whether tensions, like these in Alexandria and those that arose four hundred years earlier between Jews and Egyptians regarding bull sacrifices on the island of Elephantine, constituted anti-Semitism as it is meant today is doubtful. It was part of the rhetoric of the times to demonize rival groups with hateful and wildly creative assertions (Goldstein, 2012). It would be difficult to document a particularized hatred for Jews that did not have some parallel dislike for any of several other groups living in ancient Eurasia.

Of course, tensions between the Jews of the Holy Land and Rome continued to escalate, mostly as a result of the Judean extremists like the Sicarii (e.g., Rapoport, 1989), as well as the continued insistence on worshipping their god and observing his commands. Judean Jews revolted in 66 CE, leading to the destruction of the second temple and the bloodbath of Masada in 70 CE. Resentment smoldered, and between 115 and 123 CE Jews throughout the Roman-occupied Holy Land rebelled against Rome (Goldstein, 2012). Around 132 CE Hadrian moved to rename Jerusalem "Aelia Capitolina" (see Fredriksen, 2012). Jewish partisans now made open asymmetrical war against Rome until Julius Severus and his eclectic army, dispatched by Hadrian, finally laid siege to Bethar in 135 CE. In the slaughter that followed capitulation, every Jew there was killed.

Again, it would be irresponsible to portray Roman action as anti-Semitic in the modern sense. It is fair to say, however, that some of the negative sentiments and stereotypes regarding Jews (like perhaps that the Jews scheme to take over) may have emerged from this time period. In essence, then, the beginning of anti-Semitism may be rooted in nothing more ugly than communities of Jews desiring merely to maintain their own identity as such.

Another source of negative affect toward Jews takes the form of the "deicide charge," the assertion that it was the Jews who had killed Jesus. In the first century after Jesus the embryonic Christian faith operated in ways as an appendage of wider Judaism. With time, though, and with mutual resentment over past issues, the new faith moved to become its own endeavor. Some Jews felt separation should be made, and thus modified the *Shemoneh Esreh* to include a "blessing" declaring as heretical any observant Jew who also hailed Jesus as messiah (Goldstein, 2012). Melito, Christian Bishop of Sardis offered a "Homily on the Passover" in which he seems to have been the first to level the deicide charge. This was a little before 170 CE; around one hundred and fifty years later (as of this writing, roughly the age of Canada and of Michael's university), Constantine had his ecstatic vision of a cross and a command "in this sign conquer" (Goldstein, 2012). Regarding which faith was favored across the empire, Constantine made his preferences only too clear.

The deicide charge gained inertia from the fledgling Christian community, seeking in part to make themselves distinct from their parent faith. In the interest of deepening the divide between Jews and Christians, as well as in order to increase their own influence, John Chrysostom and Augustine of Hippo (inter alia) leveled scathing charges against the Jews. They'd killed our lord, Chrysostom raved, how could they be anything but criminal evil murderers? Augustine did not want Jews dead. He wanted them to live and witness God's favor shift to the Christians. Recall that both Chrysostom and Augustine were skilled rhetoricians; Chrysostom's name is really a description: literally "golden-mouthed" in Greek (Goldstein, 2012, p. 35); Augustine was hailed as the finest arguer of his day anywhere in the world. Either one could charm the scales off a trout, regardless of whether what they were saying made any real sense.

It goes without saying that the Jews as a community were not in any way responsible for Jesus's death. Jesus was killed by the Roman authorities: he was tried by the Roman prefect, Pontius Pilate, and he was crucified in the Roman fashion; stoning was the preferred Jewish manner of execution at the time. If *any* Jews were involved at all it would have been some of the Jewish leadership, possibly the Sadducean members of the Sanhedrin (Barton, 1922)—one might be thinking of Caiaphas—still somewhat diminished in the force of its authority. The wider Jewish community would have had no influence on Pilate himself. As for the "crowd" described in the Gospels that did seem to have an influence on Pilate's final decision making, its composition is never defined in any reliable way (though clearly Jewish, Jerusalem was an international city even then). In any event, in the Gospels there is considerable imprecision regarding the trial(s?) and condemnation of Jesus (e.g., Gaston, 1986). For instance, in places the term "high priest" is substituted for "the Jews" (e.g., Granskou, 1986). Whereas in Mark (15:8–15) we hear that the chief priests had influenced the crowd to choose Barabbas over Jesus, in John (18:38) we are told only that Pilate transacted with "the Jews" (possibly just the Sadducees) regarding Barabbas. That there are questions about the number of trials Jesus had and whether Barabbas's freedom and Jesus's execution were in any way connected (Gaston, 1986) underscores the dubious nature of biblical accounts of the events, and the room for polemical elaboration. The interest in creating a divide between Judaism and the incipient Christianity weighed on its first chroniclers (Gaston, 1986). It becomes defensible, then, today to view critically *any* portrayal of Jewish involvement with Jesus's trial and execution, save perhaps that of a handful of Sadducean authorities.

To this point, then, we have a people held in contempt merely for choosing to maintain their identity, a people thus fitted with stereotypes like "scheming" that in fact are more properly descriptive of those who authored them, and the deicide charge that makes no historic sense. Considering the latter, one might understand that negative portrayal having legs, merely because it appears to be codified in scripture. The former should have enjoyed a truly short life. It did not. Although we have identified two main justifications for latter-day anti-Semitism, it feels we are hardly closer to a sense of understanding for modern day hatred.

Arendt's Analysis. Let's skip forward in history somewhat and pick up Hannah Arendt's narrative. The centuries between Augustine and Arendt's treatment do not contribute appreciably to our understanding of anti-Semitism, as they contain only pogroms.

Reiterating a tasteless joke, the Jews-as-scapegoats idea is raised before Arendt's readers and then summarily dashed to bits. The logic of scapegoating is that the scapegoat could have been any group; that, akin to general deterrence, culpability was never part of the sanguine calculus. And caution is called for, she says, in treating the history of ideas of the past century, as many seemingly prominent ideas have been little more than "desperate efforts to escape responsibility" (Arendt, 1979, p. 9). Citing Plato and giving one a bit of a chill, she says old charlatans concerned themselves with distorting ideas, whereas today's brand of charlatan seeks to obliterate history itself, targeting facts. One is irresistibly compelled to add "and create alternative facts." So we will be wary, and follow closely in her footsteps.

As indicated earlier, Arendt links the fate of the Jews with the life course of the European nation state. More to the point, because of their statelessness, and because of historic limitations placed on Jews, Jews found themselves in something of a dual relationship with the incipient institutions of the nation-state. These new nation-states granted to their inhabitants equal rights under the rule of law, linked with citizens' identity as members of that nation-state. This was a new idea in the European landscape. The idea of a state within a state, to wit, a distinct people who were stateless, was problematic for the incipient nation-states. At the same time, wealthy Jews ended up serving in the courts of monarchs as financiers because nation-states did not yet have adequate financial resources to operate on the new stage (Arendt, 1979). Jews, then, beginning during the seventeenth century found themselves both constrained as a group and relied upon as bankers, both discriminated against and privileged at the same time.

The nineteenth century was witness to emancipation for Jews, Arendt tells us. They could own property and were less limited in the occupations to which they could aspire, but the need for Jewish financial leadership for nation-states had not abated, though the scale of the finances meant only a handful of families were viable lenders. Jews continued to exist as Jews, meaning they were not permitted to assimilate in the same fashion as other groups had done during the formation of class identities. People became identifiable by their status in the class system, not by their "position in the state or within its machinery. The only exception to this was the Jews" (Arendt, 1979, p. 13). While keeping their *social* identity, the Jews were blocked from attaining a *class* identity, and instead became associated with their perceived role in the state. The state, she argues, needed the Jews to remain outside the class strata as part of the state that sought increasingly to be separate from and above all peoples. For their part, the state's interest in keeping Jews separate from the class framework "coincided with the Jewish interest in self-preservation and group survival" (Arendt, 1979, p. 13).

Again, of course, only a handful of extremely wealthy Jewish families had the capacity to bankroll the nation-states of Europe; each state had their need for Jewish bankers. The Jews in this small group constituted something of a supranational force, with families working in several states at once. Eventually states had no need for loans, but these influential Jewish families tended to remain around as advisors. This unique positioning meant that they might have had influence on international affairs. But being stateless and largely apolitical they did not act on that potential. "The Jews, without knowledge of or interest in power never thought of exercising more than mild pressure for minor purposes of self-interest" (Arendt, 1979, p. 24). In the main, the Jews were "the only group in the population [of the nation-states of Europe] that did not indulge in expansionist fantasies and in the thoughts of destroying other peoples" (Arendt, 1979, p. 41). More ominously, they tended not to sense the increasing acrimony between the state and lower classes. As class awareness increased among poor and working-class peoples of Europe, odds with the state and its agents increasingly were sought. Because of their unique stateless but state-wedded dual status, the Jews became suitable targets of disfavor. Again, recall that the number of Jews involved in state affairs at high levels was very small, though their prominence overshadowed their numbers and tended to paint all Jews in light that cast only a tiny handful of people.

Modern anti-Semitism as we mean it today, then, though it borrows heavily from its ancient influences, begins in the last decades of the nineteenth century, primarily in Germany, Austria, and France (Arendt, 1979). Arendt's assertion should not be read to diminish the suffering of the Jews in pogroms like the one that followed the people's crusade in 1096, in the main powered by the deicide charge (Runciman, 1996). In Germany, for instance, Bismarck had taken on the aristocracy of his new nation, and true to form for new nation-states, maintained a close relationship with Jews while he was in office. The aristocracy fought back, accusing him of taking bribes. Adolf Stoecker, Lutheran theologian and court chaplain, was sympathetic for the aristocracy, and in his efforts to garner popular support against Bismarck, he found that anti-Jewish rhetoric (leveraging aspects of Christian doctrine bent for the purpose by thinkers like Chrysostom and Augustine) worked well on the working-class crowds (Arendt, 1979). In Austria, Georg Schonerer was also finding that anti-Semitic rhetoric, targeting the Rothschild family in particular, found a home with his working-class constituents. Gesturing, Arendt is adamant we note that although for Stoecker the anti-Semitic appeal was in large part accidental, Schonerer was a true believer in his arguments against the Jews. Once class conflict was overt, once the German state failed so utterly to honor the interests of the masses, and eventually once national identities codefined everyone but the Jews, who were seen as part of the state apparatus, the Holocaust was, tragically, only a matter of gravity. Versailles was not the only provider of blame for Germany to allocate.

And what of the Jews themselves and their understanding of identity? It is most forgivable, we think, to seek understanding of anti-Semitism from a social vantage, but such a framework alone leaves one without clarity. "It has been one of the most unfortunate facts in the history of the Jewish people that only its enemies, and almost never its friends understood that the Jewish question was a political one" (Arendt, 1979, p. 56). The vast majority of Jews, like any people a bounteously diverse community, were not Rothschilds or were not involved in advising national leaders. They existed as people and as a people, but were not permitted to be other than Jews. Oddly to us today, there was a time in the very late nineteenth century when Jews were seen by Berliner liberal intelligentsia as an exotic Asian people, even though they had been neighbors for generations (Arendt, 1979). What it has meant and what it means to be Jewish is fully beyond this volume to trace, but it is manifestly evident that what Jewishness means has not always been within the capacity of the Jews to define. That capacity changed only marginally as a result of the events of May 14, 1948, but more on that in a moment.

Critique of Arendt's Analysis. In fairness, Arendt was not a historian, and some of her arguments do not enjoy rich evidentiary support (Avineri, 2010). Avineri claims Arendt insufficiently addresses the link between anti-Semitism and nationalist movements in Eastern Europe. Fair enough. He also seems to feel as if Arendt is overly general with her treatment of "the Jews." She speaks of "the Jews" but refers merely to the wealthy class of Jews involved in banking, then in advising, national leaders. Although she is not overt in her differentiation, and does not explain that she understands the Jewish community to be richly diverse in nature and influence, it is evident in her writing, we feel, that she understands this. To the point, she fully grasped the fact that she tended to think about Jewish identity in ways some other Jews found challenging (e.g., Arendt, 2006). More, she is portraying a social phenomenon, where generalities work in shorthand (although again, this can be dangerous). Yet another argument in her defense deals with the use of "the Jews" to evidence how Stoecker, Schonerer, and their audiences might have thought; they seemed unable or unwilling to differentiate between the handful of state advisors and the millions of others who are also Jewish, but were schoolteachers, shop clerks, fishermen, and cobblers. In any event, it would strain credulity to argue that Arendt, herself a Jew, did not appreciate the distinction between the wider Jewish community and "the Jews" she traces through European history.

Avineri (2010) argues that the antithesis of Arendt's claims, that the involvement of Jews in socialist and liberal politics, could also be made. Pointing to Marx and Eduard Bernstein as well as others in France, he observes that this was in fact one of the anti-Semitic canards that helped the Nazis build their hate-filled narrative. He argues her treatment of anti-Semitic German authors is sorely lacking as well, and that she uses Nazi historian Walter Frank as a source several times.

These latter concerns are, of course, not without merit, and indeed the use of Nazi narratives seems wholly irresponsible (although the most bizarre lies of dictators, both then and now, often rely on germs of something like truth). Remember her earlier caution regarding the tracing of twentieth-century ideas? Perhaps she (and we) stepped afoul. *Origins of Totalitarianism* remains a powerful and important book, and her analysis is compelling if data-thin in places. Coupling her analysis with Avineri's (2010) short but cogent critique provides us with a unique perspective, though. Both may possess aspects of truth in their claims. It is possible for a large and diverse community to be perceived as monolithic by an even larger and diverse community, and for that monolithic idea to be both diametrically opposite and yet in consonance with the ideas held by yet another large and diverse community. Avineri (2010) points to individual Jews who were deeply involved in politics, whereas Arendt gestures to a family of Jews (the Rothschilds) who were *thought* to be involved in politics. In both cases "the Scheming Jew" narrative is discussed, at least at a distance. Neither instance, of course, is relevant to the millions of Jews just seeking to make a living and watch their children blossom. What becomes increasingly clear is that how the Jews as a community are understood by others and how they understand themselves is a negotiated, co-created thing. As an aside, referencing our early conversation about "mesearch,"Arendt's thought regarding the Holocaust would qualify, at least to a degree, as identity thought; it is an open question whether Avineri provided her adequate space merely to be heard. Our sense is that he did not.

Let's Sartre Again. As any proper torture session begins with the ample display of the devices to be used, they were rather off-footed to find themselves in a single room decorated in French Second Empire style: ornately traced wall panels, indulgently elaborated chair rails and crown moldings, swan-caked chairs. The couches that in time will come to mean so much to three of the characters in *No Exit* are rather far from comfortable affairs; the colors are . . . regrettable, and the devices themselves, the only evident means for comfort in the room, are stuffed hard and thin with scrolling arms and decorative headrests of hardwood, obviously designed more to be seen than used. In any event, the valet does as valets do, and shortly the room has its three occupants: Garcin, Estelle, and Inez. They share this rather ornate windowless, mirrorless, sleepless room in Sheol.

They're all dead, of course, the three characters, and all new to Hell. Estelle died from pneumonia, Inez the victim of murder-suicide, and Garcin knows for sure which soldier had the blank. At first they put on stoic faces: they know they're in Hell, and there's little point in shows of false contrition now. Very shortly, though, facades fall away and Inez figures out their circumstances: they are in this room together, eternally crushed under the pressing weight of the light, of time, and each other's presence. They are quite certainly each other's torturers, thus the famous line from the play, so often taken out of context: "Hell—is other people" (Sartre, 1989, p. 45). Garcin holds dear his self-image as pacifist, which turns out to be less . . . precise . . . than one might desire. A no-nonsense gal, Inez seems always willing to tell the other characters about the scatological habits of bears in buckwheat, but her unrequited attraction to Estelle and Estelle's desire for Garcin grinds on Inez's spirit. Estelle, accustomed to pleasure and status, denies the appropriateness of her predicament, and as in life needs a man to be complete. Garcin will do, even if he is a coward and deserter. Locked in the room with only a capricious valet bell as connection to the outside, when the door opens of its own accord later on in the play, so ensconced are they in their roles as mutual destroyers no one chooses to leave.

Truth never being too far away, we soon discover each has done unspeakable things in life. Under the tectonic pressure of the light they cave, each of them in turn; acting as each other's physical and spiritual mirror, each is confronted with her or his own ugliness never having seen their likeness. In their role as mutual torturer for the others in the room, Garcin, Estelle, and Inez act also as mutual definers for each other as well. Each is mirror both for purposes of judgment and for what remains of their sense of self. Self, as defined formerly by those with whom each character lived, is visible as if through a crystal ball, but only to the degree that those still alive still remembered them; each character strutted and fretted his or her hour of life until he or she could see no more, as he or she no more was seen in anyone's living memory. Only the regard of the other two in the room carried any signal for defining who each character was.

Recall above when we contemplated the defining of Jewishness and the Jewish community's capacity to define themselves? It turns out that not only are we as communities by whatever label we choose not fully and exclusively able to define ourselves, we as individuals are both defining ourselves and defined by others as well. Our identities are negotiated things. We co-create each other, every minute of every day, though sometimes the process is too subterranean to perceive with any real clarity. Right now, we the authors have influenced each other as we shared ideas and drafts back and forth. You, kind reader, have influenced how we seek to frame our ideas, as have our students and our interactions with colleagues at conferences and strangers on Twitter. Were an understanding of love's meaning and power more complete, we might be making an altogether different set of claims in this work, or perhaps not writing it at all. We understand the task before us in terms not only of how we understand the content of the task, but also in terms of who our audience is, what you need, what you might be willing to hear and take on board. In a very real way, we are putty in each other's hands.

But we are not merely crafted according to others' visions. Sartre (1995) cares very much about how human freedom is navigated in the space allowed by situational constraints. That navigation can be authentic or inauthentic (Sartre, 1995, p. 90). To live authentically is to claim an identity as meaningful in itself, perhaps even to love that identity or that community. Authenticity is evidenced not only by adherence to values and practices common to others with the same identity (e.g., believing as Christians do), but also by claiming that identity in the face of consequences. The authentic Jew, for Sartre, imbibes and wears the Jewish identity, and does Jewish things, regardless of how others feel about that identity. The inauthentic Christian, for example, might disdain forgiving those who harmed him, or might deny his Christianity before the teeth of a Roman lion.

When a person forgives a grievous harm, though, is it the man or the Christian who forgives? Might our forgiving Christian, also an American, serve as definitional example for other Americans? Do Americans seek to know him as an American, or is his act more meaningful to Christians? In Sartre's example, was the Jew who fought the Nazis as a member of the Maquis fighting as a Jew or as a Frenchman? Resistance, Sartre says, was seen as so clearly in service to Jewish interests that some hesitated, wanting to be sure that their acts of resistance were understood as a function of their Frenchness. We would like to be able to say the question is silly, that of course each person navigated her own meaning for the dangers she assumed. We would like to be able to say that, but sadly, for most audiences, the Jew was unable (not allowed) to liberate himself from his Jewishness sufficiently to fight for France.

Our co-created identities, themselves convincing evidence of our communal nature as a species, can precipitate for some as a species of violence.

It would be natural, even tempting we think, to contemplate overlaying identities in terms of intersectionality (e.g., Potter, 2015). We understand intersectionality to refer to "the conception . . . that each person has an assortment of coalesced socially constructed identities that are ordered into an inequitable social stratum" (Potter, 2015, p. 3). Identities are vertically layered things, penetrating horizontally; each identity acts in different contexts but potentially has a multiplicative effect regarding inequity. Intersectionality is a vital component in the continuing process of crafting a criminological/zemiological discourse that serves all of us, but the contribution of intersectionality is predominantly a hygienic correction to stayed and desiccated narratives authored by old white men (itself an intersectionality, but one of privilege). Here, in this conversation, we must go further.

We must go further because the problem of oppressive identities is not with the identities themselves, but as we witnessed in the cold light of Sheol, where souls were crushed between the scrutiny of others and Second Empire monstrosities, the problem is with the authors of those identities. Sartre quotes Richard Wright: "There is no Negro problem in the United States, there is only a White problem" (Sartre, 1995, p. 152).

Sometimes the identities we craft for others are intentionally constricting and oppressive, as in the example of race in the United States, crafted specifically to protect the interests of the new white American aristocracy. Sometimes purpose is occluded, at most dimly felt by the authors; sometimes identities are drafted with little sense at all of anything like purpose. Sartre worried about the authenticity of those who live with an identity, but it is fair to say his book ended too soon. He did not worry as deeply about the authenticity of those who drape identities on peoples. To be sure, one can detect that concern in *No Exit*; each character skewers each other mostly accidentally by just being themselves, but clearly these three poor souls were put together for the express purpose of impaling each other on themselves. Love precludes violence in all but the most extreme contexts, so we would read the word "militant" to indicate "dedicated"; in the very last pages Sartre (1995, p. 152) impales his post-Holocaust Gentile audience: "It is not up to the Jews first of all to form a militant league against anti-Semitism. It is up to us."

We are co-creators of each other through a continual process of negotiation. Why and how we undertake the process, the authenticity with which we make and carry identities matters very much to a complete understanding of justice. Let us now turn to two more voices related to identity, and to Jewish identity, in order to deepen our understanding . . . and reverence . . . even further.

Buber/Levinas

It is a wonder, though perhaps no wonder at all upon reflection, that Emmanuel Levinas is not a household name like Hegel or Husserl. One hopes in earnest, probably in vain, that his localized celebrity is itself evidence of anti-Semitism. Such a price to pay, really; to deprive one's self of such rich and powerful insights is yet another cruelty upon cruelty directed back again onto hate's author.

There is something of a self-defeating aspect to Levinas's larger project, though it is one for which we all should be grateful. Perhaps "self-defeating" is imprecise. "Quixotic" might be more apt, from the challenge to Jewish identity it presents. The fellow who cuts Michael's hair is only too familiar with issues of anti-Semitism. As a Jew who is well versed in Judaic studies and has experienced at least his fair share of in-your-face anti-Semitism, he proved a more-than-apt sounding board for the writing of this section. He put things succinctly: it is for him the collective decision to cling to Jewish culture and its ancient and treasured cultural riches regardless of consequences, and thus not to fully assimilate into other communities that has given over the Jewish people to the many iterations of suffering to which they have been put. This treasure trove of cultural wisdom, or at least part of it—one might point to the Talmud as example, but the Talmud is only a sample—was at Levinas's fingers while studying at Freiburg, and even might be seen as something of a muse; he sought a "Jewish moment" (Barnes, 2016), a chance to merge Jewish wisdom into the already fertile and churning philosophical cauldron that was early twentieth-century Germany. Taking what he had been given by Husserl and Heidegger at Freiburg, like Buber had done, he lensed phenomenology through Jewish wisdom, but came to his own unique formulation. The result was not a simple mapping of rabbinical wisdom onto Husserl. It was a sharing of that treasure trove so intensely cherished and so carefully protected by the Jewish community out into the wider world. What if he succeeded? What if Levinas's thought obliterated all recollection of Heidegger? What if Jewish wisdom became the Wisdom of the Masses? Would his "Jewish Moment" also present the greatest challenge to Jewish identity since the Holocaust? It is, we think, a profound and immeasurable act of kindness and of self-sacrifice (albeit one of deep pride) to seek to mainstream a community's treasured wisdom with the obvious possibility of it being readily accepted, and the walls they justified thus coming tumbling down.

Where Heidegger found the immediate, the locus for understanding being, to be predicated upon self, the simplest shorthand for Levinas's thought is that being for us is founded on, and perhaps more critically, experienced in the confrontation with the Other (Barnes, 2016). Whereas Heidegger has his *Dasein*, Levinas has his *Il y a*. Heidegger's situationalized being, which sees others only at some remove (and somewhat downhill), is replaced by the "there is" (Dews, 2010). Human relations for Levinas are "shot through with traces of infinity" (Barnes, 2016); his interest is far less ethical and far more sacramental (e.g., DeValve, 2017b). And perhaps it is natural then that his concern for justice is a very granular one, bridging the divide between Idea and lived experience. Between the two, for Levinas, is ritual.

Levinas's *Il y a* has a kind of quantum particle physics to her. She lives in Copenhagen, of course, she paints her house, shops for groceries, suffers an occasional toothache, wears yoga pants, and binge-watches Real Housewives, but also keeps her pistol close by at night. Like a photon striking a detector, though, she is defined, and perhaps more crucially we can come to witness her immanence, only in the moment in which she collides face to face with an Other. And for Levinas quite literally this is so: the human face is prepotent to human language; we speak or write because the face of the Other has called us, has moved us precognitively to find a way to answer. She is transformed in the presence of the Other, and becomes a worthy vessel for her own divinity.

What is striking about Levinas's thought is that he discovers holiness in a coming together from his initial effort to escape. Escape is something naturally sought by one who was a prisoner of war, as he was. *On Escape* was, it seems, an effort to isolate and thus preserve in amber the affective and intentioning self by separating it from its shell. The I/Oneself distinction he employs seems to us akin to the I/me distinction in Mead (e.g., 1934). What Levinas found, though, was for us of great significance. In overly simple terms, our existence creates needs, and we experience these needs acutely (Bergo, 2017). These needs give rise to the desire to escape, but escape is illusory. These needs instead are the framework for human existence, and as such create, not tidal movement away, as in away from our suffering selves, but instead a movement toward, specifically toward others. Needs become the dark matter, the *Il y a* of community. We would understand this connection in the form of responsibility.

Responsibility, for Levinas, is unmediated fraternal transcendence (Bergo, 2017). It is unmediated because it precedes the subject's subjectness (Levinas, 2009). Moreover, its anteriority makes it a precondition to freedom: "Responsibility for the other . . . is human fraternity itself, and it is prior to freedom. The face of the other . . . is an unrepresentable trace, the way of the infinite. It is not because among beings there exists an ego, a being pursuing ends. . . . It is because in an approach, there is inscribed. . . the face of infinity" (Levinas, 2009, pp. 116–17). This anteriority also answers an ancient question: how do we recognize "the good?" (αγαθος). Because responsibility is anterior to freedom, we need not ask after what is good, because the good finds us (Levinas, 2009, p. 122). Responsibility, then, is transcendent vertically (to God), but because it is first transcendent horizontally (to each other).

In Levinas, there seems to be an almost direct parallel to incipient Buddhist thought. It is almost as if the discoveries under the Bodhi tree occurred for Levinas independently more than 2,500 years later. We need only squint a little to see the two arguments line up when overlaid: need stands in for dukkha, Gautama's early privilege and search for answers parallels Levinas's young life: his Hebraic studies, his time as a French officer and POW, as well as the loss of his family in the Holocaust. For both men, it was a running *away* from something that led them to greater wisdom. What they both saw is also in close parallel: both saw human need/suffering as the organizing principle through which to understand the nature of human existence. Both saw divinity most clearly in the face of a stranger.

Buber joins the conversation by adding something of a typology of relations. Of course Buber, like Levinas, breathes Hebraic wisdom into his arguments about I, It, and You (and, by extension, We). Resemblance to Levinas is inevitable, even desirable, but his own tack brings its own shape, manipulability, and delicious opaqueness. In some ways it is unfair to treat Buber in Levinas's shadow as that is not where he belongs; Buber influenced Levinas, not the other way round. They drank from the same wellsprings, too, both flourished in European philosophical communities yet maintained a foot in Rabbinical thought. Still, between them important differences existed. Aside from some key substantive differences that will be evident here only insofar as they advance our narrative, Buber has a caressing ruthlessness in his voice not to be found in Levinas, and in fairness, is rarely present in philosophical writing anywhere. We treat Buber after Levinas because Buber's narrative is more direct, in some ways more relevant to justice practice, and unquestionably far more movingly poetic (so perhaps you will forgive us for quoting him so prolifically as we do below).

The typology, of course, is straightforward: we can understand the ways in which humans encounter each other can be conceived as being of two categories: I-It and I-You. I-It relations occur most commonly among humans. The It is a fixed and inanimate thing to be used, studied, known. Although It relations are not in Buber's words "evil," and indeed are necessary precursors to greater wisdom, much to its detriment, much of criminology rarely seems to move beyond an I-It relation to suffering, even to those who suffer. The alienation many feel is the result of being an It in relation to the I of others. I-It encounters bleach the objects of encounter of their humanity; if I am not Here, You are not There. I-You relations, in contrast, function at a higher and more total level—You is seen as a whole living being, indeed one in which the whole universe dwells. As Michael wrote these words, he sat at a bar in the Albany airport, waiting for a flight back to his beloved Lindsay. A man in a very white shirt and pressed slacks walked up beside him and stood. Visibly impatient he stood while the staff ran about unable to attend to him. He coughed, clearing his throat, evidently in order to be addressed. He could scarcely have been more demeaning had he snapped his fingers or summoned staff with a sexist appellation. Unironically, he glanced down to the cover of *I and Thou*, open and face up next to Michael as he writes, and then back up again to the bartender delivering him his beer, his arrogant indignation fully intact. The beer came, but no thanks followed; from all one could tell by watching, the beer was vastly more important to him than the human that delivered it. A beer. That must have been one hell of a beer.

Again, though, It relations are not inherently problematic in themselves. It is when we fail to move beyond perception of It to a more complete rendering of the Other when we run into difficulties. And of course these difficulties occur all the time in contemporary America; they are so common they are scarcely noticeable to us. We might have a difficult time connecting with each soul we pass moving to, through, and from the subway, but things become considerably easier when meeting a clerk or customer in a dyadic interaction. Yet we often fail to bother meeting eyes, listening authentically to the other's voice. We ask "How are you?" and proceed with our order without waiting for a response, offering a thoughtless "You too!" over one shoulder. At the most, we might pause to process the news, suddenly off-footed by the stutter-step imposed by the mini-narrative that we did not actually want, that we have absolutely no use for.

How do we move from It relations to relations with You? Like for Levinas, for Buber the magic is in the encounter; it is in encounter with other that we are created: "In the beginning is the relation" (Buber, 1996, p. 69). The languages of "primitive" peoples give voice to this primacy while they skewer our Eurocentric haughtiness. What matters, though, is the authenticity of the lived relations to which they point. Objects are abstract only until they are made bodily relevant. The Creature opens the blinds and his somnolent creator stirs; terror or sweetness follows, and only as this sensory experience is the Creature understood. From this point the Creature develops, both in corporeal space and in the mind of the creator; the creator creates the Creature not once but twice. "In conscious life cosmic being recurs as human becoming. Spirit appears in time as a product, even a by-product, of nature, and yet it is spirit that envelops nature timelessly" (Buber, 1996, p. 75).

The movement from It to You is a function of choice: "The You encounters me by grace—it cannot be found by seeking. . . . The You encounters me. But I enter into a direct relationship to it. Thus the relationship is elective and electing, passive and active all at once" (Buber, 1996, p. 62). But Buber also honored Kant's categorical imperative against treating humans as means to an end. So like some (e.g., DeValve, 2015) have said regarding forgiveness, I-You is both an imperative and gift of grace precisely at the same time. The Creature's creator had a choice to see the Creature's beauty and needs or to regard him as a horrific defilement of nature. It is the thrust of Mary Shelley's tender and appalling tale to trace the consequences of Frankenstein having made poor choices (and at first perhaps none at all). The grievous irony, of course, is that Frankenstein received such love and adoration throughout his own childhood, and then failed to reciprocate that care when he himself became a parent.

For Buber, co-creation of both I and You (for both come to a kind of fruition when they interact in I-You relations), spirit and love do not dwell within either the subject or the object, but in the space between them: "Jesus' feeling for the possessed man is different from his feeling for the beloved disciple; but the love is one. Feelings one has; love occurs. Feelings dwell in man, but man dwells in his love. This is no metaphor but actuality: love does not cling to an I, as if the You were merely its 'content' or object; it is between I and You" (Buber, 1996, p. 66). Even more directly: "Spirit is not in the I but between I and You. It is not like the blood that circulates in you but like the air that you breathe" (Buber, 1996, p. 89). The relationship is co-created and is never the property of either party. And what becomes available to both I and You, between them, is nothing short of divinity.

The quintessential example of I-You, perhaps, might be the child in the womb. The child and mother are one, and the child is "a pure natural association" (Buber, 1996, p. 76). The space between them is so small as to be undetectable; the space between them is so large that it encompasses them both. The relation between them is so transcendent, Buber says, that it invokes the old Jewish idea that the child in the womb knows the universe totally, and forgets what she knows at birth.

But why? Why is it that so powerful an ontological understanding is lost at birth? Of course, you might be saying, we should remind ourselves that it is all figurative, that it is a poetic trope; it is not as if childbirth bleaches all wisdom from a fetus' mind, that each of us is Buddha, lotuslike floating in amniotic fluid, but once bathed in cold fluorescence each is transfigured into a tiny troglodyte. After all, does the fetus *know* a *thing* that she can *share* with others? Can she demonstrate empirically a capacity that somehow evaporates with the loss of fetus status? Certainly not. We argue that we should not understand this knowledge or forgetting as merely metaphorical, even if it is not a knowledge measurable in terms of cortical activity. It is a knowledge of being, rooted in belonging, not owned but shared communally with all incipience, with all that is becoming. And if it is at all responsible to talk in terms of deliberateness, *it is a knowledge that is lost so that it can be remembered.*

The co-created identity, this spirit, founded in encounter, rediscovered from the fog before childhood, and dwelling in silence, remains divine in silence and becomes It when response is offered. "That is the melancholy of man, and that is his greatness" (Buber, 1996, pp. 89–90). The transformation to an It is not a dehumanization process, but instead is where what was You is made elemental and momentarily static, to be made spirit again once encounter in silence is restored. It-relations are necessary for science (and for criminology in particular), as "only as an It can [something] be absorbed into the store of knowledge" (Buber, 1996, p. 90). But criminology fails when it stops at It relations to its subjects and does not return to the encounter. Scientific It-based knowledge is necessary, "but [science] should do its work faithfully and immerse itself and disappear in that truth of the relation which surpasses understanding and embraces what is understandable" (Buber, 1996, p. 91). Criminology must begin with It, but *never* forget to embrace the You.

With regard to justice service institutions, Buber creates a distinction for us. He gestures to institutions, external formations and settings where human life occurs, where action verbs live in some kind of order "where, with the manifold participation of human heads and human limbs, the round of affairs runs its course" (Buber, 1996, p. 93). He also points to feelings, things inside us "where one lives and recovers from the institutions" (Buber, 1996, p. 93). Of course the levy between the two, Buber observes, is rather more porous than we might like; feelings intrude upon the business of . . . business. "*But the severed It of institutions is a golem, and the severed I of feelings is a fluttering soul-bird.* Neither knows the human being; only one the instance and the other one only the 'object'" (Buber, 1996, p. 93). But our confusion regarding what justice should look like has a natural source: "That institutions yield no public life is felt by more and more human beings, to their sorrow. . . . [However], that feelings yield no personal life has been recognized by few so far" (Buber, 1996, p. 94). Among those who have detected calamity, some have sought solution by leveraging feelings to "loosen up or thaw or explode" institutions (Buber, 1996, p. 94); "when the automatized state yokes together totally uncongenial citizens without creating or promoting any fellowship, it is supposed to be replaced by a loving community" (Buber, 1996, p. 94). Not so. "True community does not come into being because people have feelings for each other . . . but rather on two accounts: all of them have to stand in a living, reciprocal relationship to a single living center, and they have to stand in a living, reciprocal relationship to one another" (Buber, 1996, p. 94). And to clarify, the builder, really each of us, is that single living center. Justice organizations, if they seek to offer justice, are only possible when each member reveals their You to every Other. Justice built on any other arrangement among humans is not meaningfully distinguishable from tyranny.

Conclusion

Lines scratched on a page, almost thrown down by a gifted child. A pencil held obliquely rubbed with precision raises smudgy shadows. A room is silent but for her breathing and the intermittent sibilance of pencil on paper. Soon a nightstand emerges, with a lamp and an upright bass, all in forced perspective. Faint blue lines run horizontally through the work, offering a hint as to the tender age of the artist. None of her parents can draw, least of all her father. Her grandmother is a talented artist. Her great-great-grandmother studied art at the prestigious Cooper Union in New York City. Is it really possible that she might have her grandmother's and great-great-grandmother's gift? What is certain is that this kid can draw. She has the muse.

A child who has known little more than abuse and neglect for her first most delicate years is shown patient lovingkindness by a couple of willing strangers and almost before her new mother's eyes she becomes a fountain of lovingkindness herself. Her lineage is of little significance because the light that is her mother and father has filled the dark places, banishing shadow. A child who had only learned to blame herself now has begun to feel the strength of her limbs through the love of her adoptive parents. What is certain is that this little girl is mighty. She will change the world.

It takes one aback when a child does something that stops your breath. A ten year old picks up a guitar and rips like he knows what a broken heart feels like. We will talk a little about prodigies later on, but that's not really what we mean here. Beethoven's genius was earned. He grunted and struggled with his art; for his pains often Beethoven's works are more evocative, moving, more human. But again, we will get to suffering later, in the next chapter. No, we need to talk about something altogether different here first.

Roger Scruton (2017) holds the biological accountings of human design up for scrutiny and finds them sorely wanting. The "selfish gene" arguments of Dawkins and others reduce humanity to gene-friendly traits, but fail to account adequately for things like laughter and music. Atomistically we have our constituent components, some of which are functional in the context of gene reproduction and expression. One might argue that music might be a means whereby a suitor woos a mate. In point of fact, Michael learned recently that he owes his existence to his grandfather's adroitness with a baritone ukulele. Scruton uses painting as an analogy for how he views the human condition. Indeed, we have constituent parts, as does a painting: lines, swirls, color, and canvas. There is also a face, perhaps, smiling back at the viewer. It is this faceness, this nonconstituent phenomenon, that he regards as an incarnate part of us. It is not a gestalt, it is more verstehen. But that raises a key point for us: the identities we have discussed, these constituent constructs that compose our meaning, where do they reside? Does the face reside in the painting, or is the face, the subject of the art, in us?

Can the same be said of each of us? Where is Michael? Where is Tammy to be found? Indeed, we are not mere canvas and pigment, and Scruton's metaphor is only that. But where is me? Where is you? After all, Mead (1934) has already made sure that there is more than one chunk of us floating about. It seems obvious to us that although there is an empirically demonstrable portion of any one of us where we tend to think it is, there is also an equally demonstrable portion of any one of us in others, and elsewhere. This is not metaphor: Tammy's existence is not Tammy's alone. There is Tammy in her students, in her children, in her spouse, in her parents, in her colleagues. . . . Likewise, there is each of them in her. She is not merely different from those parts of others that land on her soil, she is more vital, more fertile for it.

The teacher sits in silence, legs crossed on the mat. The student beside him waits; a hand is raised, crooked finger launches a line that traces from his shoulder across the quarter-million miles between shoulder and moon. The finger is not the moon; the teaching is not the lesson. But the moon is not to be found at the end of the teacher's finger, nor at the end of the running line his finger authors. The moon is not in the sky, but is in the student; the pond reflects the moon, just as does each drop of dew on each bending leaf. The moon is the student, and the moon is the teacher. Identity matters immeasurably and it matters not at all.

Chapter Four

Justice, Crime, and Striving

We worried earlier, in chapter 2, contemplating the criminal law. Proximate causes could be its only real concern, and though unavoidable, really, this locality of focus represents both fatal flaw and implicit admission of our critique of contemporary ideas about justice. With the tender brilliance to which we have become accustomed, Camus contemplates suicide in *The Myth of Sisyphus*. Suicide is like a work of art, he tells us, in that "it is prepared in the silence of the heart" (Camus, 1991, p. 4). It lives secreted in the breast until it emerges in the authoring act. And like selfism we examined in chapter 1, and its antecedent conditions fear, ignorance, and avarice, "The worm is in the man's heart. That is where it must be sought" (Camus, 1991, p. 5). But who can know, Camus asks, if on that particular day, he might've received indifferent treatment from a friend; perhaps a simple, thoughtless gesture drew darkness from the silence to crawl up the back of the throat bile-like and hot. The penultimate, the moment right before the act, may well matter more than extant theory allows.

It is called labor for a reason. Michael was born a male, and as he is also not a seahorse, he is physically incapable of bearing children. He was in the delivery room when his daughter, Kinsela, was born. He was *right there*, watching. Labor was relatively short; only about eight hours (says he). Contractions came and went, as did pain medication. When the time came, he held Kinsela's mother's back and one leg in order to help her push. He was physically as involved in events as he could be. So although Michael cannot fully understand what it means to bear a child, rest assured he is *well aware* of what he does not understand.

Each of us enters the human world through the hearth of life; invariably there is struggle. Even in instances where childbirth is smooth, there is pain, shock, effort, tearing, tension, and trauma. Everyone has their own share: mother bears the brunt of things of course, while the child veritably receives the shock of her life coming into the cold light as father sits anxious and bemused, desperate for a joyous conclusion. Living means striving, struggling. Life's continuation for one being means life's end for something else, even if that something is a carrot. Buddhists tell us that *dukkha*, suffering, is the hallmark of the human condition. For them, suffering is both a thing to transcend and an invitation to wisdom. As living things, we are made to strive, in fact, and it is good for you. Taleb (2012) observes the antifragility of living things; broken bones reknitted are stronger at the breakpoint; a daily spoonful of local honey can ease symptoms of allergies for the allergens it contains. And yet we do break, we do succumb. Suffering and striving is penultimate to death and blossoming.

THE STRUGGLE

Like Bentham, some people might say that Beethoven was irascible, toxic, petulant, and often short-fused. More directly, he was *not* Mozart. Whereas Mozart's manuscripts are near flawless, almost as if he were merely taking dictation, Beethoven's manuscripts, in contrast, are cluttered with scratch-outs, arrows, and rewrites. His creative process was more akin to childbirth; creation was a laborious, sweaty struggle. Mozart just wrote what he heard in his head, it just leapt out of him, like a sneeze. Beethoven grunted, sweated, and farted his way to brilliance. If Mozart is Superman, Beethoven without question is his Batman. Both are musical geniuses in their own right. Neither lay persons nor professionals consider Mozart a greater composer merely because of the volume of his work relative to Beethoven; Beethoven "managed" only nine (which is also an important lesson for us in the assessment of scholarly contributions of criminologists). When it comes to showcasing music's velvet might and its gargantuan gentleness, at least for Michael, Beethoven the Struggler is preferred all day long.

Few knew that Beethoven was losing his hearing, even as early as 1814 (Burkholder, Grout, & Palisca, 2014). By the time of the debut of his ninth and final symphony, he was as deaf as a stone. Ludwig von Beethoven, the man whose name is practically synonymous with human musical accomplishment, spent half his life slowly losing the one sense he needed most. He never heard his last works performed; he never heard the roaring applause they generated. Conducting the premier of the ninth symphony, he finished several measures ahead of the orchestra. At the end, he stood, unknowingly staring at the orchestra in tomblike silence. He could not hear the adoring thunder of his audience behind him; the concertmaster had to turn him around so he could see them having leapt to their feet, cheering.

There is something, then, in struggle, with which we should concern ourselves if we seek to understand our own nature, and make no mistake, the study of crime/harm/suffering is also the very struggle to understand ourselves fully. Struggle invites ethical compromise, just as it spurs us to true greatness. But it would be far from a complete description of the human condition, and indeed, a very dismal and menacing existence indeed if human life were little more than strife, little more than moments of joy to be found only in those brief interludes between onslaughts. In this chapter, we will examine a few ideas of crime and of justice that contain some notion of striving or of struggle. (We could not hope to come close to covering them all, though.) And we will seek to understand the nature of that something in us that struggle reveals. What we will discover will be an indispensable insight into the crafting of a loving justice. Again, ideas here are accomplished for the insights they make possible into the nature of human striving and its role in understanding ourselves, why we hurt, and what we must do about it.

CRIME AND STRUGGLE

Just as he approaches the ATM, he feels someone slide into the space behind him; the cold touch of steel followed almost instantly as an answer to the unexpressed question. "*We* are making a withdrawal," growled the figure. The muzzle pressed hard into his back, urging him toward the machine. Across the street, another man should never drink so much as this. He rages and stumbles, roaring unintelligible insults at his tiny girlfriend. She retreats, but even in his compromised state he is quicker than she. Before she has the chance to process her peril, his right hand grips her throat, her delicate neck almost disappearing behind his calloused palm. With his other hand he deflects her wobbly attempt at counterattack, and raises his arm with fist clenched. Down the block, two rival gangs square off in a pitched battle over a few hundred feet of curb. Around the corner, a teenager mumbles to himself about how little his parents understand about the world. He reaches into his pocket to feel the loose wad of small bills he snatched from the register not an hour ago. Digging down farther, he can feel the bulge of his new pipe and the bag of weed destined for it. In the dining room of the very same house, a man stares at his hands, gnarled and hard like tree roots. Unfamiliar emotions ricochet around inside his skull, only picking up energy as they fly; is it rage he feels, or helplessness that has leeched the will from his limbs? He breathes but he has no breath. Today he found out that the 401K that was to provide his pension had been plundered. After thirty-plus years of hard work as a welder in the shipyard, the net value of his retirement account is a tragicomically puny $78.13. Never having been one to cry, even when his folks died unexpectedly a few years ago, the first tear startled him when it struck his palm. He could lay TIG welds that looked like perfect stacks of dimes lined up like little soldiers, but after decades of mastery he had nothing but pocket change to show for it. By what earthly power will he find the strength to tell his wife that the life they had envisioned has vanished? As if an answer to his question, his left arm begins to go numb.

There is a City of Crime. No, we don't mean Chicago. The City of Crime is a place co-created by criminologists and their mental avatars. David Matza's drifting delinquents live here, along with the Kallikaks, Lombroso's tattooed "slope dummy," Merton's innovators, Sherman's defiant ones, Hirschi's LSC-ites, Sutherland's differentially socially organized, and the rest. As it is a big, if troubled, city, it has two baseball teams, perpetually squaring off against each other in the World Series: the Adolescent Limiteds always seem to have a deeper bullpen than the Life-Course Persistents. There are subways to stalk, eateries to rob, victims to predate, children to consume, and banks to plunder. Not all citizens are people, either. *Citizens United* (558 U.S. 310) (2010) makes rather more sense here: there are avatars of politicians, politburos, corporations, and even entire governments. In more senses than one, it is verily a land of misfits.

Most of the residents of the City of Crime know a thing or two about struggle. Merton's avatars are understood in terms of how they navigate struggle, and Agnew deepens this contemplation by making a study of the kinds of struggles they face, whereas Sellin's avatars wage war with each other in constant cultural collision. For us to pay homage to every criminoetiological claim that had some element of struggle, it is likely we would be able to do little else here in this volume. We have met key figures and their avatars already, of course; Merton, Hirschi, Sutherland, and the list goes on. The shape of this discussion, then, will be somewhat different. We will look more cursorily at ideas and the role struggle plays in them, more as something of a reading of their claims taken together than as a detailed treatment of each argument.

After all, should it surprise us that struggle is at the heart of so much of criminology as we understand it currently? Speaking in the most general terms, crime as it is contemplated contains a collision of interests. Whether we are thinking of a mugging, delinquent boys smoking in the boys' room, rape, graft, war making, spear phishing, polluting, stealing unmentionables, or stealing elections, some collision of claims is involved. Moreover, often the reasons given for the existence of the collision itself finds roots in some form of struggle. Without question, of course, the former is often a function of the latter; criminoetiological arguments are closely related to the types of collisions they contemplate, but they are, to be clear, not the same things. Gottfredson and Hirschi (1990) have their avatar: dirty jeans and a Metallica t-shirt. Sporting greasy hair, greasy spine, and dirty nails, he lives in a single-wide behind the old Food Lion. Sometimes he steals; more often he panhandles. When it is dark, he jiggles car door handles at the nearby Walgreen's until he finds one that is unlocked, then he grabs what he can and bolts. He lacks self-control, just as Gottfredson and Hirschi envisioned; his actions create a conflict, a collision of claims between himself and those he impacts, and abstractly between himself and the state. At the same time, the struggle at work within him to steal or not to steal, at any given moment, is the focus of Gottfredson and Hirschi's attention. Any given crime he commits is the result of a struggle lost between his compromised criminological immune system and his baser urges. When he finds an unsecured car, when he reaches in, and when he takes the iPod sitting naked on the front passenger seat, a struggle has already unfolded, its outcome already decided.

Of course, struggle has been the engine of the advancement of criminological theory. Shortcomings in early theory created conceptual and empirical misfits, leading to further theoretical development. As Lombroso's theory slowly unwound into eddies and roils of exception after exception, thinkers concerned with crime looked elsewhere. Even as Hooton (1939) and Sheldon (1949) sheltered the candle of the biological explanation, acolytes of Durkheim were busy in Chicago laying the foundation for much of the rest of twentieth-century criminology. The deeply flawed and often blatantly racist theories of the individual showed themselves to be of little use, and so it became necessary to craft a new narrative, one not polluted with racism and social Darwinism. Struggles arising from the assumption of legal consensus gave rise to theories that posited law functioned primarily as a tool of subjugation. Struggles arising from the shortcoming of some radical claims lead to a more refined historic understanding of original and coopted institutional purpose, just as Hegel would argue.

For criminology, one form of struggle (to wit, that of the sovereign to maintain order, and for people to be free from predation) led to its creation, which itself is the struggle to see ourselves sufficiently well to understand the struggles each of us faces that harm ourselves, each other, and our world, and to turn that understanding into wisdom and, eventually, healing. Struggles gave rise to criminology; struggles are an integral part of the narrative, and it is itself one limb of the human struggle to eradicate struggling.

In this section, then, we will trace a brief narrative of struggle in criminoetiological discourse. In no way will it be complete, but we view that incompleteness as an invitation to you, kind reader, to participate in this work. We will make reference to authors already discussed as well as works we have not yet contemplated. True to the form of the book, works that receive more than passing reference here we might defend as "accomplished" works of criminology, even though we will offer critique, primarily because they have in some fashion turned their gaze to the nature of human struggling in order to understand crime. Even if they did so incompletely, they were on a path toward wisdom.

'Tis the Season for Treason

Before besieged Harfleur, Shakespeare portrays King Henry V of England seeking to make good his claim to the throne of France. "Warlike Harry" in full armor shouts from astride his war horse, demanding that they capitulate after this, "the latest parle [they] will admit" (Shakespeare, 2017, III, iii). Capitulate, he roars, or "look to see the blind and bloody solder / Defile the locks of your shrill-shrieking daughters, your fathers taken by their silver beards / And their most reverend heads dashed to the walls, / Your naked infants spitted upon pikes / Whilst the mad mothers with their howls confused do break the clouds. . . . What say you? Will you yield and this avoid, / Or guilty in defense be thus destroyed" (Shakespeare, 2017, III, iii). Guilty *in defense*. Beloved Harry was a soldier, but in his war making he was anything but wanton. In his imitation of the action of a tiger, he asked weightily if his claim be a righteous one, and bore the sin should his cause be unjust (even if his subjects' souls were their own). The French withheld from him what was rightfully his, and if he must, he would rake for it wherever they hid it, so we are told. He worried scrupulously about the justness of his claim before making preparations for war, but once settled, once his claims were in his mind made irrefutable, every bloody deed was permissible, and worse, the guilt for the many deaths that were to come impended solely around the necks of the indisposed French. Once his claim was justly made, every brutality in service to that claim was defensible (we can hear Fluellen pop up behind him and add "within the laws of war"); any mitigation of suffering of the enemy obscured truth. About that suffering, in October of 1415, at the culminating battle of Henry's adventures, between 8,000 and 10,000 French soldiers were killed, to England's own loss of fewer than thirty.

It was, as we have said already, a radical enough idea that Beccaria felt the need to publish his work anonymously at first: "every act of authority between one man and another that does not derive from absolute necessity is tyrannical" (Beccaria, 1986, p. 8). During the Age of Kings, any harm between subjects was a breach of the King's Peace, and thus viewable as a mini-treason. Poor Damiens's travails bear testament to the sanguine logic; for an act so heinous as attempted regicide, the offender should die once for every subject he would de-patriate by his royal aggression. As such a thing is practically impossible, he will be made to come near death as frequently and as horrifically as technology allows. Although, say, petty theft dwells in a realm far removed from regicide, like Dante's inferno, you can most certainly get there from here.

Initially, then, with regard to crime, the only struggle that really mattered was the initial one; if the claim of righteousness could be made by the sovereign, then nothing else mattered, and all force necessary to appease the sovereign's sense of justice was permitted. Again, Beccaria's royal estoppel was radical indeed, as it took away the sovereign's right of self-pleasuring at others' expense. Crucially, it did so by injecting another collision, another struggle, into the conversation. As we have discussed already, the social contract is a bank of rights surrendered by each citizen as a protection against the struggle of all against all. And for Beccaria, a sovereign may punish only insofar as that punishment helps to maintain the social arrangement that made that bank possible. Now the sovereign had to struggle also with the leviathan.

A Signal Shift

Individual-level explanations of crime then available to science had shown themselves to be vacuous at best and toxic at worst. Imprecision in the understanding of the human body and the human soul produced one of two outcomes: either the findings were of scarce value (save the elimination of the possibility of simple explanations), or they cast a light on the uglier sectors of human reasoning. We either found nothing of lasting value, or we found the more grotesque parts of ourselves.

In response, three Durkheim-soaked vectors of thought emerged from the first decades of the twentieth century, all of which ordained some form of struggle as the engine for crime. With regard to the first two, exogenous forces created conditions where crime was a natural, even quasi-functional behavior (e.g., Matza, 1969). For the third, both endogenous and exogenous forces are in play. We have, of course, made reference to the Chicago School already in the conversation about Edwin Sutherland; we spent time talking about strain in our discussion on Merton (e.g., 1938); and we referenced a more contemporary version of control theory in our talk about Gottfredson and Hirschi (1990) and their low self-control theory. Let us briefly contemplate the thought of one theorist from each vector in order to see the role struggle plays for them.

What If It's Not Just Me but Rather My Neighborhood

As Tammy walks her dogs each morning, she contemplates the nature of crime as she watches the plumes of smoke rise from the smokestack near her home. Like a dinosaur, out of time and space, the smokestack stands juxtaposed against the brightly colored houses of her neighborhood. It serves as a reminder that less than two decades ago where she stands was a housing project, McCallie Homes, known for extreme poverty and violent crime; a place where, after dark, the police often refused to enter. Today, this picturesque neighborhood, the Villages, is reminiscent of an early 1900s community with Bungalow-style housing, tree-lined streets, and newly paved sidewalks. In the morning light, it is an idyllic community, quiet and welcoming; her neighbors wave to her on their commute to work. In reality, however, the crime that was endemic to this area did not vanish; it simply moved three streets over. Her neighborhood sits adjacent to one borough of the City of Crime, an area filled with dilapidated housing, poverty, and violence. More often than she would like to admit, she has heard the sound of gunshots echo out in the distance only to discover in the morning news that lives have been lost. The sound has become so common that she doesn't even flinch anymore. While she may have been raised in the projects, these are not the projects of her childhood.

Chattanooga, like many other cities across America, began to experience the gentrification of the downtown over the last several decades; areas within the inner city that were previously deemed uninhabitable became trendy. Gentrification has led to a revitalization of the riverfront, increased tourism, and stabilization within the area. It has also resulted in an increase in home prices, unaffordable rent, and a white-washing of historically minority neighborhoods. The return of the white, middle-class suburbanite to the inner city has, in essence, led to the displacement of many of the low-income and minority residents previously residing in the area. To quell the critics, a few meager attempts have been made to build and provide housing for low-income families; Tammy's community was one of those efforts. The Villages, a failed Hope VI attempt to revitalize a housing project community into mixed-income housing, was an alternative to traditional gentrification efforts with the promise of combined affordable and market-rate housing, retail opportunities, and outdoor developments such as public golf courses and parks to increase the livability within the area. Not surprisingly, many of the promised plans never came to fruition as a result of financial mismanagement and changing governmental priorities, leaving the surrounding area underdeveloped and prone to continued criminal activity. The area was never merged with the rest of the revitalization efforts occurring throughout the city proper. Instead, it remains an island sandwiched between an industrialized and high-crime residential area. The irony is not lost on Tammy that this area of poverty, crime, and hopelessness is set at the base of Lookout Mountain, leaving Chattanooga's most affluent to look down upon the residents, both literally and figuratively.

Cities change . . . we understand that. Gentrification, whether you are in Chattanooga or Chicago, has changed the landscape of how cities are depicted. No longer is crime radiating out from the Zone of Transition. The City of Crime is no longer a static entity in location. When entire communities are displaced, it does not solve the crime problem, but rather pockets of crime emerge. Crime merely shifts to another location as displacement disperses criminal cultures out from zones deemed criminogenic and into what has been historically considered middle-class neighborhoods. So, we want to know, is it possible to eliminate the City of Crime or do the attempts to do so just mutate into something new?

Burgess and the Zone of Transition

With the shift from an agrarian to an industrial society, droves of people, including immigrants, people of color, and unemployed farm workers, flocked to cities to find jobs during the Industrial Age. As noted by Palen (1981), again Chicago, a city that had around four thousand occupants at its incorporation in 1833, increased to over two million in less than a century (see, e.g., Cullen & Agnew, 2003). As the majority of those were unskilled laborers, many of them clustered in the inner city where stockyard, slaughterhouse, and factory jobs were available. Immigrants settled where they worked with most residing in tenement houses, characterized by overcrowding, unsanitary conditions, and crime, within the center of the city; tenement houses would later be replaced by subsidized housing, but many of the same issues would still plague residents. Thus, rather than finding economic relief, workers who had come to Chicago for a better life were met with poor working conditions, low wages, long hours, and safety and health issues.

As noted by Cullen and Agnew (2003), sociologists working at the University of Chicago began to think that crime was not a matter of individual characteristics but a matter of the traits of neighborhoods as the rapid influx of immigrants had created numerous problems within the urban landscape. In his seminal work *The Growth of the City* (1925), Ernest Burgess, a member of the Chicago School, argued that urban development is not a haphazard occurrence but rather a social pattern of distinct areas. Drawing on the work of his colleague Robert Park and his work on plant communities, Burgess argued that cities expand from the city center, slowly moving outward, in patterns known as concentric circles through a process of invasion, dominance, and succession. Economic competition would determine where people lived within the city. Burgess broke these zones into six distinct groups: Zone I was the central business district made up of commercial areas and factories with access to transportation; Zone II, the zone of transition, which was typically considered the oldest part of the city, continuously experienced the process of invasion, dominance, and succession. This "slum" area is characterized by dilapidated housing and is typically occupied by a transitioning immigrant population. Residents are poor and as a result cannot leave the area unless displaced by an ever-growing wave of incoming immigrants. Zone III is made up of those who were able to escape the poverty of Zone II; it is filled with single-family homes and apartments of modest size. Zone IV is a residential area of single-family homes and makes up the final zone within the city itself. Zone V, known as the commuter zone, is the suburban area beyond the city limits. Middle- and upper-class residents live outside of the city as they have the resources to commute to work (see Akers, Sellers, & Jennings, 2016; Bernard, Snipes, & Gerould, 2010; Lilly, Cullen, & Ball, 1995).

It was, however, the zone of transition in which Burgess and later sociologists would spend much of their focus. Due to a constant influx of immigrants, and an ever-changing population, the ecological pattern present in the zone of transition led to a destabilization of the area weakening family and communal ties resulting in the process of social disorganization. The imbalances present within these communities would lead others to study the area with regard to crime (Bursick & Grasmick, 1993; Kornhauser, 1978; Sampson & Groves, 1989; Shaw & McKay, 1942). Now, we know that the majority of you are familiar with the work of Park and Burgess and their academic descendants. Unquestionably, we can trace crime and delinquency to the inner city. As noted by Shaw and McKay (1942), delinquency rates are highest in areas immediately adjacent to the central business district and high concentrations of poverty and foreign-born and/or African American families. Even today, on the nightly news, we see these areas of social disorganization on display, their criminogenic nature projected creating fear throughout the community. But as noted, the cities of today are not as they once were.

Critics have long noted the inherent problems associated with the theory even though this simplistic cartographic explanation was never truly intended to describe life outside of fully developed cities (e.g., Chicago). Burgess's concentric zones were not applicable to cities outside of the United States; the failure to account for all forms of crime, and to acknowledge race, gender, and class issues were—and continue to be—major critiques of the model. It is the criticism of the failure to acknowledge power and its relationship to race and class that carries the most weight, in our eyes at least. Spatial distribution is anything but natural. Community and neighborhood development is intentional. Burgess did not anticipate the changing climate cities would experience with gentrification. The powerful often shape where people live and what benefits they can receive; retail is not wasted on the poor. Segregation of minorities and the poor is simply a historical truth. Crime and delinquency is a direct result of isolating the "dangerous classes" from the mainstream. Industrialization just made it easier to detect. For instance, Judith and Peter Blau (1982) found in their study on urban crime that violence was more prominent in areas where there was racial and economic inequality. Studies have repeatedly found that public housing is associated with residential instability, especially when developments are placed in poor neighborhoods (Bursick, 1989; McNulty & Holloway, 2000). But would you expect anything else? We know what happens when public housing efforts are proposed for middle- and upper-class neighborhoods. Even our most liberal friends start to balk at the notion of having "those people" move into their area. It never ceases to amaze us that many ivory tower ideas collapse under the pressure of reality.

The Zone of Transition as described by Burgess and his successors no longer exists. Gentrification has seen to that. Today, much of the inner city is lined with rows of overpriced, renovated apartments and newly built homes to meet the needs of the young metrosexual. The inner city is now developed around the idea of "live where you work" rather than "live where you can afford to live." Street crime, which has largely been associated with concentric zones and social disorganization theory, has, in theory, been priced out. Yet, it remains. Pockets of crime spring up on the fringes of these newly developed areas. Residents are shocked that criminal behavior is occurring within the area. Attempts are made to eliminate the problem: homeowner's associations impose restrictions to target undesirables, residents sign petitions to have the local homeless shelters removed from the area, and the local university oftentimes creates policies that makes those deemed as "other" unwelcome on campus property. Crime still remains. Much of this may be due to economic segregation created by gentrification efforts of the time. More problematic is that crime is no longer concentrated in the inner city. Pockets of criminality still exist within the downtown corridor; however, crimes historically only associated with the inner city have now come to suburbia. Gentrification, in essence, did not eradicate the behavior but only displaced it. Now, we realize that this is counterintuitive in relation to some of the recommendations made by Sampson and colleagues that supported dispersing public housing throughout the city rather than in poor neighborhoods. Logically that makes sense. Housing projects were found to be a miserable failure; however, few are anxious to square off against the real problem. The crimes that people most fear may not be acts of criminality but acts of desperation, acts that are a result of systemic poverty that has mauled generation after generation.

We are only too well aware that not all areas of the city are deeply riven by crime and delinquency, or at least the crime and delinquency that makes the nightly news. But why is this so? Research and sound criminological thinking (e.g., Bursick & Grasmick, 1993; Kornhauser, 1978; Sampson & Groves, 1989) indicates that strong networks of social relationships prevent, or at least reduce, conditions that give rise to crime and delinquency. Intuitively, we would assume that eliminating public housing from certain areas and dispersing it throughout the city would eliminate crime; however, that would require allowing low-income housing to be placed in high-traffic, economically desirable areas. Few residents are clamoring for these developments to be built in their area. Again, even some of our more liberal-minded friends would balk at the idea . . . and have. Might it also be possible that gentrification has not only displaced populations but also has eliminated the valuable social networks once prominent in lower socioeconomic and minority communities? Based upon Freudenberg's (1986) research on rural communities, we might say yes. It seems to be the case that displaced and transient communities often lack the informal controls typical of more settled, middle-class neighborhoods marked by home ownership and long-term dwelling. The transitions of populations do not allow for neighbors to get to know each other and to develop a sense of community. But step back for an instant. There is something there; there is a code. At least, there was. No longer is informal surveillance the albeit questionable force once present in many communities. It is often presumed that values don't exist within these high-crime areas, but that may simply be a reflection of cultural differences (e.g., Sellin, 1938; Sutherland, 1947). Left to their own devices without community supervision (e.g., churches), delinquency appears to be a likely option for youths. Thus, neighborhood and the relationships established in them matter.

If crime was simply a function of the deficiencies of individuals, finding a solution would be easier, or at least we might be able to isolate those who have criminal traits from the population. It is, however, myriad factors, both endogenous and exogenous, that contribute to crime, and as a result, we often find that there are no direct and obvious solutions. Displacement has created new problems for communities, criminal justice practitioners, and academics alike, as trying to isolate the social causes of crime is as likely as stumbling upon a unicorn. And it is here that we find the brilliance of Burgess and his successors in their formulation of social disorganization theory. While flawed, "the Chicago criminologists leveled a powerful challenge—backed by some convincing data—to explanations that saw crime as evidence of individual pathology. They argued cogently that where people grow up and with whom they associate cannot be overlooked in the search for the origins of crime" (Lilly, Cullen, & Ball, 1995, p. 49). We saw with these theorists a change in how crime was viewed. Social problems became more important than individual traits in explaining criminality. While traditional theories may no longer apply on the surface as society has changed, aren't the social problems that plagued us a century ago still manifest? Without understanding the reason for struggle, why it occurs, and individual responses to those factors, we may never understand the nature of crime.

The Chicago School brought our attention to suffering in relation to crime, and as we have said, it sought to understand that suffering with the tools it had available to it. Although they may have made strides, the nature of human suffering is both changing and nuanced. Perhaps the biggest mistake we might associate with the Chicago School was its end; had it continued, praxislike, to refine its understanding and apply its discoveries, the human world might well be a very different place.

Like the water in a river, human suffering is not where we last left it, even with the insight that it changes. It can stay unmoved like a rock in one's shoe for a time and then flit moment by moment like a malevolent butterfly. It becomes incumbent on us in our effort to understand it to recognize the perpetually changing and unpredictable nature of human pain.

The Struggle to Contain Delinquency

All of us at one point in our youth have heard our parents utter the phrase, "So, if all of your friends jumped off of a bridge, would you?" Most kids respond with a sullen "no," or at least they attempt to give a justification of how this does not apply to their situation. Of course, parents aren't really talking about doing literal harm, but the question is often in response to something that we once may have wanted to do that seemed ludicrous to them. 'Tis the nature of youth. We all have done or wanted to do something to which our parents did not agree, and as parents, we find ourselves repeating the same conversations with our own children. Being a teen was a struggle; most of us would never consider reliving their "glory days." Could you return to a life of overactive hormones, acne, awkwardness, and trauma of high school? Most of us, especially the authors, would never go back to that time period. And do you want to know why? We might not survive it the second time around. We, like many youths today, engaged in "dumb kid shit," or worse, deliberate acts of delinquency. It doesn't matter if you grow up in the suburbs or the "zone of transition," youths seem to always be looking for a place to belong, and that often involves behavior that may be deemed as deviant. And sometimes, adolescents do engage in delinquent activities, especially when delinquent peers are present and/or delinquent behavior is normalized.

Growing up in the projects, you are often characterized by your surroundings, sometimes for good reason, and sometimes not. People often look at you differently when they know where you are from. And if you ascribe to the teachings of Burgess and his descendants like Shaw and McKay, delinquent behavior would be attributed to the neighborhood in which you belong. But is that true? While evidence seems to indicate that crimes may be higher in some socially disorganized neighborhoods, can we stereotype every youth that grows up in "the hood" as delinquent? Obviously not. We know that there are "good kids" growing up in "bad neighborhoods"; many will never succumb to criminal behavior that surrounds them (Cullen & Agnew, 2003). The question then becomes, "How did they resist engaging in such behavior?" Walter Reckless attempted to answer this question.

Like social disorganization theorists, Reckless emerged from the Chicago School perspective on studying crime. His work *Vice in Chicago* (1933) emerged from his dissertation examining fraud, prostitution, and organized crime in Chicago's "vice" districts; however, it was his work on juvenile delinquency that would lead him to notoriety. Like so many of his era, Reckless shifted his focus to the study of juvenile delinquency. He cowrote *Juvenile Delinquency* (1932), which examined juvenile court dispositions and the characteristics, both physical and social, of these delinquents. He would not begin work on his seminal work, containment theory, until the mid-1950s. Drawing on the works of other social control theorists, Reckless argued that social control acts as a constraint against deviance, delinquency, and crime. Like most social control theorists, Reckless did not attempt to explain why crime occurs. Reckless was more interested in why crime does not occur than offering a theory on crime causation. According to Reckless, previous control theories had two major limitations: (1) previous theories had failed to operationalize their variables, and (2) previous theories had not been able to adequately determine which individuals would engage in delinquency as a number of biological, psychological, and social factors were responsible for delinquency.

And here we get to the idea of struggle. How is it that some people in the same community, the same family, and/or the same household react differently to struggle? For instance, how does one child end up as a drug addict, dependent of the state while another child obtains her doctorate in criminal justice? We, especially Tammy, are equally baffled at these outcomes considering the social community in which these two different siblings developed. Reckless argued that he knew the answer. Containment theory attempted to remedy the flaws of previous theories as it argued that individuals are subject to "pushes" and "pulls" that lead them to crime. These "pushes" and "pulls" toward delinquency were instrumental in understanding the motivations to commit crime. These pressures, or as Reckless would define them, pushes, "consist of adverse living conditions such as poverty, unemployment, economic insecurity, group conflicts, minority group status, lack of opportunities, [and] inequalities" (Reckless, 1967, 1972, p. 479). For example, exposure to violence would push an individual into engaging in delinquency and future violent behavior. Conversely, positive enticements toward crime or pulls "draw a person away from [their] original way of life and accepted forms of living. [They] consist of prestige individuals, bad companions, delinquency of criminal subculture, deviant groups, mass media, [and] propaganda" (Reckless, 1967, 1972, p. 480). Similar to other theories we have discussed (e.g., Sutherland, 1947), delinquent peer associations can pull individuals into a life of deviance.

Thus, individuals who are frequently exposed to delinquent behaviors, live in socially disorganized neighborhoods, and learn that deviance is an acceptable means of behavior will be more likely be pushed and/or pulled into crime. Well, not exactly. Reckless noted that only a small number of adolescents, regardless of exposure to pushes and pulls, become involved in delinquency. Reckless characterized these individuals as having weak inner and/or outer containments. That is, social control mechanisms are either not present or have been weakened to a point where they are ineffective. Similar to Reiss (1951) and Nye (1958), Reckless's containment theory is founded on the idea that internal and external controls prevented youth from engaging in delinquent behavior. External controls or outer containment include informal and formal regulations, supportive group relationships, and moral guidance. Internal controls or inner containment are characterized by factors such as self-concept, goal orientation, frustration tolerance, and norm retention (Lilly, Cullen, & Ball, 1995). "Internal containment involves the ability to withstand pressures and pulls, to handle conflicts, to divert oneself from exciting risks, and to stay out of trouble" (Reckless, 1967, 1972, p. 51). It is here where Reckless is able to explain why "good kids" can emerge from "bad neighborhoods." While pushes and pulls make delinquent behavior more likely, it does not guarantee that the behavior will occur. And, if proper social controls are present, it will not.

Outer and inner containments serve as a barrier to the pushes and pulls toward crime. Youths are "pushed" and "pulled" toward delinquency and without strong inner and/or outer containment, youths are more likely to engage in criminal activity. While outer containment is considered to be an important factor in preventing delinquency, Reckless argued that juveniles could still resist engaging in delinquency if outer containment was not present as inner containment, in itself, would be sufficient to ensure that a youth could resist temptation. All youths in socially disorganized neighborhoods are exposed to the "pushes" and "pulls" toward delinquency. Yet, still some juveniles refrain from engaging in criminal activity. Inner containment is thus considered the principal mechanism for social control; regardless of an individual's external environment, strong inner containment will prevent delinquency (Reckless, 1967, 1972). This "last line of defense" (Cullen & Agnew, 2003, p. 221) against criminality is indicative of the self.

A strong self-concept is, at least according to Reckless, the key factor in preventing delinquency. A positive self-concept has been found a vital component in the prevention of delinquency (Carrol, Houghton, Wood, Perkins, & Bower, 2007; Levy, 2001; Reckless, Dinitz, & Murray, 1956). Drawing from the work of Cooley (1902/1964) and his conceptualization of the "looking-glass self," Reckless (1967) constructed self-concept as a protective factor against delinquency. Adolescents with "insulated" self-concepts possess self-control and view themselves as law-abiding citizens; youths with favorable self-concepts were found to be less likely to come into contact with law enforcement and exhibit delinquent behavior (Reckless et al., 1956; Dinitz et al., 1962).

And this is what we love about containment theory. Imagine a world of self-reliant youths who believe in themselves. Reckless was adamant that containment theory could prevent juveniles from engaging in delinquency. Early identification of poor containment could be identified, and programs would thus be set up to protect at-risk youth. Whether intentional or not, containment theory appears to be the cornerstone for many of the nonprofit programs used to target our most vulnerable youth. From Headstart to the YMCA, organizations have promoted programs that focus on developing favorable self-concepts among our most at-risk adolescents. As most of us already know, at-risk youths often reside in socially disorganized neighborhoods characterized by structural disadvantage where academic and institutional resources are limited thereby exposing them to negative outcomes such as delinquency (Ford & Browning, 2011). These programs promote the belief that these youths can be successful, academically and personally, if positive self-concepts are developed. Ensuring success among our most at-risk populations is often daunting. But it is the willingness to try that must command respect. And it is here where Reckless, not the programs implementing many of his theoretical concepts, fails.

Let's return to this notion of self-concept and family. The research of Reckless and his colleagues and descendants suggested that parents were the most influential sources of favorable self-concepts (Lilly et al., 1995, p. 87). And this makes sense. Our parents in our formative years unquestionably have the most influence on who we believe we are. But just as Reckless begins to test his theory, the testing stops; at least, it stops outside of testing beyond the idea of favorable self-concepts. We know that there are a number of programs out there focusing on establishing a positive self-concept, but if parents are the most influential source, can any program compensate for bad parenting and the development of negative self-concepts? Reckless is not the only control theorist to fall prey to the failure to acknowledge that bad parenting can have a significant impact on juvenile delinquency. Just think about Hirschi and his attachment to criminal parents. Strong bonds don't necessarily prevent delinquency in these instances. As much of the extant literature has noted (see Cullen & Agnew, 2003), "self-concept as an insulator" was the only proposition of the theory to be tested. Yes, we know that there was support for this part of the theory, but Reckless ignored much of the other propositions. Perhaps the propositions were too difficult to measure, but wasn't that the critique that Reckless had applied to other theories? It is easy to criticize. Creation is much more difficult.

But like us, we don't feel as if Reckless was being condescending. He really wanted to know why many youths exposed to the worst of possibilities can disassociate from the chaotic world around them. It was not simply a handful of youths, but the majority who were able to find self-worth and escape the pitfalls of a socially disorganized world. In the face of struggle, they were able to succeed. Now, containment theory remains problematic as one cannot tell where outer containment begins and inner containment ends, and yes, it may be tautological in nature. It does, however, give us hope that in the struggle of life, one can succeed, or at least refrain from engaging in delinquency even if the deck has been stacked against our youth. Perhaps this is idealistic and a bit naïve, but we recommend reading Geis's account (Geis & Dodge, 2002) of working with Dinitz (and Reckless) on the research of containment theory to see that even the best of us may cling to subjective ideas even if the research is not supported. Intention really does matter.

Struggling to Cope: Agnew and General Strain Theory

Romantic love is fickle. One minute you have butterflies swirling in your stomach, and the next you are crying, drowning your sorrows in a vodka tonic. While this book is about love, sometimes finding and maintaining love, at least the romantic variety, is a difficult task. Let's revisit the story of Theseus and Ariadne. Although we would like to believe that love conquers all, and that the mythical heroes lived happily ever after, we are more apt to accept the version of the story in which the relationship did not last; most accounts have Theseus abandoning Ariadne on the island of Naxos. Ariadne was willing to give up everything for true love; Theseus was not.

Even though he promised marriage, his intentions were not honest as he was a selfish man. Ariadne, being true of heart, sacrificed her family for the idea of love, yet it was not reciprocated by the man whose life she had saved. Most of us can empathize with Ariadne's heartbreak: left alone in her bed, on the island, betrayed by the man she loved, as we too have in some form or another experienced the sorrow of losing the one we love. Unrequited love can be dangerous as it may turn to hate out of the anger experienced by loss. As expressed in anger by Ariadne, "So you left me—you traitor! Me, taken from my family altars—You traitor! On a deserted beach! Thesesus!" (Cantullus, 1997). Anger, despair, hopelessness, and regret are only a few symptoms of the suffering created by the loss of a romantic partner; for some, it is one of the most painful events that will affect one's life. Ariadne was no different; she wanted nothing short of revenge. Some versions of the story have Ariadne ending her own life as a result of being abandoned while others have her being saved by the god Dionysus, with whom she would be joined in marriage. In one story, she crumbles from the loss while in others, she rises above her struggles only to become transformed to a higher being. For us mortals, some of us are able to come to terms with this suffering while others are not. One person will move on to the next relationship, while another may engage in self-destructive behaviors doing anything (e.g. drug and alcohol abuse) to ease the pain even if it means eventually taking one's own life. Even though many of us feel the same emotions from loss, why is it that individuals cope differently with the struggles (and strain) of life?

Drawing on the work of Merton (1938), Robert Agnew (1992) proposed an individual explanation of strain, general strain theory, that emphasized the negative relationships with others. Strain, as noted by Agnew (1992), is a result of "relationships in which others are not treating the individual as he or she would like to be treated" (p. 48). It is, thus, a result of factors outside our control, those relationships that cause us strain that are often responsible for crime and delinquency. According to Agnew (2001), general strain theory holds that "strains or stressors increase the likelihood of negative emotions like anger and frustration" (p. 319). In an attempt to correct these negative emotions, offended parties react and sometimes crime is the result. Though Agnew (1992) relies upon the work of his predecessors, he argues that Merton and subsequent strain theorists fail to acknowledge the natural limitations inherent in their conceptualization that strain simply occurs as a result of the failure to achieve positively valued goals. Status frustration and failure to achieve monetary success are only two ways that strain occurs. Agnew expands on traditional strain theory to include strain as not only the result of failing to achieve positively valued goals but loss and other negative experiences. According to Agnew (1992), strain may occur as the following: the actual or anticipated failure to achieve positively valued goals, "the actual or anticipated removal of positively valued stimuli from individuals," or "the actual or anticipated presentation of negative or noxious stimuli" (pp. 57–58). While the failure to achieve one's goals is unquestionably a stressful event, we cannot discount the strain from loss. The loss of a romantic partner or death of a loved one may be unbearable for some. While Ariadne, at least we hope, went on to find another love, this is not always the case for others. Take for instance the story of Medea. When she is cast aside by Jason (of the Argonauts) for another, she falls into a fit of rage, seeks revenge against her transgressors, and eventually kills them along with her own children. Almost everyone can relate in some way to this loss of a loved one regardless of whether it is through heartbreak or death. Love hurts and the struggle to cope is real.

While loss is often unbearable, Agnew would argue, and we would agree, that the presence of negative or noxious stimuli cannot be discounted as a source of strain. Domestic violence, bullying, and workplace harassment are all examples of the presence of noxious stimuli. Trauma is a precarious phenomenon. One only has to examine the literature on ACE scores, which we will discuss later, to see how trauma affects individuals in their struggle to survive. While we try to quantify the outcome of traumatic events, the effects of experiencing such harmful events may be immeasurable, and disconcertingly, we may never know how an individual will respond to the presence of noxious stimuli. Human nature is funny like that. For instance, children raised in houses where domestic violence in present may go on to live healthy, productive lives; however, the literature has noted the link between childhood exposure to intimate partner violence and offending later in life (Hamby et al., 2011; Murrell et al., 2005). The same goes for bullying. Being a victim of bullying does not guarantee that one will engage in suicidal or homicidal ideation; however, there are notable cases in which exposure to bullying played a part in horrific outcomes. For instance, Phoebe Prince, Tyler Clementi, and Kenneth Weishuhn all committed suicide as a direct result of bullying and/or cyberbullying. Others, however, react in a more externalized manner to remove the noxious stimuli. Take for instance one of the Columbine shooters, Eric Harris. Early reports after the event indicated that Harris had been a victim of bullying. What we know is that Harris was a disturbed individual suffering from mental health issues, but the extent that bullying played a part in the massacre has been questioned. Critics often argue that Harris and his friends would engage in bullying themselves, so how could they be considered victims of bullying? What we know from the literature is that victims are often bullies as well (see Haynie et al., 2001). These bully/victims are often more likely to engage in aggressive and externalizing behaviors as well as experience depressive, acceptance, and self-worth symptoms (Austin & Joseph, 1996; Kumpulainen et al., 1998; Haynie et al., 2001). General strain theory would argue their inability to cope positively with noxious stimuli often creates a negative reaction to the strain, which may lead to criminal behavior. Thus, internal and external violence is something to be expected, especially for those struggling to cope.

General strain theory may be able to identify strain, but what it cannot do is predict how those affected may react. Free will gets in the way of the quantifiable especially when strain and emotionality are mixed into the recipe. This failure to be able to predict exactly how people will react is not necessarily a criticism of Agnew but is simply stating the limitations of human insight into ourselves. Most of the time, individuals do not even know how they will respond in stressful situations until they occur. The struggle to survive after a strainful event is all too real, and for some, too much to bear. But Agnew does try to address this as best he can. The theory can, however, be criticized on its broadness as everyone is exposed to strain in some form. At what point can we attribute strain to criminality? This is the great unknown and where general strain theory falters. Yes, general strain theory has stood up to numerical empirical testing and received tremendous support (Agnew, 2001; 2006; 2013; 2016; Agnew et al. 1996; Agnew & White, 1992), but it still cannot predict who will offend and who will not in times of struggle.

What is novel regarding Agnew's theory is not only that it takes into consideration new forms of strain, but that the theory also maintains that anticipated negative relationships may cause as much stress as the actual event. As illustrated in Frank Herbert's 1965 novel, *Dune*, fear may really be the mind-killer. We get so worked up in what may be that we actually forget what is. It is in this that we are reminded of the (fake) Buddha quote, "The past is already gone, the future is not yet here. There's only one moment for you to live and that is the present moment." Now, this does not mean that the past does not shape our lives, and the look to the future does not have an effect on our actions, but that the anticipation based on our past experiences may result in strain. The struggle to overcome what has happened or what may be is often overwhelming. Strain, as noted, does not illicit the same emotional response from everyone. Agnew (2001) argues that the same event (or anticipated event) may occur in two individual's lives, but this does not guarantee that these two people will evaluate an event in the same manner. While both may be affected negatively, their reaction to their experience may vary.

Take for instance the tales of Ariadne and Medea. Both were betrayed by men for whom they had sacrificed everything. While both wanted revenge, Medea chose a more lethal alternative. While many have argued that female responses to strain are often internalized, Agnew's original vision found that strain and the responses, including crime, are "largely a function of the characteristics of the individuals experiencing the strain. In particular, strain is most likely to lead to crime when individuals lack the skills and resources to cope with their strain in a legitimate manner, are low in conventional social support, are low in social control, blame their strain on others, and are disposed to crime" (2001, p. 323).

Most of us are faced with strain whether it be failing an exam, not being promoted or tenured, being bullied, or, similar to Ariadne and Medea, being betrayed by the one you love. Yet most of us do not engage in crime. Life is about struggle, but it is, in essence, about how we choose to react to this struggle, at least for Agnew and his supporters, that ultimately makes a difference. There are days that we, Tammy in particular, want to choke the living daylights out of those with whom we interact. It is often a struggle not to do so. Somedays it seems as if this optimistic scholar is possessed by the ghost of Medea looking to get revenge on everyone. So why does she smile and go about her own business? This is where Agnew ends, and a new theory must begin. We all know what deterrence theorists would say, but is there more to overcoming the strains of life than fear of punishment? Of course, sometimes access to a mental health professional is a good start. While we jest, it is here that we must look beyond individual struggle as each life touches on another. Strain will always be present in life as humans have an inexplicable tendency to create their own "hell on Earth." While some will be able to cope, at times, using positive behaviors, others will not. Struggle is inevitable, but it is at that point when strain is overwhelming with which we should truly be concerned. Where do we go when we cannot cope, cannot find meaning, and how does the system react to us when we falter especially when many of our most at risk have no access to mental health professionals? The struggle to find a simple solution is daunting indeed.

Al and the Boys

Albert Cohen begins his seminal work (1955) with a similar and vexing problem. Specifically, he contemplates the collision of Mrs. Jones and her beloved Johnny. Johnny, in contemporary parlance, is acting out, showing his ass. He isn't a bad kid, really; he grew up in a "normal" home. He isn't defective or dense or deranged, but he is spending time with bad kids and doing bad things: he smokes in the boys' room, he hangs out with the toughs on the corner, and he talks back to his mom. There is something of a clash of norms at center stage for Cohen. But remember that he is only echoing a burning question that sits on a million dinner tables in million homes. He reflects the fear too appalling to which to give voice, carried in the *sanctum sanctorum* of every mother's heart: what if our dear boy becomes delinquent? How can

I arrest his icy slide into a living tomb? Even a mother's arms cannot reach inside a prison cell.

There is in Cohen an unmistakable grandeur, a certain assuredness akin to that of the learned and confident physician who knows in a moment just what is wrong and just how to remedy it. And his assurances seem to be as much about the capacity of contemporary sociology, including its epistemic sidecar, as about relieving the worrisome mother or anxious dad. He feels the certainty of his method in the strength of his limbs, and it is part of his medicine. Looking around the kitchen, he even draws examples from their common surrounds: "For example, when we explain to a child why the rubber safety valve on a pressure cooker pops off when the interior of the cooker reaches a certain critical temperature, we first tell him that there are certain well-established relationships between pressure and temperature . . . and then we show him that the behavior of the valve is exactly what we should expect if the rules . . . were true" (Cohen, 1955, pp. 49–50). There is also an evident and marked gentleness in his tone; he seems intent on cooling the fears that indirectly gave rise to his meditations; he is a sage physician with a steady bearing, sure hand, and velvet bedside manner. That his medicine is incipient, that his assurances were hollow, is no fault of his own.

> Our really hard problems are those for which we have no ready-at-hand solutions which will not leave us without tension, frustration, resentment, guilt, bitterness, anxiety or hopelessness. These feelings and therefore the inadequacy of the solutions are largely the result of a frame of reference through which we contemplate these solutions. It follows that an effective, really satisfying solution must entail some change in that frame of reference itself. The actor may give up pursuit of some goal which seems unattainable, but it is not a "solution" unless he can first persuade himself that the goal is not worth pursuing; in short, his values must change. (Cohen, 1955, p. 54)

After all, to whom is he speaking here? It might seem he is offering his medicine to a worrisome mom or providing crucial theoretical details to a colleague. He might just as easily be speaking to an attentive juvenile delinquent, offering some sense of clarity as to why he is showing his ass. Maybe he speaks to us all.

That damned iPad. Michael's folks bought his and Beth's daughter one for Christmas several years ago, and the cursed thing refuses to die. When she got the device, her aspiration was to become an entomologist. Now she wants to be a YouTuber. Sure, she will be able to care for her aging old man in style if she chooses the latter and gets millions of views, but he would be lying if her change in dreams did not grieve him a little. Cohen makes the point that in a democracy like the United States, the "status universe" of the average middle-class kid is far wider than it would have been in a more primitive feudal society; although kids live better now than before, they may not feel the difference, as their comparison schema is somewhat off kilter. More than a half-century later, technology has made the status universe of the American kiddo even weirder. Almost automatically and almost feebly he defends the democratic idea of character and achievements being the means whereby we would seek to measure a person, but recognizes the existence of "competing standards for judgment" (Cohen, 1955, p. 84) as well, like the Protestant work ethic.

The plot thickens. Cohen spends considerable effort in comparing the values of the middle class to those of the working class. The former, for example, contains what he calls the "ethic of individual responsibility" whereas the latter has an "ethic of reciprocity" (Cohen, 1955, p. 96). The individual responsibility ethic asserts that it is incumbent upon each member of society to earn through work his own supply of goods, to achieve what Cohen graphically calls "congealed labor" (Cohen, 1955, p. 93). In contrast, the ethic of reciprocity is the result of a community living in an environment of scarcity; when one member needs, say, a meal, it is provided by the wider community. Now it turns out, Cohen argues, that American and indeed Western society is founded on middle-class norms and assumptions; those who have internalized those norms and operate from those assumptions tend to be more culturally fluent. Those who operate from the working-class subculture (he emphasizes that the working-class subculture is far from monolithic) will have a harder time reaping the benefits of a society that in the main values middle-class ideals. "The ability to conform to these norms and therefore to achieve status in these terms does not depend on a simple effort of will" (Cohen, 1955, p. 94). The middle-class culture thus functions both as measuring rod and ramrod, forcing itself against those for whom it arguably should not apply. "It is a plausible assumption, then, that the working class boy whose status is low in middle-class terms *cares* about that status that this status confronts him with a genuine problem of adjustment" (Cohen, 1955, p. 128, emphasis in original).

Corner kids, then, are faced with a struggle that authors something of an existential choice, one with which college kids simply don't have to grapple. Regarding this struggle, corner kids have two basic choices, Cohen tells us. They can choose either to brave the unknown college-kid landscape, be culturally illiterate in unfamiliar country while alienating those they leave behind, or to stay home, embrace the corner as it were, and participate in aspirations they can more plausibly achieve. It is for them a struggle they did not create, one they did not seek. All the corner boy really can be sure to possess is his choice; in this choice, though, the corner boy who chooses the corner has not so much chosen to avoid a struggle as much as chosen a side.

The kindly physician enters the examination room: "Well, I have good news and I have bad news." It turns out that your fretting over Johnny's truancy, rabble-rousing, and tomfoolery is pointless, as his behavior is fully functional and natural. The bad news, ma'am, is that his delinquency is in response to joistlike, load-bearing components of our culture. One almost hears Pete Townshend lamenting the drug-induced stupor of the Isle of Wight and Woodstock throngs: "Don't raise your eye / It's only teenage wasteland" (Townshend, 1971). In truest Cohen-esque style, Townshend's audience did not take his meaning and instead claimed "Baba O'Reily" as a celebration of teen rebellion, the obverse of what was intended (Scapelliti, 2009).

The struggle continues, as again little Johnny has merely chosen a side. He has chosen to lose, though he has no awareness of this. The oppositional nature of the corner culture only reinforces the very hegemony at which he kicks his heels. Cohen also contemplates the real possibility of reaction formation within individual corner boys, rendering in miniature the struggle being played out on a cultural stage, a struggle with a foregone conclusion. The middle class in Cohen's analysis wins before the game begins. They even have their media game tight (e.g., Cohen, 1955, pp. 124–25).

In the end, though, Cohen comes up short of making the final crucial connection; in the end, though he implicates aspects of middle-class culture as criminogenic, he never commits to the *critique* to which his reasoning has led him. He gestures limply to the changing of middle-class anatomy and ideology, but demurs, "*If* these things are possible, we must then ask: What price are we willing to pay for this or that change?" (Cohen, 1955, p. 177, emphasis in original). After his diagnosis, the able physician seems almost to become senile as you look on, mumbling something unintelligible about the death of a salesman. Raising his eyes, he asks, "Are you *sure* you want this ingrown toenail fixed?"

Messner and Rosenfeld: And the Crowd Goes Mild!

Others are not so abashed about completing the line of reasoning Cohen begins with such majesty. Though much of the reasoning would be familiar already to fans of Merton, Messner and Rosenfeld (1997) offer cogent critique where Cohen failed to do so. Where Cohen gestured meekly to American culture's criminogenic components, Messner and Rosenfeld laid the blame squarely at the doorstep of the American Dream. Cohen illustrated the hypocritical struggle between how Americans think they want American culture to function and how it often actually does; Americans like to think in terms of a fair racetrack, but conveniently forget about the inside lane as well as those who begin the marathon thirty feet from the finish line. Yes, this is a struggle to which Cohen turns our attention, but he almost seems to apologize in doing so, his noted gentleness lulling the patient into a false sense of security. Messner and Rosenfeld, however, offer no apologies. They will not be misunderstood: "The thesis of this book is that the American Dream itself and the normal social conditions engendered by it are deeply implicated in the problem of crime" (Messner & Rosenfeld, 1997, p. 6). They, like Cohen, end their analysis somewhat anemically, failing to offer little more than some good but overbroad ideas regarding how to reduce crime, given their analysis, but we will enlarge on that shortly. For now, let us revel in the clarity of their forceful critique.

Even for Messner and Rosenfeld, Merton said it best: "In the words of sociologist Robert K. Merton, 'a cardinal American virtue, "ambition," promotes a cardinal American vice, 'deviant behavior'" (Messner & Rosenfeld, 1997, p. 7). They indicate that critiques leveled against Merton's anomie are cogent, and then endeavor to refine the idea for use in contemporary America. It is fair to observe, of course, that Merton's initial writing about anomie and the modes of adaptation uses as its first and clearest example American culture (Merton, 1938). The clash of claims Messner and Rosenfeld trace are different in detail but quite similar to the clash of claims offered initially by Merton. What they add is some sense of whose oak tree to adorn with toilet paper: "Furthermore, we argue that the anomic pressures inherent in the American Dream are nourished and sustained by a distinctive institutional balance of power dominated by the economy. The interplay between the core cultural commitments of the American Dream and its companion institutional balance of power results in widespread anomic, weak social controls, and ultimately, high levels of crime" (Messner & Rosenfeld, 1997, p. 61). That means that certain ideals (to wit, the American Dream), coupled with certain institutional power relations create a weakening of other ideas and power relations, leading to a weakening of exogenous controls, further leading to an increase in crime. A toxic idea set, then, coupled with institutions that give that idea set space and leverage to operate, erode exogenous controls against criminality. Logically, modifying or abandoning the idea set, or modifying or obliterating the institutional arrangements that give the ideas play, will curtail the weathering of exogenous constraints on crime.

In the classic American marketplace setting, competing institutions vie for market share. Competition is the cauldron of truth, the market is the field of tilting where the mighty always emerge victorious. Importantly, this collision of capacities also generates a loser. For the capitalist losing is an indication of inferiority, of incapacity, of incompetence. The loser has been adjudicated by the marketplace and found to be wanting. The struggle to achieve a market share is presumed to be a fair one, of course, but as Cohen has reminded us only too gently, often that presumption does not serve. The American Dream and its value set encourage a by-any-means-necessary (Messner & Rosenfeld, 1997, p. 17) approach to commerce, and indeed to the navigation of American culture more generally. Here again is an iteration of the struggle, familiar to Cohen and Merton, and even Marx: the ostensible benefits of competition are tilled under in a free market, precisely because its members do not seek a truly free market. Capitalism encourages market players to garner for themselves every advantage, to make the race as unfair as possible. It is assumed that truth comes from the collision of equal forces, just as it is in an American adversarial courtroom. As influential as it has been on the American sense of ordered liberty, this assumption is, of course, ridiculous on its face. But even granting the most charitable reading of facts, the basic premise of free market capitalism (and the adversarial courtroom) is almost never reality.

There is also a commodification process whereby invaluable things are forced into a marketable shape and made sellable. Messner and Rosenfeld rightly (but very briefly) bemoan the commodification of education. Today, of course, only a decade later, the commodification of education has reached sickening levels. Private for-profit colleges force students into deep debt that simply cannot be repaid on the strength of the degrees they offer. By free market logic, places like the University of Phoenix and Miller-Motte College would have been shuttered long ago as they offer a far inferior product at a far higher cost. The use of tax vouchers for private schools is yet another form of commodification of the uncommodifiable. Another is the college credit system itself. Ostensibly, employers crave creative and competent workers, yet they do not trust higher education merely to certify individuals when they are truly ready to face difficult challenges. Calls for graduate competence are answered by policy efforts that are *directly* oppositional, and even active hindrances, to the sought goal: a deepening of structured curricula and deepened accountability schema. As we have done in our prisons, we give the sick patient a broken leg or another debilitating disease. In education and in justice, we still prescribe leeches.

Thus we are left with another kind of struggle, something of a layered affair: Americans want to believe in the nobility of their values, and that they live according to them, when in fact not only are the ideas of a free market and an adversarial courtroom horrible ideas at the outset, but Americans make little effort to live by even these flawed values. Messner and Rosenfeld make the point that this hypocrisy is illustrated by both Merton and Marx, but for those who succeed, for those who do earn wealth and power, there is little impetus to change practices. Indeed, these toxic ideas, like the Protestant work ethic, give ample defilade to the privileged from claims of unfairness and calls for wealth redistribution. Neither Cohen nor Messner and Rosenfeld discuss the idea of providence. God's favor is shown in the form of wealth to those who work hard. If one has come upon wealth, it is God's will that this be so as a reward for living according to God's design. Such an idea is a species of violence, as it guarantees yet another struggle: in a debt-based economy like the current American economy, by definition there is never enough money to "pay" all the "debts" that exist. That means that there is never going to be enough money in circulation for everyone to have a reasonable crack at a defensibly provisioned life. Saving money beyond a threshold virtually assures that someone else will not have enough money. On the scale on which we are discussing, of course, a few thousand in a bank account does not offend, but when corporations horde tens of billions of dollars, it is a virtual certainty a nontrivial segment of the American populace will miss dinner. We are hypocrites, using wacky, Calvinist logic to justify our abject failure to care for those who suffer.

Of the four moving parts in Messner and Rosenfeld's model (idea, institutions, exogenous controls, and crime), clearly their reasoning guides attention to the first two: revise the American Dream and modify the institutions that amplify its influence. Here, again, we could find yet another struggle, related in part to the one just above. Treasured ideas like those that comprise the American Dream do not always go quietly onto the Heap of Really Bad Ideas, and boilerplate institutions of American culture are unlikely to be loosened easily, like the armor of a battleship's turret. For Messner and Rosenfeld, some of the epoxy should be weakened by the simple realization that these ideas and these institutions are themselves criminogenic: ". . . the logical solution is social reorganization. This will entail, in our view, both institutional reform and cultural regeneration" (Messner & Rosenfeld, 1997, p. 88). It is perhaps the greatest misfortune of this work that although they identify correctly key criminogenic forces, in the end, the treatment plan offered by these physicians is rather less than robust. Policies and social changes should be wrought, they tell us, that will "vitalize families, schools and the political system" (Messner & Rosenfeld, 1997, p. 97) in order to redistribute power from the realm of economic interests into other realms of society. Such a revitalization will dilute the influence of the American Dream idea set. Worker protection, family leave, flexible schedules, child care, and unnamed services like meaningful health care, whistleblower protection, equal employment opportunities, and the like are emphasized. Oddly, they emphasize free market logic regarding schools; as we have already mentioned, were that logic sound, universities that emphasize student actualization and faculty teacher/scholar models would outperform even Ivy League institutions. In the end, their analyses of the problem conclude with a discussion of solutions that are bland even from the most generous reading. The physicians have a proper diagnosis: you have early stage lung cancer. The treatment? "Don't smoke so much."

It is likely that traditionalists would view Messner and Rosenfeld's conclusions with a jaundiced eye; the indictments they hand down are for treasured ideas and institutions. The radical reader is also equally dissatisfied, but for the opposite reason: Messner and Rosenfeld failed to go anywhere close to far enough with their conclusions. Actually, both critiques are spot on. Indeed, there are ideas and institutions that are going to require vast overhaul, even rebuilding from the keel up, but the Milquetoast approach to reform offered by Messner and Rosenfeld is likely to be considerably worse than maintaining a status quo or reducing existing institutions to rubble and smoke. The struggles that would result would be from all sides, rather than one or two, and the fruits of that struggle would be scarcely different from the current state of dysfunction.

Speaking of dysfunction, though, the idea that we might simply re-author the Dream held not only by Americans, but by most members of Western culture, increasingly to include China, may be, well, daft. Although in our criminological musings we should be attuned to the struggle of the Other, Hall (2012) rouses us from our beautiful daydream: "In the hurly burly of everyday life in the ubiquitous capitalist marketplace, where, should important things not get done, the individual, or indeed the whole nation can fall through a hole in the bottom into relative poverty and insignificance, strict deontological and empathetic ambitions regularly collapse into evasive and compromised felicific calculations" (Hall, 2012, p. 12). That we have fallen into felicific mumbling before and failed to realize the musings of our better angels does not mean that we should give up being guided by them. Further, we have done well in learning from our failings, and have built a sound sense of what is practically needed to manufacture loving institutions.

Cultural Criminology

It's Tuesday morning and Tammy is halfheartedly grading this semester's assignments. The television is playing in the background when she peers around the corner of her laptop to view the day's story on *Megyn Kelly Today*. Normally, she would pay this type of programming no mind, but today on *Today* (pun intended), the program catches her attention: Black female police chiefs. Sounds like an oxymoron, doesn't it? At best, this is an outlier, as the mainstream conceptualization of what a police officer, especially a police chief, should be neither Black nor female. Conventional depictions overwhelmingly portray men as being police officers, and even more so when these portrayals are of police chiefs. And for good reason . . . statistics indicate that whereas women account for approximately half of the general population, they only make up about 13 percent of police officers. Additionally, while African Americans account for approximately 20 percent of police officers within urban areas, the rates are much lower throughout the rest of the country (Gabiddon & Greene, 2013). When you factor gender into the equation, African American women make up less than 5 percent of police officers. While this may be proportionate to a population (see Gaines & Kappeler, 2005), female officers, in North Carolina at least, are seemingly beating the odds and breaking the glass ceiling as six African American women have been appointed to head their respective police departments. But this really isn't the point of the story.

Under the traditionally constructed criminal justice mantle, we as a society seem to have a dichotomous view of policing: male or female, white or nonwhite, just or unjust . . . you get the picture. The majority of us are aware of the lack of diversity in policing and understand that policing is primarily performed by white males who more often than not embrace an outdated identity of us versus them in which they stand as the last defense against chaos . . . the thin blue line. But who and what are they protecting? Wouldn't it be more apt if they saw themselves part of the collective rather than being outside of it? And, it is the dichotomy that creates many of the issues present in our criminal justice system, today. Human nature is not simply black and white, literally and figuratively.

The public servant role versus the social control role distinction for law enforcement has rarely functioned clearly. We may condemn those within the system for their dichotomous construction, but isn't everyone just as guilty? Even among criminologists and the authors of this book, the role that police play in our society can be debated. Much like who should be employed as a police officer, the image of what police officers do, whom they serve, and their origins are often bifurcated if not multivalent. Among members of the criminological community, we disagree regarding the true origins of American policing. Did American policing emerge from the professional traditions of Robert Peel, or is it simply an extension of the slave patrols that emerged during the founding of our country? Is it both? What we can say for certain is that how we identify police origins often impacts how we view the police. Choosing a middle ground is not an option for most. As we examine human ideologies, similar to that of *The Matrix* (1999), most consumers would argue that they have taken the "red pill" and that their constructions of reality are based in knowledge and truth, even if that construction is a painful one. But how do we really know? What if you really took the "blue pill," and your argument while you find it quite logical is based on the illusion of truth? Of course, you would never be wrong, but isn't that the beauty of the Matrix; we don't know whether our reality is truth or simply the illusion of it. We often assume that our viewpoints are based on truth, fact, and science, but in reality, much of this is largely shaped by our interpretation of the world around us. Media and popular culture portrayals or the cultural norms in which we were raised or which we currently embrace often influence what we believe, and our perceptions of crime and the criminal justice system is no different.

Images of crime and crime control agents are omnipresent. As criminologists, we are aware of the constructions of crime in popular culture mediums. It is funny, however, that no matter how much we protest the false constructs presented in these depictions of crime and criminal justice agencies, we are still apt to support these images. Crime-related images on the nightly news, primetime television, and in the morning paper, or in this day and age, our designated media app, seem to consume our lives. Many of us find ourselves glued to the television daily, watching reruns of our favorite primetime crime drama while recorded episodes of our current favorites sit unwatched on our DVR. Or worse, we get fixated on the media loops that perpetuate pseudo-images of reality. Somehow we get sucked into watching and re-watching these constructed images of crime. And for good reason . . . Neilson ratings during the 2013–2014 season reported that half of the top ten primetime television shows were crime dramas. These crime dramas included shows such as *NCIS*, *NCIS: Los Angeles*, *Blacklist*, *Person of Interest*, and *Bluebloods*. Other primetime crime dramas including *Criminal Minds*, *Castle*, *Crime Scene Investigation (CSI)*, *Elementary*, and *Hawaii Five-O* have ranked in the top twenty-five primetime programing (Garland, Blackburn, Browne, & Ammons, 2017). While we are aware that this is fiction, sometimes, it is a struggle to separate fact from the imaginary world. More disconcerting is determining how to establish what is real. We would argue *science* of course! But we must admit that most of those whom we encounter are not concerned with science, statistics, or objective analysis; they are concerned with crime and its sanguine and seemingly ubiquitous nature. Even the most educated will watch the news and based on their ideas of crime will automatically deem a person guilty regardless of the evidence. But why? Although crime has been steadily decreasing for the last thirty years, the perception that crime is on the rise is the reality . . . even members of our own families seem to argue the fact. How many of you working in the field have found yourselves engaged in argument about the criminal justice system only to be informed that your knowledge of the system is biased? It is frustrating at minimum. And it seems that in this world where fake news is accepted and political rhetoric can rely on embellished ideology, the social construction of crime and the criminal justice system becomes more like a Quentin Tarantino film than a PBS documentary. This isn't more apparent than in relation to perceptions on policing.

One would think that these constructed images would be clear as to who is considered to be the good guy; doesn't the hero always wear a white hat just like Roy Rogers in old western films while his nemesis is clad in black? Like reality, popular culture has a way of dichotomizing characters into either the protagonist or the antagonist. And, at least in the movies, the good guys always wear white or, if you are a true believer, blue. But in reality, identifying the hero is not so easy (e.g., DeValve, 2017c). Shouldn't those representing criminal justice agencies be identified as being the protagonist? Of course, but this is not always the case. If only it were that easy to tell the good guys from the bad, all of us criminologists and criminal justice practitioners just might be out of a job. Sadly, sometimes, the villain wears blue.

Media images of policing are anything but straightforward. From the nightly news to reality crime programming, we are bombarded with images that support a bifurcated image of what policing is meant to be. As noted by Ferrell and Sanders (1995), "With their mix of street footage, theatrical staging, and patrol-car sermonizing, reality crime programs . . . generate conventional, though at times contradictory, images of crime and policing" (408). While he is referencing reality crime television, images of policing regardless of what medium we choose often create this same sense of paradoxical imaging. One cannot watch the nightly news without seeing images of a semi-schizophrenic system in which law enforcement officers are portrayed in some of the most extreme circumstances. In one moment, officers are portrayed as the hero carrying citizens out of burning buildings (e.g., 9/11 terrorist attacks) or across flooded streets (e.g., Houston hurricane victims); they are often depicted as willing to sacrifice their own lives to save those they have sworn to protect. Yet in another moment, police are seen violating the civil rights of individuals and engaging in deadly force (e.g., Michael Brown, Tamir Rice, Walter Scott). So, how is it that policing can be both heroic and unjust? The simple answer is that this is reality, but this disjunctive reality doesn't sit well with most of the population. What we often perceive people, organizations, and ideas to be does not always align with our reality; police deviance is real. Just because an individual puts on the uniform and carries the perceived mantle of justice doesn't necessarily mean that the individual is just. It means that he is human, and humans are often flawed, immersed in their own biases, and capable of violating the same laws that they have sworn to uphold. Now, this is in no way an attack on police officers in general as many would lay down their lives to protect our own, but there is no denying that there are corrupt officers, and the subculture of policing creates a veil in which those engaging in criminal activity are not only protected but have their behaviors justified. And the research has supported this. From theft and extortion to sexual violence against women and murder, studies have shown that police officers not only engage in criminal activity, but are protected by a system that is supposed to safeguard them from consequences (Kraska & Kappeler, 1995; Kappeler, Sluder, & Alpert, 1998).

The failure to acknowledge police corruption and individual rights violations has led the public, especially minority populations, to view policing as an institution as not only corrupt but a means to (re)enslave populations. And popular culture mediums have reinforced this paradigm shift. For instance, forty years ago, police corruption and brutality was being explored in films such as *Serpico* (1973). It was the classic good-cop-versus-bad-cop film in which police officers may have been criminal, but a single officer was able to stand against a corrupt system and ensure justice was met. Even Dirty Harry doesn't believe that there is a line that police cannot cross, and he was willing to cross it. Thus, the institution of policing, at least on the big screen, maintained the perception of justice . . . well, sometimes the acceptability of vigilantism in the name of justice. In the past, one simply had to tune into classic films such as *Magnum Force, Copland, Training Day*, and the cult classic *L.A. Confidential* to realize that while all police officers may not be the hero, there is always one who will stand up to the corruption of many. Now we know that Hollywood does not equate to reality, but in the movies, things may have changed within the last decade . . . well, maybe just our perception. Regardless of how many officers are willing to risk their lives on a daily basis, there appears to be an unlimited number of media accounts that create an idea in which police are no longer the hero but rather the villain. And, as criminologists, we know that policing in America has not been a fairytale. One simply need only recall the riots in Chicago and the south during the 1960s to recognize that policing has not always been just (and see Barlow & Barlow, 2000; Shelden, 2008; Zinn, 1999). Regardless, public confidence, minorities excluded, has remained relatively stable over the past thirty years. People of color have grown increasingly skeptical of law enforcement (Crow et al., 2017), however. With high-profile fatal incidents, the nightly news is filled with stories of police violence, and it is not surprising that minority populations may be more fearful of the police. These images are not limited to the news media but expand across all popular culture mediums. Take, for instance, the portrayal of the Decepticon Barricade in the *Transformers* (2007) film franchise. The character, who was originally depicted as a Formula One racing car, was reimaged in the film series as a Saline S281E police cruiser. The traditional police motto "To Protect and Serve" was replaced with the menacing "To Punish and Enslave." Not only was this Deception depicted as the stereotypical "bad cop," but it is apparent that enslaving the human population is the goal. Also included on the patrol car is the phrase "Incorporated since June 1865." This is a clear reference to the continuation of slavery after the American Civil War; the date alludes to the last Confederate surrender. Images such as this coupled with real-life incidents of police violence, especially against minority populations, create a perception of injustice. Whether real or not, these images have a tangible impact on how our justice system is perceived. The question is what impact do these perceptions have on crime and criminal justice–related issues? Cultural criminology attempts to answer this question.

According to Hayward and Young (2004), cultural criminology is "the placing of crime and its control in the context of culture; that is, viewing both crime and the agencies of control as cultural products—as creative constructs" (p. 259). While it is rooted in British cultural studies (see Cohen, 1972; Hall et al., 1978), deviant subcultural studies (see Becker, 1969), and criminology, cultural criminology emerged during the mid-1990s (see Ferrell & Sanders, 1995) drawing elements from varying perspectives and methodologies to examine the meaning of crime and crime control by using images, textual analysis, and other cultural and media representations. Through this process, we are able to examine deviant subcultures, the social construction of crime through popular culture mediums, and how our constructed perceptions influence the reality of crime (Ferrell, 1999). This "new" perspective takes into account the theoretical foundations of the past and couples it with innovative methodological techniques to not only analyze the world around us but to determine how our experiences and the meanings we attach to what we see shape our reality. Cultural criminology takes methodological approaches such as ethnography and textual/visual analysis and turns how we view the reality of crime and crime control upside down. Rather than promoting objectivity, it rejects positivist thought and allows us to revel in our subjective existence acknowledging that we bring our own biased ideologies to the table; it is not simply what we see in the mirror, but how we interpret the images that are reflected back at us (Ferrell, 1999; Phillips & Strobl, 2006).

Although innovative in its attempts to explain crime and crime control, cultural criminology is rooted in a history where popular culture media have systematically been sanctioned as a means of preventing criminality and controlling the dangerous classes. From dime novels to comic books to music videos, popular culture media have been linked to violence against women, juvenile delinquency, and other forms of violent crime . . . just think of the hysteria caused by Frederic Wertham's (1954) commentary on the comic book industry in *Seduction of the Innocent*. His inflammatory commentary, in conjunction with other media constructions like Rush Limbaugh and Alex Jones, has contributed to a world in which opinions about crime have the same market value as scientifically derived criminological assertion. So, while the truth may be out there, just ask Fox Mulder, it is often distorted by our own personal opinions and the images in which we associate them. Regardless, the amalgamation of these constructs allow individuals to shape their perception on crime and criminal justice agencies thereby creating a reality in itself. Yet, all is not lost as cultural criminology allows a scientific approach to analyzing what has often been considered fiction. It is through the lens of cultural criminology that we can examine the relationship between media depictions of reality and the actuality of the criminal justice system. With this being said, cultural criminology, as noted, is not simply used to analyze media, but is also a technique allowing ethnological research to guide our interpretations of crime and crime control. Numerous ethnographic studies have been conducted under the umbrella of cultural criminology (see Ferrell & Hamm, 1998; Ferrell, 1996), and it is here in which we are able to understand not only crime but the realities of these subcultures involved in crime.

Much of how we view the criminal justice system is based on how we culturally construct our reality. But while we may be fascinated with the idea of how culture shapes our ideas of crime and the criminal justice system, cultural criminology falls flat when providing an answer to how we "fix" a broken system that may be a result of our own bias and the structural inequalities inherent in a capitalistic society. Although it acknowledges these inequalities that exclude those defined as "other," it has often been criticized for excluding those who are often the most disenfranchised: women. While this critique may have been originally true, cultural criminology has been expanded to incorporate feminist constructs and methodologies (Hayward, 2016). As a result, a plethora of feminist research, by feminist scholars, has emerged that incorporates the principles of cultural criminology into ethnographic and media studies (see Brown, 2011; Phillips & Strobl, 2013). More aptly, the perspective has been criticized for having little statistical rigor with even less impact on policy and real-world change. While we would certainly agree with Hayward (2016) that cultural criminology serves as "a rejection of classical, one-dimensional Marxist/macro theories or criminal causality" (p. 302), we would, albeit begrudgingly, agree that cultural criminology has had little impact on crime policy. For us, cultural criminology is reminiscent of the snake eating itself, only to go around and around without any solutions. As noted in our discussion of Carlen (2013) in chapter 3, we are often uncomfortable in the science with this form for "mesearch." Now, does that mean the approach to crime and the justice system does not have value and is not methodologically grounded in the scientific method? Hardly. Even cultural criminologists themselves recognize the inherent problems with the theory, especially in regard to policy (see Hayward, 2016). Let us not forget that the foundational elements of the perspective (e.g., symbolic interactionism) have also faced similar criticisms. Relying on the quantitative mechanisms accepted within the field, cultural criminology, like its theoretical predecessors, may have difficulty illustrating its impact on policy. As noted by critics, cultural criminology may provide true descriptions of social phenomena, but its impact may often be negligible. According to Hayward, "for unless the relationship between data and theory is entirely clear, and sufficient attention is paid to ensure that research findings travel from the specific to the more generalizable level, it will remain difficult for cultural criminologists to have their say in policy discussions" (Hayward, 2016, p. 308). Thus, in order to be viable, cultural criminology must adhere to more rigorous methodological approaches. In her assessment of Jock Young's contribution to criminology, Carlen (2014), who may have disagreed with Young in his approach, was able to appreciate the ever-changing sociological method in which he approached the field. It was not enough to simply embrace the number-crunching, quantitative methodologies conscripted by mainstream and often armchair academics, Young and his colleagues challenged the accepted doctrine, the obsession with quantitative approach, while embracing the humanity of those involved in the system. Thus, while the tangible benefits of the theory cannot truly be measured, the need to assess the system through a sociological and often ethnographic lens is not lost on us. Recognizing that there is a problem is always the first step in coming up with a solution; Hayward (2016) in his response to the critiques of cultural criminology has not only provided responses to those critiques but also possible solutions; one way, as he observes, to further develop the perspective would be to incorporate techniques such as cartography and demography. Although these new techniques may provide new insights into the perspective, it should be reemphasized that examining the demographic correlates of crime from an ethnographic or media analysis has value. While cultural criminology may not give us concrete, statistical absolutism about why crime occurs and the policies that emanate from these scientific observations, it does give us a humanistic perspective of how individuals are affected by crime and the practices that often codify people as other and the impression that this leaves on our souls.

Conclusion

Burgess, Shaw, Sutherland, Merton, Cohen, Messner and Rosenfeld, Agnew, and their fellows did away with one form of struggle, arguing varyingly but essentially that crime is a functional adaptation to noxious conditions. It is not a challenge to the state, not a mini-treason. Instead, crime is the residue of economic disadvantage, the "corporation pudding" lining the city streets;

it is just another form of pollution. It is the sum of the remainder of billions of transactions in the marketplace. If wealth is "congealed labor" in Cohen's terms, then surely crime is "congealed shortfall."

Struggle is the leitmotiv as well for much of criminology, including discourses we have not addressed here. The centrality of struggle in these narratives is plain; tracing it here serves only to bludgeon a point already made: the contemplation of struggle is at the very heart of the contemporary discourse on criminology, whether one views that discourse from a traditional or a critical perspective. That struggle-ology has produced modest impacts on lived experience should concern us. That struggle is so endemic to criminological thought should lead us to ask "So what are you going to do now?" The understanding that struggle is at crime's core should compel us to act. Now it is with some measure of joy that we can point to journals like *Critical Criminology* as containing an increasing number of works that attend to the amelioration of human suffering (e.g., Leon & Ken, 2017). As heartening as this turn is, more is required of us.

Part of the reason why the struggle insight has not guided research or activism (and yes, academics can and must be activists when conditions call) is because that insight has not had purchase on the hearts of criminologists. Most criminologists have not grappled with the meaning of this struggle, and thus have not made the choice to struggle for meaning.

JUSTICE AND STRUGGLE

That struggle for meaning is related to individual survival, as we will see later on, but it is also a duty performed for others who are not able to struggle as mightily as we. It is something we will never understand: why someone would engage in criminological research, discover human brokenness, and do little more than write it up for publication. If by absurd we intend the assertion of sanity on static, meaning in the background microwave radiation, as we shall see it is an act of absurdity to confront pain and do nothing but shrug. But our assertion of meaning itself may be insane, could it not?

The Absurd and Justice

It is raining, harder now than before, and colder. Exiting a car one is immediately drenched as if stepping fully clothed into a morning shower. I hold an old copy of *Rolling Stone* over my head as I jog feebly to the front door of the Barnes & Noble. I am absolutely soaked, wetter outside than in; what little dignity I had has been washed from me and now traces a pale thin line into the gutter. I stamp my feet, as if doing so would make me even a bit drier, yet even as I do so, I realize the sickening futility of my painful stomping. I have mixed my metaphors in a sense: stomping might have freed snow from shoe surfaces. But as cold as I am I am only, and unalterably, wet. Snow can be tricked into releasing its grip. There is no hope for me.

Dripping from arms, scalp, and chin, I recover from my momentary musing, give my suit jacket a shake, and move to the door. At the door I stop, remembering the soggy magazine in my right hand, now utterly unreadable. I turn on my heel and head to the garbage can. It makes a sickening slap when it hits whatever was on top of the waste pile inside. I had meant to read the cover article.

Inside, the air is almost welcoming: the smell of books and of baking cookies is incongruously bucolic. For what seems like an hour I stand, agape and unsure at the entry. People move in and out past me as if I were an unfortunately placed memorial, fit for pigeons. Eventually a gravitational tug, weak at first then growing, pulls me to my left and slightly forward, and I relent. Riding my legs to where they ceased moving, possibly for a spot of green grass, I found myself, by myself, in the journals section. Stacks upon stacks of bound journals, wordless and silent, were piled on shelves and stacked on the floor; books bound with not a single jot of ink anywhere upon them sat and stared at me with the eyes of Holocaust victims. They began to move, insensate and dumb, but now stirred to life by my presence. They welled like surf and began to tower over me as if to swallow me under their denseness. A short, high-pitched shriek leapt from me before I knew it was coming. The cashier, a soft, wide, shiny cherub of a fellow, arrived at my elbow in seconds.

"Sir, are you . . . ?" His voice trailed off, I can only presume after seeing something unspeakable in my eyes. He swallowed hard and gathered himself, his voice catching in his throat: "—lright? . . . Are you . . . alright, sir? Can I get you some . . . some . . . something?" He swallowed hard again. His face was safe and almost familiar. I turned back to the tsunami of silence expecting it to be upon us both, moving as if to shield him, but it had recessed again into the walls.

I had not realized, but my fingers had clenched into knurled, arthritic claws, rasping at my chest. As fingers released, I could feel my stomach begin to churn and tumble. Mucus and bile mingled at the back of my throat; I spun round past the cherub, streaked for the door.

The entry chamber ripped past on all sides, but for an instant, though I was in full flight, I became acutely aware of every detail within, as if my nausea were someone else's and I had been given leave to study this chamber with the detail and care of an archaeologist. Discount books lay in shelves on both sides of the chamber, stacked unevenly; I was offended by the lack of care shown with the display, as surely it is not an inordinately obtuse expectation for the very *first* books one sees at a bookstore to be orderly. *Discover Egypt* was plastered with garish tourist brochure photos of the Sphinx and the pyramids of Giza. There was a book about cars, with a race car on the cover. Another book detailed the history of firearms; it was bedecked with small illustrations of Colt single-action pistols, Remington rifles, Browning Hi-Powers, and AK-47s. In the northwestern corner, up by the ceiling, the wallpaper had lost its fight with some past moisture leak, had turned a ruddy brown and begun to peel. The rubber floor mat was slightly askew, just enough for one corner to flap against one of the doors. I worried vaguely whether that flap would get stuck in the door as I exited.

I thrust myself headfirst back into the rain, landing on my knees just in front of the curb. I tried to vomit, but nothing came forth. School was out for Thanksgiving. Children ambled past contemplating Christmas lists. Some stared at me as I knelt in the deepening puddle unable even to master my own viscera. Breath came deep and fast as the rain continued to fall.

Roquentin, Sartre's protagonist in *Nausea,* discovers moments where he is aware of every single thing: ships at sea ringing to their gunwales with music, cities again ablaze with lights, combatants ripping each other to pieces in the ruins of Berlin, women in Paris and each single stroke of their kabuki brushes. Everything, all of it, moves to the pace of his footsteps. He moves like a conquering army through the streets. Waking from such moments like from a febrile dream he is sickened. What is it, precisely, that sickens him? "Having been so sublime last evening" is what he says (Sartre, 1969, p. 56), but we (and he) are not fully clear as to why yesterday's revelry would result in nausea today. In this, we think, there is much to do with meaning, with what Camus concerns himself with in *Sisyphus*. Roquentin seeks something he cannot find in those moments of sublime revelry where he feels not only connected to all things, but as if he were the puppeteer, granting breath via royal dispensation, in those moments something was both true and untrue. His illness came from a realization that there was untruth that underlay any truth he had beheld last night, that the narrative that buoyed his spirit was mostly fiction. Perhaps it was a kind of foolishness he felt, but if so it was likely quite a bit more profound.

Roquentin's sickness came from seeing untruth under what truth he understood. Without doubt, he had touched something real in each of his moments of his seeing, of revelry, but the untruth worked to greater effect than it deserved, invalidating more than itself. Was truth untrue? Was the untruth the greater wisdom? Was any of it meaningful?

"If man realized that the universe like him can love and suffer, he would be reconciled" (Camus, 1991, p. 17). Ah, then: so it is not so much a question of which truth is truer, but whether or not we, meaning-bearing beings, can find reconciliation with a universe that is insensate and dumb. Is it possible that we might be able to look into the abyssal icy dark and see something we recognize looking back at us? Such reconciliation, Camus tells us, is not to be. When one recognizes the existence of the unbridgeable space between the certainty of one's existence and the meaning one seeks to project on that existence, in that moment one touches the absurd. And in light of the absurd, suicide is a rational act. Using a scattergun to scatter meaning-seeking matter like the contents of a shattered jam jar is something of a confession of failure, but it is also an affirmation of a kind. Rather, it can be an affirmation, depending upon the meaning of the act for the actor. "For a man who does not cheat, what he believes to be true must determine his action" (Camus, 1991, p. 6); the universe confronts (perhaps the better word is affronts) the reasonable person with its unwavering and impassionate unreasonableness.

If it is not an act of cowardice, seeking to leave the world of the unreasonable can mean that the idea of reasonableness is more revered than is its perception. Sure, reasonableness may rule on the far bank of the Styx, but it is unlikely to be the ferry ride one seeks when one chooses suicide. Don't forget Hamlet's famous dilemma; and don't forget even he chooses to live, *knowing* Dad was on the far shore, waiting. Suicide, for Camus, is more about the *here*, about the ideals we treasure in this place than it is about ever attaining them in full, here or elsewhere. Were it not, the more reasoned response to the divorce between the meaning we crave and the meaninglessness of the universe would be to embrace the void and live an indulgent and sybaritic life. Damn the torpedoes and pour me another martini.

In trying to say what we have learned regarding the absurd, even in this we are frustrated; if we seek to say what we know, we find only that we do not know anything definitively. We can lay hands on truths, but not Truth, yet we sense not only the presence of Truth, but that Truth is somewhere nearby, behind the veil. Perhaps that is why Camus and Sartre, and as we will see soon Kafka as well, all relied on novels in order to explore the vertiginousness of the absurd; it is certainly why we began this section with a nonsequitur narrative, so that you would feel a tiny pinch of vertigo. But something has to be the constant in our model. If our senses are to be believed, and in the end our senses are all that we possess, it is not the world that must be absurd, then, or the person, but the gravity that binds the two together. It is the absurd that hires the divorce lawyer in the same gesture as it arranges the romantic introduction.

So we have before us now the human, the universe, and the construct; three things coexisting, ennobling, competing, colliding. This sense of a separation between human, human creation, and universe is a leitmotiv for

Kafka. Setting this separation off in high relief is the juxtaposition of human tenderness and human callousness common in his works. Now a cockroach, poor Gregor is eventually undone by a rotting apple embedded in his chitinous back, hurled at him *by his father*. His death was a happy event, and his remains likely were thrown into the garbage, though in truth we never do find out. A lawyer himself, Kafka offers scathing critique of the law's footprint in humanity, its cruel deafness to compassion. "Like a dog!" Joseph K. is deprived of even dying with a shred of dignity, even though he knows not a thing about why he is being executed. He never met his judge, never heard his charges, and almost didn't feel the blade enter his side.

Not long before his end, Joseph K. speaks to a prison priest. Though he is not in prison, but only visiting the prison cathedral, they speak as to the nature of the law. The priest seeks to set Joseph straight in his grasp of the law through the use of parable. There was, the priest says, a seeker of the Law. He approaches an open door, the way to the Law; the doorman guarding the door says it possible to enter, but that it is not available to him at the moment. The seeker peers into the open door and the doorman invites him to try to force his way in, only the next hall is guarded by a much more formidable doorman, and each hall after by even more fierce guards. So the seeker waits. He waits his entire life to enter, giving up everything, in vain. With his last breath the seeker asked the doorman why over the many years he waited no one else came. The doorman explains as the seeker's sight dims for the last time that this door was intended for him only, and that now he was gone, the door could be closed.

In *The Trial,* the priest offers several interpretations of the parable, just as one who has contemplated it at length might have done. Yet just like one who has contemplated a parable at length he seems to have failed in the effort to grasp the deeper and yet more blatant illness evident with the parable. And why not after all? The priest ostensibly works for a religious institution that exists as a functional part of a totalitarian regime. Even if he might have become attuned to shortcomings of the process, just like the lawyers in Kafka's earlier courtroom scenes, never would he dream of suggesting a change to practice, as it would only benefit future seekers and irreparably harm him. No, the parable isn't meant to be a source of insight. It is heroin for the junkie priest and his pals.

The priest posits that the doorman had done his job admirably. He also offers that the doorman and the seeker were one and the same. All of their musings in the end fail to recognize the fundamental nature of law: it is made by us for us. The purpose of law is to facilitate the nurturance, healing, and transformation of human suffering. In this dystopic-realm-come-to-life, though, the law is its own means and its own end. It is of us, true, but it exists apart from us, even beyond us, like a demiurge cooked in a crock pot. It is as insensate as Camus's cold universe and as emetic as Roquentin's self-judged folly. Joseph K.'s efforts to find reason in the unreasoning uber-reason that is the law come to nothing, even as his executioner twists the blade in the tender flesh of Joseph's beating heart. "I don't know whether this world has a meaning that transcends it, but I know that I do not know that meaning and that it is impossible for me just now to know it" (Camus, 1991, p. 51). These are Camus's words, but they might as well have been Joseph's last thoughts as he bled out like a dog on the cold and thirsty rocks.

The criminal law as constituted currently is not misguided to concern itself with proximate things, then. In all fairness, it may not have much choice, but it is not in this narrow sense misguided. The error and folly lie elsewhere. The law, too, has its avatars, and like others in use today, culpability is pinned to proximate moments. Now it is not an error to see in the moments of culmination of destructive endeavors as being central to the understanding of responsibility: in the moment where one with nefarious intent breaks a lock to enter a store there exists in microcosm the rest of what occurs subsequently. Yet it is not the only moment so pregnant. Given time and care, we might find other moments, in fact, far more fecund with this crime than the one that represents at law the consummation of evil. If it is anything, the law (and perhaps the criminal law in particular) is an effort to project reason on an unreasonable world, to compel smooth Cartesian geometry from a jagged, moiling, and obdurate world.

But wait: the criminal law projects Cartesian grid over broken ground, surely, but it is not the broken ground of the insensate universe that gives it fits. It is the fractious tempest of people—of you and me—that puts the lie to the calm, austere, beshelved reason that is the criminal law. If anything is absurd, it is the law, at the very least in terms of its capacity of mapping human brokenness. The order it seeks is not even a pleasant fiction.

In our nausea, though, there is to be found clarity, like a diamond gleaming at the bottom of a rain-drenched gutter. The law projects its order over human folly and fractiousness, but in this it can be seen that we ourselves *are* the universe. We are the insensate. We are also the reason sought. We are the projection. "If I were a tree among trees . . . ," muses Camus, "this life would have a meaning, or rather this problem would not arise, for I should belong to this world. I should *be* this world to which I am now opposed by my whole consciousness and my whole insistence upon familiarity" (Camus, 1991, p. 51, emphasis in original). He need not worry. He isn't a tree. Today.

And he isn't opposed to this world at all, or if he is, it is because he has taken on an understanding of himself as distinct from the rest of the universe. He has consumed and adopted his identity as an independent and distinct individual.

He has imbibed a lie. Nausea's cause has thus revealed itself: food poisoning. In the end, the absurd is not the gravity slamming Newton's apple into churlish turf. It is the meaningless distinction between Newton, his apple, and the turf. Which of the three did the falling and which did the learning is a useful question only abstractly and only for a limited time. In time, Newton eats the apple, eventually dies, and, just like Camus did, he becomes a tree.

So the law, like science and practically any other human institution, is an embodiment of a form of struggle. Both science and law struggle to wrest order from the universe; the former operates from the premise that the universe is prolific but deaf and dumb. The latter, however, seeks to demand the universe take on a human shape. The irony, of course, is that it already has; it confuses audience and performer, it offers vocal lessons in the *schweinsteiger.* By its existence, by its insistence, the law as it exists today invalidates itself.

What could possibly be just, then, about the absurd? Perhaps the question is better asked another way: what can the sense of the absurd teach us about what justice might mean for us? We have concluded that the absurd stems from the misperception of separation, from the false distinction between self, universe, and construct. The absurd can be perceived only when one has taken on as part of her marrow the untruth that we exist as beings separate from each other and separate from the rest of the universe. Indeed, it is an illness that leads to the sour stomach that results from eating that lie, and as such is likely a common experience for those who embrace the wisdom of compassion but fail to follow Ariadne's string all the way into the labyrinth. It is a vertiginousness, a feeling of being clobbered. The vertigo tends to dissipate with the lifting of the veil, though; as we reckon our connectedness to all that is, emetic symptoms abate. The absurd points to desideratum: our inter-belonging. Lest we forget, Camus leaves Sisyphus at the base of the mountain, probably smiling. Savoring the "wholly human origin of all that is human" (Camus, 1991, p. 123), he, his rock, and his mountain are one. We are nauseous because separation is not our natural state. When we remember correctly (*smrti*), we are reconciled in our choice to turn to True North and find more than our appetite.

If justice is what each of us is due, then the recalibration of our compasses points us toward *reconciliation.* For Barth who concerns himself with the reconciliation of the scoundrels we are with God, "salvation is fulfillment, the supreme, sufficient, definitive, and indestructible fulfillment of being" (Barth, 2004, p. 9). Reconciliation is the bringing together of those things that have been separated against their nature, but that reconciliation is undertaken as part of the ultimate aim of fulfillment. Barth's perspective is a Christian one, but the longing for reconciliation is not unique to Christianity, taking many forms both sacred and secular. Justice, then, true justice, must be concerned with achieving human reconciliation. Along with human connection, we will return to the task of contemplating what reconciliation means for us in the next chapter.

Hegel

At the outset, though, reconciliation likely seems an incomplete or partial aim point for us in the undertaking of uniting love and justice. It seems perhaps that a turning point is of rather less importance as it would be of greater concern to contemplate what followed reconciliation's admittedly magical moment (in Kornfield's [2001] words, after the ecstasy, the laundry). Such a sense, though, may be illustrative of desideratum: we need to talk about method, about process. Lest there be confusion, we have pursued for ourselves something of an understanding of mind; an understanding of harm requires it. Whether we approach harm from a criminological view, a political view, an anthropological view, or a philosophical view, some measure of phenomenology is demanded of us. We can be forgiven, perhaps, for having put off a conversation on phenomenology until now, as none of us is a phenomenologist. Again, our aim in this work is to set up love as the quintessential seamstress; love knits together broken discourses, closes holes in threadbare narratives, and binds together edges of thought systems, thus making a single narrative, useful in its unity.

Without question, Hegel's writing is . . . opaque . . . to say the least, but again, this is by design. Some ideas are not so far from traditional, though. In our rather brief use of Hegel here in the effort to understand justice, we will not seek his counsel on justice directly; his understanding of justice, as far as the *Phenomenology* goes, is somewhat akin to the striking of an equilibrium, an idea with which we have already dispensed. Instead, we should take note of his larger endeavor: he is seeking to free us from our misconceptions so that we might be more truly free. Truth's development is only possible through a striving for it. Truth's unfolding must be undergone; there is no shortcut, no Cliff's Notes to Truth. Inscrutability may not be *the* point, but it certainly serves his larger end. In this sense, the process of coming to understand Hegel is both content and process.

To be sure, many of his ideas are unlike those that came before in the Western tradition. His word *use*, the meaning he gives to a number of the words he uses, along with their subtext, also makes Hegel challenging. Words like "science," "spirit," "sublate," "mediation," and "knowledge" are all laden with meaning that is both intricate and not immediately obvious. What is more, readings of Hegel are plentiful; Eisenberg (1990), while asking whether Hegel was a panlogicist, concludes that Mind was not the fundamental metaphysical firmament of Hegel's system; that there was for Hegel a God that had an outer component, parallel to and interpenetrating with, the inner one. Contemplating whether or not Hegel was a transcendentalist, and whether the *Phenomenology* was an introduction to transcendental philosophy, Williams (1985) demurs somewhat, though he wants to answer in the affirmative. As non-Hegelian readers, Hegel's archipelago of ideas presented something of a challenge to us, akin at times to cat-and-mouse. Often, though, Hegel hid gems for us to find. That is until we came across what can only be amply described in scatological terms: "The only essential connection that has existed and continued between the Negroes and the Europeans is that of slavery. In this the Negroes see nothing unbecoming them, and the English, who have done most for abolishing the slave trade and slavery, are treated by the Negroes themselves as enemies" (Hegel, 2004, p. 94). Fully regarding the historical context, we are aware that efforts to paint a rich and authentic portrait of Hegel and struggle were changed fundamentally for us by statements like this, and by his slight regard for Buddhism despite what some might argue is a considerable similarity to his thought. Hegel's ideas became a struggle, but in a very different and unintended way.

Putting aside all of that, though, what is the nature of the struggle as Hegel intended? Hegel's task, particularly in the *Phenomenology*, is the discovery of a process whereby Mind can know itself, can regard itself from the cool isolation of first principles. The struggle exists at two levels, one individual, one socio-historical. It is part of the genius of Hegel's system that the two can be seen in something of a part-whole relationship. On the individual level, sense certainty collides with concepts, resulting in perception. The tension between perception and concept tends to lead to a sense of uncertainty and thus a suspension of judgment. The suspending of judgment in turn creates space for the determinate negation (*aufheben*). This negation is both an opposition to and a preservation of that which came before. What follows is the synthesis of the first moment and its determinate negation. At the socio-historical level, the same three moments are discernible throughout history; just as we ourselves come to know ourselves dialectically, so does the Absolute come to know itself through history.

Central to Hegel's thinking was the linkage between substance and process. One might be tempted to claim that Hegel would argue that if there is no process, there is no truth. Such an understanding of the relationship between process and content is closer to yet vitally different from an Eastern view relative to other, non-Hegelian Western ideas. Eastern phenomenology tends to hold that process and content are one and the same. Now that we understand the process in its fullness, he says, the Absolute is within our grasp; the completion of knowledge, even in something of an eschatological sense, is now possible (Berthold-Bond, 1988). We might note with some amusement that Hegel was fully right in his wrongness, at least with regard to this completion of knowledge. At the time of publication of the *Phenomenology*, all that could be understood in terms of who we are as beings was rendered. Except not. At that moment, he was spot on. The globe, for many, had now been invented; the idea itself of a phenomenology of the mind now existed. That we have continued to grow and change only means that our new state of the understanding of ourselves in relation to the absolute is also in a sense "done," even though we also know that it is not. Hegel's completeness assertion is challenged not by technological growth itself, but by the understanding about ourselves such technology offers. Hegel's ideas are threatened not by the *f*MRI, but by the neuroplasticity in humans it discovered. But more to the point, his assertion that at any given moment the knowledge possessed by a culture is complete is true. Perhaps it is not as extensive as the knowledge it will have in a century, or the knowledge possessed by the alien visitors disembarking from their flying saucer, hands extended in greeting. It is, however, fully complete at that moment. This distinction matters more than it might seem, and is quite a bit more than a play on words.

You see, Kant perceives a difference between absolute knowledge and the conditioned experience of that knowledge; we can only know the absolute as it presents itself to us and only as our capacity to render it authentically allows. There is objective reality, but it is only a sketchbook version of it that we can grasp ourselves. True, we struggle to increase in our capacity to perceive, but only to a limit. We can factor out the medium between cognition and truth, but even then we are left with a gap between us and Truth. In essence, we may be able to shrink the size of the gap, but however big or small it is, it remains unspannable. Of course, here we come to Hegel's critique: the effort to understand cognition, the process he creates to grasp *Geist*, itself functions as a barrier to its own success; Mind (*Geist*) is, itself, an object to itself. If cognition is itself a conditioned construct, then the use of cognition to understand cognition is doomed to failure from the start. Unlike Sisyphus, we can't even budge our rock as the fulcrum and the rock are one and the same. Intuition, then, or nonmediated ways of knowing are of less value, and indeed, are siren songs as they proffer a sense of knowing that is illusory. As there is no process, no mediation, there is no truth.

Nevertheless, we have to commit ourselves to *some* arrangement of things regarding knowledge, simply because the train won't ever stop. But the quest for epistemic security is misguided, Hegel tells us. The fear of error is in fact a fear of Truth, in Hegel's terms; clinging to certainty ends up as a rejection of reality. The only way to manage such a thing is not to choose our arrangement in advance, but through trial and error (the dialectic). For Hegel it is to be celebrated, then, that we get it wrong, just so long as we know it to be wrong. Risk invites error which is the humus of growth. To modify a phrase common to workout spaces, mistakes are error leaving the body.

Of course, for Hegel the totality of human history is the narrative whereby the Absolute comes to know itself. For Hegel, insight, development toward truth is hard-won. It is, again, a struggle, and it must be so, for the struggle itself is the process whereby God is rendered. The world, meaning the place and the beings in it, is a thing that is only somewhat capable of self-determination. We are constrained in our choice making; one cannot teleport one's self to Paris for a cappuccino and croissant or stroll the Mariana Trench. In contrast, God is unlimited. Necessarily then She must enjoy unlimited self-determination. She must be free of confining relations to other beings, and thus is not in the most concrete sense a being at all (because a being like Tammy, Beth, Michael, or Steve Buscemi is a negotiated, mutually created thing). Self-determination matters; how else could something be all powerful if it is not capable of total self-determination? Reason (mediated knowing) provides that missing fulcrum for self-determination, and therefore for omniscience. We humans are capable of touching this reasoned divinity at times and to a limited degree. This capacity is for Hegel some measure of evidence that God is. Perhaps we should say instead that it provides evidence that God is *possible*. God, for Hegel, is the biomass of actualized self-determination of all the beings capable of it; She is the highest and most complete reality, the most crystalline and perfect reason, both accessed and made via the same process. Limited beings, then, struggling together create the unlimited.

We can see then that Hegel's God is incomplete, but not for Hegel's idea about process. He has a bigger problem. Hegel's conception of God does not offer a completely unlimited God after all. Hegel's God is unlimited in the same way a number line is unlimited: potentially infinitely long, infinitely precise. Yet She needs that fourth grader to pick up a number-two pencil and draw; wavy lateral line, greater-than and less-than carrots capping each end, vertical line scratched down the middle, and numbers complete with hash marks. God's Achilles heel is us. It is not She who reaches for us through the veil between realms, but we who drop a line into the ether for Her. Another way of saying the same thing is that you are the breath of God.

It turns out this is no problem at all; it is profound insight. As beings, we are limited, but as sentient beings we are in possession of the power of choice: we choose to increase our own capacity (for Hegel, that means mediated knowledge) and, crucially, *to participate in the increasing of the capacity of those around us*. God is rendered by our action, *by choice*, through the process whereby we are reconciled with each other. Such an idea of God would seem to have roots in Hebraic thought. Eden's message for us may not be what most Christian interpretations claim it to be (see, e.g., Cooper, 1998). As we shall see later in chapter 5, rabbinical treatments of the tale focus not on the theft of fruit and the concomitant punishment but on the choice made by Eve (and eventually explained to Adam) to accept the conditions of service, as it were. To bring light to the darkest places comes at a cost, you see, and only by *knowingly choosing* service with full knowledge of its consequences does the light truly reach through the dark; only then does God truly exist.

Where the mapping of Mind's phenomenology is a crucial early step, the play of many minds together creating history, millions of silken strands winding together, shuttle dancing deftly back and forth, is the ultimate aim. History is a narrative of the Absolute, a Phenomenology of God. Thus it seems to us that Hegel's posthumously assembled *Lectures in the Philosophy of History* is something of a bookend counterpoint to the *Phenomenology of Spirit*; the latter establishing the nature of the fibers, the former describing the loom's ordinances.

We would be well served, then, to regard in Hegel a fundamental theme: reconciliation. It is reconciliation, a coming to understanding, as well as a coming into being. What is being in the *Phenomenology* is the becoming of the *Lectures in the Philosophy of History*. Even if his own thought is distastefully biased, his *system* of thought unifies local and global, individual and historical. It portrays an end as means, showing how each of us coming to understand ourselves is related to the progress of history toward perfect reason. We might pick a fight with Hegel regarding his conception of beings like us being discrete things (and we will take a rather different position in chapter 5), but meeter for our purposes here, we would observe Hegel's disdain for nonmediated ways of knowing. In fairness, his allergy to some of the metaphysical claims in the water during his lifetime is altogether appropriate.

Critique of Hegel

In this work we have examined impoverished and accomplished thought regarding justice and crime, grappling with authors and ideas as we went. In our struggle, we have attempted to render in miniature some measure of a developmental process, one that Hegel might recognize. Something akin to the dialectical three step can be seen here occasionally, but of greater concern is that the struggle with particulars is seen, at least in places. Were time available, we might, as Hegel does, walk through history and trace dialectical dances and granular details, and we can hope to be fairer and kinder in our storytelling than he has been. Our project is less ambitious: we intend this work to be a sign by the side of the road, a simple arrow and caption: "This Way to Elysium." We have not taken to task every argument about justice nor held up for scrutiny every criminoetiological claim. Our sense is that encyclopedic critiques tend to be of little value, even for the rather narrow audience for which they would be intended. They leave work done. They miss the opportunity to invite readers into collaboration. Hegel very intentionally tore down the author's fourth wall; what kind of nuts would we be if we failed to do the same in our discussion of him? What, for instance, would left realism look like were it lensed through love? You, kind reader, are invited to bring yourself to the conversation, and to envision your thought, your favorite models and prized constructs lensed through love. Just as Hegel writes as he does in support of his agenda, so we too write to fold you into ours.

There's the problem of the beautiful soul, though (e.g., Milne, 2002). It may be Hegel's beloved sister also haunted him to a degree; she seems to have been the muse for his contemplations of the beautiful soul (Rabate, 2014), the "unreconciled immediacy" (Hegel, 1807/1977, p. 407), the inspired and super-reasoned creativity. Mediation is the blood of reason for Hegel, but then in wanders Mozart, or Samuel Barber, or Isaac Stern, or Kieron Williamson, Vic Wooten, Joe Bonamassa, Derek Trucks, or Seongha Jeong. . . . A boy or girl who can paint so as to make the hardened heart melt, a child who can tell you deep secrets through his guitar: these creatures break the bonds of Hegelian gravity and simply wander among the planets. One might be willing to offer Hegel something of a variance, a get-out-of-jail-free card here, especially as he contemplates the beautiful soul for some time, and beholding the example of his sister he almost audibly shrugs. We should not be so quick to give a pass, though, as this seeming verdant variant gestures indirectly to a far larger concern.

Hegel makes a rather fundamental assumption at the outset of the *Phenomenology*, one so fundamental it is not stated, one so crucial the justification of the project hinges upon it. He assumes that the nature, and thus the experience, of Mind is the same for us all, and that this nature and experience of Mind is constant over the life course, even if sophistication can increase over time. Although one might be tempted to point to the functionality of language and the power of art as evidence of the similitude of our phenomenological anatomies, in fact evidence indicates quite the opposite may be the case (e.g., Fuchs & Flugge, 2014; Kolb & Gibb, 2011). More to the point, as clever as he was to craft a narrative of a phenomenology of mind that was demanding to procure precisely because the procurement of an understanding of mind itself must necessarily make us work, he has assumed that the endpoint is one that will be universally (or at least generally) meaningful vis-à-vis his readers' own experiences, and universally constant lifelong. Such an assumption, however, is not defensible. The evidence of a prodigy violinist or blues guitarist or mathematician also creates the possibility of other forms of exceptionality, other kinds of brilliance, other beautiful souls. Michael failed shop class in middle school. His friend and fellow bandmate is a master luthier. Another bandmate is a master HVAC technician. Is it not possible that other souls, souls not gifted in painting or math, might otherwise be just as beautiful? It turns out that "unrealized immediacy" is not so rare as Hegel supposed, his exception is quite a bit closer to the rule; it is all around us in full flower.

With regard to achieving anything akin to an understanding of the Absolute, all one can ever attest to meaningfully is where She found it herself, as well as something like a manifest of what one found. Hegel was right: understanding mind is hard indeed. It is so hard in fact that each of us must do it on our own. Where Hegel offers a cramped tome, the wiser teacher sits, extends one arm, one finger, and points to the moon. We can read the *Phenomenology* as *his* map of *his* mind, but there is no reason to assume that his mind and yours or ours bear any resemblance to each other. There is no small sense of irony here: Hegel's *Phenomenology* is intentionally inscrutable, possibly even cacographic, and often commentators are loath to untie too many knots for others in honor of the author's intention for the work, yet the very work itself is problematic even for its own end because no one phenomenology of mind can account for all minds. In essence, then, Hegel builds a mighty castle, complete with generations of Swiss guards, protecting nothing more than Hegel's own private Idaho.

Even if Hegel's battlements exist to thwart an army of allies, his insight into the fertility of struggle should not escape our gaze. And there are some attributes of mind in common between you and him and us. But it is not enough to assume that one map describes all terrain. Art provides perhaps the clearest illustration. Although we have some measure of similitude sufficient perhaps even to process shape and color in similar ways (although we know of course that such similitude is not common among all humans), the meaning derived from sensory input is not manufactured in the same fashion, to wit, a collision of input and concept. An observer of mind might refrain altogether from imputing any concept and merely experience the sensory drama before her; instead of ramming stimulus into idea, yet another might craft a new idea altogether. To observe that humans take particular data from senses and process it in relation to generalized data in the form of concepts and to hold that up as a universal phenomenological model is only slightly more meaningful than to say that humans only create things while wearing pants. Even if viewed as a dialectic, the process described is not universally true, even if it is a common process; further it is unlikely to be connected to the processes whereby Minds do their really interesting things. Ultimately, where a work of art represents for one a message regarding freedom of expression, for another it is blasphemous, incendiary offal. Oh, and that wise teacher we mentioned earlier, the one pointing to the moon . . . where did the accomplished student *find* the moon? Not in the sky.

Lest we forget, relatively recently we have come to understand the vast capacity of the human mind to change itself through "behavioral medicine" (Davidson, Kabat-Zinn, Schumacher, Rosenkranz, Muller, Santorelli, Urbanowski, Harrington, Bonus, & Sheridan, 2003). Humans (and very likely other sentient beings) possess a far greater degree of neuroplasticity than we thought possible even a decade before (e.g., Fuchs & Flugge, 2014). The experience of Mind and its development is very likely to be a rather changeable thing, making the project of a standard phenomenology of Mind a project of very limited value indeed. The most one might offer is one's own map to Mind; one might find value in seeing where another traveler found wisdom. Michael has been fortunate to offer a brief and clumsy sketch of his own phenomenology (DeValve, 2017b).

So struggling for wisdom is the greater wisdom, and the reconciliation that results is, without question, holy. Here Hegel has given us much. It is likely, though, that although some basic structural things may be in common among us, a proper universal phenomenology is likely out of the question. Indeed, struggle itself to grasp Mind probably changes the Mind's map at a basic level, and it seems Hegel even assumes as much in the introduction to the *Phenomenology*. It might appeal to some to attempt a mapping of those things likely held in common; although some might be learned from such an effort, our emphasis would instead be elsewhere. Justice understood as we envision it does not depend on commonness derived from comparisons, but instead upon a divine unity that commands of us and inspires from us the cultivation of each individual toward her actualization. Such a cultivation effort may attend at times to elements in common, but will be guided by the growth of each individual to her fullest capacity.

CONCLUSION

So in the end what are we to make of it all? We have seen struggle make Sisyphus smile; we have seen it generate progress toward reason; we have seen it function as the engine of brokenness; and we understand that it quite literally can make us *more robust* against brokenness. Are the different thinkers discussed here actually contemplating a similar human phenomenon? Did a semantic shell game get us here? We think not. Each is contemplating human striving and struggling, but each witnesses it operate rather differently on the human heart. Crucially, none of them draws irresponsible conclusions from her musings. Each of them offers a valid piece of the puzzle, although it would be something of a stretch to argue that each piece is equally valid. How are we to put them together?

Let us consider one last contributor, just briefly, for something of an answer. Viktor Frankl survived many months of internment at Auschwitz. A psychiatrist, he was an able observer of humanity; as things turned out, he was to be his own most significant subject. He recounts experiences from his time in Auschwitz sufficient to bring the mightiest to ruin. In light of the extraordinarily cruel and inhuman conditions in which he and his fellows were kept, he observed that among camp prisoners it was common to let fate navigate. At arrival, prisoners were sorted right and left, but had no idea what that might mean . . . initially. Quickly it became only too clear; many rejoiced when they noted actual water dripping from shower heads in the shower room. It would be reasonable, Frankl (2006) observes, for his reader to conclude from his recounting of events that humans were merely a product of their environment. Human thought and action is merely a response to stimuli, just as Skinner argued. Not so, Frankl intones. But what of human freedom? Does it exist in a place like Auschwitz? It turns out that yes, especially in a place of darkness, human freedom exists, and indeed becomes lifesaving. He speaks of individuals who moved through camp huts offering encouragement, even giving their last crumbs to others more in need than they. Frankl had been given a visa to emigrate to the United States to continue his work and in order to avoid the inevitable, but he demurred and chose to remain in Austria with his aging parents who could not leave. What cannot be taken from a person, regardless of the direness of her environs, is her choice how to respond. *Choosing intentionally to have authentic purpose in the midst of the struggle to survive was what reconciled him with God and humanity and saw him though to true freedom, even while in chains.*

Well, then, how are we to resolve the evident tension between the conception of strain as criminogenic, moderated by coping, resistance, or susceptibility factors, with the idea that strain can keep someone alive under the most inhuman conditions? Striving and struggling underscores the existence of one key human attribute: choice. Humans and other sentient beings enjoy choice. But choice is not commonly understood, in part because the kinds of choices contemplated are not, strictly speaking, the fully comparable. Constraints may exist on the space for one choice relative to another; knowledge of options may be limited, foresight possibly even nonexistent.

More than the existence of choice, though, is the manner of the choice in relation to the nature of the struggle, the sense of agency it creates. Recall (Cooper, 1998) that Eve *chose* the unpleasant consequences of the land outside of Eden. Frankl *chose* his parents and grave suffering over safety without them. Once interned, he *chose* to survive for the benefit of his manuscript, for his ideas. He chose to survive so that he might offer to others what he was learning about the human condition; he chose to live for those who could not and for those who had yet to be born.

Contemplating choice is less about whether humans enjoy a measure of indeterminism, whether it is soft or hard, and quite a bit more about whether and how that choice is understood, and what it means in the moment of choice. Rational choice theorists like Felson or Cornish and Clarke depend much of their thinking on the idea of choice, but they keep the nuanced and plastic anatomy of choice at arm's length. Merely asserting humans have choice is as scientifically meaningful as asserting that humans have hats. In fact, as things stand currently, it seems as if the biomass of mainstream criminology has become woefully interbred to the point that arguments about social pushes toward crime (strain), pulls toward crime (learning), and restraints to crime (control) have begun to appear as if each is merely a variation on themes of another, spiraling increasingly in upon itself.

Most importantly, choice must contemplate the thing chosen; the real benefit for criminology/zemiology is in the understanding of the degree to which people understand their own choice making. For Frankl, it was meaningfulness, or rather, a specific meaning. Those who chose to see life as meaningful, and more to the point, to see that their survival was in some way instrumental toward some other end, tended to have a greater chance of surviving the hell of Nazi concentration camps. Whether that meaning be the completion of a manuscript (in Frankl's case), being alive for a beloved thought to be waiting, or some other goal, survivors lived *for* something. Each person chose to cling to the meaningfulness that appealed to their heart. And when they chose to release it, often they succumbed. Frankl tells of a fellow prisoner who had dreamed the end of the war would occur on March 30, 1945. As the date approached and news did not bode well for his prediction, he fell ill. His war ended early in the morning of March 31, 1945.

What does not kill us makes us stronger; a little struggle is a good thing for humans, at least as Frankl (2006) sees things. An existential vacuum, Frankl claims, is the result of a lack of meaningful struggle. Our guides (like instinct or tradition) are either no longer present or are of little practical use in contemporary society. We are now left in a state of choiceless boredom. Camus sees the absurd as something of a collision between the human need for meaning and the insensate and meaninglessness of the universe in which he finds himself. He craves meaning so badly in fact that without it his very skin feels to him like a waxy, soiled parchment.

Meaning, though, comes and in plentitude through Hegel. We discover our meaning in a gritty, mediated dialogue between idea and determinate negation. Meaning, Hegel seems to insist, is ours for the asking if we only choose to do the hard work necessary to get it. Meaning, yes, and in its pursuit, reconciliation; we reconcile actuality with potential both locally and globally, mine, yours, and ours.

In 1957, Albert Camus was the second youngest person to receive a Nobel for literature; he was certain his life's work had not yet begun. He was killed in a car crash just after the turn of the new year, 1960. He, his wife, and their two young children were returning to Paris; though he hated cars, he had been persuaded by his publisher and friend to go with him by car (Simpson, 2017). The unused return-trip ticket was found in his coat pocket.

The next tree you pass might very well have a dot or two of Camus. Not saying hello would be absurd.

Part III

JUSTICE THAT LOVE GIVES

Here we are, then, moving together into the last portion of this work. Together we have surveyed a fair chunk of the criminological and justice landscapes; we have found some ideas to be woefully wanting, some to be rather better fits. Even with the better fitting dialogues, though, thought about justice and thought about crime have remained separate garments, even when they have had some measure of their anatomy (e.g., identity or struggle) in common.

What we hope to demonstrate in this section is that what has been dysfunctional in both discourses not only can be resolved, but the two discourses necessarily made one, when justice and love are seen to be synonymous. We will take material from what we have discussed as well as introducing some new ideas to weave a new garment with Ariadne's thread: a garment that comforts and covers each of us without padding or flattery.

Chapter 5 is the place where our final argument will be made regarding love and justice. The sixth and final chapter, informed by the penultimate chapter, is something of a gallery of "epic wins" of justice and crime.

Chapter Five

A Unified Theory of Justice and Crime

Here we are now, together, at the denouement. If you're reading this, you've more than paid your dues. Up to this point, we have examined theories of crime and theories of justice as separate dialogues, often kept separate by the very incompleteness of the ideas themselves. The incompleteness that challenges them and affronts us is rooted in the nature of the avatars used in the theory making. The philosophical dress forms that gave shape to selfism and balance in different iterations look little like us. As homunculi, they are twisted grotesquely out of shape in an attempt to stretch the logical positivist metaphor over them. No fault is to be found here, though, whatsoever. The thinkers who endeavored to create abstractions and thus make empiricism more useful did so for the same reason we write this, for the same reason Jonathan Livingston Seagull flew: in order to learn. It turns out that through the striving itself, through the act of reaching for understanding itself and less because of what we find in the effort, we discover our truest selves.

Here in this chapter we will examine ideas related to the unification of justice and love. We will examine some theorists whose ideas equate justice and love, or at least bring them into very close alignment. We will conclude with our own unified theory of justice and crime, possible only because we equate justice and love. In our efforts, we will do all we can to learn from the mistakes of others with regard to their avatars. We do not want to add any citizens to the City of Crime. In truth, we hope to set the occupants all free so that they may find peace.

If we return to Aristotle's assertion, that justice occurs when we give to each what is due, we can now see that he was absolutely correct, but with a crucial caveat (whether he intended this caveat is altogether a different issue). Deservedness does not depend upon actions done, virtue possessed, or some other conditional state. What is due to any one person is not a function of their wealth, their bravery, their achievement. What is due is due merely and wholly because each person *is*; each sentient being is due our highest honor of service, merely because she exists as such. What is due to us is due because we *are,* not because we have or have not done or been something.

That might sound to some suspiciously like entitlement. The idea that one deserves resources on which to live merely because one lives seems deeply unfair to the person who has worked long, difficult, physical days in order to earn a meager living for his family. But his anger is aimed in the wrong direction. He, along with many, have been lied to. We have lied to ourselves, and to each other. We have married the sense of what we should receive to the sense of what we have given, but lawyers, judges, and one notary public are ready, and the time for divorce has come. Recall from chapter 2 the idea we call equity theory (Adams, 1965); it asserts that justice is understood to be a function of the perceived ratio of inputs invested and outputs received for each relevant individual. The idea has a striking and intuitive appeal. As we saw, though, in chapter 2, the idea is fundamentally flawed. The assertion that truest justice could come from perceptions of equity is utter and unmitigated hogwash. At best such justice is a poor understudy for truest justice.

So what then? On what foundation shall we build, what firmament is sound enough to justify entrusting to it so vital and so worthy a thing as the dignity of our children? If you are thinking of a political or economic system, such as communism, then you have missed much of the point of this book as we can find as much fault in communism as capitalism. To get to the answer, you must return to the childlike innocence you once possessed. The very reason we are compelled to ask the question contains the answer: love. It is the how just as it is the why and the when. Surely it cannot be that simple, though, can it? If it were just that easy, we would be doing it already, and probably so for centuries. Yes, in truth, it is just that simple, and yet it is the hardest, most demanding thing one might be asked to do.

A society founded on love is our birthright. It is also our responsibility to fashion it in grand and tiny acts every moment of every day. It is our natural state to nurture, as we are essentially social beings, but we must actively choose to do so, to take the risk of extending one's hand. With that extended hand, of course, we co-author each other and that loving society to which we are heir. And crucially we must fashion our institutions of social welfare to have ensconced in them these capacities, to facilitate the granular, and to enact the grand works of love. In choosing the difficult task of honoring our responsibility to each other we find meaning, and through meaning, freedom. It is choosing to love even though we are aware of one's faults; we do not love blindly like our animals, but choose to love and embrace the imperfectness of humanity wide-eyed and aware. More than a few of our readers will find such a claim, even now, to be outlandish. More is required of us, the authors, in the effort to present our unified theory. Specifically, it will serve our ends to offer fresh ontological and epistemological ideas through which to view the future we envision.

LOVE'S ONTOLOGICAL PROJECT

Although there are many mighty voices that make similar arguments, several of whom we will turn to soon for support, the particular argument that love and justice are synonyms tends to wipe away much of what has come before. It is necessary for us, then, to offer something of an ontological model that would place love at the center of the human universe. Such a project as submitting an ontological model is daunting, and many would argue that it is no humble task. Rest assured, beloved readers, that we undertook the project with the greatest humility.

Let us begin these contemplations with something of an admission: Beth, Tammy, and Michael differ somewhat with regard to our faiths. For each of us, though, our spiritualities are central to who we are as thinkers, parents, teachers, and spouses. Others who have set out their own ontologies have tended to make assertions about the nature of God. Well, we will get there, but it is important to note at the trailhead that your guides here are not seeking to affirm any given religious worldview in this effort.

Love's ontological project relies upon several assertions:

1) *The fundamental nature of existence is connection.* We exist as part of the universe, itself perhaps part of an even wider and grander scheme. We are fully part of the universe that surrounds us; the iron in our blood was forged in supernovae or neutron stars billions of years ago, and the simple act of respiration assures that we are perpetually transacting with the space around us. At a far finer level, discerning the place where we begin and end becomes increasingly difficult, increasingly meaningless. We are nodes in what Buddhists call the Net of Indra. Nothing we do, nothing done to us, can ever alienate us from connection to all that is. Like it or not, convenient or not, we are in each other's care because, well, we are each other.

Thich Nhat Hanh (e.g., 1987; 2007) relies upon a powerful metaphor to illustrate what he calls interbeing: each of us is a wave on the surface of an ocean stirred. Each wave is easily discernible as such, with a beginning, a life course, and an end, but never at any time does any wave cease being water. At birth a wave arises from waterdom, and at its death it returns there, but never did the wave depart from the water. So are we, the triquetra: birth, death, life

. . . we have a discrete and observable course, but never at any time do we cease being part of the earth, the universe. There is no coming from, and there is no returning. And there is no you or me. We are all intertwined, interconnected; our essences touching and affecting each and every life we encounter.

2) *Divinity exists, and its nature is love*. Each of us carries in us the divine in miniature, in us, inalienable from our being/nonbeing. Each divine flame is both part and whole; it is not divinity entire, but each divine flame is complete and contains the full divinity of God. It is connection, reconciliation, wholeness. It is actual and potential, being and becoming, both at the same time. We might liken our sense of God to a hologram: the whole contains an image, but if broken into smaller pieces, each piece also contains the whole image. When brought together again, they form again the one single image. Michael does not possess a clear sense of what that divinity looks like beyond the totality of individual divine bits in each sentient being, whereas Tammy tends to view God from a Christian perspective. But consider: what if Michael and Tammy were *both* "correct"? What if both of us understood divinity as we were disposed to, even as we needed to? The conclusion, of course, is that the universal divine exists precisely and only as each of us needs it to (as Paul would tell us, God is, quite literally, love). In a phone conversation not long ago, Michael mentioned this thought experiment to his father, John. John paused, almost audibly smiling: "It is just like you said when you were a small boy . . . God speaks to each person on his own phone."

Yes, we are presuming the existence of a divine force (and yes, we sense a need to address doing so). Few philosophers offered sound evidence for their own assertions of God's existence; many simply presumed Him to be. Pascal merely weighs costs and benefits and finds that, although God is unlikely, the benefits of getting it right are extreme. Such logic barely rises to the name. Those few arguments that did offer some reasoning are saddled with unresolvable weaknesses. Descartes's *cogito* yields a boundless idea of God, and this boundless idea proves God's boundlessness. Ideas about the divine are necessarily pinned to our ontology, but we do not inquire after proof, nor do we fail to recognize our assumption as such. We simply assume that all understandings of divinity, from Nietzsche to Kierkegaard, are absolutely flawless . . . for each author. Our presumption of divinity is not particularized; the atheist and the devout may here share ground. For each, the divine appears just as that person needs it to appear. We presume no particular form of divinity. More to the point, we presume your idea of divinity, whatever it may be, is perfect.

We assert, however, that the divine, whatever its nature for any given being, enters the social world through action. When we do loving things, and for selfless reasons, there love resides. In Matthew 25:36–40 we are told it is not simply enough to love God, but to love mankind and offer assistance to those in need: the poor, the hungry, the sick, the imprisoned. In helping your fellow man, you are, in essence, accepting, embracing, and even reuniting with God and bringing Her to bear on human harm and suffering. Tolstoy's Martin Avdeich dreamed he would see Jesus in the morning (Tolstoy/Parini, 2009). During his day, he lived in love, giving of himself to passersby according to their need. When the sun had sunk low and Avdeich began to return to his Bible, he thought about his dream; as he did so, each of the people whose lives he touched emerged from the shadows, "It is I." It is in the doing, and the doing without thought of self or return, that the divine is authored into corporeal form. "Truly, I say to you, as you did it to one of the least of my brothers, you did it to me" (Matthew 25:40). God is love, but love is praxis.

It is not the case, however, that the existence of a divine force or phenomenon implies some larger overarching purpose. Rather, divinity itself is its own purpose, if it is even meaningful to speak of one at all; there is no struggle, no Manichaean Verdun between darkness and light. Just as the light of the divine is within each of us and rendered real by our thought and action, so too is the darkness. We project a struggle onto the universe only when one exists within the lamphouse of our hearts.

3) *We are.* There is no "because." If Kant is correct in his assertion that human beings are ends in themselves, then it stands to reason that asking after a why—why are we here—is meaningless. "I am here because . . ." instantly turns the speaker into a means to an end, something that is impermissible, because it is a species of violence. We perceive, we experience, we process, we create, we distill; we do all of these things simply because we do them.

4) *We are perfect.* Each sentient being is perfect. This is not to say we do not make mistakes or that we are immortal. Clearly such an assertion would be folly. Some Christian doctrine tends to convey the message that we are deeply flawed and sinful beings, irreparably tainted by an act with which we had no involvement. Augustine (2006) argues we, all of us, were present in the Garden, mostly because he must, or the rest of his Christological Jenga would crash down; the idea of our indelible stain otherwise simply holds no water. No, we are perfect even in our damage, our confusion, our imperfections. Each of us carries a part of the divine, and in that part, the whole of the divine. As we are more than vessel, we are divine, and thus perfect.

Think back to Hegel's assertion that knowledge was now complete. As we observed, his knowledge with regard to the races was *far* from mature, just to begin. His thin treatment of Buddhist thought is all the more remarkable given the temptation felt by more than a few Hegelian scholars to align Hegel's ideas with Eastern ideas like interbeing. No, Hegel didn't have all the answers. He didn't have most of them, actually. Nevertheless, he was complete and perfect as a being, as he was, at that moment. And to his point about human knowledge, it too was perfect. At that moment. Although we cannot allow harm to follow from his words, say, regarding the many millions who hail from Africa, we can honor his beauty as it was. His racism is the last thing from beautiful, but his being, distinct as it is from his confusions and attachments, is radiant. So is yours.

5) *Life's continuation presupposes life's end.* As something of a corollary of interbeing, for any given organism to continue its life, the end came for some other organism. Eat a simple salad and life ends under a blanket of ranch dressing. Something dies in order for something else to live. Even as we struggle and thus succeed to continue our lives today we know that such victories are temporary. Each of us, however robust and successful we are, will end, and the king will go a-progress through the guts of a beggar. Generally we hold ourselves apart from this realization, possibly in part because holding such a realization in mind as we struggled might well diminish our verve and taste for the fight. Our sense of a singular consciousness and our selective forgetfulness are utile incapacities that aid us in some contexts, but run us aground in others.

The idea that life's continuation presupposes life's end does not somehow ratify the killing process or cheapen life; indeed quite the opposite is true: life's end in the continuation of life (to wit, eating) must be undertaken with the most earnest reverence. Every salad is a gift, every orange is precious medicine, and the fatty muscle of an animal made our larger brains possible. Instead of dwelling on meat as murder, let us honor animals that die to give us life; let us discard factory farming, let us touch the animal's life and its death even as we consume it. And instead of dwelling on the dark end awaiting us all regardless of what we eat, let us honor our continuation now and the sacrifices that made it possible by living as sustainably, as lovingly as we can, in every minute of every day.

In a remarkable and transformative little book, Wohlleben (2015) shows us trees that make friends, trees that warn each other of danger, even trees that sustain nearby stumps with lifegiving sap. We aren't saying the carrot in your salad tonight had feelings and is staring back at you with big, wet, cow eyes as you devour it remorselessly. Is your dinner table made of wood? Michael's is. This much is certain: all life is noble, that privileging meat-producing life as somehow more blessed than beech trees is a distinction we are not comfortable making. All life is precious, but life's continuation presupposes life's end. In time we too will be dinner (or a dinner table).

It is worth noting as an aside that in terms of our ancestors, it is likely they were hunters and scavengers. We have evolved to eat both vegetable and animal materials. The many arguments for and against vegetarianism in the main are rationalizations of preferred arrangements, and very little more. As descendants of hunter/scavengers, we are omnivores. The challenge before us is not to cease meat intake and then to rationalize that decision (although cutting red meat considerably is environmentally wise), but to choose to approach the consumption of animals and vegetables mindfully and with authentic reverence.

6) *It is well.* Our connectedness is total, unavoidable. No struggle offered by humans can alter it even minutely; no art can give shelter from love. Ayn Rand spent the last years of her life on Medicare and Social Security, and lived in state-subsidized housing. But it is alright. Truly, it is okay. Whatever weights you carry right now as you read this, it is well, and it will be well. Life ends for a carrot, or for a child. Pain may be crushing, debilitating. Life may never return to "normal." Yet it will be well. It is okay to live; it is not treasonous to laugh again. Where it is not well is where we find confusion, suffering, avarice; and it is where we find confusion, suffering, and avarice that we find also opportunities for love's healing to act, for justice to be done. Forgiveness for harm, as Michael observed in *A Different Justice*, is both a categorical imperative and gift of grace at the very same time. The capacity to forgive meaningfully, however, is not necessarily a thing easily cultivated. Such a capacity comes in large part from the discovery that all is well.

Perhaps it is noteworthy to clarify that we do *not* assert the universe to be inherently good or bad. Such labels are meaningless, and thus offer no use for us here. Love does not honor such distinctions.

7) *It is in you.* Hours of practicing behind him, hours more yet ahead, Michael peered balefully through the window of his Ithaca College practice room at his cello resting against the single chair in the room. Dvorak awaits. In this moment, Michael had a realization that contributed to his decision not to pursue music professionally, and instead to pursue his interest in criminal justice. In the Michael-and-cello team, the member that held the team back from performing perfectly the canon of cello music . . . was Michael. It is a good cello: made, as such instruments are, by hand by a skilled luthier. This particular cello was made by Jan Juzek, a Czech luthier of some renown, sometime in the first few decades of the twentieth century. It is, in fact, more cello than Michael had chops for. If YoYo Ma or Mistislav Rostropovich were to sit down behind the instrument, it could sing so as to move one to tears. Michael's Carpathian companion stared back at him through the window, waiting in silence. It waits still; Michael never really returned.

Not long ago, Michael was practicing his electric bass and watching master classes on YouTube. He came across a video of Victor Wooten . . . being Victor Wooten. Now, for the uninitiated, Vic Wooten is, well, the Man. Kind, humble, brilliant, inspiring, he is the truest example of a bass guitar virtuoso. During one master class, he modified the attention of a student, really only slightly, by telling him to focus on the drummer in his head, and not on his bass. The difference was striking. He had the student stop playing, then he dropped a bomb. He observed that the change that had occurred in the quality of his groove was a function of his shift of attention away from the tool in his hands to the music in his head. As the student stood there, smiling, the instrument made no sound. Wooten observed this, saying that the music does not reside in the instrument. It resides *in you*. Michael realized in that moment that he had been completely wrong all those years ago to abandon his friend in that practice room.

We would be remiss if we did not pause just a moment to observe the power of a simple idea to change entirely how one views one's self in relation to the world. Michael probably still would have chosen criminology/zemiology as a home, and in truth he is grateful for his earlier error aiding him in his life choices, though as pointless as they are to contemplate, one can never be completely sure of such things. This particular lesson in a bass guitar master class bears rich criminological significance, of course. We have contemplated above where art resides (Scruton, 2017), and where justice resides. Justice, like art, like music, resides solely within you. What does it mean to say justice resides solely in you? Like music, Fromm (2006) tells us, love is an art requiring discipline, care, dedication, practice, preparation, creativity, and ultimately freedom from the instrument of practice; forget the bass and be with the music. Each of us must take ownership of the idea of justice, not with eyes of vengeance or of comparison, but of love. We assert that justice and love are one and the same thing; it would stand to reason, then, via simple replacement, that justice is an art requiring discipline, care, dedication, practice, preparation, creativity . . . and freedom.

8) *Truest freedom is a birthright*. Most of us never taste true freedom, however, at least currently, because so many of us cannot recognize or even perceive our fetters. Truest freedom is a state where we exist articulably free from conditionings, habit energies, assumptions. In such a state, our natural inclination is to turn to love, like flowers follow the sun across the crystal summer sky.

9) *Choice is the gift, charge, and commission of sentience*. We, along with many countless beings, have the gift of choice. And indeed choice is at the very heart of the problem of crime and the human understanding of justice. From the foregoing, it should be evident that choice is absolutely central to love, and choice matters not at all.

Remember that treatment of Genesis we discussed earlier? Two people stand in a garden, verdant and yielding. The two, a woman and a man, are not alone. God is there, choruslike, to set the scene. All this is yours, God says. Eat and live. But of this tree over here, this one with the figs (figs are the only fruit mentioned by name in the account), do not eat of this tree. The day you eat of this tree you will die.

Let us pause to consider circumstances thus far. Two beings, just like us save for being brand new, are set into an ideal circumstance, with all humans could ever need freely provided in abundance. There is but one law, a one-statute criminal code, and a capital offense at that. This one law forbade the sampling of a single tree in the garden. Chapter 14 of the North Carolina General Statutes, the criminal code, contains sixty-one articles, and hundreds of subsections. Under ideal conditions, two humans violated *the only law*, ostensibly punishable by death, *within an hour*. Why would God introduce such a dangerous thing as a tree that kills in the middle of a garden built to sustain? But what is death, after all, to a being only an hour old? Either this is a horrible story, or there is more to things than meets the eye.

Rabbi Friedman (2011; see also Cooper, 1998) offers help. Adam and Eve, he asserts, were given a mission. The mission was to go to earth, to the lowest place, and there to work to elevate it. It was Eve, it seems, who figured out the purpose of the tree. She eats, and she presses Adam to eat as well. The reason? Choice. They had to choose to suffer in order to elevate. Childbirth pangs and stubborn soil are conditions to be borne so as to bring light by action, by choice, into being.

Yet choice cannot be used as a cudgel against one who has chosen to cause harm. Advocates of rational choice are not in error about the existence of choice. Indeed, as noted earlier, they focused much of their corrective action on the conceptualization of "rational." But the fact that a person chose to visit harm cannot be used as justification for punishment, mostly because punishment, as we have already shown, is masturbation, but also because choice is a function of freedom; even Hegel did not fully grasp what freedom means. Even if punishment ever made sense, it would be bizarre to punish a person for not being wiser than Hegel.

9) *Growth is the tendency of living, loving things*. Speaking of Hegel, his dialectical framework, noble and useful though it may be, is itself something of an abstraction of the process whereby God comes to know herself through history. Certainly we agree with him that development, our negative-entropic vector if you prefer, is not linear, and that his iterative dialectic can be discerned in part through an examination of history. It is, however, only as a function of analysis that the dialectic exists; we perceive it in retrospect, though it is somewhat less precise a technology for purposes of extrapolation of future humanity. In his treatment on Buddhism (Hegel, 2004, pp. 161–65), for example, we might assume the principles as he lays them out

(incomplete and imprecise though they may be) to be thesis, yet such a treatment would be like one hand clapping without some antithesis to presage the synthesis that is Navayana. Of course, only once Navayana is established as a result of the suffering confronted by Buddhist thinkers, only then can the dialectic troika be discerned. It is a useful tool for historical analysis, but not so robust for understanding the nature of choice made at the time.

Instead of the iterative dialectic, then, let us conceive of choice not as a result of dialectic, or of rationality (cost and benefit), of as a vector with turning points (e.g., Sampson & Laub, 1993). Human choice is the mechanism whereby we author divinity, unity, reconciliation, wholeness, or darkness, pain, divisiveness, isolation. Choice is the chisel with which we fashion the human universe, the cello with which we sing the song of ourselves. We are at times rational, at times emotional, at times clear-eyed, at times lost to ourselves; and we make choices under these and other conditions all of the time, big and small. Often we get better at making choices as we do it. Those who harm choose, those who react to harm choose, those who craft the law choose. And each choice, momentous and trivial alike, has its own anatomy, its own history, present and future. Each choice lives like a child born to a single parent; part in whole and whole in part.

Love's Epistemology

As a direct consequence of our fundamental connectedness, each of us both is and is not discrete. There is no fully discernible self, and yet we can speak of some attributes of self-ness. We are, and we are not. We arise, we live, we die, but we are not separate from the whole at any given time. It is natural, then, to ask *who*, when we contemplate knowing. *Who* is doing the knowing?

The best neuroscience available at the time of writing indicates that our bare consciousness is related to three separate regions of the brain working in concert (Fischer, Boes, Demertzi, Evrard, Laureys, Edlow, Liu, Saper, Pascual-Leone, Fox, & Geerling, 2016). Examining a dozen coma-causing lesions in comparison to twenty-four controls, it was found that a tiny portion of the rostral dorsolateral pontine tegmentum was associated with wakefulness. Also functionally linked to this portion of the brain stem were the ventral anterior insula and the pregenual anterior cingulate cortex. Connections among these sites were disrupted in comatose patients, and not for healthy controls. Although we tend to experience our consciousness as a single voice, a directed will, such sensation is mere illusion. At the very least, consciousness is the result of the interaction of several sites in the brain.

But even this specificity, the identification of organic sites for bare consciousness, just does not satisfy. Wakefulness and basic awareness of self is rather far from the plastic and creative din of mind activity that often resembles the trading room floor on Wall Street. Our minds defy description; such a thing it is for matter to grasp its own capacities, and yet find the description daunting. Time in contemplative practices reveals the experience of multiple voices, multiple subroutines within the umbra of consciousness. In our silence, we can witness and even identify several distinct voices, even characters, that negotiate awareness, meaning, action, and memory. Our knowing, then, is not performed by a singular controlling part of us, there is no captain of the ship. Our knowing is negotiated by committee. *What* we know, *how* we know, *that* we know . . . all are negotiated within, *in camera*, in the vault of the mind. Certainly agreement is possible, and even agreement with other committees (other sentient beings), but it is agreement within where knowing begins.

Within Michael, for instance, one can find (inter alia) a cowboy, a frail, angry, and frightened old man, a young Henry Miller, a Sammy Hagar–esque character, a monster, a young boy, a Buddha, and what he has taken to calling Gollum, the sad, grasping shell of a being that was once Tolkien's Sméagol. Often it is the quiet voice in the back of the room, the Buddha, who receives attention (at least that is the intention), although on occasion the cowboy or the angry codger steals the mic. Who, then, is he who knows? Each of the voices within, each of the subroutines knows, and each to a different degree.

Just as there is often cacophony, a collision of voices, so too is mighty serenity possible. Contemplation offers the opportunity to find a deep and abiding silence within, and within that silence, a wisdom deeper and more exquisite than words can corral. In this silence, what is known is not merely known. It is felt, echoing through joints, ringing in bones, radiating from life into life.

Asking after what is known, then, seems a natural next step. We do not *know* about God. We *think* we understand *how we respond to the idea* of God, but we can only either presuppose God's existence, or not. Assertions we make about God's nature or the nature of the universe generally are, for all the verve and certainty we may offer, actually and unavoidably mediated by our perception capacity. Humans know symbols, patterns. Humans know emotions, yet when healthy they are not ruled by them. Humans know beauty. Humans know sensations. But in any of these is at best partial insight, at most portions of truth. Sentience is inseparable from its constituent parts. The perceiver *is* the perceived.

If the perceived is beautiful and perfect, as we have asserted, then, *modus ponens*, perceiving, experiencing, processing, and creating are all beautiful. Sentience is magnificent. And it is, but it rises to its fullest magnificence when it is regarded in its fullness. In an age of increasing specializations and intellectual balkanization, it remains the case that fullest understanding exists where empiricism, art, faith, and metaphor overlap, and mutually fertilize each other.

The tendency is for examinations of epistemic inquiries to relate almost directly to empirical ones. Although perhaps natural, we will not thus privilege scientific knowing. We know, we feel, we believe, we surmise, we reason, we infer, we fear, we abstract. We do all of these things and more. The emphasis on logic, rationality, data reduction, pattern finding, sequentiality, and the like has tended to privilege one kind of "knowing" but at the expense of other kinds of knowing, like abstract, symbolic, artistic knowledge. Unless injured or surgically modified, our corpus callosum welds our capacities into a formidable whole: we can use logic and art, data analysis and intuition, math and song, in order to discover human truth. Indeed, using our total capacity is the only way to understand fully our universe and our place in it, and particularly when it comes to the problems of justice and suffering. When we embrace our total selves, when we accept lovingly who and how we are, our capacity for understanding increases exponentially. There is some hint of precedent for such a stand in Hegel: he crafts space for truth for both philosophy and religion; one provides conceptual truth whereas the other offers representative or symbolic truth.

Perhaps some of the confusion lies in semantics: after all, science is the pursuit of knowledge. But we are capable of much more than mere knowing. Rather, knowing is often illusory. Before Einstein, scientists *knew* Newton's laws explained planetary motion. Before the Kansas City Preventive Patrol Experiment, everyone *knew* police patrol prevented crime. Instead, we must seek something grander, more complete, more ancient.

What, then, does it mean to know something? As the saying goes, recognizing that a tomato is a fruit is knowledge; wisdom, however, means not putting it in a fruit salad. As consciousness is itself nonwhole, as there are several distinct parts to it, clearly "knowing" is not a uniform thing. Having possession of a fact is appreciably different from understanding how best to nurture a spouse or child. Moreover, knowing is often a volatile thing, both from within the knower and with regard to the known. How deeply one understands facts, concepts, feelings varies over time. Any empirically derived understanding of an aspect of the human condition is useful only until it isn't; often within two decades most empirical findings lose their traction unless bolstered by insights from other sectors of human inquiry.

Understanding the human world, what we will call *human truth*, is fully and unalterably human. Seeking objectivity or relying upon subjectivity or intersubjectivity alone produces an incomplete awareness, and relying upon a particular kind of knowledge to carry the day is foolishness. Hegel's idealist version of *Geist* is not wholly dissimilar to the idea of human truth, either in nature or in the means of derivation. Where difference tends to reside is in the shape of the guardrails, and in terms of the diversity of ends sought. Progress, we would agree, is not linear, but its generalized vector is not on rails of reason toward highest reason as Hegel would assert, but love: "*The salvation of man is through love and in love*" (Frankl, 2006, p. 37; emphasis in original). (Let us pause just for a moment and recognize that a man who lost his family in the gas chambers of Auschwitz, who himself suffered to the limits of his physical frame, explains to the rest of us that our salvation is in and through love.) True, we can reason to love, and Hegel holds this out as even ideal, but love exists beyond reason, and navigates free of its constraints. Borrowing meter from cummings, love is more true than Truth.

Now we must be cautious: the assertion that love is more true than Truth does not obliterate the physical sciences as an endeavor. Of course not. Love sublates it. More, we should not take from the limitations of science some ill-informed claptrap about science being a politically driven enterprise. Objectivity, though, is not all it promises. Objectivity, like Newton's laws, function well for us but within a bandwidth of human experience. Newton's laws and quantum mechanics seem to collide conceptually, but in fact the former is a natural consequence of the latter. As we grow in understanding, both of ourselves and of our universe, we will find increasingly that simpler ideas like objectivity, rational choice simply lose their appeal as we no longer see ourselves in them.

FOR THE FURIOUS

Shakespeare's Henry V evidenced his rage, ripping the herald from his horse. The squires in the luggage had been killed, expressly against the laws of war and chivalry. Against this French perfidy he fired "I had not been angry since I came to France / Until this instant" (*Henry V*, IV, vii). There is a vein of righteous anger—strike that—righteous fury detectable in our discipline. A number of critical criminologists openly call for the "pound of flesh" from police officers who fail cataclysmically, or they demand that the institutions that so concern and vex criminologists should be obliterated utterly, and only *maybe* be rebuilt, but vastly differently.

Let us begin with a clarification: we are angry, too. Livid in fact. Institutions and their actors today are arrayed and equipped in such a way that it is well possible that another Tamir Rice could be liquidated without consequences; as we write in fact young Jordan Edwards, an honor-roll student, was killed by a rifle bullet fired by a Balch Springs police officer. *Yet another* beautiful young life ended. Under such circumstances the only sane response is fury; that and an abyssal sadness. Fundamental recrafting of justice is necessary, from its very genetics to its largest iterations, but the question we must concern ourselves with is not whether these institutions should be radically repaired or blown up and rebuilt, as both will give us about the same thing in the end. What matters is not what we do, but rather when we do it relative to our development. And that means that the question of how and who we are at the time is *absolutely central.* Were we to dismantle and rebuild policing today, perhaps some of the genetic code of the slave patrols could be excised, but the institution would look much like the institution we have today because we are still who we are now.

Radical criminological thought, like that of Kramer, Michalowski, and Kauzlarich (2002), discerns a greedy and small figure in the contemplation of a white-collar or a corporate criminal. He is as skeevy as Shkreli; a demon in a Kiton suit. In his quieter moments, Michael will admit that he has fantasized about open-hand slapping Shkreli hard enough to loosen his molars. Michael would never, but there is a very small part of him that would deeply relish the moment. It is this very voice in each of us that has been the author of so much of the impoverished thought we have discussed. It is the crafter of broken justice, the architect of ruins. It is a dark fiction that vengeance or comparative calculi somehow result in anything close to justice, but the author of that fiction is you and us.

And it is natural to stare unbelieving into the maw of hate and wonder where God might be hiding. How could a loving God let young Tamir Rice be executed? How could a loving God let Michael Brown lie for hours in the street like roadkill? Where is God when so many people hurt so badly? Does He offer no solace? Some might find God in scripture, but that is not His real home. God dwells in choices. God lives among us in the tiny moments where we choose to smile to a passerby, when we choose to hold a quaking hand, when we choose to connect with another despite risk to ourselves. When we respond authentically to the question "why do I hurt," with compassion, commitment, and capacity, that is where justice is, where love is, where God is. The divine exists when all hope seems to be lost, when our fellow man has disappointed us beyond repair, when the system convicts an innocent man; God is there to pick up the pieces, and She does this through you and me.

A UNIFIED THEORY

Equipped as we are now, let us return finally to our question regarding Ariadne's string. Considering all that has come before, taking lessons learned from impoverished and accomplished but incomplete thought on justice and crime, we can finally bring these two discourses together into a unified theory of justice and harm. What allows us to do this is setting a simple equivalency: justice and love are synonyms.

Well, perhaps it is more precise to say that justice, like our children, is the fruit of love. Cornel West has famously said that justice is what love looks like in public, which some of us (e.g., DeValve, 2017c) have taken as something of a barometer of the quality of our inner states: a dysfunctional justice system evidences a desiccated capacity to love. Quite so. But identifying the relationship between justice and love is only the first step on the path of a thousand miles. Can we say anything more?

Quite so. First, let us recap briefly what we mean when we say "love." Love is "the artlike, individualized, unconditional, aware, and end-less praxis, whereby a human or organization mindfully, assertively, and continuously labors for the actualization of another human being as an end in herself, without thought of return, without reliance upon authority, without fear, or possibility of cessation" (DeValve, 2015, p. 103). Love is not affect alone, nor is it action alone. It is a constant, authentic struggle for insight into how to facilitate the actualization of another without thought of benefit to one's self.

Love's Theory of Criminoetiology

The creation of a criminoetiology of love occurred in *A Different Justice*, specifically in the ninth chapter. An avatar was present there as well—actually at least two were used as dress forms for the theory. The first was Michael's father who has often asserted that humans do what they do because they believe it to be self-enhancing. The second avatar was Michael himself, not an alien construct. Michael learned somewhat recently, for example, that a marriage is akin to two people juggling scissors in a lightless broom closet: never is harm intended, but just as surely as no harm is intended, someone is going to get hurt.

Harm, including crime, is the result of human action or inaction. Harm, including crime, happens. It is not any more causatively tied to any other thing any more than is any other complex human activity. People do what they do (or don't do what they don't do) because they believe that what they do (or don't do) is in some way self-enhancing (DeValve, 2015). Harm or not, crime or not, we do things that we think to be self-enhancing. Even suicide can be understood in this way, as it might be undertaken to end one's ceaseless and excruciating pain. Humans live their lives acting and reacting, self-enhancement as a behind-the-scenes reason for it all. Shopping at Food Lion instead of Harris Teeter saves you money; listening to a CD in your car instead of the radio insulates you from vacuous and repetitive commercials. Kissing your beloved before leaving for work is retaking the oath of love again in miniature.

Self-enhancement, however, is not necessarily well understood (DeValve, 2015) by each human. It is in our collective best interest (and thus is self-enhancing) for us to stop driving gasoline-powered vehicles in order to minimize human greenhouse gas emissions. Michael for one surely could benefit from putting his ample ass on a bicycle now and again, and pedaling it to and from work. But he does not. Indeed, even writing these words for publication has not made it a scintilla more likely that he ever will do so. Fear of insane drivers . . . and laziness . . . prevent the idea from ever rising to the point of active contemplation. So he buys a small car and hopes for the best, smugly proud of not driving the big Jeep he actually wants. In *A Different Justice*, Michael iterated his experience making bread pudding for the local homeless breakfast kitchen. The bread pudding went over like a fart in church. No one got sick, of course, but food was wasted along with a couple of afternoons, and some people actually skipped eating for fear of the brown, bready mound on their plates (DeValve, 2015). Even when we intend well, we can cause harm.

We increase the likelihood of harm, to ourselves, to others, and to the wider world, though, when we act from greed, fear, or ignorance (DeValve, 2015). Being afraid does not guarantee we will harm another or ourselves, but it makes the perception of our truest nature harder to perceive; it occludes our real best interest. Greed, desiring more, nicer things and more money, hides from us what truly has value. Of course, greed is a form of fear (e.g., of not having), fear is interwoven with ignorance. Each of these three "criminogenic" constructs are themselves interpenetrating each other to the point where one term might best be used to describe the entire phenomenon: *dukkha*, or suffering.

We increase the likelihood of harm through our own suffering, but it would be imprecise to say that greed, fear, and ignorance (or *dukkha*) is causative of crime (or other harm). As we have already observed, harm can be utterly unintentional and come from the very best of intentions. The National Highway Traffic Safety Administration reports that in the United States, 10,265 died in alcohol-related accidents in 2015 (National Highway Traffic Safety Administration, 2015). It would strain credulity to argue that a nontrivial portion of these deaths were intentional. One more bourbon will be just fine.

Love's Theory of Justice

If harm (and the special case of crime) is a natural result from human interaction, but more often occurs in particular interactions that are impacted by the impairments brought on by *dukkha*, how should the wider human community (e.g., seek accountability and allocate its resources) respond to that harm? Given the foregoing, we can understand that justice is a kind of activity as well as a result from that activity. It is a thing we do that seeks to render meaning from the suffering it confronts. That meaning is, like our individual identities, co-created in authentic action toward both harmer and harmed that seeks to transform suffering into wisdom and insight. The justice action must be intentioned toward transformation of suffering into insight, and although that action cannot be conditional, it is reciprocal when conditions require (the justice professional is as likely to be harmer or harmed).

The action of justice that leads to the outcome of justice is endless (or at least not temporally constrained) and is rarely easy or simple; far more often the action of justice involves struggle and striving. It is in that understood and intentional choice to strive, to struggle, though, that justice (and we) find meaning, and in which we are reconciled to each other; harmer to harmed, justice agent to harmer, and all to the wider human world.

Certainty, authority, specificity, comparison, predetermined outcome, anger . . . all of these take us far afield of true justice, and lead us instead to barren fields of their own where what passes for justice is toxic, dishonest, cheap, masturbatory, and emetic. We will know true justice when we choose to do the hard thing, to be the breath of God in our granular thoughts and actions toward those we do not know, even those who we fear. The action of justice resides, then, in you, in us, but the fruits of that justice dwell in the spaces in between.

CONCLUSION

Somewhere between realizing the existence of a Coke delivery button and the establishment of a presidential library, each American president has an epiphany (or we might hope an Epistrophe?): each one realizes that they etch a new Rushmore in time with their words and actions; they sculpt history with every gesture. That means their daily activity, the letters, the emails, the tweets, even the hand-scribbled notes are fodder for libraries, and may end up in history books and beheld by generations to come. You and we are not such people as kings; we do not issue history with every sneeze, but we do have access to a similar realization, a similar invitation. Future criminologists, philosophers, or zemiologists, or whatever we will call ourselves, will, just as we have done, look back at the ideas and actions of others, and they will judge us, just as we have judged. To be sure they will critique our reasoning ability, our empirical prowess, our sophistication, and our integrity, just as we have assessed the generations before us. In fact, although it sounds dysfunctional, it is an important part of the scientific process: concern regarding future scientists tossing aside our life's work as childish, uninspired, dishonest, or hopelessly inured in our own psycho-social swamps keeps good social scientists up nights, and keeps them sharp (if sleepless) in their work.

Of course, science does not operate on such concern alone, or even primarily, but that need for securing our immortality or something like it resides somewhere in the darker recesses. It would be inimical to our arguments to claim that the attachment to self of which we speak should be intentionally created or manipulated for outcomes. It is real, however, and it is a thing to which we must respond. We must recognize that a time will come when we will be held accountable for our fruits as scientists and as a science. We will be held accountable not only for the quality of our science, but of the quality of our hearts.

In Japan, there is a practice called kintsugi, or kintsukuroi. A clay bowl is dropped and breaks into pieces, some big, some small. The Zen master weeps tenderly for the nobility of a dented old teapot, still anxious to carry your tea, but for its broken handle. It is the art of broken pieces, or the art of embracing damage. In the practice, potsherds are reassembled using gold foil, or gold-dust-impregnated lacquer. The result is often far more beautiful than the original bowl.

It turns out that trees make friends (Wohlleben, 2015). Beech trees in particular will share access to nourishing light. Trees also warn each other of danger. They will even provide life-sustaining sap to a nearby stump, supporting its life for years.

People are not pots. People are not trees. The challenges humans face often are multifaceted and seemingly intractable. They are not more profound, however, than those faced by the stump or the shattered pot, for these are problems of the existential variety. If we can learn to tend to a bowl with the tenderness of kintsugi and trees can sustain the life of a neighbor when hope is ridiculous, might we also see past our complexity and offer ourselves in love?

Chapter Six

Notes from the Field

Epic Wins in Justice Practice

One of the most fascinating aspects of the study of justice and harm today is that there are instances of human growth, blossoming, and healing interspersed amid the cold and unyielding stone of contemporary justice practice. Humans *do* succeed, they *do* grow, and they *do* heal in the most barren and desiccated environs. Often, however, it is *despite* conditions rather than because of them. Criminologists/zemiologists in search of empirical research might do well to consider this one: akin to epidemiologists confronting a confounding illness, they may, as an alternative, consider studying instances of survival and humans blossoming *despite* exposure to noxious conditions. It is the human condition to thrive. And it is here we criminologists must learn to re-approach our studies on the human condition with the same zeal. Positivists have long studied humans as if they were inanimate objects rather than living, breathing, sentient beings. The *why* of becoming involved in the justice system and the *punishment* of wrongdoers have been the focus within our field for too long. And, while many argue the various ways to do so, in the end, we, as practitioners, simply impose varying methods of punishment in order to *rehabilitate* seemingly damaged individuals; we use verbiage similar to that used in medicine, but rather than a healing practice, the criminal justice version of *rehabilitation* is more akin to taking a sledgehammer to an already shattered ankle. Under the best of circumstances, treating a broken leg is easy compared to treating the harms done to the soul. We must offer care, *loving kindness*, and nurture the soul back until it is made whole . . . we must *rehumanize* rather than *rehabilitate* those who are lost. Even a fracture site will grow stronger if nurtured correctly.

While we believe in the human condition to overcome, sometimes the deck is stacked and everyone does not play fair (or is not even playing the same game) including those who are supposed to adhere to justice. Thus, we would be remiss were we not willing to address instances of catastrophic failure of justice practice. Many critics (e.g., Alexander, Stevenson, Williams, Shelden) argue that our justice system is not at all broken, but it is designed to function precisely as it does, that the damage to the low-wealth, gender and sexual minority, racial, and ethnic communities is fully intentional. This is in no way a new argument, of course, and the recent iteration of thinkers making waves neither goes far enough, nor in the main does it offer cogent solutions. Still, the sentiment that the criminal justice system destroys as it was intended is both correct yet not precisely accurate. Sir Robert Peel and Patrick Colquhoun had no intention of creating an institution bent on oppression; their version of policing was based on professionalism in which police officers, not apart but of the people, were public servants entrusted to enforce the law. But in contrast to a professionalized system, the American slave patrol emerged (Hadden, 2003); this (in)justice system is both an unabashed effort to oppress and also the precursor and parent of our American police, incorporating an *us* versus *them* mentality. Whereas some policies may be intended to oppress, other failed practices are conceived by humans with noble plans to help their fellow humans reach their intended, God-given destiny. The Quakers had only good and loving intentions when they conceived of the penitentiary, a penitence structure designed to render God's servants from the raw materials of the Devil's legion. While things didn't go as planned, and the hopeful intentions of the penitentiary system became more of a waking nightmare than a path to salvation, the failure paled in comparison to other versions. The post-reconstruction South put prisons to a far darker use than the Quakers could have ever envisioned remotely possible; a system created to embrace the last vestiges of slavery, the Southern prison system reenslaved a population to meet its own political and economic agenda. It is fairer, then, to say that criminal justice institutions function in a distorted, inhumane way because their purposes, while often well-intended, have been coopted by those in power and are the result, intent considered, of a failure to understand our own humanity. The genuinely well-meaning if misguided visions of the founders of keystone institutions in criminal justice have been sublimated and drowned out by fear-drenched and greed-driven calls for "controlling the negro" or "getting tough on crime" in the name of justice.

We should be angry. Tammy, Beth, and Michael are beyond furious. It has become common to fear CNN news bulletins for fear of reading about another beautiful life ended by "justice agents." As much as it sickens us, it is necessary to hold up instances of abject failure of justice practice to produce anything akin to justice, as from these instances, we may also learn something. We do not intend to hurt anyone with the examples we will contemplate, and we seek to cast no accusations upon individuals or institutions not discussed here. Paraphrasing Dr. King, it is in the darkest night that we can best see the stars; learning, wisdom, and insight can be derived, and more importantly, human hearts can be reclaimed.

This final chapter, then, is about epic wins of justice practice, offered with the intent of learning something valuable from them. It is by no means a complete listing of such instances. Some recent and some historic and iconic examples will be contemplated here. Sometimes, time and distance will provide rich insight and healing; sometimes recency will have its own rewards.

EPIC WINS

It is our hope that we can repair the harms perpetrated not only by crime but by the system. In chapter 5, we established our assumptions for developing a theory of justice as love. But it is not enough to simply propose a theory of justice. We must also make sure a mechanism of justice is available to implement change; love as praxis. We are cognizant that we are not the first to promote such ideas, as Braithwaite (1999) would argue that restorative justice has been a prevailing model of justice throughout human history. Communitarian (e.g., Aboriginal, Maori, and other First Nations and Native Americans) and religious believers (e.g., Jewish, Christian, and Buddhist) have implemented ideas of love and justice for centuries. It is only in the last thirty years that we have placed them under the umbra of restorative justice practices, so modern restorative justice traditions are a good place to start in our application of the justice as love principle.

Restorative justice is a transactional process rooted in reintegrative shaming (Braithwaite, 1989), exchange, and social disorganization theories (e.g., collective efficacy; Bazemore & Schiff, 2005). In this process, harm is identified and steps are taken to repair this harm in an attempt to seek justice for *all* stakeholders. According to Zehr (2005), crime is a violation of people and their relationships; we would argue that this applies not only to crime but the injustice committed by the system in the name of a socially constructed pseudo justice, the criminal justice system. It is in this violation that we do harm as we violate our contract with the divine and our fellow man. Justice does not simply affect single actors, the victim and the offender, as we must acknowledge that a violation against another wounds the entire community as we are all connected. And we agree with Zehr that we have an obligation to "make things right." But we have come to see that more is possible, that transformation is possible through the transaction of restoration. What is needed, though, is not exchange but truth: authentic honoring of connection, brave confrontation of harm, true contrition. These things are not always possible, as each participant in a mediation comes to that mediation with their own store of gifts and capacities, but when capacity and spirit allows, the mediator can serve as the facilitator of divine transformation. Thus, restorative justice practices, based in divine justice, can be a means "to promote reconciliation, repair, and reassurance" (Zehr, 2005). It is an instrument to emphasize accountability, making amends, and possibly forgiveness. It can reestablish the connection between the divine and ourselves when harm has been done. But we must be cautious here in our dichotomous definition of who has been harmed and who has committed the harm as the term "victim" is often convoluted. We would argue that those who seek to do harm can also be a victim as harm has been done to them. Even in their victimizing another, harm, maybe justly, will continue. Now, Zehr (2005) argues that restorative justice is not simply about forgiveness, as forgiveness is not a requirement. It is here where we must depart, because to love is to forgive. As noted, restorative justice is based on returning to a pre-offense status, but in reality, that is not possible, especially without forgiveness. Things can never return to the way they were. Even with forgiveness, you will be well, but you may never be the same. So, when we talk about forgiveness, we don't intend to imply that the offending act never happened, but rather forgiveness allows us to see an individual for the (im)perfect being that the divine intended and understanding that change can occur. Seeing that harm affects us all in our connection (or loss of) to the divine. Justice, for us, is about reducing harm for the "least of these" as victims and offenders are often one and the same. Below, we attempt to give examples where wins have occurred within the criminal justice system. Out of darkness, light emerges, sometimes even unintentionally.

Alternative Dispute Resolution/Mediation Practices

Perhaps an ideal, albeit obvious, epic win of the justice system lies in the practice of alternative dispute resolution/mediation, a restorative justice technique discussed earlier in this book and found most frequently within the court function of the justice system. To recap, the core premise of victim-offender mediation practices relies on the cooperation between the harmed and the harmer to come to a mutually agreed upon resolution to their situation with the assistance of a trained, unbiased facilitator (Dhami, 2016). Mediation is often used in concert with traditional justice approaches and may be reliant upon referrals to victim-offender mediation programs by the court or corrections agents (Umbreit, Vos, Coates, & Armour, 2006). The goal of this style of restorative justice programs is to begin the healing process for both the victim and offender, and in some iterations the community itself. Healing leads one to assume that compassion or concern for the "other" is at the core of this practice—not punishment or atonement, but healing. How does healing begin? Typically, healing begins with an acknowledgment that someone has been harmed or "wronged." However, even in the earliest of societies gaining acknowledgment for a "wrong" has been complicated (Wright & Brightman, 2018). The need for a victim to accuse someone of a transgression and to bring this transgression to the attention of an authority figure (a clan or tribe leader, an elder, a religious figure) has led to acknowledgment of the "wrong" coming from an outsider, someone not involved in the incident itself.

Whereas crime victims were much more involved in the overall process in earlier civilizations, feasibly most important being identified as the specific entity that has been harmed, the introduction of nation-states and communities under greater control of a more formalized government structure led to crime victims not being able to engage with the accused to receive that formal acknowledgment. This contributed to the demise of discourse between the victim and offender and took away the opportunity for the victim to experience the relief that may have come from the offender's acknowledgment of the harm felt by the victim overall (Wright & Brightman, 2018). Instead, the state became the aggrieved party and the victim was a tool used to illustrate that fact. The purpose of this change grew out of the need to quash blood feuds between victims and offenders (or those close to them) and was developed to decrease continued resentment and retribution experienced by both parties (Wright & Brightman, 2018). So, the intention was good. However, it took away the ability of victim and offender to work together to resolve a conflict or remedy a harm. Perhaps, most catastrophic was the removal of the recognition that the victim was hurt, because once that was removed there was a failure to focus on what needed to be done to assist the victim (and the community and offender) to recover from the perpetrated harm. Decades of research have illustrated that crime victims have been suffering as a result of their sidelined role and that judicial outcomes that hold offenders accountable for their transgressions are not sufficient in and of themselves to help victims recover from the harm they experienced (Wright & Brightman, 2018).

Mediation, and other restorative justice practices, have built upon the principle of restoration—that the actual parties involved in the incident can benefit from interaction with each other because there is acknowledgment of the act of harm and intention to work together to heal all parties involved—recovery for the victim and assistance for the offender, so that he/she may not harm another. Integral to the mediation meeting is the acknowledgment that harm has been perpetrated against the crime victim, not just the state (Choi, Green, & Kapp, 2010). With that acknowledgment comes accountability, and with accountability comes recognition of and atonement for the harm perpetrated. Indeed, Shapland et al. (2006) (as cited in Dhami, 2016) found that both victims and offenders had an expectation that a mediation session would involve some type of apology within it, and that this was a motivating factor for participating in a mediation session overall. Similarly, Choi, Green, and Kapp (2010) found that the need to receive an apology was paramount in the group of victims participating in VOM that they interviewed. It was the receipt of the apology that was most valued as an outcome of the process. While a conviction does accomplish the goal of holding one accountable in a public fashion (and the power of that cannot be diminished), it does not follow that accountability automatically will provide the crime victim with a sense of well-being, satisfaction with the system, or a guide toward healing. Mediation, however, does appear to offer some of these things. In an evaluation of mediation programs over twenty-five years, Umbreit, Coates, and Vos (2004) found that in the vast majority of studies, upward of 80 to 90 percent of victims reported higher levels of satisfaction with the mediation process than victims reported in traditional justice approaches overall. Victims reported satisfaction with the overall process and the outcome of the session itself (Umbreit, Vos, Coates, & Armour, 2006). Additionally, in an analysis of sixty-three studies of restorative justice programs (VOM being the predominant form of program), Umbreit et al. (2002) found that offenders were more likely to complete their obligations of restitution that had been agreed upon within the session, as well as to have higher rates of desistance from future crimes. Direct satisfaction with restitution receipt is more often realized by crime victims participating in VOM and as such is a third element of increased satisfaction with mediation over traditional court processes as well. Choi, Green, and Kapp (2009) reported that victims felt satisfied with the ability to receive answers to questions that persisted from the beginning of the traditional court processes and for which there were no other mechanisms by which they could communicate with the offender. One of the participants in their study indicated that it provided a sense of relief, a way to quell some of the anger that remained after the traditional proceeding because the questions remained and resulted in unresolved emotions for the victim. Umbreit, Vos, Coates, and Armour (2006) reported that across multiple studies, personal crime victims reported that they were satisfied with the ability to express themselves and to "feel" heard, and that they were able to transform how they saw the offender—as a person as opposed to a monster. It increased their ability to trust others and it reduced their anger. There appeared to be a sense of release—VOM appears to provide for some victims the opportunity to move on.

Mediation has been found to be healing to victims, offenders, and communities overall (Gerkin 2009). While initial victim-offender mediation programs tended to focus on seemingly minor and/or nonpersonal types of crimes, today mediation is used across all types of crimes. In fact, personal crime victims (and those who are survivors of individuals who were victims of homicide) report very high levels of satisfaction with the process and outcome of mediation overall (Umbreit, Vos, Coates, & Armour, 2006). An important element that contributes to high levels of satisfaction is the interaction between the victim and offender that offers the opportunity for connection and resolution. In contemporary court processes the victim is often relegated to the role of witness. While he or she may have the opportunity to express how the crime has affected him/her in a victim impact statement, there is no opportunity for the offender and victim to truly communicate. The system, and this process, remain adversarial and healing is not a goal. Justice—meaning the correct outcome, which may be relative and based on the perspective of the participant—is the goal and winning by the prosecution is the goal. Gerkin (2009) reminds us that restorative justice is a needs-based perspective where "the thoughts and feelings of all people are vital" and "the psychological and emotional needs of victims and offenders . . . vary from person to person, which is part of the reason why participation in the restorative process is so significant" (p. 227). Mediation provides victims and opportunities a forum in which to identify their needs and develop a plan to achieve them.

The beautiful thing about mediation is that it can be a holistic approach toward healing. It is not an either/or process. In traditional court processes, a conviction is sought with punishment as an outcome; this is what the system offers to the crime victim—a public acknowledgment of accountability, even though the state plays the role of aggrieved party, and punishment. The sentence describes the punishment the offender will receive and it is then placed upon corrections agents to sort out the details of the court order to determine how to send an offender back to the community in a way that will decrease harm to the rest of the community. While rehabilitation of the offender may be a part of the court order, there is no guarantee that an offender will receive what is needed to "heal" (heal in the sense of resolving whatever ailment may have contributed to perpetration of the act of harm). So we see that aspects of the court process either deal with the victim OR the offender—but typically not in concert or in a way that allows for them to heal together. It is restorative justice programs that bring these parties together for healing. The traditional court process pits victim against offender, two parties always at odds, but that is not necessarily how all victims and offenders see themselves, and mediation allows for them to participate in a process that eliminates that distinction. For instance, Van Camp (2017) found that victims chose to engage in mediation with the prosocial mindset of helping the offender—both in property and personal crime offenses. Many victims in Van Camp's study had indicated they themselves were "fine" but when the offender reached out, or they thought they could have an impact on the offender's future, they agreed to participate in the sessions. This truly speaks to the justice as love concept as in these cases, there was very little "direct" benefit to the crime victim aside from helping the offender to recover and/or evolve. Bouffard, Cooper, and Bergseth (2017) found that any type of restorative justice mediation program utilized with a large sample of juvenile offenders was found to be effective at reducing recidivism among participants for a significant period of time when compared to a matched population of juvenile offenders participating in traditional court proceedings only. Umbreit, Vos, Coates, and Armour (2006) report that offenders participating in VOM reported that the process allowed them to feel good about something they did, that they were able to help as opposed to harm, and that they developed a sense of clarity about the impact of their offense on the person(s) they harmed.

The effects of crime are not all tangible, such as the loss of an item, destruction to property, or a physical harm. The research on the impact of mediation informs us that psychological/emotional harm and the lack of true resolution that can only come from direct interaction between a victim and offender can limit the ability of both victim and offender to heal. The ever-increasing presence of victim-offender mediation in the justice system is a huge win as it illustrates that those in charge of the justice system have broadened their view of what is needed in order for true justice to occur.

Specialized Courts

Another potential "win" operating within the court function of the justice system is the increase in use of specialized courts that place a strong focus on healing and transformation. Specialized courts are those courts that focus on a specific type of offender and require said offenders to engage in targeted and skillfully crafted programming with enhanced supervision by the court to assist them in getting back on the right track toward becoming more whole (Kaiser & Holtfreter, 2016). The first specialized courts (established in 1989) focused on dealing with drug-related offenses, specifically offenders with substance abuse issues. Since then, specialized courts have grown to include domestic violence courts, mental health courts, veterans courts, teen courts, and reentry courts and they continue to expand (Kaiser & Holtfreter, 2016). Operating under the theoretical framework of therapeutic jurisprudence (e.g., Wexler & Winick, 1996), it is the goal of these specialized programs that offenders receive treatment for their offending behavior with the ultimate outcome being desistance of the behavior overall. The drug court programs deviated from traditional court processes by creating a "non-adversarial structure, team decision-making, the use of non-incarcerative sanctions and incentives, and judicial involvement and interactions with offenders" (Kaiser & Holtfreter, 2016, p. 46). An additional powerful component is the interaction between the judge and the participant/offender (Hueston & Burke, 2016). This judge-offender interaction is evidence of the power of justice as love. The interaction, the getting to know the person behind the offense, is what helps to develop a plan with the highest probability of success and it is this interaction that requires genuine regard from one human to another. To demonstrate, Hueston and Burke (2016) write:

> The atmosphere during drug-court hearings is dramatically different; it is often didactic, motivating, and healing. While in court, the judge is engaging and instructive, and the defense and prosecuting attorneys are collaborative, not adversarial. The approach is therapeutic, built on praise, not punishment; and built on treatment, not threats. (pp. 44–45)

The need for specialized courts arose in part out of the frustration of judicial officials from seeing the same offenders return to court for subsequent offenses and/or for failing to abide by court order restrictions and thus falling through the cracks. No remedies were evidenced, no improvement, and judges in generalist courts were expected to dole out punishments in a fair and just way through band-aid style rulings that didn't necessarily address the root causes of defendants' offending in the first place (Mirchandani, 2005). Another significant contributor to the developing of specialized courts came from the crime spike in the 1990s and the sheer volume of cases focusing on drugs, domestic violence, etc. (Olson, Lurigio, & Albertson, 2001). The volume of cases warranted an evaluation of court functioning as the courts were simply not able to handle the vast increase in cases (Barnes, 1996; Mirchandani, 2005; Olson, Lurigio, & Albertson, 2001). It was proposed that speed and efficiency could be improved through the specialized focus on a particular type of offense as court personnel would be better equipped with knowledge to address offense-specific challenges. Additionally, a defendant (and victim) wouldn't end up coming before multiple judges unfamiliar with their histories and/or multiple courts dealing with related issues (Barnes, 1996). Mirchandani (2005) states, "The nationwide push to institutionalize special courts or courts whose docket is devoted to one social problem stems from an increase in docket size and a decrease in resources" (p. 393). Baldwin and Rukus (2015) suggest that for veterans treatment courts specifically, officials recognized that veterans were coming before the court with multiple issues that contributed to their criminal behavior. When a courtroom is focused on one social ill or one specific offense or group of offenses, it allows for the workgroup to increase their knowledge regarding root causes, treatments, and resources available and to thus develop a plan that is problem solving versus assembly line in nature.

The court process is required to affect the necessary shift in the specialized court environment. Whereas the traditional courtroom allows for the courtroom workgroup to work together because of their familiarity with each other, the specialized court requires a team approach wherein the workgroup develops a coordinated plan for the defendant/offender, with graduated sanctions for rule infractions and more of a case management style approach to supervision that persists beyond the sentencing phase of court. The group convenes to discuss the defendant's progress on a regular basis versus the defendant having to be self-reliant in full to follow the orders of the court. Speaking specifically about drug treatment courts, Olson, Lurigio, and Albertson (2001) state that common components of this type of specialized court include: "immediate interventions, a non-adversarial process, a hands-on judicial role, drug treatment with clearly defined rules and goals, and a team approach" (p. 174). These same components can be seen in other types of specialized courts with variation in the treatment rules and goals.

Mirchandani (2005) also reports how specialization of courts allows for court officials to get to know the defendants more closely, thus gaining a better foothold on what works and does not work for any given individual. No longer are offenders able to slip by unnoticed because they are before, and accountable to, someone with whom they are familiar and, perhaps more importantly, who is familiar with them. Once again, the concept of human connectedness is the focus with high importance being given to the intimacy that comes from repeated contacts, even in the court environment.

The goals and approach to specialized courts certainly conform with the justice as love principle wherein the focus is on healing and a high value is placed on human potential. So, how do specialized courts "perform" in the realm of goals of the justice system overall? Additionally, how satisfied are the participants? Baldwin and Rukus (2014) found that for veterans, the specialized court appeared to be effective. The participants felt as if they were surrounded by a support system and that this was a motivation to be successful in the program. Similarly, Tutty and Babins-Wagner (2016) found a significant improvement in recidivism rates for batterers involved in specialized domestic violence courts versus those in traditional courts (approximately 8 percent for specialized court participants versus approximately 41 percent for traditional court participants). Tutty and Babins-Wagner (2016) attribute the difference to the focus on treatment and availability of services in the specialized court process. In addition to benefits for offenders, Cissner, Labriola, and Rempel (2015) suggest that previous research on domestic violence (DV) specialized courts have reported that victims of domestic violence have higher rates of satisfaction with the specialized court experience. They felt more supported and were also provided services to assist them in recovering; the program included enhanced safety measures in the overall treatment protocol for the offenders. Regarding offenders, the authors reported that the DV specialized courts evidenced lower rates of recidivism when they were both treatment and accountability focused (Cissner, Labriola, & Rempel, 2015). They further stated that one major benefit of the specialized court was that judges became more familiar and immune to the particular manipulation tactics used by DV defendants overall, leading to higher rates of accountability overall. Gover, Brank, and MacDonald (2007) found heightened levels of satisfaction for both victims and defendants in their assessment of a specialized DV court. Participants in the study indicated that they felt heard, respected, and pleased with the outcomes of their cases.

Critics of specialized courts suggest that judges may hold too much power in the courtroom workgroup, that the coercive element of compelling participation in treatment programs is contrary to true restorative justice principles, and finally that participants' sentences might end up being longer than what they could have received in traditional court processes if participants are not immediately successful with treatment programming. Despite these critiques, it appears that specialized courts with the focus on human value appear potentially to contribute positively to improved circumstances for defendants engaged in them and to decreased presence in the justice system overall.

Police Body-Worn Cameras (Possible Double Win . . . Sort of)

Largely in response to police killings of unarmed Black males across the United States, public outcry for transparency and accountability brought about an increased use of body-worn cameras (BWCs) by law enforcement officers in the United States (Culhane, Boman IV, & Schweitzer, 2016). Akin to Sir Robert Peel's vision regarding the use of officer-assigned badge numbers as a means by which citizens could hold particular officers accountable for their bad behavior, the BWC offers citizens a means by which citizens may feel empowered as officers' actions may be reviewable. BWCs are cameras that are worn by officers on their lapels or protective vests and record interactions between officers and community members. Now, in no way are we saying that technology in itself is a win; they are simple cameras after all. However, it is the willingness for law enforcement agencies to reach out through transparent methods to mend their broken relationships with communities and the community trust that may follow that is truly the win. In fact, Ariel, Farrar, and Sutherland (2015) report that the College of Policing in England and Wales stated that BWCs were precisely THE tool to use to help repair the reduction of public confidence in the police; this is especially true among minority communities. BWCs turns out to be advantageous for two reasons: (1) they provide the public with video and audio footage of encounters between individuals and a law enforcement official and allow for the public (including justice authorities) to examine an interaction to determine whether or not the actions of any given officer are justified, understandable, reasonable, and/or fair; and (2) they provide an opportunity for law enforcement to stand up to unfair accusations of brutality and/or misconduct by showing the public the actions of the individual interacting with the police officer (Headley, Guerette, & Shariati, 2017). In this sense, BWCs *may* provide a double win: they can help the public hold law enforcement officers accountable for their actions, and they can support an officer when his or her act was justified but falls under suspicion. In this sense, the justice as love principle works both ways to provide evidence for community members when police act in a harmful manner and for police when a citizen's actions lead to the harm of other citizens or officers. We can examine an interaction to assess how the people involved are treating each other—in a loving or harmful way. Hedberg, Katz, and Choate (2017) echo this by stating that supporters of BWCs suggest that they can help agencies identify continuing problems (namely problematic officers) without having to rely on citizen complaints. This takes the onus off the community and places it more appropriately on organizational leaders. It also gives them the justification they may need to require additional training for problematic officers and/or justification for letting an officer go.

The overall goals of police agencies' use of BWCs are: (1) increased transparency and accountability; (2) reduced use of force complaints; and (3) improved police-community relations as an "objective account" of an interaction is made available (Hedberg, Katz, & Choate, 2017). Culhane, Boman IV, and Schweitzer (2016) report that in a pilot project conducted by the New York City Police Department (NYPD), BWCs had a significant impact on improved relations between police and community members and contributed to a substantial reduction in use of force incidents. They state that the study of the pilot project found that complaints against officers decreased by 88 percent while use of force incidents decreased by 50 percent as well—thus "reducing the risk of physical injury to both officers and the public" (p. 255). Again, a win-win. Headley, Guerette, and Shariati (2017) found that officers wearing BWCs were more likely to use less intrusive methods of resolving incidents and to engage in more field contacts (self-initiated dealings with the public) than those who did not wear BWCs. Other studies have found that use of force complaints have been reduced by upward of 90 percent in multiple communities (see Sutherland, Ariel, Farrar, & DeAnda, 2017). Arial, Farrar, and Sutherland (2014) suggest that this may be attributed to the possibility that we are less likely to act in a negative manner, both socially and morally, when we are being watched. Hence, the BWC acts as an external conscience to which the officers are constantly subject while on the job.

BWCs and studies to assess effectiveness have been implemented in large, medium, and smaller departments across the country (Ariel, Farrar, & Sutherland, 2015; Culhane, Boman IV, & Schweitzer, 2016; Sutherland, Ariel, Farrar, & DeAnda, 2017). In support of the use of BWCs by departments, the federal government distributed upward of $19 million to police agencies to enhance or implement BWC programs, and it is estimated that over $70 million will be allocated overall to support the BWC initiative (Sousa, Coldren Jr., Rodriguez, & Braga, 2016). Hedberg, Katz, and Choate (2017) report that of the eighteen thousand law enforcement agencies across the United States, approximately four to six thousand utilize BWCs.

One might propose that it makes sense to see a decrease in adverse behavior in the initial stages of "being watched" but that the impact of surveillance may fade over time. However, research suggests that BWCs are successful at attaining decreased levels of use of force and citizen complaints against police. Moreover, Sutherland, Ariel, Farrar, and DeAnda (2017) report that complaints against police and decreases in police use of force persisted for four years after the implementation of BWCs in the agency they studied. This suggests that the improvements noted by several authors investigating the impact of BWCs (namely decreased use of force complaints, improved police-community relations) are not attributable to the "newness" of the technology and protocol, but become an operating feature of the agencies that utilize the technology. While reliance on technology as a means to love's end is not completely ideal, the beneficial effects of BWCs that have been found seem to suggest that this mode of technology has reduced harmful interactions between police and the community.

Although we include the implementation of BWCs as a win because they are a potentially powerful tool for accountability . . . in both directions, we must realize that every individual working for or with the criminal justice system may choose to simply ignore the evidence (as seems to be the case with the police shooting of Alton Sterling). It is when controversial images appear that we should be the most careful in our use and interpretation of evidence obtained. Sometimes, it is difficult to understand what we are seeing especially in the heat of the moment (e.g., the police-involved shooting of Daniel Shaver). And that is part of the problem with solely relying on BWCs. Humans make mistakes and BWCs are only a tool, but a tool to be used in conjunction with other police technologies, all ultimately used to inform people utilizing the highest possible wisdom. Humans may not always choose to hold other humans accountable, especially if there is not a clear picture of what has occurred, and the evidence is not sound. 'Tis again, part of the human condition. Sometimes, we fail to see what goes against our construction of reality as we are well aware that juries even with sound evidence are unlikely to convict. Thus, it is important that police officers, prosecutors, juries, the media, and others use this tool authentically to ensure justice is served. Hopefully, the use of this technology will help contribute to transparency and create positive perceptions of policing in the future. As BWCs are implemented across the country, we hope we are able to find truth in the images they capture.

Juvenile Justice System Wins and the Impact of Trauma-Informed Justice

Although the modern-day juvenile justice system ostensibly is based on the principles of *parens patriae*, the state as parent, and was established to serve the best interest of the child, what has emerged during the last century since its formal inception has been anything but just or restorative. As the Supreme Court held in *Kent v. US* (1966), juveniles receive the "worst of both worlds"; they are afforded neither the same constitutional protections of adults nor the care and treatment claimed for children. This disjunctive nature of the juvenile system has created a process in which the juvenile court has no clear identity. Rather than healing the wounds that have been inflicted, as a loving parent should, the process of holding juveniles accountable has not only failed to restore offenders to the community, but instead has created a never-ending game in which juveniles are unable to prevail. As opposed to receiving the care they need from the system and emerging as viable adults, they are unlikely to come out unscathed, if they come out at all. Proponents of a more formalized juvenile system have long criticized the system as being too soft and have argued that youths receive excessively lenient dispositions. And with the rise in juvenile violence in the mid-1980s/early 1990s, their critiques were answered, and a new system of social control emerged. The public began clamoring for harsher punishments and legislators bent on appearing tough on crime and curbing this socially constructed juvenile violence were more than willing to address the concerns of their constituents. These "get tough" policies led to a shift in the juvenile system reflecting a more retributive ideology similar to that of the adult criminal system. It appears as if there was a "shift from individualized justice to just deserts, from offender to offense, from amenability to treatment to public safety, and from immature delinquent to responsible criminal" (Feld, 1999, p. 17). Fear of the juvenile super predator led to the expansion of punishments for juveniles, and the line between the juvenile and adult courts were further eroded. State governments began to toughen their laws and enacted more punitive policies such as lowering juvenile age limits for prosecution, eliminating confidentiality safeguards, and modifying the requirements for juveniles to be transferred to adult courts. Additionally, we saw a net-widening effect in the system in which juveniles, who would never have come into contact with the formalized system, were being brought before the court for petty offenses such as disruption of school classrooms or curfew violations. As a result, youths, especially minorities, have increasingly been placed in residential facilities even though crime has been steadily decreasing for over three decades. African American or Hispanic youths represent over 62 percent of youth detained or committed to residential placement (Sickmund, Sladky, Kang, & Puzzanchera, 2017). We know the system is broken as the data indicate that approximately 45 percent of juvenile offenders recidivate after their primary adjudication (Abrams, 2006). Thus, punishment isn't working. To expect a different outcome, as there has been little effort to create policies that effectively address juvenile crime, would be futile. So, if the juvenile system doesn't work, then there must be alternatives. Now, we hope that the system's inadequacies are not equated with the "nothing works" doctrine of Robert Martinson as our assertion is more of a critique on the juvenile process rather than rehabilitative efforts (sometimes a lack thereof). Not surprisingly, however, the belief that the juvenile system does not work has resulted in calls to eliminate the juvenile system altogether in favor of placing juveniles in the adult system (Whitehead & Lab, 2015). Now, we find this suggestion preposterous, as we could not imagine our own children being held to the same standards as ourselves, but seemingly public opinion has embraced holding juveniles accountable. We must not forget that at the height of the panic regarding juvenile crime, an increasing number of transfer laws were put into place resulting in thousands of juveniles being waived to the adult system. During the 1990s, almost all states had expanded legislation that made it easier to waive juveniles to adult court. Juvenile waivers reached their peak in 1994 but have steadily decreased since then; however, a number of juveniles, including female and minority populations, have been affected. But interestingly enough, female transfers have increased since the height of the transfer movement although they only make up approximately 10 percent of the transfer population (Adams & Addie, 2010). Take, for instance, the case of Cyntoia Brown: unredeemable, unloved, and seemingly unworthy of being tried in the juvenile justice system. At the age of sixteen, she was convicted of the murder of a forty-three-year-old man who had paid her to have sex. While it is apparent that Cyntoia was a victim of sex trafficking, the nature of the crime resulted in her being transferred to adult court and being sentenced to life in prison. Cyntoia was not only a victim of childhood abuse, but she also suffered from the lack of control and reasoning that Fetal Alcohol Syndrome brings. And it is her history of abuse and neglect that concerns the authors. Somewhere the social service and juvenile justice systems failed Cyntoia as it has done numerous juveniles. Mitigating circumstances were ignored and at no point were attempts made to try to heal the harms that had been inflicted on this young woman of color. Now, most of our readers wouldn't expect any other outcome as, time and time again, the system has shown to be biased in its judgment of minorities; however, this transfer, like many others, has bothered us as the past and current trauma that Cyntoia was experiencing was all but ignored. While early intervention may not have altered her life trajectory, it saddens us that she was simply thrown away. No attempts at rehabilitation were made, which seems counterintuitive to the nature of the justice system. Obviously, Cyntoia did not deserve a free pass, but no attempt was made to treat her and remedy the harms done; had she had a broken leg, surely, some form of medical care would have been offered not only to fix the fracture but to ease her pain. But nothing other than continued harm was provided. Although Cyntoia has been incarcerated for more than a decade, recently social media has brought this case to the forefront of public attention. It is funny that in just over a decade later, the manner in which the public perceives this case is vastly different. Whereas this may be a result of Hollywood activists becoming involved, such as with the case of the West Memphis Three, we have hope that the status quo has changed.

There is hope as it appears as if the pendulum has swung back to a more balanced approach for treating juveniles. Within the last decade, it appears as if society has evolved, and our attitudes toward punishing juveniles has softened, maybe even leaning toward a more restorative and healing approach. For instance, during the late 1980s, we saw "three strikes" laws expanded and the juvenile death penalty reembraced with the decisions in *Thompson v. Oklahoma* (1988) and *Stanford v. Kentucky (1989)*; however, something changed and hope was renewed. In 2005, based on the ideas of a national consensus, evolving standards of decency, reduced juvenile culpability, and international opinion, the Supreme Court ruled in *Roper v. Simmons* (2005) that sentencing a juvenile to death was unconstitutional. Four years later, similar justifications were used in *Graham v. Florida* (2010) to determine that life without the possibility of parole for a nonhomicidal crime was unconstitutional as well. Critics of sentencing juveniles to death or imprisoning youths for inordinate lengths of time have long argued that juveniles do not have the mental reasoning, maturity level, or life experience to be held to the same standards as adults (Horowitz, 2000). And they are correct. Research has long documented that juveniles are impulsive, and as a result, often exhibit poor judgment. When presented with possible negative outcomes for violations, they truly do not understand the consequences of their actions; this applies to all juvenile offenders, not just those who have committed violent crimes and are considered to be unredeemable (Whitehead & Lab, 2015). Expanding on this discussion of culpability of juveniles, one final systemic win is the legislative action by individual states to reconsider the minimum age level at which juveniles may be held to account for their delinquent/criminal acts at the adult level. According to Kelly (2017), only five states remain that consider persons under the age of eighteen to be "adults" in the justice system. This number has been steadily declining since 2007, when fourteen states held that certain minors could be tried as adults without exception and/or automatically based on the crime. The five states that retain laws that enable minors to be handled by the adult criminal justice system all have bills submitted to raise the age of jurisdiction to eighteen. Steinberg (2017) argues that the US Supreme Court has made rulings that reflect the consideration of scientific research into the neurological development of adolescents and the impacts of said development on both their understanding of and resulting culpability in their harmful acts. This too is a potential win: the authentic consideration of an offender's capacity for understanding harm he has done used to inform the organized response to that harm can work to effectively reduce or eliminate future acts of harm. But how do we change a system that has traditionally sanctioned and used punishments as a means of rehabilitation? We would argue that the answer is simple . . . love. Loving your own child is easy even on our worst days, so why can we not take this approach and support a system that truly acts in the best interest of the child? It really does take a village, and loving your neighbor, or in this case, your neighbor's kid, is paramount to ensuring justice.

Proponents of a restorative justice approach to the juvenile system (see Bazemore, 1999) have long argued for programs that mend communities and victims that have been affected by crime. And for good reason. . . . As we have discussed, deterrence does not work even for adult offenders; it also does nothing to mend the harm inflicted on the victims. So how do we expect juveniles to adhere to rules that their adult counterparts cannot often conceptualize? Juveniles are less culpable as they have not developed physically and psychologically, and by sentencing a juvenile to excessive punishments, the system has guaranteed that there is no chance of rehabilitation; this ensures that the offender, the victim, and the community will never be able to reconcile the crimes that have been committed as harm is increased. While the overall goals of the justice system, at least in theory, are to hold youths accountable for their actions, promote public safety, and reduce recidivism (Dierkhising & Branson, 2016), past and current approaches have failed to ensure that these objectives are met. There have been attempts to reconcile juveniles back into the community such as peer, drug, and mental health courts, community service programs, and other restorative justice programs, which we will consider mini-wins, but generally, we fail to adequately support these programs for political and financial reasons (see Feld, 1999). It is not a failure of programs to curtail the harms inflicted by juvenile crime, but a lack of effort (and funding). Investing in a juvenile and preventing future crime is a choice that will serve us well in the end as it costs less to educate and rehabilitate a child than it does to incarcerate him for life. But even if we were to invest in a system that focused on rehabilitation, would we really curtail juvenile crime? Yes, but there is a catch.

Whereas all of these alternative juvenile programs are a "win" for the system, they still fail to get to the heart of the offending behavior. Well, that was until trauma-informed justice became an option when dealing with juvenile offenders. Now, don't get too excited. The use of trauma-informed justice to assist in the care and rehumanization of juveniles is a relatively new concept and is not widely practiced at this time. Whereas most juvenile justice programs are absent of this approach (Ford et al., 2007), there is hope as recently the Department of Justice (DOJ) has called for research on the issue and has begun implementing training on trauma-informed justice for criminal justice professionals. As a result, the stakeholders (e.g., American Bar Association, International Chiefs of Police, and National Council of Juvenile and Family Court Judges) have begun to call for the implementation of trauma-informed practices in the juvenile court system (Dierkhising & Branson, 2016). This is a step in the right direction as those involved in the justice system, including juveniles such as Cyntoia Brown, have significant histories of trauma. And it is here that we see a glimmer of hope, hope to ensure that the needs of all are met by recognizing and healing the harms inflicted by others.

Trauma-informed justice is based on the premise that negative outcomes for juveniles involved in the juvenile justice system are diminished by working with youth to reduce the effects of posttraumatic stress and other trauma-related mental health issues (Dierkhising & Branson, 2016). Trauma "results from an event, series of events, or set of circumstances that is experienced by an individual as physically or emotionally harmful or threatening and that has long lasting adverse effects on the individual's functioning and physical, social, emotional, or spiritual well-being" (Substance Abuse and Mental Health Services Administration, 2014, p. 7). Thus, trauma creates an inability to cope and often results in one acting out to suppress the suffering triggered by such events. Traumatic experiences such as exposure to domestic violence, sexual violence, neglect, racism, and a number of other individual and community-level issues are prevalent among delinquent youth (see Oudshoorn, 2016) and often create long-lasting damage for victims (Zehr, 2009) especially those who are detained and suffer further victimization at the hands of the system. An estimated 90 percent of juvenile offenders have been subjected to trauma during their lifetime (Abrams et al., 2004; Dierkhising et al., 2013); prior trauma is linked to delinquency and future violence (see Crosby, 2016). Further, placement within the juvenile system "may expose youth to additional traumatic stressors, such as peer violence, abuse by staff, and shackling and restraints" (Ford et al., 2016, p. 32). Thus, it is imperative that we consider not only the harm that has been inflicted on society, but also the harm that has already occurred and will continue to occur when we punish juveniles using methods that are punitive and often excessive. Shifting from a punitive-based system that neither rehabilitates youthful offenders nor prevents recidivism to a system that focuses on trauma-based practices may assist in actually reducing future harms experienced by youths and allow them to thrive. Applying methods that moderate the trauma experienced and avoid re-traumatization is key to reintegrating youth back into society.

As previous scholars have noted (e.g., Braithwaite, 1999b), shaming individuals into submission rather than reintegrating them fails to achieve systemic goals. When you take into consideration the trauma and harms that youthful offenders have experienced, it is unlikely that punishments are going to be effective. Not only must we consider the criminogenic risk factors, but we must also determine what service needs must be met when dealing with trauma-inflicted youth (Dierkhising & Branson, 2016). And this has started to take root. While trauma-informed justice is not endemic to working with juvenile offenders, it is likely to be successful as the harms that have been inflicted may also be remedied especially if these youths are kept out of a formalized system. And it is a trauma-informed approach developed under a restorative justice framework that is most likely to restore offenders to the community. "Because restorative justice sees the task of repair of relationships as central to the project of justice, a trauma-informed approach is not only profoundly compatible, but absolutely essential to its theory and, especially, its practice" (Randall and Haskell, 2013, p. 506). Juveniles, especially minority populations, must be perceived by criminal justice professionals as a vulnerable population in need of assistance rather than the stereotype (Crosby, 2016). It is, thus, necessary for the system at all levels (e.g., police, corrections, and courts) to buy into the process of treating the disease, providing proper care, and nurturing the youth back to health rather than simply responding to the symptoms of juvenile delinquency. By implementing a restorative approach focusing on trauma, it is possible that we may be able to heal the wounds inflicted on our youth and ensure this vulnerable population receives the help it so desperately needs.

CONCLUSION

The examples of epic wins, as stated previously, are by no means an exhaustive examination into the successes of the justice system as it currently exists. Additionally, the wins chosen while done so with the intention of illustrating (or highlighting the lack of) the justice as love principle are completely subjective. The takeaway here is for you, the reader, to understand that when we invest in each other, progress in both the justice system and the social fabric can be achieved. When we fail to acknowledge each other's perfection we rip a hole in our social fabric; what might have been a potential win becomes something rather more grotesque very quickly.

FINAL THOUGHTS

Fast friends from graduate school and forever students, Beth, Tammy, and Michael are now also teachers. One of the most rewarding things about teaching is the experience of beginning to weave a conversation with students and having them pick up the thread and begin weaving on their own. When teaching, often we get to see that moment happen before our eyes in real time, giving us immediate gratification. With a project like this, our aim is hardly different—we seek to begin a conversation, not resolve one—but the instant gratification, which is more aptly understood as co-teaching, is not present. The wins you identify and analyze according to our arguments here are easily as important, if not decidedly more so, than the ones we have chosen.

But instead of wins, fails will be tragically plentiful. As we were preparing this work for submission, sixteen-year-old Joseph Edward Haynes was shot by a police officer following a scuffle in a courthouse. As of June 26, 2018, there have been 501 police shootings in 2018 leading to the death of the individual shot (*Washington Post*, 2018). Whereas all of these deaths are tragic for all parties involved, it is the shootings that involve the death of an unarmed person that society finds most disconcerting and garner the greatest amounts of justified scrutiny as we strive to understand (in hindsight) whether that amount of force was necessary. Indeed, great amounts of discussion, arguing, and blame-throwing occur when these incidents are publicized. Twenty-eight of the 501 shootings involved shootings of unarmed persons (approximately 5.5 percent of all shootings). In fifteen of those instances, police or others were being attacked by the decedent, and, in an additional eleven cases, the act fell under the threat level "other" indicating that it was in the course of a domestic dispute, suicide by cop, traffic accident or dangerous situation. In only two cases were the shootings conducted in an "undetermined" threat level (approximately 0.4 percent of incidents). When we approach each other outside of the bonds of love and tragedy ensues, we fail. We fail as a collective society when any death occurs within the context of an interaction between an individual and a law enforcement agent. We fail because we—society—allowed for a situation to develop that led to a person's demise, no matter if the shooting was justified or not, whether the decedent was aggressive and uncooperative or not, whether the officer felt there was no other option to ensure his or our safety . . . or not. We fail because that person is gone and if only the situation had not been allowed to arise, that person would still be with us. The failure, really, is one: it is all of ours, police, yours, and ours alike. It is seen in skylit moments of great import, but the failure lives in the tiniest of moments and interactions. We kill Joseph Haynes yet again when we fail to offer ourselves authentically to one another. We kill NYPD officers Wenjian Liu and Rafael Ramos when we cower behind a gun, a law, an office, a wall. When our fear rules us, we have failed in the most complete way possible. We cease to be all we are and begin to resemble some of the malformed and sclerotic avatars viewed earlier. We are not such things as these.

There will be more wins, too, to inspire us to do better, to be truer to our better angels than we have been. That's because we *are* better than that; we *are not* cowards. The men and women of law enforcement, of the courts, of community and institutional corrections are, in the main, noble and heroic people doing an exceptionally hard job with few resources often under dire conditions. They are heroes. Rather, they have the makings of heroes; whether they choose to be heroes is up to each of them in every single moment. We can help them, of course, by honoring true bravery (the willingness to assume risk, to put others' lives before one's own), integrity (being worthy of the trust invested in one), and service (skillfully identifying human need and authoring skilled responses).

Choice is indeed our problem, but it is also our truest salvation. And in the choice to love beyond the moment, to connect authentically, to serve through praxis. We will make mistakes; though we are perfect, we are human. We will pass on invitations to love; we will love unskillfully. The only real failure is when we fail to learn from mistakes and try again, or when we simply give up. We would like to say that such things are simply not options, but of course they are. That's part of what makes love so powerful. After mistakes, and after failure, when we do finally choose to equate love and justice, we will finally begin to experience the kind of peace we so desperately desire for our children. And there is something else, too: with the turn toward a loving justice, those of us who have struggled and failed and hoped and prayed and cried so often, we will find a thing as well for us: reconciliation.

References

Abram, K. M., Teplin, L. A., Charles, D. R., Longsworth, S. L., McClelland, G. M., & Duncan, M. K. (2004). Posttraumatic stress disorder and trauma in youth in juvenile detention. *Archives of General Psychiatry 61*, 403–10.

Abrams, L. S. (2006). From corrections to community: Youth offenders' perceptions of the challenges of transition. *Journal of Offender Rehabilitation 44*, 2–3, 31–53.

Adams, B., & Addie, S. (2010). Delinquency cases waived to criminal courts, 2007. *Fact Sheet*. Washington, DC: US Department of Justice.

Adams, J. (1965). Inequity in social exchange. *Advances in Experimental Social Psychology 2*, 267–99.

Adkinson, C. (2008). The Amazing Spider-Man and the evolution of the comics code: A case study in cultural criminology. *Journal of Criminal Justice and Popular Culture 15*(3), 241–61.

Aeschylus, Morshead, E. D. A., Landes, S. H., & Landes, Willa (1998). *The Eumenides*. Studio City, CA: Players Press.

Agnew, R. (2016). A theory of crime resistance and susceptibility. *Criminology 54*, 2, 181–211.

Agnew, R. (2001). Building on the foundation of general strain theory: Specifying the types of strain most likely to lead to crime and delinquency. *Journal of Research on Crime and Delinquency 38*(4), 319–61.

Agnew, R. (2006). *Pressured into crime: An overview of general strain theory.* Los Angeles, CA: Roxbury.

Agnew, R. (2013). When criminal coping is likely: An extension of general strain theory. *Deviant Behavior 34*, 653–70.

Agnew, R., Cullen, F. T., Burton, V. S., Evans, T. D., & Dunaway, R. G. (1996). A new test of classic strain theory. *Justice Quarterly 13*, 681–704.

Agnew, R., & White, H. R. (1992). An empirical test of general strain theory. *Criminology 30*, 475–99.

Akers, R. (1991). Self-control as a general theory of crime. *Journal of Quantitative Criminology 7*(2), 201–11.

Akers, R., & Sellers, C. (2012). *Criminological theories*. 6d. Chicago: Fitzroy Dearborn.

Akers, R., Sellers, C., & Jennings, W. (2016). *Criminological theories: Introduction, evaluation and application*. New York: Oxford University Press.

Albright, W. F. (1915). The home of Balam. *Journal of the American Oriental Society 35*, 386–90.

Al-Talib, N. I., & Griffin, C. (1994). Labeling effect on adolescent's self-concept. *International Journal of Offender Therapy and Comparative Criminology 38*(1), 47–57.

American Civil Liberties Union (2013). A living death: Life without parole for non-violent offenses. Retrieved from https://www.aclu.org/files/assets/111813-lwop-complete-report.pdf

Amnesty International (2012). Death penalty facts, updated May 2012. Accessed April 9, 2016, 7:45pm, from http://www.amnestyusa.org/our-work/issues/death-penalty/us-death-penalty-facts

Amos, J. (2016). Ig Nobel win for Alpine "goat man." BBC News, Science & Environment, 23 September. Accessed June 10, 2017, 11:16pm, from http://www.bbc.com/news/science-environment-37443204

Anderson, J., Myowa-Yamakoshi, M., & Matsuzawa, T. (2004). Contagious yawning in chimpanzees. *Proceedings of the Royal Society of London*. (Suppl.) *271*, S468–S470.

Anti-Defamation League (2013). A brief history of anti-Semitism. Accessed July 29, 2017, 10:27pm, from https://www.adl.org/sites/default/files/documents/assets/pdf/education-outreach/Brief-History-on-Anti-Semitism-A.pdf

Anti-Defamation League (2015). Price tag attacks. Published online March 16. Accessed April 16, 2015, 10:09am, from http://www.adl.org/israel-international/israel-middle-east/content/backgroundersarticles/price-tag-attacks.html#.VS_AcNzF-E6

Arendt, H. (1979). *The origins of totalitarianism*. Orlando, FL: Harcourt, Brace, & Co.

Arendt, H. (2006). *Eichmann in Jerusalem: A report on the banality of evil*. New York: Penguin Classics.

Ariel, B., Farrar, W. A., & Sutherland, A. (2015). The effect of police body-worn cameras on use of force and citizens' complaints against the police: A randomized controlled trial. *The Journal of Quantitative Criminology 31*, 509–35.

Ashford, E., & Mulligan, T. (2012). Contractualism. Stanford Encyclopedia of Philosophy. Accessed July 18, 2016, 7:59pm, from http://plato.stanford.edu/entries/contractualism/#HowDoeConDifOthSocConThe

Augustine of Hippo (2006). *The city of God*. (M. Dods, Trans.). New York: Barnes & Noble.

Austin, S., & Joseph, S. (1996). Assessment of bully/victim problems in 8 to 11 year-olds. *British Journal of Educational Psychology 66*, 447–56.

Avineri, S. (2010). Where Hannah Arendt went wrong: Hannah Arendt's analysis of totalitarianism remains innovative and brilliant, though she failed abysmally to understand modern anti-Semitism. *Haaretz*. March 3. Accessed August 1, 2017, 4:08am, from http://www.haaretz.com/where-hannah-arendt-went-wrong-1.264075

Bach, R. (2014). *Jonathan Livingston Seagull: The complete edition*. New York: McMillan.

Baldwin, J. M., & Rukus, J. (2015). Healing the wounds: An examination of veteran's treatment courts in the context of restorative justice. *Criminal Justice Policy Review 26*(2), 183–207.

Barlow, D., & Barlow, M. (2000). *Police in a multicultural society: An American story*. Long Grove, IL: Waveland.

Barnes, M. (2016). Levinas by Michael Barnes. YouTube video. Accessed August 7, 2017, 2:42pm, from https://youtu.be/heHJm4ge-L0 St. Johns Nottingham.

Barnes, P. G. (1996). It may take a village . . . or a specialized court to address family problems. *ABA Journal*, December 22–23.

Baron, S. W. (2010). Street youth's control imbalance and soft and hard drug use. *Journal of Criminal Justice 38*(5), 903–12.

Baron, S. W., & Forde, D. R. (2007). Street youth crime: A test of control balance theory. *Justice Quarterly 24*(2), 335–55.

Barth, K. (2004). *The doctrine of reconciliation*. Trans. G. Bromiley. New York: Continuum.

Barton, G. (1922). On the trial of Jesus before the Sanhedrin. *Journal of Biblical Literature 41*(3/4), 205–11.

Bartusch, D. J., & Matsueda, R. L. (1996). Gender, reflected appraisals, and labeling: A cross-group test of an interationist theory of delinquency. *Social Forces 75*(1), 145–76.

Bazemore, G. (1999). The fork in the road to juvenile court reform. *Annals of the American Academy of Political and Social Science 564*, 81–108.

Bazemore, G., & Schiff, M. (2005). *Juvenile justice reform and restorative justice: Building theory and policy from practice*. Portland, OR: Willan.

Beaver, K., Al-Ghamdi, M., Kobeisy, A., Alqurashi, F., Schwartz, J., Connolly, E., & Gajos, J. (2015). The effect of low self-control and delinquent peers on alcohol, tobacco and drug use in a sample of Saudi Arabian youth. *International Journal of Offender Therapy and Comparative Criminology*, 1–19

Beccaria, C. (1986). *On crimes and punishments*. Translated and introduced by D. Young. Indianapolis, IN: Hackett.

Beck, A. (2016). PREA data collection activities, 2016. U.S. Department of Justice, Bureau of Justice Statistics. NCJ 249872.

Becker, H. (1969). *The other side: Perspectives on deviance*. New York: Free Press.

Becker, H. S. (1963). *Outsiders: Studies in the sociology of deviance*. New York: Free Press.

Beckett, K., & Evans, H. (2014). *The role of race in Washington state capital sentencing*. Commissioned report. Law, Societies, and Justice Program and the Department of Sociology, University of Washington. Accessed April 9, 2016, 8:27pm, from http://www.deathpenaltyinfo.org/documents/WashRaceStudy2014.pdf

Benjet, C., & Kazdin, A. (2003). Spanking children: The controversies, findings, and new directions. *Clinical Psychology Review 23*, 197–224.

Bentham, J. (1948). *The principles of morals and legislation*. New York: Hafner.
Bergo, B. (2017) Emmanuel Levinas. *The Stanford Encyclopedia of Philosophy* (Fall 2017 Edition), E. Zalta (Ed.). Accessed August 28, 2017, 1:36pm, from https://plato.stanford.edu/archives/sum2015/entries/levinas/
Bernard, T., Snipes, J., & Gerould, A. (2016). *Vold's theoretical criminology*. 7d. New York: Oxford.
Berthold-Bond, D, (1988). Hegel's eschatological vision: Does history have a future? *History and Theory 27*(1), 14–29.
Bettelheim, B. (1976). *The uses of enchantment: The meaning and importance of fairy tales*. London: Vintage Books.
Blau, J. R., & Blau, P. M. (1982). The cost of inequality: Metropolitan structure and violent crime. *American Sociological Review 47*(1), 114–29.
Bohm, R. M., Clark, L. J., & Aveni, A. F. (1991). Knowledge and death penalty opinion: A test of the marshall hypothesis. *Journal of Research in Crime and Delinquency 28*(3), 360–87.
Bouffard, J. (2007). Predicting differences in the perceived relevance of crime's costs and benefits in a test of rational choice theory. *International Journal of Offender Therapy and Comparative Criminology 51*(4), 461–85.
Bouffard, J., Bry, J., Smith, S., & Bry, R. (2008). Beyond the "science of sophomores": Does the rational choice explanation of crime generalize from university students to an actual offender sample? *International Journal of Offender Therapy and Comparative Criminology 52*(6), 698–721.
Bouffard, J., Cooper, M., & Bergseth, K. (2017). The effectiveness of various restorative justice interventions on recidivism outcomes among juvenile offenders. *Youth, Violence, and Juvenile Justice 15*(4), 465–80.
Bowers, W. J., Vandiver, M., & Dugan, P. H. (1994). New look at public opinion on capital punishment: What citizens and legislators prefer. *American Journal of Criminal Law 22*(1), 77–150.
Braithwaite, J. (1989). *Crime, shame, and reintegration*. Cambridge, MA: Cambridge University Press.
Braithwaite, J. (1997). Charles Tittle's *Control Balance* and criminological theory. *Theoretical Criminology 1*(1), 77–97
Braithwaite, J. (1999a). Charles Tittle's control balance and criminological theory. *Theoretical Criminology 1*(1), 77–97.
Braithwaite, J. (1999b). Restorative justice: Assessing optimistic and pessimistic accounts. In M. Tonry (Ed). *Crime and justice: a review of research*. Chicago: University of Chicago Press.
Brown, M., & Rafter, N. (2011). *Criminology goes to the movies: Crime theory and popular culture*. New York: New York University Press.
Brownsey, P. F. (1978). Hume and the social contract. *The Philosophical Quarterly 28*, 111, 132–48.
Buber, M. (1996). *I and thou*. New York: Touchstone.
Burgess, E. W. (1925). The growth of the city: An introduction to a research project. In R. E. Park, E. W. Burgess, & R. D. McKenzie (Eds.). *The city* (pp. 47–62). Chicago, IL: University of Chicago Press, 1967.

Buckingham, S. (2016). Trauma informed juvenile justice. *American Criminal Law Review 53*, 641–92.

Bureau of Justice Statistics (2015). Police use of nonfatal force, 2002–11. NCJ249216.

Burkholder, J., Grout, D., & Palisca, C. (2014). *A history of Western music.* 9d. New York: W. W. Norton.

Bursick, R. (1989). Political decision-making and ecological models of delinquency: Conflict and concensus. In S. F. Messner, M. D. Krohn, & A. E. Liska (Eds.). *Theoretical Integration in the Study of Crime and Delinquency*. Albany, NY: Albany State University Press.

Bursick, R., & Grasmick, H. G. (1993). *Neighborhoods and crime: The dimensions of effective community control*. New York: Lexington Books.

Camus, A. (1991). *The myth of Sisyphus and other essays*. Trans. by J. O'Brien. New York: Vintage International

Cantullus. (1997). *The marriage of Peleus and Thetis* (Poem 64). Retrieved from http://www.stoa.org/diotima/anthology/cat64.shtml

Carlen, P. (2011). Against evangelism in academic criminology: For criminology as scientific art. In M. Bosworth & C. Hoyle (Eds). *What is criminology?* (pp. 95–108). New York: Oxford.

Carlen, P. (2014). Just criminology: The legacy of Jock Young. *Crime, Media, and Culture 10*(3), 191–202.

Carrol, A., Houghton, S., Wood, R., Perkins, C., & Bower, J. (2007). Multidimensional self-concept. *School Psychology International 28*, 237–56.

Champagne, M., & Gladstein, M. (2015). Beauvoir and Rand: Asphyxiating people, having sex, and pursuing a career. *Journal of Ayn Rand Studies 15*(1), 23–41.

Child Welfare Information Gateway (2017). *Foster care statistics 2015*. Washington, DC: US Department of Health and Human Services, Children's Bureau.

Christie, N. (2000). *Crime control as industry: Toward gulags, Western style* (3rd ed.). New York: Routledge.

Christie-Mizell, C., Pryor, E., & Grossman, E. (2008). Child depressive symptoms, spanking, and emotional support: Differences between African-American and European youth. *Family Relations 57*, 335–50.

Choi, J. J., Green, D. L., & Kapp, S. A. (2010). Victimization, victims' needs, and empowerment in victim offender mediation. *International Review of Victimology 17*, 267–90.

Church, W. T., Wharton, T., & Taylor, J. K. (2009). An examination of differential association and control theory: Family systems and delinquency. *Youth Violence and Juvenile Justice 7*(1), 3–15.

Chwaszcza, C. (2013). Hume and the social contract: A systematic evaluation. *Rationality, Markets, and Morals 4*, 108–30.

Cissner, A. B., Labriola, M., & Rempel, M. (2015). Domestic violence courts: A multisite test of whether and how they change offender outcomes. *Violence against Women 21*(9), 1102–22.

Citizens United v. Federal Elections Commission (2010). 558 U.S. 310

Cohen, A. (1955). *Delinquent boys: The culture of the gang*. New York: Free Press.

Cohen, G. (2011). Fairness and legitimacy in justice, and does option luck ever preserve justice? In G. Cohen. *On the currency of egalitarian justice, and other essays in political philosophy* (pp. 124–43).
Cohen, L., & Felson, M. (1979). Social change and crime rate trends: A routine activities approach. *American Sociological Review 44*, 588–608.
Cohen, S. (1972). *Folk devils and moral panics*. London: Macgibbon & Kee.
Collins, A. (1998). Shielded from justice: Police brutality and accountability in the United States. NCJ 178727.
Cooley, C. H. (1902/1964). *Human nature and the social order*. New York: Schribner.
Cooper, D. (1998). *God is a verb: Kabbalah and the practice of mystical Judaism*. New York: Riverhead.
Cornish, D., & Clarke, R. (1987). Understanding crime displacement: An application of rational choice theory. *Criminology 25*(4), 933–47.
Cornish, D., & Clarke, R. (2005). The rational choice perspective. In S. Henry & M. Lanier (Eds). *The essential criminology reader* (pp. 18–29). Boulder, CO: Westview.
Costello, B. (1998). The remarkable persistence of a flawed theory: A rejoinder to Matsueda. *Theoretical Criminology 2*(1), 25–92.
Crosby, S. D. (2016). Trauma-informed approaches to juvenile justice: A critical race perspective. *Juvenile and Family Court Journal 67*(1), 5–15.
Crow, M. S., Snyder, J. A., Crichlow, V. J., & Smykla, J. A. (2017). Community perceptions of police body-worn cameras. *Criminal Justice and Behavior*, 1–22.
Culhane, S. E., Boman IV, J. H., & Schweitzer, K. (2016). Public perceptions of justifiability of police shootings: The role of body cameras in a pre- and post-Ferguson experiment. *Police Quarterly 19*(3), 251–74.
Cullen, F. T., & Agnew, R. (2003). *Criminological theory: Past to present*. Oxford: Oxford University Press.
Davidson, R., Kabat-Zinn, J., Schumacher, J., Rosenkranz, M., Muller, D., Santorelli, S., Urbanowski, F., Harrington, A., Bonus, K., & Sheridan, J. (2003). Alterations in brain and immune function produced by mindfulness meditation. *Psychosomatic Medicine 65*, 564–70.
De Beauvoir, S. (1976). *The ethics of ambiguity*. (B. Frechtman, Trans.). New York: Citadel/Kensington.
Death Penalty Information Center (2016a). Execution List, 2015. Accessed April 7, 2016, 8:03pm, from http://www.deathpenaltyinfo.org/execution-list-2015
Death Penalty Information Center (2016b). Facts about the death penalty, updated April 7, 2016. Accessed April 8, 2016, 8:40pm, from http://www.deathpenaltyinfo.org/documents/FactSheet.pdf
DeFleur, M. L., & Quinney, R. (1966). A reformulation of Sutherland's differential association theory and a strategy for empirical verification. *Journal of Research in Crime and Delinquency 2*, 1–22
DeHaan, W., & Vos, J. (2003). A crying shame: The over-rationalized conception of man in the rational choice perspective. *Theoretical Criminology 7*(1), 29–54.
Delisi, M., & Hochstetler, A. (2002). An exploratory assessment of Tittle's control balance theory. Results from the National Youth Survey. *Criminal Justice Studies 15*(3), 261–72.

Delisi, M., Hochstetler, A., Higgins, G., Beaver, K., & Graeve, C. (2008). Toward a general theory of criminal justice. *Criminal Justice Review 33*(2), 141–58.

Department of Investigations of New York (2016). An analysis of quality-of-life summonses, quality of life misdemeanor arrests, and felony crime in New York City, 2010–2015. Retrieved from https://www1.nyc.gov/assets/oignypd/downloads/pdf/Quality-of-Life-Report-2010–2015.pdf

Derrida, J. (2001). *Writing and difference*. Trans. A. Bass. New York: Routledge

DeValve, M. (2015). *A different justice: Love and the future of justice practice in America*. Durham, NC: Carolina Academic Press.

DeValve, M. (2017a). Love/power. *Critical Criminology 25*(3), 375–91.

DeValve, M. (2017b). Epistrophe: Desiderata for a loving justice. *Journal of Theoretical and Philosophical Criminology 9*(2), 118–27.

DeValve, M. (2017c). O for a muse of fire: Revolution as sacrament. *Critical Criminology 25*(1), 87–102.

DeValve, M., & Brightman, S. (2018). The little things: Deconstructing Christian doctrine and theorizing a loving justice. *Journal of Theoretical and Philosophical Criminology 10*, 34–52.

Dews, P. (2010). Phenomenology crash course: Levinas. YouTube video published August 9, 2010. Accessed on July 11, 2018: https://www.youtube.com/watch?v=lGRu7xZnp5I.

Dhami, M. K. (2016). Apology in victim-offender mediation. *Contemporary Justice Review 19*(1), 31–42.

Dierkhising, C. B., & Branson, C. E. (2016). Looking forward: A research and policy agenda for creating trauma-informed juvenile justice systems. *OJJDP Journal of Juvenile Justice*, 14–30.

Dierkhising, C. B., Ko, S. J., Woods-Jaeger, B., Briggs, E. C., Lee, R., & Pynoos, R. S. (2013). Trauma histories among juvenile youth. *European Journal of Psychotraumatology 4*, 1–12.

Dinitz, S., Scarpitti, R., & Reckless, W. C. (1962). Delinquency vulnerability: A cross group and longitudinal analysis. *American Sociological Review 27*, 515–17.

Donner, C., & Jennings, W. (2014). Low self-control and police deviance: Applying Gottfredson and Hirschi's general theory to officer misconduct. *Police Quarterly 17*(3), 203–25.

Durkheim, E. (1997). *Suicide: A study in sociology*. Florence, MA: Free Press.

Eisenberg, P. (1990). Was Hegel a panlogicist? *Nous 24*(1), 159–67.

Eitel, A. (2016). Virtue or art? Political friendship reconsidered. *Journal of Religious Ethics 44*(2), 260–77.

Erikson, K. T. (1964). Notes on the sociology of deviance. In H. S. Becker (Ed.). *The other side of deviance* (pp. 9–21). New York: The Free Press.

Feld, B. (1999). *Bad kids: Race and the transformation of the juvenile court.* New York: Oxford University Press.

Felson, M. (1987). Routine activities and crime prevention in the developing metropolis. *Criminology 25*(4), 911–31.

Felson, R. B. (1985). Reflected appraisals and the development of the self. *Social Psychology Quarterly 48*(1), 71–78.

Felson, R. B. (1992). Kick 'em when they're down: Explanations of the relationship between stress and interpersonal aggression and violence. *Sociology Quarterly 33*(1), 1–16.
Ferrell, J. (1996). *Crimes of style*. Boston, MA: Northeastern University Press.
Ferrell, J. (1999). Cultural criminology. *Annual Review of Sociology 25*, 395–418.
Ferrell, J., & Hamm, M. (Eds.) (1998). *Ethnography at the edge: Crime, deviance and the field.* Boston, MA: Northeastern University Press.
Ferrell, J., & Sanders, C. (1995). *Cultural criminology*. Boston, MA: Northeastern University Press.
Fischer, D. B., Boes, A. D., Demertzi, A., Evrand, H. C., et al. (2016). A human brain network derived from coma-causing brainstem lesions. *Neurology 87*(23), 2427–34.
Ford, J. L., & Browning, C. R. (2011). Neighborhood social disorganization and the acquisition of Trichomoniasis among young adults in the United States. *American Journal of Public Health 101*(9), 1696–703.
Ford, J. D., Kerig, P. K., Desai, N., & Feierman, J. (2016). Psychosocial interventions for traumatized youth in the juvenile justice system: Research, evidence base, and clinical/legal challenges. *Journal of Juvenile Justice 4* (3), 44–62.
Ford, J. D., Chapman, D. F., Hawke, J., & Albert, A. (2007). Trauma among youth in the juvenile system: Critical issues and new directions. National Center for Mental Health Research and Program Brief. Retrieved from www.ncmhjj.com
Foucault, M. (1979). *Discipline and punish: The birth of the prison.* New York: Vintage.
Fox, K. A., Nobles, M. R., & Lane, J. (2016). Control balance behind bars: Testing the generality of Tittle's theory among incarcerated men and women. *Crime and Delinquency 62*(7), 925–53.
Frankl, V. (2006). *Man's search for meaning*. Boston: Beacon.
Fredriksen, P. (2012). *Sin: The early history of an idea.* Princeton, NJ: Princeton University Press.
Freudenberg, W. R. (1986). The density of acquaintanceship: An overlooked variable in community research. *American Journal of Sociology 92*(1), 27–63.
Friedman, M. (2011). Adam and Eve: What were Adam and Eve thinking? YouTube video published January 7, 2011. Accessed July 11, 2018: https://www.youtube.com/watch?v=3zyuvNnTcNY.
Fromm, E. (2006). *The art of loving*. New York: HarperCollins
Frum, D. (2016). The seven broken guardrails of democracy. *The Atlantic*, May 31. Accessed September 6, 2017, 11:32am, from https://www.theatlantic.com/politics/archive/2016/05/the-seven-broken-guardrails-of-democracy/484829/
Fuchs, E., & Flugge, G. (2014). Adult neuroplasticity: More than 40 years of research. *Neural Plasticity* 2014, Article ID 541870.
Furman v. Georgia. (1976). 428 US 153
Gabiddon, S., & Greene, H. (2013). *Race and crime*. Thousand Oaks, CA: Sage.
Gaines, L., & Kappeler, V. (2005). *Policing in America.* Cincinnati, OH: Anderson.
Garland, D. (2012). *Peculiar institution: America's death penalty in an age of abolition.* Cambridge, MA: Harvard University Press.

Garland, T., Blackburn, A. G., Browne, J. A., & Ammons, C. D. (2017). Prime-time representations of federal female police officers. *Feminist Criminology*, 1–23.

Gaston, L. (1986). Anti-Judaism and the Passion narrative in Luke and Acts. In P. Richardson & and D. Granskou (Eds). *Anti-Judiasm in early Christianity* (pp. 127–54). Waterloo, ON: Wilfried Laurier.

Gauthier, D. (1977). The social contract as ideology. *Philosophy and Public Affairs 6*(2), 130–64.

Gaylord, M., & Galliher J. (1988). *The criminology of Edwin Sutherland.* New Brunswick, NJ: Transaction.

Geis, G. (1955). Pioneers in criminology: VII Jeremy Bentham. *The Journal of Criminal Law, Criminology, and Police Science 46*(2), 159–71.

Geis, G., & Dodge, M. (2002). *Lessons of criminology*. New York: Routledge.

Geld, B. C. (1999) *Bad kids: Race and the transformation of the juvenile court*. New York: Oxford University Press.

Gerkin, P. M. (2009). Participation in victim-offender mediation: Lessons learned from observations. *Criminal Justice Review 34*, 2, 226–47.

Gershoff, E. T., & Grogan-Kaylor, A. (2016). Spanking and child outcomes: Old controversies and new meta-analyses. *Journal of Family Psychology 30*(4), 453–69.

Gibbs, J. P. (1966). Conceptions of deviant behavior: The old and the new. *Pacific Sociological Review 9*, 9–14.

Gibbons, J. J., & Katzenbach, N. (2006). Confronting confinement: A report on the commission on safety and abuse in America's prisons. *Washington University Journal of Law and Policy, 22*, 385–562.

Glossip v. Gross (2015). 576 U.S. ___ (2015). 135 S.Ct. 2726. (14–7955).

Goffman, E. (1963). *Stigma: Notes on the management of spoiled identity*. Englewood Cliffs, NJ: Prentice-Hall

Goffman, E. (1969). *The presentation of self in everyday life*. New York: Anchor Books, Doubleday.

Goldstein, P. (2012). *A convenient hatred: A history of anti-Semitism*. Brookline, MA: Facing History and Ourselves.

Goleman, D. (1996). *Emotional intelligence: Why it can matter more than IQ*. New York: Bantam.

Gottfredson, M. (2013). A note on the role of basic theory in thinking about crime prevention. *European Journal on Criminal Policy & Research 19*, 91–97.

Gottfredson, M. R., & Hirschi, T. (1990). *A general theory of crime*. Stanford, CA: Stanford University Press.

Gover, A. R., Brank, E. M., & MacDonald, J. M. (2007). A specialized domestic violence court in South Carolina: An example of procedural justice for victims and defendants. *Violence against Women 13*(6), 603–26.

Graham v. Florida (2009). 560 U.S. 48

Granskou, D. (1986). Anti-Judaism in the Passion accounts of the Fourth Gospel. In P. Richardson & D. Granskou (Eds). *Anti-Judiasm in early Christianity* (pp. 201–16). Waterloo, ON: Wilfried Laurier.

Grasmick, H., Tittle, C., Bursick, R., & Arneklev, B. (1993). Testing the core empirical implications of Gottfredson and Hirschi's general theory of crime. *Journal of Research in Crime and Delinquency 30*(1), 5–29.

Gray, A., Durbin, K., Call, J., Evans, H., & Melton, W. (2015). Differential association and marijuana use in a juvenile drug court sample. *Applied Psychology in Criminal Justice 11*(1), 1–8.

Gray, K. (2014). *Race, gender, and deviance in Xbox Live: Theoretical perspectives from the virtual margins*. New York: Routledge.

Greenwood, A. (2014). What it means to say a dolphin committed suicide. *Huffington Post*, June 13. Accessed January 19, 2016, 1:17pm, from http://www.huffington post.com/2014/06/13/dolphin-commits-suicide_n_5491513.html

Gusfield, J. (1963). *Symbolic crusade: Status politics and the American temperance movement*. Urbana: University of Illinois Press

Hadden, S. (2003). *Slave patrols: Law and violence in Virginia and the Carolinas*. Cambridge, MA: Harvard University Press.

Haigh, A. E. (1896). The Oresteia: A synopsis and analysis of the trilogy of Aeschylus. Accessed on October 8, 2015, 5:32pm, from http://www.theatredatabase .com/ancient/aeschylus_004.html. Originally published in A. E. Haigh (1896). *The Tragic Drama of the Greeks* (pp. 114–21). Oxford: Clarendon Press.

Hall, S. (2012). *Theorizing crime and deviance: A new perspective*. Thousand Oaks, CA: Sage.

Hall, S. (2014). Synopsis of "Theorizing Crime and Deviance." *Journal of Theoretical and Philosophical Criminology 6*(2), 145–55.

Hall, S., Critcher, C., Jefferson, T., Clarke, J., & Roberts, B. (1978). *Policing the crisis: Mugging, the state, and law and order*. London: MacMillan.

Hambry, S., Finkelhor, D., Turner, H., & Ormond, R. (2011). *Children's exposure to intimate partner violence and other family violence*. Washington, DC: Office of Juvenile Justice and Delinquency Prevention.

Harcourt, B. (2013). Beccaria's *On Crimes and Punishments*: A mirror on the history of the foundations of modern criminal law. *Coase-Sandor Institute for law and Economics Working Paper No. 948*. Chicago: University of Chicago Law School.

Havelock, E. (1978). *The Greek concept of justice: From its shadow in Homer to its substance in Plato*. Cambridge, MA: Harvard University Press.

Haynie, D. L., Nansel, T., Eitel, P., Crump, A. D., Saylor, K., Yu, K., & Simons-Morton, B. (2001). Bullies, victims, and bully/victims: Distinct groups of at-risk youth. *The Journal of Early Adolescence 21*(1), 29–49.

Hayward, K. J. (2016). Cultural criminology: Script rewrites. *Theoretical Criminology 20*(3), 297–321.

Hayward, K. J., & Young, J. (2004). Cultural criminology: Some notes on the script. *Theoretical Criminology 8*(3), 259–73.

Headley, A. M., Guerette, R. T., & Shariati, A. (2017). A field experiment on the impact of body-worn cameras (BWCs) on police officer behavior and perceptions. *Journal of Criminal Justice 53*, 102–9.

Hedberg, E. C., Katz, C. M., & Choate, D. E. (2017). Body-worn cameras and citizen interactions with police officers: Estimating plausible effects given varying compliance levels. *Justice Quarterly 34*(4), 627–21.

Hegel, G. (1807/1977). *Phenomenology of spirit*. Trans. A. Miller. New York: Oxford.

Hegel, G. (2004). *Philosophy of history*. New York: Barnes & Noble.

Heimer, K., & Matsueda, R. L. (1994). Role-taking, role commitment, and delinquency: A theory of differential social control. *American Sociological Review 59*(3), 365–90.

Henberg, M. (1990). *Retribution: evil for evil in ethics, law, and literature*. Philadelphia: Temple University Press.

Hickman, M. J. (2006). Citizen complaints about police use of force. Bureau of Justice Statistics Special Report, NCJ 210296.

Hickman, M., & Piquero, A. R. (2001). Exploring the relationships between gender, control balance, and deviance. *Deviant Behavior 22*(4), 323–51.

Higgins, G., Fell, B., & Wilson, A. (2007). Low self-control and social learning in understanding students' intentions to pirate movies in the United States. *Social Science Computer Review 25*(3), 339–57.

Higgins, G., Jennings, W., Tewksbury, R., & Gibson, C. (2009). Exploring the link between low self-control and violent victimization trajectories in adolescents. *Criminal Justice and Behavior 36*(10), 1070–84

Hirschi, T., & Gottfredson, M. (1993). Commentary: Testing the general theory of crime. *Journal of Research in Crime and Delinquency 30*(1), 47–54.

Hirschi, T., & Gottfredson, M. (2000). In defense of self-control. *Theoretical Criminology 4*(1), 55–69.

Hirschi, T., & Selvin, H. C. (1967). *Delinquency research: An appraisal of analytic methods*. New York: The Free Press.

Holtfreter, K., Reisig, M., Piquero, N., & Piquero, A. (2010). Low self-control and fraud: Offending, victimization, and their overlap. *Criminal Justice and Behavior 37*(2), 188–203.

Hooton, E. (1939). *Crime and the man*. Cambridge, MA: Harvard University Press.

Horowitz, M. A. (2000). Kids who kill: A critique of how the American legal system deals with juveniles who commit homicide. *Law and Contemporary Problems 63*, 133–77.

Hueston, J., & Burke, K. (2016). Exporting drug-court concepts to traditional courts: A roadmap to an effective therapeutic court. *Court Review 52*(1), 44–50.

Hughes, E. C. (1945). Dilemmas and contraductions of statuses. *American Journal of Sociology 50*, 353–59.

Ingraham, C. (2017). Jeff Sessions personally asked Congress to let him prosecute medical marijuana-providers. Retrieved from https://www.washingtonpost.com/news/wonk/wp/2017/06/13/jeff-sessions-personally-asked-congress-to-let-him-prosecute-medical-marijuana-providers/?utm_term=.a122a96cfd83

Jensen, G. F. (1999). A critique of control balance theory. *Theoretical Criminology 3*, 339–43.

Jones, D. (1986). *History of criminology: A philosophical perspective*. New York: Greenwood.

Kafka, F. (1995). *The trial*. Trans. W. & E. Muir. New York: Schocken.

Kaiser, K. A., & Holtfreter, K. (2016). Using procedural justice and therapeutic jurisprudence to promote offender compliance and rehabilitation. *Criminal Justice and Behavior 43*(1), 45–62.

Kappeler, V. E., Sluder, R. D., & Alpert, G. A. (1998). *Forces of deviance: Understanding the dark side of policing*. Long Grove, IL: Waveland.

Keegan, J. (1989). *The second world war*. New York: Penguin.

Kelly, E. (2009). Criminal justice without retribution. *The Journal of Philosophy 106*(8), 440–62.

Kelly, J. (2017). 19 states have narrowed juvenile involvement in adult system since 2015. October 10. Retrieved from https://chronicleofsocialchange.org/juvenile-justice-2/19-states-narrowed-juvenile-involvement-adult-system-since-2015/28413

Kelsen, H. (1941). Causality and retribution. *Philosophy of Science 8*(4), 533–56.

Kennan, G. (1946). 861.00/2–2246: The charge in the Soviet Union (Kennan) to the Secretary of State. Telegram sent from Moscow, February 22, 1946—9 p.m. to the United States Department of State. Accessed August 26, 2016, 3:14pm from http://nsarchive.gwu.edu/coldwar/documents/episode-1/kennan.htm

Kent v. US (1966). 383 U.S. 541

Kierkegaard, S. (2009). *Works of love*. New York: Harper Perennial.

Klofas, J., Hipple, N., & McGarrell, E. (2010). *The new criminal justice: American communities and the changing world of crime control*. New York: Routledge.

Kolb, B., & Gibb, R. (2011). Brain plasticity and behavior in the developing brain. *Journal of the Canadian Academy of Child and Adolescent Psychiatry 20*(4), 265–76.

Kornfield, J. (2001). *After the ecstasy, the laundry: How the heart grows wise on the spiritual path*. New York: Bantam.

Kornhauser, R. (1978). *Social sources of delinquency: An appraisal of analytic models*. Chicago: University of Chicago Press.

Kramer, R., Michalowski, R., & Kauzlarich, D. (2002). The origins and development of the concept and theory of state-corporate crime. *Crime & Delinquency 48*, 2, 263–82.

Kraska, P. B., & Kappeler, V. E. (1995). To serve and pursue: Exploring police sexual violence against women. *Justice Quarterly 12*, 85–111.

Kubrin, C., Stucky, T., & Krohn, M. (2009). *Researching theories of crime and deviance*. New York: Oxford.

Kuhn, T. (1996*). The structure of scientific revolutions*. 3d. Chicago: University of Chicago Press.

Kumpulainen, K., Rasanen, E., Hentotten, I., Almqvist, F., Kresanov, K., Linna, S. L., Moilanen, I., Piha, J., Tamminen, T., & Puura, K. (1998). Bullying and psychiatric symptoms among elementary school-age children. *Child Abuse and Neglect 22*, 705–17.

Lanier, M., & Henry, S. (2010). *Essential criminology* 2d. Boulder, CO: Westview Press.

Lansford, J., Wager, L., Bates, J., Pettit, G., & Dodge, K. (2012). Forms of spanking and children's externalizing behavior. *Family Relations 61*(2), 224–36.

Larson, M., Vaughn, M., Salas-Wright, C., & Delisi, M. (2015). Narcissism, low self-control, and violence among a nationally representative sample. *Criminal Justice and Behavior 42*(6), 644–61.

Laub, J. (2006). Edwin Sutherland and the Michael-Adler Report: Searching for the soul of criminology seventy years later. *Criminology 44*(2), 235–57.

Lemert, E. M. (1951). *Social pathology.* New York: McGraw-Hill.

Leon, K., & Ken, I. (2017). Food fraud and the Partnership for a "Healthier" America: A case study in state-corporate crime. *Critical Criminology 25*(3), 393–410.

Levi-Strauss, C. (1966). *The savage mind.* Chicago: University of Chicago Press.

Levinas, E. (2009). *Otherwise than being: Or beyond essence.* (A. Lingis, Trans.). Pittsburgh, PA: Duquesne University Press.

Levine, J. (2014). Deconstructing the politics of three-strikes sentencing reforms in California. *ACJS Today 39*(2), 29–33.

Levy, K. S. (2001). The relationship between adolescent attitudes towards authority, self-concept, and delinquency. *Adolescence 6*, 333–46.

Lewin, K. (1951). *Field theory in social science.* New York: Harper and Brothers.

Liazos, A. (1972). The poverty of the sociology of deviance: Nuts, sluts, and perverts. *Social Problems 20*, 103–20.

Lilly, J., Cullen, F., and Ball, F. (1995/2015). *Criminological theory: Context and consequences.* 6d. Thousand Oaks, CA: Sage.

Longmire, D. R. (1996). Americans' attitudes about the ultimate weapon: Capital punishment. In T. J. Flanagan & D. R. Longmire (Eds.). *Americans view crime and justice: A national public opinion survey* (pp. 93–108). Thousand Oaks, CA: Sage Publications.

Lynch, M., & Haney, C. (2015). Emotion, authority and death: (Raced) negotiations in mock capital jury deliberations. *Law and Social Inquiry 40*(2), 377–405.

MacKenzie, M., Nicklas, E., Brooks-Gunn, J., & Waldfogel, J. (2015). Spanking and children's externalizing behavior across the first decade of life: Evidence for transactional processes. *Journal of Youth and Adolescence 44*(3), 658–69.

MacMillan, H., Boyle, M., Wong, M., Duku, E., Fleming, J., & Walsh, C. (1999). Slapping and spanking in childhood and its association with lifetime prevalence of psychiatric disorders in a general population sample. *Canadian Medical Association Journal 161*(7), 805–9.

Magnezi, A. (2015). Jewish teens who set fire to Palestinian café sentenced to community service. *YNet.* Accessed April 16, 2015, 9:31am, from http://www.ynetnews.com/articles/0,7340,L-4647006,00.html

Mankoff, M. (1971). Societal reaction and career deviance: A critical analysis. *The Sociological Quarterly 12*, 204–18.

Matsueda, R. (1982). Testing control theory and differential association: A causal modeling approach. *American Sociological Review 47*(4), 489–504.

Matsueda, R. (1988). The current state of differential association theory. *Crime and Delinquency 34*(3), 277–306.

Matsueda, R. L. (1992). Reflected appraisals, parental labeling, and delinquency: Specifying a symbolic interactionist theory. *American Journal of Sociology 97*(6), 1577–611.

Matsueda, R. (1997). "Cultural deviance theory": The remarkable persistence of a flawed term. *Theoretical Criminology 1*(4), 429–52.

Matza, D. (1969). *Becoming deviant.* Englewood Cliffs, NJ: Prentice Hall.

McNulty, T. L., & Holloway, S. (2000). Race, crime, and public housing in Atlanta: Testing conditional effect hypothesis. *Social Forces 79*(2), 707–29.

Mead, G. H. (1934). *Mind, self, and society*. Chicago, IL: University of Chicago Press.

Merton, R. (1938). Social structure and anomie. *American Sociological Review 3*(5), 672–82.

Merton, R. (1996). *On social structure and science*. P. Sztompka (Ed.). Chicago: University of Chicago Press.

Merton, R. (1997). On the evolving synthesis of differential association and anomie theory: A perspective from the sociology of science. *Criminology 35*(3), 517–25.

Messner, S. (1983). Regional and racial effects on the urban homicide rate: The subculture of violence revisited. *American Journal of Sociology 88*(5), 997–1007.

Messner, S., & Rosenfeld, R. (1997). *Crime and the American dream*. Belmont, CA: Wadsworth.

Midianite. (2015). In *Encyclopædia Britannica*. Accessed May 27, 2015, 3:54pm, from http://www.britannica.com/EBchecked/topic/381574/Midianite

Miller, J. (2013). Individual offending, routine activities, and activity settings: Revisiting the routine activity theory of general deviance. *Journal of Research in Crime and Delinquency 50*(3), 390–415.

Mill, J. S. (1993). *Utilitarianism*. Rutland, VT: Everyman/Tuttle.

Mills, C. W. (1959/2000). *The sociological imagination*. New York: Oxford.

Milne, D. (2002). The beautiful soul: From Hegel to Beckett. *Diacritics 32*(1), 63, 65–71, 73–82.

Mirchandani, R. (2005). What's so special about specialized courts? The state and social change in Salt Lake City's domestic violence court. *Law and Society Review 39*(2), 379–417.

Mitchell, W. (1918). Bentham's felicific calculus. *Political Science Quarterly 33*(2), 161–83.

Moon, B., & Alarid, L. (2015). School bullying, low self-control, and opportunity. *Journal of Interpersonal Violence 30*(5), 839–56.

Montesquieu, C. L. (1748/2011). *The spirit of the laws*. Accessed October 21, 2015, 3:48pm, from http://lf-oll.s3.amazonaws.com/titles/837/Montesquieu_0171–01_EBk_v6.0.pdf

Moskos, P. (2011). *In defense of flogging*. New York: Basic Books.

Murrell, A. R., Merwin, R. M., Christoff, K. A., & Henning, K. R. (2005). When parents model violence: The relationship between witnessing weapon use as a child and later use as an adult. *Behavior and Social Issues 14*, 128–33.

National Highway Traffic Safety Administration (2015). Drunk driving. Accessed September 22, 2017, 11:43pm, from https://www.nhtsa.gov/risky-driving/drunk-driving

Newman, G. (2008). *The punishment response*. New Brunswick, NJ: Transaction.

Nhat Hanh, T. (1987). *The miracle of mindfulness*. (M. Ho, Trans.). Boston: Beacon.

Nhat Hanh, T. (2007). *The art of power*. New York: HarperOne.

Norbury, A., Manohar, S., Rogers, R., & Husain, M. (2013). Dopamine modulates risk-taking as a baseline sensation-seeking trait. *The Journal of Neuroscience 33*, 32, 12982–986.

Nozick, R. (1974). *Anarchy, state and utopia*. New York: Basic Books.

Nozick, R. (1992). Distributive justice. In S. Avineri & A. de Shalit (Eds.). *Communitarianism and individualism* (pp. 137–50). New York: Oxford.

Nye, F. I. (1958). *Family relationships and delinquent behavior*. Oxford: John Wiley.

Olson, D., Lurigio, A., & Albertson, S. (2001). Implementing the key components of specialized drug treatment courts: Practice and policy considerations. *Law and Policy 23*(2), 171–96.

Oudshoorn, J. (2016). *Trauma-informed juvenile justice in the United States*. Toronto: Canadian Scholars' Press.

Ozbay, O., and Koksoy, O. (2009). Is low self-control associated with violence among youths in Turkey? *International Journal of Offender Therapy and Comparative Criminology 53*(2), 145–67.

Palen, J. J. (1981). *The urban world*. New York: McGraw-Hill.

Palmara, F., Cullen, F. T., & Gersten, J. C. (1986). The effect of police and mental health intervention on juvenile deviance: Specifying contingencies in the impact of formal reaction. *Journal of Health and Social Behavior 27*(1), 90–105.

Park, R., Burgess, E., & McKenzie, R. (1925). *The city*. Chicago: University of Chicago Press.

Paternoster, R., & Bachman, R. (2001). *Explaining criminals and crime: Essays in contemporary criminological theory*. Los Angeles, CA: Roxbury Publishing.

Paternoster, R., & Iovanni, L. (1989). The labeling perspective and delinquency: An elaboration of a theory and an assessment of the evidence. *Justice Quarterly 6*(3), 359–94.

Pedneault, A., & Beauregard, E. (2014). Routine activities and time use: A latent profile approach to sex offenders' lifestyles. *Sexual Abuse: A Journal of Research and Treatment 26*(1), 34–57.

Phillips, N., & Strobl, S. (2006). Cultural criminology and kryptonite: Apocalyptic and retributive constructions of crime in comic books. *Crime, Media, and Culture: An International Journal 3*(2), 304–331.

Phillip, N., & Strobl, S. (2013). *Comic book crime: Truth, justice, and the American way*. New York: New York University Press.

Piquero, A. R., & Hickman, M. (1999). An empirical test of Tittle's control balance theory. *Criminology 37*(2), 319–42.

Piquero, A. R., Hickman, M., & Piquero, A. R. (2006). Control balance and exploitative corporate crime. *Criminology 44*(2), 397–430.

Potter, H. (2015). *Intersectionality and criminology: Disrupting and revolutionizing studies of crime*. New York: Routledge.

Potter, N. (1998). The principle of punishment is a categorical imperative. *Faculty Publications, University of Nebraska–Lincoln Department of Philosophy*. Paper 22. Accessed on January 20, 2016, 3:20pm, from http://digitalcommons.unl.edu./philosfacpub/22

Quinney, R. (1970). *The social reality of crime*. Boston: Little, Brown.

Rabate, J. (2014). *The Cambridge introduction to literature and psychoanalysis*. New York: Cambridge University Press

Radelet, M., & Lacock, T. (2009). Do executions lower homicide rates? The views of leading criminologists. *Journal of Criminal Law and Criminology 99*, 489–508.

Rand, A. (1964). *The virtue of selfishness*. New York: Signet/Penguin.

Randall, M., & Haskell, L. (2013). Trauma-informed approaches to law: Why restorative justice must understand psychological coping. *The Dalhousie Law Journal*, 502–33.

Rapoport, D. (1989). Terror and the Messiah: An ancient experience and some modern parallels. In D. Rapoport & Y. Alexander (Eds.). *The morality of terrorism: Religious and secular justifications* (pp. 13–42). New York: Columbia University Press.

Rawls, J. (1997). *A theory of justice*. Cambridge, MA: Belknap.

Rawls, J. (2001). *Justice as fairness: A restatement*. Cambridge, MA: Belknap.

Reckless, W. C. (1933). *Vice in Chicago*. Chicago: University of Chicago Press.

Reckless, W. C. (1967, 1972). *The crime problem*. New York: Meredith Publishing.

Reckless, W. C., Dinitz, S., & Murray, E. (1956). Self concept as an insulator against delinquency. *American Sociological Review 21*, 744–46.

Reckless, W. C., & Smith, M. (1932). *Juvenile delinquency*. New York: McGraw-Hill.

Reiss, A. J. (1951). Delinquency as the failure of personal and social control. *American Sociological Review 16*, 196–207.

Remnick, D. (2014). Going the distance: On and off the road with Barack Obama. *The New Yorker*. Retrieved from http://www.newyorker.com/magazine/2014/01/27/going-the-distance-david-remnick

Richardson, H. (2016). John Rawls (1921–2002). Internet Encyclopedia of Philosophy. Accessed July 27, 2016, 7:52pm, from http://www.iep.utm.edu/rawls/

Righetti, F., Finkenauer, C., & Finkel, E. (2012). Low self-control promotes the willingness to sacrifice in close relationships. *Psychological Science 24*(8), 1522–40.

Rios, V. (2011). *Punished: Policing the lives of Black and Latino boys*. New York: New York University Press.

Ritzer, G. (1992). *Sociological theory.* 3d. New York: McGraw-Hill.

Roper v. Simmons. (2005). 543 U.S. 551.

Runciman, S. (1996). *The first crusade*. New York: Cambridge University Press.

Sampson, R. J., & Groves, W. B. (1989). Community structures and crime: Testing social disorganization theory. *American Journal of Sociology 94,* 774–802.

Sampson, R. J., & Laub, J. H. (1993). *Crime and the making: Pathways and turning points through life*. Cambridge: Cambridge University Press.

Sartre, J. (1969). *Nausea*. Trans. L. Alexander. New York: New Directions.

Sartre, J. (1989). *No Exit and three other plays by Jean-Paul Sartre*. Kindle edition. New York: Vintage.

Sartre, J. (1995). *Anti-Semite and Jew: An exploration of the etiology of hate*. New York: Schocken.

Savelsberg, J. J. (1996). Review: Control balance: Toward a general theory of deviance. *American Journal of Sociology 102*, 620–22.

Scapelliti, C. (2009). The Who: Interview with Pete Townshend. *Guitar World 30*(9). Accessed May 29, 2017, 2:47am, from http://www.guitarworld.com/pete-townshend-interview-the-who

Scheff, T. J. (1966). *Being mentally ill: A sociological theory*. Aldine

Schild, W. (1981). History of criminal law and procedure. In J. Fosberry (Trans.) *Criminal justice through the ages: From divine judgment to modern German legislation*. Burgasse, Rothenburg, Germany: Mittelalterliches Kriminalmuseum.

Schmit, K., Wansaula, Z., Pratt, R., Price, S., & Langer, A. (2017). Centers for Disease Control and Prevention: Tuberculosis—United States, 2016. Accessed September 6, 2017, 10:58am, from http://eds.b.ebscohost.com/ehost/pdfviewer/pdfviewer?vid=8&sid=45219cbb-55ae-4e75-b5dd-9588cd2be982%40sessionmgr104

Schur, E. M. (1971). *Labeling deviant behavior: Its sociological consequences*. New York: Harper & Row.

Scruton, R. (2017). *On human nature*. Princeton, NJ: Princeton University Press.

Sebba, L. (1984). Crime seriousness and criminal intent. *Crime and Delinquency 30*(2), 227–44.

Sellin, T. (1938). Culture conflict and crime. *American Journal of Sociology 44*(1), 97–103.

Sevier, J. (2014). The truth-justice tradeoff: Perceptions of decisional accuracy and procedural justice in adversarial and inquisitorial legal systems. *Psychology, Public Policy and Law 20*(2), 212–24.

Shakespeare, W. (2017). *The Life of King Henry the Fifth*. Accessed May 30, 2017, 1:05pm, from http://shakespeare.mit.edu/henryv/henryv.3.3.html

Shakespeare,W., & Siemon, J. R. (2009). *Richard III*. London: Metheun Drama.

Shakespeare, W., & Hubler, E. (1987). *The tragedy of Hamlet, Prince of Denmark*. New York: Penguin Group.

Shaw, C. (1930). *The jack-roller: A delinquent boy's own story*. Chicago: University of Chicago Press.

Shaw, C., & McKay, H. (1942). *Juvenile delinquency and urban areas: A study of rates of delinquents in relation to differential characteristics of local communities in American cities.* Chicago: University of Chicago Press.

Shaw, C., McKay, H., & McDonald, J. (1938). *Brothers in crime*. Chicago: University of Chicago Press.

Shaw, C., and Moore, M. (1931). *The natural history of a delinquent career.* Chicago: University of Chicago Press.

Shelden, R. (2008). *Controlling the dangerous classes: A history of criminal justice in America*. New York: Pearson.

Sheldon, W. (1949). *Varieties of delinquent youth: An introduction to constitutional psychiatry*. New York: Harper.

Sickmund, M., Sladky, T. J., Kang, W., and Puzzanchera, C. (2017). Easy access to the census of juveniles in residential placement. Retrieved from https://www.ojjdp.gov/ojstatbb/ezacjrp/

Simon, H. (1945/1997). *Administrative behavior*. New York: The Free Press.

Simon, H. (1946). The proverbs of administration. *Public Administration Review 6*(1), 53–67.

Simon, H. (1947) Administrative behavior. In S. Avineri & A. de Shalit (Eds.). *Communitarianism and individualism* (pp. 29–50). New York: Oxford.

Simpson, D. (2017). Albert Camus (1913–1960). Internet Encyclopedia of Philosophy. Accessed May 30, 2017, 11:57pm, from http://www.iep.utm.edu/camus/#H1

Sousa, W. H., Coldren Jr., J. R., Rodriguez, D., & Braga, A. A. (2016). Research on body worn cameras: Meeting the challenges of police operations, program implementation, and randomized controlled trial designs. *Police Quarterly 19*(3), 363–84.

Stafford, M., & Warr, M. (1993). A reconceptualization of general and specific deterrence. *Journal of Research in Crime and Delinquency 30*(2), 123–35.

Stanford v. Kentucky. (1989). 492 U.S. 361.

Straus, M., & Paschall, M. (2009). Corporal punishment by mothers and development of children's cognitive ability: A longitudinal study of two nationally representative age cohorts. *Journal of Aggression, Maltreatment and Trauma 18*, 459–83.

Steinberg, L. (2017). Adolescent brain science and juvenile justice policymaking. *Psychology, Public Policy and Law 23*(4), 410–20.

Stern, J. E. (2015). The cruel and unusual execution of Clayton Lockett. *The Atlantic*. Retrieved from https://www.theatlantic.com/magazine/archive/2015/06/execution-clayton-lockett/392069/

Substance Abuse and Mental Health Services Administration (2014). Trauma-informed care in behavior health services. Retrieved from https://store.samhsa.gov/product/TIP-57-Trauma-Informed-Care-in-Behavioral-Health-Services/SMA14-4816

Sutherland, A., Ariel, B., Farrar, W., & DeAnda, R. (2017). Post-experimental follow-ups—Fade-out versus persistence effects: The Rialto police body-worn camera experiment four years on. *Journal of Criminal Justice, 53*, 110–16.

Sutherland, E. (1947). *Principles of criminology*. 4d. Chicago: Lippencot.

Sutherland, E., & Cressey, D. (1978). *Criminology*. 10d. New York: J. D. Lippincott.

Swift, A. (2016). Support for marijuana legalization up to 60% in the US. Retrieved from http://www.gallup.com/poll/196550/support-legal-marijuana.aspx

Taibbi, M. (2013). Cruel and unusual punishment: The shame of three strikes laws. *Rolling Stone*, March 27. Accessed on April 2, 2015, 4:21pm, from http://www.rollingstone.com/politics/news/cruel-and-unusual-punishment-the-shame-of-three-strikes-laws-20130327?page=5

Taleb, N. (2012). *Antifragile: Things that gain from disorder*. New York: Random House.

Tannenbaum, F. (1938). *Crime and the community*. Boston, MA: Ginn

Taylor, C. (1992). Atomism. In S. Avineri & A. De-Shalit (Eds.). *Communitarianism and individualism* (pp. 29–50). New York: Oxford.

Thibaut, J., & Walker. L. (1978). A theory of procedure. *California Law Review, 66*(2), 541.

Thompson v. Oklahoma. (1988). 487 U.S. 815.

Tittle, C. (1975). Deterrents or labeling? *Social Forces 53*(3), 399–410.

Tittle, C. (1995). *Control balance: Toward a general theory of deviance*. Boulder, CO: Westview.

Tittle, C. (2004). Refining control balance theory. *Theoretical Criminology 8*(4), 395–428.

Tittle, C., Burke, M., & Jackson, E. (1986). Modeling Sutherland's theory of differential association: Toward an empirical clarification. *Social Forces 65*(2), 405–32.

Tolstoy, L. (2009). *Last steps: The late writings of Leo Tolstoy*. J. Parini (Ed.). New York: Penguin.

Townshend, P. (1971). *Baba O'Reily*. London: Polydor Records.

Traub, S. H., & Little, C. B. (1994) *Theories of deviance*. Itasca, IL: F. E. Peacock Publishers.

Trop v. Dulles. (1958). 356 US 86.

Tutty, L. M., & Babins-Wagner, R. (2016). Outcomes and recidivism in mandated batterer intervention before and after introducing a specialized domestic violence court. *Journal of Interpersonal Violence 1*, 1–24. DOI: 10.1177/0886260516647005

Umbreit, M. S., Coates, R. B., & Vos, B. (2002). The impact of restorative justice conferencing: A multi-national perspective. *British Journal of Community Justice 1*(2), 21–48.

Umbreit, M. S., Coates, R. B., & Vos, B. (2004). Victim-offender mediation: Three decades of practice and research. *Conflict Resolution Quarterly 22*, 1–2, 279–303.

Umbreit, M. S., Vos, B., Coates, R. B., & Armour, M. P. (2006). Victims of severe violence in mediated dialogue with offender: The impact of the first multi-site study in the U.S. *International Review of Victimology 13*, 27–48.

Unnever, J., & Gabbidon, S. (2011). *A theory of African-American offending: Race, racism & crime*. New York: Routledge.

Van Camp, T. (2017). Understanding victim participation in restorative practices: Looking for justice for oneself as well as for others. *European Journal of Criminology 14*(6), 679–96.

Vasoli, R., & Terzola, D. (1974). Sutherland's professional thief. *Criminology 12*(2), 131–54.

Vazsonyi, A., & Belliston, L. (2007). The family → low self-control → deviance: A cross-cultural and cross-national test of self-control theory. *Criminal Justice and Behavior 34*(4), 505–30.

Vera, E., & Moon, B. (2013). An empirical test of low self-control theory among Hispanic youth. *Youth Violence and Juvenile Justice 11*(1), 79–93.

Vollum, S., & Adkinson, C. (2003). The portrayal of crime and justice in the comic book superhero mythos. *Journal of Criminal Justice & Popular Culture 10*(2), 96–108.

Vollum, S. & Buffington-Vollum, J. (2009). An examination of social-psychological factors and support for the death penalty: Attribution, moral disengagement, and the value-expressive function of attitudes. *American Journal of Criminal Justice 35*, 1–2, 15–36.

Vollum, S., Longmire, D. R., & Buffington-Vollum, J. (2004). Confidence in the death penalty and support for its use: Exploring the value-expressive dimension of death penalty attitudes. *Justice Quarterly 21*(3), 521–46.

Vollum, S., Mallicoat, S., & Buffinton-Vollum, J. (2009). Death penalty attitudes in an increasingly critical climate: Value-expressive support and attitude mutability. *Southwest Journal of Criminal Justice 5*(3), 221–42.

Von Hirsch, A. (1976). *Doing justice: The choice of punishments*. New York: Hill and Wang.

Wallace, D. (2015). A test of the routine activities and neighborhood attachment explanations for bias in disorder perceptions. *Crime and Delinquency 61*(4), 587–609.

Walters, G. (2015). Proactive criminal thinking and the transmission of differential association: A cross-lagged multi-waved path analysis. *Criminal Justice and Behavior 42*(11), 1128–44.

Washington Post (2018). Police Shootings 2017 Database. Accessed January 18, 2018, 12:17pm, from https://www.washingtonpost.com/graphics/national/police-shootings-2017/

Weisburd, D., & Piquero, A. (2008). How well do criminologists explain crime? Statistical modeling in published studies. *Crime and Justice 37*(1), 453–502.

Wertham, F. (1954). *Seduction of the Innocent*. New York: Rinehart & Co.

Wexler, D., & Winick, B. (Eds.) (1996). *Law in a therapeutic key: Developments in therapeutic jurisprudence*. Durham, NC: Carolina Academic Press

Whitehead, J. T., & Lab, S. P. (2015). *Juvenile justice: an introduction.* 8d. New York: Routledge.

Williams, R. (1985). Hegel and transcendental philosophy. *The Journal of Philosophy 82*(11), 595–606.

Wilson, E. O. (1998). *Consilience: The unity of knowledge*. New York: Knopf.

Wilson, J. Q., & Kelling, G. (1982). Broken windows: The police and neighborhood safety. *Atlantic Monthly 249*(3), 29–38.

Wittgenstein, L. (1922/2007). *Tractatus logico-philosophicus*. New York: Cosimo.

Wohlleben, P. (2015). *The hidden life of trees: What they feel, how they communicate*. Vancouver: Greystone.

Wolfgang, M., and Ferracuti, F. (1982). *The subculture of violence*. Thousand Oaks, CA: Sage.

Wolfson, A. (2013). "Papa John" makes no apology for wealth, Obamacare remarks. Published January 14, 2013, 2:59pm, in the Louisville *Courier-Journal*. Accessed September 6, 2017, 10:38am, from https://www.usatoday.com/story/money/business/2013/01/14/pizza-papa-john-schnatter/1566364/

World Nuclear Association (2016). Chernobyl Accident 1986. Accessed September 6, 2017, 9:50am, from http://www.world-nuclear.org/information-library/safety-and-security/safety-of-plants/chernobyl-accident.aspx

Wright, E. Q., & Brightman, S. (2018). *Crime victimization: A comprehensive overview*. 2d. Durham, NC: Carolina Academic Press.

Young, J. (1971). *The drugtakers*. New York: HarperCollins.

Young, J. (2011). *The criminological imagination*. Boston: Polity.

Yun, I., Kim, S., & Kwon, S. (2015). Low self-control among South Korean adolescents: A test of Gottfredson and Hirschi's generality hypothesis. *International Journal of Offender Therapy and Comparative Criminology*, 1–24. Published online at http://ijo.sagepub.com/content/early/2015/03/24/0306624X15574683

Zaloznaya, M. (2012). Organizational cultures as agents of differential association: Explaining the variations of bribery practices in Ukrainian universities. *Crime, Law, and Social Change*, 295–320. DOI: 10.1007/s10611–012–9386-x

Zehr, H. (2005). *Changing lenses: A new focus for crime and justice*. 3d. Harrisonburg, VA: Herald Press.

Ziliak, S., & McClosky, D. (2013). We agree that statistical significance proves essentially nothing: A rejoinder to Thomas Mayer. *Econ Journal Watch 10*(1), 97–107.

Zimring, F., & Hawkins, G. (1997). *Incapacitation: Penal confinement and the restraint of crime*. New York: Oxford.

Zimring, F., Hawkins, G., & Kamin, S. (2001). *Punishment and democracy: Three strikes and you're out in California.* New York: Oxford University Press.

Zinn, H. (1999). *A people's history of the United States: 1492 to present*. New York: Harper Perennial.

Index

About the Authors

Michael J. DeValve is dad to Kinsela, husband to Lindsay, son to Jeanne and John, meditator, mediator, musician, and zemiologist. Michael grew up in a home full of love and art of all kinds. After finding that a life of music was not for him, he turned to the study of criminal justice. He earned an MA and PhD in criminal justice from Sam Houston State University in 2004. Michael is a reluctant theorist whose focus is on love and its place in justice practice. He is also passionate about folding the arts into the justice classroom. His articles can be found in several journals, including *Police Quarterly*, *The Prison Journal, Contemporary Justice Review*, *Critical Criminology*, and the *Journal of Theoretical and Philosophical Criminology*. Michael continues to be an active musician, playing bass in a local rock band. He is an associate professor in the Department of Criminal Justice at Fayetteville State University. He lives in Fayetteville, North Carolina, with his soulmate, Lindsay, their borador, Davyn, and Kinsela whenever is possible.

Tammy S. Garland is professor and graduate coordinator in the Department of Social, Cultural, and Justice Studies at the University of Tennessee Chattanooga. She received a PhD in criminal justice from Sam Houston State University in 2004. Her current research emphasis includes victimization of the homeless, women, and children; gender, crime, and popular culture; and drug policy issues. Her publications can be found in *American Journal of Criminal Justice*, *Criminal Justice Policy Review*, *Criminal Justice Studies*, *Feminist Criminology*, and *Journal of Poverty*. Currently, she resides in Chattanooga with her husband, her children, and myriad pets.

Elizabeth Q. Wright received bachelor's degrees in psychology and social welfare from the University of Wisconsin–Madison. She earned a master of arts and PhD from Sam Houston State University in August 2004 and began her academic career at Fayetteville State University. After eleven years there, she became a faculty member in the Department of Criminal Justice Administration at Middle Tennessee State University. Her interests include: victimology and victims' studies, police-community relations, vicarious trauma, stress management, and the criminal justice response to disasters. In the field, Beth has worked as a corrections liaison with both incarcerated boys and girls. Additionally, she worked for several years as a rape crisis hotline counselor and support group facilitator and continued her victim advocacy work through board membership, grant writing, and training to rape crisis and domestic violence organizations in North Carolina and Tennessee. Beth has been published in *Women and Criminal Justice*, *Applied Psychology in Criminal Justice*, *Contemporary Justice Review*, *ACJS Assessment Forum*, and *Crime Prevention and Community Safety*; has written five book chapters exploring different victimological and victims' rights issues, including a problem-oriented policing approach to repeat victimization; is in the second edition of her victimology textbook (coauthored with Sara Brightman); and a technical report on the victimization experience presented to the Texas State Legislature.

www.ingramcontent.com/pod-product-compliance
Ingram Content Group UK Ltd.
Pitfield, Milton Keynes, MK11 3LW, UK
UKHW040154091026
15587UKWH00018B/268

9 781498 559904